INDIAN LIFE
AT THE
OLD MISSIONS

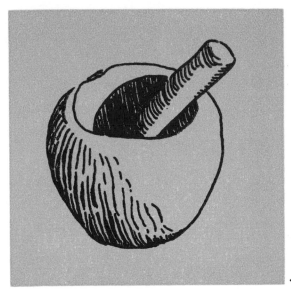

Indian life
at the
old missions

Edith
Buckland
Webb

foreword: F. W. Hodge

WARREN F. LEWIS, PUBLISHER :: LOS ANGELES

Quotations from *The History of (Lower) California* by
Don Francisco Javier Clavigero, S. J., translated and edited
by Sara E. Lake and A. A. Gray; *The Visit of the "Rurik"
to San Francisco in 1816*, by August C. Mahr; *The Mission
of San Antonio de Padua*, by Frances Rand Smith, are
reprinted with the permission of the authors and of the
publishers, Stanford University Press.

PRINTED IN THE UNITED STATES OF AMERICA
AT THE WAYSIDE PRESS, LOS ANGELES, CALIFORNIA

DEDICATED
TO THE PIONEERS OF ALL TIMES
AND ESPECIALLY
TO MY FATHER AND MOTHER, ALONDUS LAFAYETTE
AND GENEVA HARRIET (PACK) BUCKLAND

FOREWORD

FOREWORD

PUBLICATIONS on the subject of the Missions of California constitute a library in themselves, for these relatively ancient monuments stand as symbols of the introduction of civilization to the southern two-thirds of the state less than two centuries ago.

It has not been the intention of the author, a resident of California for half a century, to penetrate deeply the history and structure of the Missions, which have been treated time and again by many writers. Rather she has attempted to reveal the life of the Indian neophytes at the Missions, a subject to which she has devoted more than twenty years of research—a phase of mission history neglected to the present time.

To this end Mrs. Webb has visited all of the Missions, some of them innumerable times; she has interviewed oldtimers whose knowledge of the activities of the neophytes during their own lifetime, and through family narrations, revealed much that otherwise would have been lost forever. Nor have the Mission and other archives been neglected in this search for information. Indeed, the accumulation of materials Mrs. Webb has gathered is prodigious.

The results of these researches, embodied in this volume, reveal why and how the Missions were built; how the Indians were brought to them; the food, dress, and instruction of these natives in the useful arts—agriculture in its many ramifications, milling, cattle and sheep raising; the Indians as artists and musicians— all of which demanded the patience of their teachers, for almost everything in which the Indians were instructed was novel to them.

The volume closes with a chapter on "The Tragic Fate of the Indians," their appalling death-rate not many years after the Missions were founded, and, finally, the secularization and spoliation of the Missions.

To the researchers, as well as to the casual reader, the work will be found to be replete with information of ethnological interest and value, for it treats of many phases of the cultures of the Indians before the advent of the Padres and the attempted transformation through Christianization. It is comprehensive, conscientious, scholarly.

The illustrations with which the volume is provided are far beyond what one would expect in completeness, excellence, and illustrative quality. None of these has been selected as a means of embellishment, but solely as an aid in elucidating the text. Of exceptional interest are the photographic reproductions of models designed to depict life at the Missions; these have been made so realistically that only the time element would seem to bar belief that the photographs were made while life at the Missions was still at its climax. Many of the photographic reproductions are from negatives made by the author's husband, whose work as the Southwest Museum well knows, is nothing short of superb.

F. W. Hodge

Southwest Museum
Los Angeles

PREFACE

PREFACE

ONE OF MY EARLIEST recollections is that of listening to my little blue-eyed New England grandmother, Nancy Laura Aldrich, tell of living at Mission San Francisco, or Dolores as it was known even then. She and her mother had come to California on the ship *Brooklyn*, the first passenger vessel to enter the San Francisco Bay. Leaving New York on February 4th, with a load of immigrants, the *Brooklyn* sailed around Cape Horn, made a ten-day stop at Honolulu, and arrived at San Francisco July 31, 1846. Finding a dearth of houses in Yerba Buena, as San Francisco was called in its early days, some of the immigrants, of whom there were two hundred thirty-eight, pitched their tents on a vacant lot near the beach. Others, including my grandmother and great-grandmother, were given shelter at the old mission. There, they and three other families set up their tents in the first long room of the right wing of the mission quadrangle. In this room, on October 10, 1846, my grandmother and grandfather, Alondus D. Lafayette Buckland, were married. Not being Catholics they were not married in the mission church. Grandfather and his mother had also come to California on the *Brooklyn*.

In June, 1847, my grandparents moved to the little settlement of New Hope, on the Stanislaus River, near Stockton, California. There my father was born September 17, 1847, the first white child, it is said, to be born in San Joaquín County. Returning to San Francisco in 1848, they once more found living quarters at the old mission while grandfather was building the Buckland House, one, if not the first, of the hotels to be erected in that city.

From my maternal English-French grandmother, Mary Jane (Walker) Pack, came stories of a father, James Walker, who was master of a vessel in which he "sailed the seven seas" and brought back to his little daughter in Saint Helier, Isle of Jersey, gorgeous silk shawls, gold earrings, brooches, coral beads, and many other treasures that told of dealings in China, India, Persia, and other far-off lands. When I was a small child my grandmother gave me a strand from a coral necklace that had come from India. My sister received a pair of gold earrings for the wearing of which her ears were pierced. I still treasure some of those beads. I wish that I might add that my great-grandfather's vessel was anchored in California harbors and that he traded with the mission Padres. It is not impossible that he should have done so, but of that I have no sure knowledge.

With these cherished bits of family heritage, I came to California in 1901, counting myself not an alien, for my grandparents and my father had been here before me. Naturally I was interested in the missions, the Padres, and the Indians, and one day in 1903, when we were visiting in San Francisco, my husband, Hugh Pascal Webb, hired a horse and buggy and we drove out to the old mission. There we made our first mission photograph. Since that time we have visited all the missions along El Camino Real many times, and some of them times innumerable. I have investigated and gathered information and my husband has taken photographs, hundreds of which have been made solely for my study of the old establishments.

Encouraged by the Rev. St. John O'Sullivan, priest serving at San Juan Capistrano in 1910-1933, I began about twenty-five years ago to make a serious study of the old buildings and their former uses with the object of painting a series of pictures of the missions as they existed prior to secularization. To that end I read many books, started a modest library, and began gathering from every available source copies of early sketches and photographs, as well as surveys of the mission buildings and gardens, for I wished my paintings to be as historically correct as possible. I pasted hundreds of old photographs in four 18 x 25-inch scrapbooks and took them with me on field and investigation trips, as I soon found that they quickened the memories of many of those persons from whom I sought information.

I have been particularly fortunate in having found, in some of those communities that have grown up around the old missions, a number of long-time residents whose memories were good and statements trustworthy. Facts so gleaned, together with the study of source material—old Spanish documents, diaries, and accounts written by traders and travellers have unfolded to me an intriguing picture of mission life.

It has occurred to me that there is a place for a book wherein may be found many of the interesting facts and intimate details that I have gathered from here and there concerning the everyday life of the neophyte Indian; the various industries carried on at the old missions, together with descriptions of the old ways and customs as told by persons who wrote from their own personal observations and experiences. These details have never until now been correlated and told in one volume. Fr. Zephyrin Engelhardt, O.F.M., has written many books that deal with the great work done by the Franciscan Padres in Christianizing and civilizing the California Indians, but no one heretofore has taken up the story of the workaday life of the neophyte, his inherent capability, his adaptability, and his progress and accomplishments under the tutelage of the Padres and the artisan instructors.

In this volume I have, therefore, tried to present a truly authentic picture of the life of our Indians from the time when the Spanish explorers first saw them until they were set adrift after the missions were secularized in 1834-1837. Believing that no retold narrative is quite so good as the original, I have quoted at some length from diaries, official reports, and accounts written by early visitors to California.

I have checked and rechecked information that has been given me and, wherever possible, have made personal investigations. I have searched for the remains of old mission and rancho buildings, investigated water systems, climbed into and measured old reservoirs, crawled into and measured the penstock of Santa Bárbara's old gristmill, helped with excavating, climbed ladders to belfries, and attended numerous religious rites and ceremonies. I have, in fact, done everything within my power to make this work authentic, and in all these ventures I have been accompanied and ably assisted by my husband. For those errors that are bound to creep into human work I ask the reader's forbearance.

Before passing on to acknowledge my indebtedness to the many kind friends and even strangers who have made the writing of this book possible, I should like to speak of a work that has been a constant source of inspiration to me. Just before World War II began, Mr. William M. Connelly came to Los Angeles enthused with the desire to promote here an attraction comparable to the Holland Tulip Festival held annually in Holland, Michigan. After a number of conferences we agreed to co-operate in recreating California's twenty-one missions on a scale of an inch to the foot. All the work was to be as historically accurate as was humanly possible to make it. When completed the entire series was to be set up on a plot of land three to five acres in extent. A little Camino Real was to lead from one mission to the next, dwarf trees dotting the landscape. The illusion of life was to be created by means of figures (also made to scale) of Padres, soldiers, Indians, and many domestic animals. Indian neophytes were to be represented performing various tasks according to mission-day methods. Ceremonies and religious customs were to be depicted. Completed, these recreations should have been invaluable as a means of visual education. However, the war came and "Little Mission San Diego de Alcalá" was the only one finished.

Our son, Alfred Hugh Webb, who did the decorative drawings for this book, was technical director of the project. It was his task to coordinate the archeological, historical, and architectural data and reduce them to working drawings, as well as to supervise all the work done. For the greater part, the completed buildings were the work of his hands. The data were taken from my files—the same data that I have drawn upon for this book. Mr. Connelly financed the venture and gave of his time to see that materials and workmen were found.

In illustrating this volume I have used some of the "Little Mission" buildings and figures to create scenes of industrial and ceremonial activities of mission-day life. My husband photographed them for me. The lifelike "little people" shown are the work of the talented young sculptress and worker in ceramics, Katherine Donnell of Pacific Palisades, California. The oxen were created by Charles O. Jenney of Los Angeles, and the other animals by Peter Terry, ceramist and maker of masks, also of Los Angeles. The carts, plows, saws, doors, furniture. etc., were fashioned by Alfred Hugh Webb, Avard Ward, and Forrest Howsley. I am very grateful to these workers for their faithful and painstaking creations, I am doubly indebted to Katherine Donnell* for the loan of special groups of "little people," from her own private collection, to be used in making illustrations for my book.

I regret very much that a number of those friends who contributed so much to the accuracy of this volume will never see its printed pages. The research work was begun many years ago and in the intervening years death has taken some of those who helped me most. Among these are the Rt. Rev. St. John O'Sullivan, of San Juan Capistrano; Mr. Cave Couts, of Rancho Guajome; Mr. C. C. Pierce, Los Angeles photographer, from whose historic collection I obtained many rare photographs; Lucile Lloyd, noted mural painter and faithful researcher; Mr. E. M. Sheridan, of San Buenaventura; Rev. Patrick Roddy, O.F.M., of Mission Santa Bárbara; Mr. Frederick C. Hageman, Senior Foreman (Architect) in charge of the restoration of Mission La Purísima Concepción; Mr. E. P. Rogers and "Billy" Alberts, of San Luis Obispo; Mr. Benito A. Soberanes, of Salinas, from whom I learned much about Mission La Soledad; and Prof. B. W. Dedrick of State College, Pennsylvania, who, though more than ninety years of age and almost blind, read the chapter on gristmills and gave me many valuable suggestions.

To those whom I have mentioned here and there throughout the book, I express my sincere appreciation of their encouragement and cooperation. I am very grateful to the following for so graciously granting me permission to quote from their books and publications: Dr. Herbert E. Bolton of Berkeley, California;

---

* This little friend passed away soon after these lines were written.

Rev. Owen da Silva, O.F.M.; the Academy of Pacific Coast History; the University of California Press; the Leland Stanford Junior Press; the Society of California Pioneers; the California Historical Society; the Henry E. Huntington Library and Art Gallery; the Santa Bárbara Musuem of Natural History; the National Miller Publications of Chicago, and the University of New Mexico Press.

I am especially grateful to Dr. Elizabeth Larsson, of Los Angeles, through whose faith and skill I was given an extended lease on life and thus enabled to complete my book; to Rev. Maynard Geiger, O.F.M., Archivist and Historian of Mission Santa Bárbara, for the continued encouragement he gave me and the generous placing of old documents at my disposal, as well as for reading my manuscript for its correctness in ecclesiology; to Rev. Joseph Thompson, O.F. M., of Los Angeles, who generously gave of his time to read the manuscript for possible errors in Spanish; to Dr. Frederick Webb Hodge, Director of the Southwest Museum, who read it for its ethnological content and wrote the Foreword.

I wish also to acknowledge my indebtedness to the Most Rev. Joseph T. McGucken, of the Archdiocese of Los Angeles, for his letter bespeaking for my work the assistance of the priests at the various missions; to Mr. M. R. Harrington, Curator of the Southwest Museum, and Mr. Arthur Woodward, Chief Curator of History at the Los Angeles County Museum, for their assistance in securing photographs of rare Indian artifacts; to Mr. and Mrs. John Davidson, of the Junípero Serra Museum at San Diego, for the loan of valuable material; to Mr. Ferdinand Perret, of Los Angeles, for his unfailing interest and valued criticisms; to Dr. Owen C. Coy, Director of the California State Historical Association, and to his secretary, Miss Dorothy Caton, for the privilege of copying valuable historical material; to Mr. Harry N. James, photographer of Oxnard, who copied many old photographs for me; to Mr. H. V. Smith, formerly Project Superintendent of La Purísima State Park, who supplied me with numerous details of the mission restoration work; to Mr. Harry Downie, who has given generously from his fund of valuable information on the northern missions; to Miss Margaret O'Connor, of San Luis Obispo, who introduced me to long-time residents of that town and who has been a companion on many an investigating jaunt; to Rev. David Temple, O.F.M., and Rev. Thaddeus Kreye, O.F.M., of Mission San Miguel, for photographs to be used for illustrations; to Rev. Tiburtius Wand, O.F.M., formerly of San Miguel, for assistance in locating old mission ranch houses; to Rev. Arthur Spearman, S. J., Rev. Edward

Shipsey, S. J., and Rev. Henry L. Walsh, S. J., of the University of Santa Clara, for information about old Mission Santa Clara; to Rev. Arthur Hutchinson, of San Juan Capistrano, for his cooperation in the study of the ruins of the old stone church and the industrial structures of that mission; to Mr. H. C. Hilts, of Westwood Village, for his active interest and assistance; to our daughter, Helen Duke, for her Map of the Missions of Alta California; to the other members of my family, each of whom has, in his or her own way, contributed to the completion of this volume; and lastly, to Mr. Warren F. Lewis, who has done all that a publisher could do to help create a worthwhile book.

E. W.

N. B. In copying excerpts from the Informes and other old documents no alteration has been made either in the spelling, capitalization, abbreviation, or accentuation of the Spanish words employed.

CONTENTS

ILLUSTRATIONS

INDIAN LIFE
AT THE
OLD MISSIONS

"Set up again the walls, and rebuild the towers, and ring the bells. Cover the hills with herds and the valleys with vines. Recall the hosts of Indians and banish the American. Let the English tongue be again unheard, and put the railway so far away that even the village of Chicago, floundering in its swamp around a trading post and a fort, knows it not. Let the storm-worn ships from around the Horn prowl along the coast for their cargo of hides, the only and the infrequent visitors from the intangible and unimportant world. Bring again Spain, and make San Blas an important port and Guadalaxara a capital. Take away Los Angeles, and give the little white-washed adobe pueblo in the valley her full name and her proper people. Let only monks in robes and sandals, and soldiers in leathern jackets, and Indians bearing burdens, traverse the paths from mission to mission. Let us speak only of Yerba Buena if we mean the locality of the Pacific capital, and mention only San Carlos if we mean Monterey. Let a brown-walled rancho appear occasionally in the landscape, and let us make it a complete establishment of a feudalism almost unknown in the middle ages, perfect in independence, isolation and peace, the home of a life neither California nor elsewhere can ever know again."

JAMES STEELE (1889)

CHAPTER 1

Our Spanish Heritage: Ceremonies and Fiesta-Making
The Gray-Robed Friars Journey to Alta California

As EARLY as 1543, sailing vessels flying the Spanish flag prowled along the Pacific Coast from México to Cape Mendocino. In later years, others followed, their navigators intent on exploring and taking possession of new lands in the name of the Spanish Crown.

These explorers all kept diaries wherein they noted everything of interest concerning the voyage and the waters through which they sailed. They wrote in glowing terms of the harbors which afforded them occasional shelter, of the land, its rivers and trees, and its friendly native inhabitants. They made note of the habits and customs of the Indians, marveling at the remarkable canoes they built and used in their fishing. All that was written was delivered, at the end of each voyage, to the viceroy of New Spain (México) who in turn sent the accounts on to the Spanish king. Yet, in spite of the favorable nature of these reports, two centuries passed before an attempt was made to occupy and colonize the country discovered.

Then, in the year 1767, the missionaries of the Jesuit Order, who had been founding and maintaining missions in Baja (Lower) California since 1697, were expelled from the country. They were replaced by Franciscan friars from the College of San Fernando in Mexico City.

In the meantime Carlos III had sent one Joseph de Gálvez as Inspector-General to look into and reorganize the affairs of New Spain. In 1768, Gálvez was on his way to visit the old missions when he received "superior orders" from the Spanish king. He was directed to take steps immediately toward the occupation and defense of the upper Pacific coast down which Russia was nosing her way.

The inspector was possessed of broad powers for carrying out the king's instructions. Moreover, he was capable, energetic, and very zealous. He immediately ordered two sailing vessels made ready and provisioned for the undertaking. He called into conference Fr. Junípero Serra, newly appointed presidente of the peninsula missions, whose energy and zeal matched his own. It was decided by these two that, besides the expedition going by sea, another should go by land to San Diego. Uniting there contingents from both parties should proceed to Monterey. Both these ports were to be settled and fortified.

Furthermore, Gálvez proposed that three missions be founded—one at San Diego, another at Monterey, and a third between the two. This plan called for six missionaries, for it was a rule of the Order that no Franciscan should live alone in the missions except in case of most urgent necessity.[1] Fr. Serra enthusiastically offered to go in person with the expedition and suggested that a letter be written to the guardian of the College of San Fernando asking for more missionaries.

Then, because the viceroy had been so pleased with the methods employed by the Franciscans in the missions of the Sierra Gorda, in México, the inspector determined that the new outposts should be managed in the same way. Those missions had been furnished seeds, tools, "cows, oxen and other cattle." Accordingly, Gálvez ordered tools and implements for house and field to be boxed up and sent, also fruit tree cuttings, and seeds of all kinds, including those of vegetables, flowers, and flax.[2]

Desiring to take advantage of the favorable season for making the voyage, Gálvez decided against sending to México for supplies.[3] Instead, he named Don Fernando Rivera y Moncada, captain of the Leather-jacket Company of the royal presidio of Loreto, as commissary and directed him to visit all the old missions and procure from each what he could of cattle, horses, mules, equipment, and foodstuffs for the expedition. The inspector also commissioned Fr. Serra to go along the same route and select from the churches and their sacristies such vestments, bells, and other furnishings as could be spared. The peninsula missions were well stocked, and it had always been the custom for the old ones to help the new.[4]

Everything going by land was to be taken to Santa María de Los Angeles,[5] the most northerly of the missions established by the Jesuits in Baja California, and the one nearest San Diego. Everything going by sea was to be collected at

---

[1] Engelhardt, *Missions and Missionaries*, 1. 297-298 (hereinafter referred to as *Miss. & Miss.*).

[2] *Palou's Life of Junipero Serra* (James edition), 57-58, hereinafter referred to as *Palou's Life of Serra* (James ed.); Watson, *Junipero Serra's Expedition to California in 1769*, 43.

[3] Due to contrary winds, the trip across the gulf often consumed several months' time. In visiting the peninsula Gálvez had embarked at San Blas on May 24, 1768, and did not reach Baja California until July 6th.

[4] For what was taken from the old missions, by whom, where it went, and what was given in payment, see Bolton, *Palou's New California*, 1. 46-65 (hereinafter referred to as *Palou's New Cal.*).

[5] For location of this and other Jesuit missions, see illustration, "Map of Old California and Adjacent Mainland" copied from *Ibidem*, by permission of the author.

La Paz. Governor Gaspar de Portolá was appointed commander-in-chief of the land expedition; Don Vicente Vila was to head the one going by sea. St. Joseph was chosen as the patron saint for both land and sea expeditions.

In due time the first of the supply vessels, the *San Carlos*, was fully provisioned and ready for the trip. Then following the old custom of blessing ships about to embark on an important mission, and of blessing flags, or banners, about to be carried onto fields of conquest, Gálvez called upon Fr. Serra to perform that ancient and dramatic ceremony. The Padre Presidente, accordingly, blessed the standards and the packet, and sang Mass aboard her. Following these ceremonies the vessel sailed from La Paz on the 9th of January, 1769, and was soon on her way to San Diego subject to the vagaries of the winds.[6] The *San Antonio* sailed shortly thereafter, Mass having been sung for the success of her voyage also.

A third vessel, the *San José*, was later fitted out, loaded with provisions, christened "with the oath of the banners" and sent on her way to San Diego in order that there might be no scarcity of supplies for the great undertaking. This packet with all on board was lost at sea.

In the meantime it had been decided that the land expedition should go in two divisions. Captain Rivera had arrived at Mission Santa María with men, live stock, and supplies for the journey. Not finding proper pasturage for the animals at that place, he passed on to a spot called Vellicatá. Here the party remained for a time until the horses and mules were conditioned for the trip, and the loads of provisions packed. Fr. Fermín Francisco de Lasuén had, at the captain's request, come up from his mission, San Francisco de Borja, to prepare the people spiritually for the journey.

It was a great adventure upon which they were setting forth—an adventure and an enterprise of momentous consequence, undertaken at the command of the Spanish King, Carlos III. In our minds we may picture their departure. With banners flying, hands waving farewell, and many a last word shouted to those who had come to see them off, the procession starts. Captain Rivera with a number of his leather-jacket soldiers mounted on horses are in the lead. Following them are the Christian Indians with spades, pickaxes, crowbars, and machetes tied to their saddles, for they are to help with opening the roads. Next comes Don José Cañizares on horse, and, as befits a disciple of St. Francis, Fr. Juan Crespí astride a white mule.[7] After them plod the pack-mules, with many a groaning protest and

---

[6] *Palou's Life of Serra* (James ed.), 58; "Diary of Junipero Serra," (Lummis transl.), *Out West*, March, 1902; Bolton, *Palou's New Cal.*, 2. 13-14.

[7] Don José Cañizares was charged with observing the latitude and marking the routes to be followed. Fr. Crespí was to keep a diary of the days' happenings.

much creaking of pack-gear. They are laden with leathern sacks and hampers packed with food supplies and other necessities for the long journey. With them go the muleteers whose duty it is to see that no mule strays from the trail and no packs are lost. Shouting and cajoling they urge on the contrary beasts. Bringing up the rear are the rest of the leather-jacket soldiers and the remaining scantily clad Christian Indians. A cloud of dust rolls up behind them. Thus they go! With hand upraised in blessing, Fr. Lasuén watches them slowly disappear in the distance.

A few weeks later the second division of the land expedition was assembled at Mission Santa María. Here the herd of cattle for the new missions was made up. Then with horses and mules, they also were taken to pasture at Vellicatá until all was ready for the start.

Inspector-General Gálvez had charged Fr. Serra together with Governor Portolá to establish a mission at Vellicatá. This they proceeded to do with the customary solemn ceremony. Fr. Serra then appointed Fr. Miguel de la Campa y Cos as first minister of the new mission which was named San Fernando de Vellicatá in honor of St. Ferdinand, King of Spain.[8] This was the only mission established by the Franciscans in Baja California.

Led by the governor, the second division of the land expedition was soon under way. This time it was Fr. La Campa who waved farewell to the departing company and watched it disappear in a cloud of dust—watched regretfully, for he had expected to go to Alta California.

Governor Portolá and Fr. Serra, who with soldiers, muleteers, and Christian Indians, had accompanied him, both kept diaries of the journey.[9] On July 1st, 1769, both land and sea expeditions were united at San Diego. It was at once a joyful and a sorrowful meeting, for of the sea contingent many had died and others were still very ill. Of the land divisions, five Christian Indians had died on the way and many had deserted, returning to their homes in Baja California. On the other hand the first objective of the expedition had been achieved. The colonizers had reached San Diego, the harbor first discovered by Cabrillo in 1542. There remained the task of rediscovering and occupying Monterey. This duty accomplished, they would have played their parts in launching an enterprise whose object, according to Gálvez's instructions, was: "to establish the Catholic Faith, to extend Spanish domain, to check the ambitious schemes of a foreign nation, and to carry out a plan formed by Felipe III, as early as 1606," and the

---

[8] *Palou's Life of Serra* (James ed.), 69; "Diary of Junipero Serra," *Out West*, April, 1902; Engelhardt, *Miss & Miss.*, 1. 356-357.

[9] Fr. Serra's long-sought, original diary was recently found in the Mexican archives by Rev. Maynard Geiger, O.F.M.

▲ THE SPANISH BANNER *that was probably carried by Portolá in 1769 on the sacred expedition.*

▼ MAP OF BAJA CALIFORNIA *and the adjacent mainland, showing the location of Jesuit missions.*

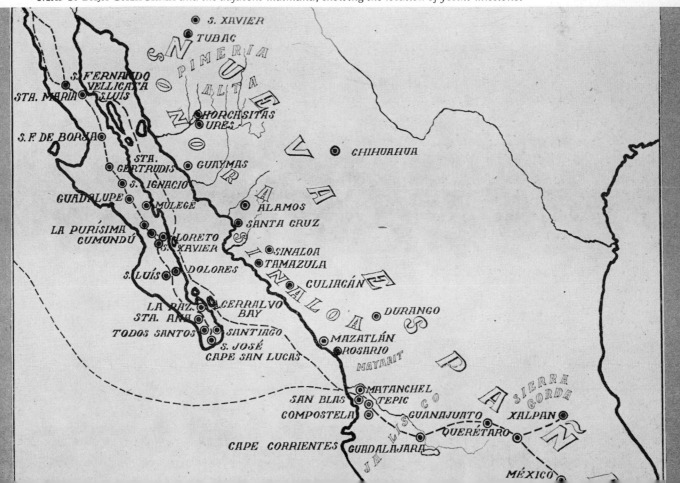

MISSIONS of ALTA CALIFORNIA.

SAN FRANCISCO SOLANO

SAN RAFAEL ARCANGEL

SAN FRANCISCO DE ASIS

SAN JOSE

SANTA CLARA DE ASIS

SANTA CRUZ

SAN JUAN BAUTISTA

SAN CARLOS DEL CARMELO

LA SOLEDAD

SAN ANTONIO DE PADUA

SAN MIGUEL ARCANGEL

SAN LUIS OBISPO

LA PURISIMA CONCEPCION
SANTA INES

SANTA BARBARA
SAN BUENAVENTURA

SAN FERNANDO REY
SAN GABRIEL ARCANGEL

SAN JUAN CAPISTRANO

SAN LUIS REY

SAN DIEGO DE ALCA

HELEN DUKE

MAP OF THE MISSIONS *founded by the Franciscan Padres for the Indians of Alta California.*

inspector-general added these significant words: "Therefore no pains can be spared with-out offense to God, the King, and the country."[10]

Much is made of "Mother México," and well it may be, for it was in México that Spanish dreams and plans for extended empire were crystallized into action that opened up a new and glorious land. For the beginnings of our California history, however, we must go back to Spain with her insatiable thirst for empire and the riches that new colonies might bring to her.

From Spain—Grandmother Spain—came the Franciscan Padres whose names are graven in the annals of our old missions. From Spain came Don Joseph de Gálvez, Don Gaspar de Portolá, and Don Vicente Vila. To this list of names others of equal luster might well be added. But for these men the beginning of California's history might have been far different from what it was. To New California, as Fr. Palóu calls it, they brought Spanish customs and laws, bandos and cédulas, rules and regulations—reglamentos without end. They brought Spanish color and fiesta making; tools and methods unchanged for centuries. With the Spanish Padres came all the magnificent pageantry of the Roman Catholic Church. They brought an architecture that suits our bright blue skies as no other ever will. Truly we owe much to Grandmother Spain.

This is the background. The remaining chapters of this book will tell the story of the Indians, our first Californians, and what the coming of the Portolá expedition of 1769 meant to them, as well as what it might have meant.

[10] Bancroft, *History of California*, 1. 129, note 7; Engelhardt, *Miss. & Miss.*, 2. 5. Gálvez to Vila, "Instruccion" January 5, 1769. *Cal. Arch. St. Pap.* 1, 28-37.

CHAPTER **2**

Our Indians as the Spaniards Found Them in 1769

Portolá's Party in Search of the Port of Monterey

IN DESCRIBING the Indians of the Santa Bárbara Channel, Fr. Font wrote: "I surmise that these Indians, who are so ingenious and so industrious, would become experts if they had teachers and suitable tools or implements, for they have nothing more than flints, and with them and their steady industry they make their artifacts. . ."[1]

So he might have written of other California natives. Much that is unjustly derogatory and erroneous has been printed about our California Indians. Fortunately, however, early Spanish explorers and discoverers of New California obeyed the injunction prescribed by the royal ordinances of July 13, 1573, and kept a daily commentary of all they found and saw, and of what happened to them on their journeys. These diaries were usually written by the commanders of the expeditions and the accompanying Religious,[2] and furnish, therefore, accounts of the natives as recorded by representatives of the two groups who were destined for so many years to control the lives of those Indians.

Within the past thirty-five years most of the diaries or narratives written by Spanish explorers of our Pacific Coast have been translated from the originals by competent authorities and made accessible to students everywhere through various publications. Thus we have one diary of the Cabrillo voyage of 1542-1543;[3] two of the Vizcaíno exploration of 1602-1603;[4] six of the Portolá expedition of 1769,[5] and twelve of the Anza expeditions of 1774, 1775-1776, including Palóu's and Moraga's accounts of the founding of San Francisco.[6] All throw consider-

---

[1] Bolton, *Anza's California Expeditions*, vol. 4, 261 (hereinafter referred to as *Anza's Cal. Exped.*).
[2] A term applied to members of religious Orders.
[3] Bolton, *Spanish Exploration in the Southwest*, 13-39.
[4] *Ibidem*, 52-103.
[5] Publications of the Academy of Pacific Coast History, Vol. 1, Nos. 3 and 4; Vol. 2, Nos. 1 and 4; Bolton, *Palou's New Cal.*, 2. 109-260; Serra, *Diary*.
[6] Bolton, *Anza's Calif. Exped.*, Vols. 2, 3, and 4.

able light on the subject of the California Indians as the Spaniards found them.

By May 1st, 1769, both packets, the *San Carlos* and the *San Antonio*, were anchored near Point Guijarros within the Bay of San Diego. Many of the soldiers and members of the crews of both vessels were ill with scurvy. Some had died. A scouting party was sent out to look for a watering-place and the two vessels moved into the inner harbor to be nearer the shore where shelters and tents were to be set up for the sick. Returning, the searching party reported that they had walked about three leagues[7] along the shore until they had come to the banks of a river lined on both sides with overspreading cotton woods. Thirty-five or forty Indian families had their homes scattered along the stream. The natives "were friendly and tractable." The country "was pleasant and green with many different kinds of fragrant herbs, wild grapes, and had plenty of game."[8]

Don Miguel Costansó, one of those who went in search of the watering-place describes the village and its inhabitants:

Within a musket-shot from the river, outside the wood, they discovered a town or village of the same Indians who were guiding our men. It was composed of various shelters made of branches and huts pyramidal in shape, covered with earth. As soon as they saw their companions with the company which they were bringing, all the inhabitants—men, women, and children—came out to receive them, and invited the strangers to their houses. The women were modestly dressed, covered from the waist to the knee with a close-woven, thick netted fabric. The Spaniards entered the town which was composed of from thirty to forty families. . .

The natives were well-built, healthy, and active. They go naked without other clothing than a belt—woven like a net—of ixtle, or fine agave thread, which they obtain from a plant called lechuguilla. Their quivers, which they stick between the belt and the body, are made of the skin of the wildcat, coyote, wolf, or deer, and their bows are two yards long. In addition to these arms, they use a sort of throwing stick of very hard wood, similar in form to a short curved sabre which they throw edgewise, cutting the air with great force. They throw it farther than a stone, and never go into the surrounding country without it. When they see a snake or other noxious animal they throw the throwing stick at it, and generally cut the animal in two. Spaniards learned after-wards from their continued intercourse with the natives, they are of an overbearing disposition, insolent, covetous,[9] tricky and boastful; and although they have little courage, they boast much of their strength, and consider the strongest to be the most valiant. They beg for any rag of cloth-ing; but after different ones on successive occasions had been clothed, on the following day they again presented themselves naked.

. . . Fish constitutes the principal food of the Indians who inhabit the shore of this port, and they consume much shellfish because of the greater ease they have in procuring them. They use rafts made of reeds, which they manage dexterously by means of a paddle or double-bladed oar. Their harpoons are several yards long, and the point is a very sharp bone inserted in wood; they are so adroit in throwing this weapon, that they very rarely miss their mark.[10]

---

[7] League—old Spanish land measurement equaling 2.63 miles.

[8] *The Portola Expedition of 1769-1770. Diary of Vicente Vila*, 91-97 (hereinafter referred to as *Diary*).

[9] Costansó's account here is colored by his remembrance of the raid made later upon Fr. Serra and his handful of supporters left after Portolá and his party had departed in search of Monterey.

[10] *The Narrative of the Portola Expedition of 1769-1770* by Miguel Costanso, Publications of the Academy of Pacific Coast History. Vol. 1, No. 4. 29, 33 (hereinafter referred to as *Narrative*).

Once more the two vessels weighed anchor and sailed in yet closer to the shore to be as near as possible to the watering-place and to the shelters which were to be erected for the sick. Don Pedro Fages, Don Miguel Costansó, Fray Juan Vizcaíno, "and the soldiers who were best able" went ashore to start work on the hospital. They gathered brushwood and earth for the roofs of the huts and returned to the vessels to report that they "had decided to build the shelters for the sick on a hillock close to the beach and a cannon shot from the packets."[11]

That morning, Captain Vila tells us, "seven or eight Indians came alongside on their rafts, and, in exchange for a few trinkets, they gave us several sea-otter skins and [skins of] other animals from their traps."[12]

Close to the beach, on the east side of the port, a small enclosure was built with a parapet of earth and brushwood, and mounted with two cannon. Some sails and awnings were landed from the vessels and, with these, two tents suitable for a hospital were made. On one side were placed the tents of the two officers, the missionaries, and the surgeon. When everything was ready to receive the sick, they were brought on shore in the launches, and were housed in the tents as comfortably as possible.[13]

Painted Indians were seen at various places on the shore and both men and women visited the lodgings of the Spaniards. The Diegueños, as the natives of the San Diego region came to be called, took a great liking to Lt. Fages and he was able to secure from them baskets, hats, fish nets, and feather head-dresses of the chief. He sent these relics to Gálvez in Mexico City.

In the meantime, in spite of Dr. Prat's ministrations, the sick soldiers and sailors continued to die at the rate of two or three a day. It was with great rejoicing, therefore, that the sadly depleted little band welcomed the arrival on May 14th, of the first division of the land expedition.

They [the members of the land expedition] rested on that day near the camp of the sick, and were supplied with food to recover their strength. The officers resolved to move the camp close to the river, which had not been done before because it was not deemed advisable to divide the small force they had for the protection at once of the vessels and of the people lodged on the shore; at the same time, the greater convenience of a shorter distance for the transportation had to be taken into consideration, in order not to tire unduly the men who were handling the launch, as the want of beasts of burden obliged them to carry on their shoulders everything that was brought on shore.

All moved to the new camp which was transferred one league farther north on the right bank of the river, on a hill[14] of moderate height, where it was possible to attend with greater care to the sick, whom the surgeon, Don Pedro Prat, did not leave for a moment and nursed with the utmost kindness.[15]

[11] Vila, *Diary*, 99, 101.
[12] Vila, *Diary*, 101.
[13] Costanso, *Narrative*, 33.
[14] This was Presidio Hill. Here it was that Fr. Serra and Portolá, coming with the second division of the land expedition, found them on July 1st, 1769.
[15] Costanso, *Narrative*, 35.

Fr. Crespí, who had come with the party arriving May 14th, and who had been charged with keeping a record of the journey, makes this notation in his diary:

> In this port and its vicinity there are many large villages of heathen. All the men are naked and most of them painted, as I have said of all the rest [i. e., those met on the way up from Baja California], but the women are modestly covered in front with woven fabrics and behind with skins of animals. They are very intelligent Indians, noisy, bold, great traders, covetous, and thievish. They all go armed with their bows and quivers of arrows, and some with macanas [the throwing stick mentioned by Costansó?]. The beach abounds in large sardines, star fish, and other species of fish, and mussels. All these heathen are fishermen, and they go to sea in rafts of tule.[16]

Fr. Serra, it will be remembered, came with the last of the expeditionary parties. On July 3rd, two days after his arrival at the port of San Diego, the Father President wrote at some length to his old friend, Fr. Palóu, who was still in Baja California. Of the Indians at San Diego he said:

> The natives are exceedingly numerous, and all of this coast of the South Sea along which we came from the Ensenada at Todos Santos, so called on the maps and charts, live well on various seeds and on fish which they catch from rafts made of tules and formed like canoes, with which they venture far out to sea. The Indians are very friendly. All the males, men as well as boys, go naked. The women and girls are decently covered as far as the breast. In that manner they would approach us with such confidence and ease as though they had known us all their life. When we wished to give them something to eat, they would say that they did not want that, but clothing. Only for things of this kind would they barter their fish with the soldiers and muleteers.[17]

It was, indeed, this very hankering for articles of clothing that led these natives to attack the small party left behind on Presidio Hill after Portolá had departed with the rest in search of the port of Monterey. The attackers were driven off but not before a servant of the Fathers had been killed and several other persons, including one of the Fathers, wounded. The natives lost a number of their men while others suffered injuries. Strangely enough they returned within a few days bringing their wounded to be treated by the Spanish surgeon, Dr. Prat.[18]

Journeying on up the coast with Portolá's party, Costansó notes:

> In general, the whole country is inhabited by a large number of Indians, who came forth to receive the Spaniards, and accompanied them from one place to another. They are very docile and tractable, especially from San Diego onward.[19]

The explorers' first camp was near the present site of Ladrillo.[20] Here natives came from a nearby village bringing gifts of fish. They were rewarded with

[16] Bolton, *Palou's New Cal.*, 2. 101.
[17] Engelhardt, *Mission San Diego*, 21.
[18] Bolton, *Palou's New Cal.*, 2. 271.
[19] Costanso, *Narrative*, 43.
[20] Identifying present day names of sites are taken from Bolton, *Palou's New Cal.*, Vol. II.

beads and articles of clothing, than which nothing pleased them more. Going on the next day the Spaniards were met by Indians from a little village in Soledad Valley. The natives greeted them joyfully, one of their number accompanying the party to their next camping place. At the end of this valley, Fr. Crespí says: "we came to a medium-sized pool of fresh water, in which we saw two pots of baked clay, very well made." Next day the travellers passed another village where they saw "pots and jugs of baked clay, well made." That night, according to Dr. Bolton, they camped by Batequitos Lagoon. And Fr. Crespí writes:

> As soon as they saw the camp was made, the whole village which was composed of eight men, three women, and four children, came down. Their chief made us a harangue, and when it was concluded they sat down as though they had always known us. One of the heathen came smoking a pipe of black clay, well made.[21]

On July 18, four days' journey from San Diego, Fr. Crespí continues:

> . . we descended to a large and beautiful valley, so green that it seemed to us that it had been planted. We crossed it straight to the north and pitched our camp near a large pool of water, one of several in the plain. At the extremities or ends of the plain are two large villages.
> Soon after our arrival the heathen came to visit us. There were more than forty Indians, naked and painted from head to foot in several colors, which is their usual custom when they go visiting or to war. They all came armed with bows and arrows, and the chief made the accustomed harangue. When it was concluded they threw their arms on the ground and sat down near us. The governor [Portolá] took out some beads, and, giving half of them to me, requested that we two should distribute them to the Indians. They gave the governor a present of a few fish nets made of thread that they make out of some fiber which, when it is spun, looks like raw hemp. Behind the men followed the women and children, who numbered more than fifty, but did not dare to come near. We made signs to them not to be afraid, and after one of the heathen spoke to them they came at once, and we gave them also presents of beads.[22]

Day after day, all along the way to Monterey, similar incidents occurred. Inhabitants of village after village came out to visit the Spaniards, bringing gifts of food of various sorts, fish nets, and necklaces of colored shells and stones like coral. They invited the travellers to stay with them and, failing in this, sent guides to show the way to watering-places, to point out the best places for fording rivers, or to lead them to passes through the mountains. Word went from one village to the next advising the natives of the approach of the strange white men who were so curiously dressed and who came riding strange animals the like of which had never before been seen in this land.

On August 2nd, the explorers halted near a river which they named Porciúncula. Dr. Bolton thinks that their camp was probably near Downey Avenue in the present city of Los Angeles. And as Fr. Crespí relates:

---

[21] Bolton, *Palou's New Cal.*, 2. 112, 114. For pottery similar to that made by the Indians of this region see *An Archeological Survey of the Twenty-nine Palms Region* by Elizabeth W. Crozer Campbell. Southwest Museum Papers, No. 7.

[22] Bolton, *Palou's New Cal.*, 2. 116-117. Years later Mission San Luis Rey was founded near this site. These Indians or their children came to be known as Luiseños.

As soon as we arrived about eight heathen from a good village came to visit us; they live in this delightful place among the trees on the river. They presented us with some baskets of pinole made from seeds of sage and other grasses. Their chief brought some strings of beads made of shells and they threw us three handfuls of them. Some of the old men were smoking pipes well made of baked clay and they puffed at us three mouthfuls of smoke. We gave them a little tobacco and glass beads and they went away well pleased.[23]

Next morning the party crossed the river and "entered a large vineyard of wild grapes and an infinity of rosebushes in full bloom." Travelling west they passed La Brea (the tar) Pits and came to a village whose inhabitants came out to meet them howling like wolves. It was a friendly howling, however, for the natives were bringing gifts of seeds. Proceeding onward, the explorers passed over into what is now called the San Fernando Valley, probably by way of Sepulveda Canyon. They camped near the spot now known as Encino and named the region spread out before them the Valley of Santa Catalina de Bononia de los Encinos. This valley, according to Fr. Crespí, was three leagues wide and more than eight leagues long.[24]

The following day they rested and held open house for the natives who came from far and near to visit them. A delegation had been sent from a little village over the pass near the present town of Newhall to invite the Spaniards to visit them, and to guide them thither. And, though it was off the road, the explorers felt obliged to visit the town in order not to disappoint the Indians who had prepared for them such foods as acorns and nuts and baskets of pinole made of sage and seeds of grasses. They also provided baskets (Indian water bottles?)[25] for the strangers to drink from.

Beyond the site of the present Camulos Rancho the party stopped, on August 11th, near a large Indian village built on the banks of an arroyo. Fr. Crespí continues:

In the afternoon seven chiefs came to visit us with a numerous following of Indians with bows and arrows, but carrying the bow-strings loose, which is a sign of peace. They brought us an abundant present of seeds, acorns, walnuts, and pine-nuts, which they spread out before us. The chiefs having learned who was in charge, offered to the commander, to us, and to the officers, several necklaces of stones, white, black, and red, whose texture and material was similar to coral. There must have been more than five hundred of the heathen; the governor gave them some beads.[26]

Beyond the place where Santa Paula now stands, the Spaniards came upon a small village of twenty houses made of grass and shaped like half an orange. A

[23] Bolton, *Palou's New Cal.*, 2. 134.
[24] *Ibidem*, 137-138.
[25] See Kroeber, *Handbook of the Indians of California*, Bureau of American Ethnology. Bulletin 78, pp. 533, 561-562, 701 (hereinafter referred to as *Handbook*).
[26] Bolton, *Palou's New Cal.*, 2. 143.

vent in the top furnished light and permitted the escape of smoke from the fire which was built on the floor in the center of the house.

On August 14th, they reached the spot where Mission San Buenaventura was later established. Here, Miguel Costansó tells us:

> We reached the coast, and came in sight of a real town—the most populous and best arranged of all we had seen up to that time—situated on a tongue or point of land, right on the shore which it was dominating, and it seemed to command the waters. We counted as many as thirty large and capacious houses spherical in form, well built and thatched with grass. We judged from the large number of people that came out to meet us, and afterwards flocked to the camp, that there could not be less than five hundred souls in the town.
>
> These natives are well built and of good disposition, very agile and alert, diligent and skillful. Their handiness and ability were at their best in the construction of their canoes made of good pine boards, well joined and calked, and of pleasing form. They handle these with equal skill, and three or four men go out to sea in them to fish, as they will hold eight or ten men. They use long double-bladed paddles and row with indescribable agility and swiftness. All their work is neat and well finished, but what is more worthy of surprise is that to work the wood and stone they have no other tools than those of flint,[27] they are ignorant of the use of iron and steel, or know very little of the great utility of these materials, for we saw among them some pieces of knives and sword-blades which they used for no other purpose than to cut meat or open fish caught in the sea. We saw and obtained in exchange for strings of glass beads and other trinkets, some baskets or trays made of reeds, with different designs; wooden plates and bowls of different forms and sizes, made of one piece so that not even those turned out in a lathe could be more successful . .
>
> We thought that this was the town which the first Spanish navigators—among others Rodrí-guez Cabrillo—named Pueblo de Canoas.[28]

Fr. Pedro Font, Franciscan friar who, in 1776, passed along this coast with Capt. Juan Bautista de Anza and his company, wrote such an excellent descrip-tion of the canoes spoken of above that it seems expedient to quote from his diary:

> The Indians are great fishermen and very ingenious. They make baskets of various shapes, and other things very well formed, such as wooden trays and boxes, and things made of stone. Above all, they build launches with which they navigate. They are very carefully made of several planks which they work with no other tools than their shells and flints. They join them at the seams by sewing them with very strong thread which they have, and fit the joints with pitch, by which they are made very strong and secure. Some of the launches are decorated with little shells and all are painted red with hematite. In shape they are like a little boat without ribs, ending in two points somewhat elevated and arched above, the two arcs not closing but remaining open at the points like a V. In the middle there is a somewhat elevated plank laid across from side to side to serve as a seat and to preserve the convexity of the frame. Each launch is composed of some twenty long and narrow pieces. I measured one and found it to be thirty-six palms long and some-what more than three palms high. In each launch, when they navigate or go to fish, according to what I saw, ordinarily not more than two Indians ride in each end. They carry some poles about two varas long which end in blades, these being the oars with which they row alternately, put-

---

[27] Kroeber, *Handbook*, 559, speaks of a wedge of whale rib and an adz of shell.
[28] *The Portola Expedition of 1769-1770. Diary of Miguel Costanso*, Publications of the Academy of Pacific Coast His-tory, Vol. 2, No. 4, pp. 33, 35 (hereinafter referred to as Costanso, *Diary*).

INDIAN ARTIFACTS. Top: *Flutes and whistles of bone and cane; ancient metate and mano.* Center: *Burden basket; ollas from the Twenty-nine Palms region.* Bottom: *Harpoon, knife, fishhook, fetishes and bowls.*

MISSION INDIAN DESCENDANTS: *The parents and grandparents of these Indians were trained in mission shops and fields.*

ting the ends of the poles into the water, now on one side and now on the other side of the launch. In this way they guide the launch wherever they wish, sailing through rough seas with much boldness.[29]

Along that stretch of coast from San Buenaventura to Santa Bárbara, Portolá and his followers were entertained with native music, dancing and speech-making. They named one village El Bailarín in honor of its chief, who was a great dancer—"a robust man of good figure and countenance, . . " One night they were serenaded with pipes and whistles, which, Costansó says, "were very disagreeable and only served to annoy us and keep us awake." Fr. Crespí, as usual, named the spot for a saint, but the soldiers called it Pitos (Whistles) Point, and so it is known today.

Near Carpintería the explorers passed two towns which were "ruined and deserted." Portolá surmised that the inhabitants of these villages had "mutually exterminated each other."[30] Essentially peaceable, the inhabitants of one village occasionally made war upon those of another for such causes as the theft of salt, acorns, or pine-nuts, a slight to a chief, or the belief that a death had been caused through the practice of witchcraft.[31]

Costansó was much impressed with the Indians of the Santa Bárbara Channel and writes at some length about them:

They live in towns, the houses of which are spherical in form, like the half of an orange, are covered with reeds, and are as much as twenty yards in diameter. Each house contains three or four families. The fireplace is in the middle, and in the upper part of the house they leave an air passage or chimney for the escape of the smoke. These Indians confirmed in every respect the affability and friendly treatment experienced in former times by the Spaniards who landed on this coast with General Sebastian Vizcayno. Both the men and the women are of good figure and appearance, and are fond of painting and staining their faces and bodies. They use large tufts of feathers, and hairpins which they put through their hair with various ornaments and coral beads of different colors. The men go entirely naked, but when it is cold they wear long capes of tanned otter-skins, and cloaks made of the same skins cut in long strips, and turned in such a manner that all of the fur is on the outside. They then weave these strips together, making a fabric, and give it the form mentioned above.[32]

The women are dressed with more modesty, wearing around the waist tanned deerskins, which cover them in front and back more than half way down the leg, and a little cape of otter-skin over the body. Some of them have attractive features. It is they who weave the baskets and vessels of reeds, to which they give a thousand forms and graceful patterns, according to the use for which they intend them—for eating, drinking, holding seeds, or other purposes, as these people do not understand the use of clay as it is used by the Indians of San Diego.

The men make beautiful bowls of wood with strong inlays of coral or bone, and some vessels of great capacity, contracted at the mouth, which appear as if turned in a lathe; in fact with this

[29] Bolton, *Anza's Calif. Exped.*, 4, 252-253.

[30] *Diary of Gaspar de Portola During the California Expedition of 1769-1770*, August 18th. Publications of the Academy of Pacific Coast History. Vol. 1, No. 3 (hereinafter referred to as Portola, *Diary*).

[31] Kroeber, *Handbook*, 236, 646, 647, 843.

[32] See Chapter XV. for Dr. Kroeber's description of the Indians' method of weaving rabbit-skin and feather blankets.

machine they could not have been turned out better hollowed or more perfectly formed. To the whole they give a polish which seems the finished handiwork of a skilled artisan. The large vessels which contain water are made of very strong texture of rushes, coated inside with pitch, and they give them the same shape as our jars.

In order to eat the seeds which they use instead of bread, they first of all roast them in small bowls, putting among the seeds red-hot pebbles or small stones; then they stir and shake the bowl so as not to burn it, and after the seeds are sufficiently roasted, they grind them in mills or stone mortars. Some of these mortars are of extraordinary size, and as well formed as if the best tools had been used in making them. The patience, exactness and energy which they exercise in making these articles are worthy of admiration. . .

In their houses the married people have their beds set apart on platforms raised above the ground. Their mattresses are some plain *petates*, or mats of rushes, and their pillows are the same kind of mats rolled up at the head. All these beds are hung with similar mats, which serve for decency, and as a protection from the cold.

The expertness and skill of these Indians is unsurpassed in the construction of their canoes of pine boards. No iron whatever enters into their construction, and they know little of its use. But they fasten the boards firmly together, making holes at equal distances apart, one inch from the edge, matching each other in the upper and lower boards, and through these holes they pass stout thongs of deer sinews. They pitch and calk the seams, and paint the whole with bright colors. They handle them with equal skill, and three or four men go out to sea to fish in them, as they will hold eight or ten [men]. They use long double-bladed oars, and row with indescribable agility and swiftness. They know all the arts of fishing and fish abound along their coast, as was said of San Diego. They hold intercourse and commerce with the natives of the islands, from whom they obtain the coral beads, which in all these parts take the part of money. They value, however, more highly the glass beads which the Spaniards gave them, offering in exchange for them all they possess, such as baskets, otter-skins, bowls, and wooden dishes. But above everything else, they esteem any kind of knife or sharp tool, admiring its superiority over those of flint; and it gives them much pleasure to see use made of axes and cutlasses, and the ease with which the soldiers felled a tree to make firewood by means of these tools.

They are also great hunters. In killing deer and antelopes they employ an admirable device. They preserve the skin of the head and of part of the neck of one of these animals, removing it with care—with the horns left attached to the skin—and filling it with grass or straw to keep its form. This mask they put on like a cap on the head, and with this odd equipment they set out for the woods. On seeing a deer or antelope, they crawl slowly with the left hand on the ground, carrying the bow and four arrows in the right. They raise and lower the head, turning it from one side to the other, and make other motions so characteristic of these animals, that they attract them without difficulty to the decoy, and having them at short range, they discharge their arrows with sure effect.[33]

Fishing was good at this time and the inhabitants of village after village turned out to welcome the explorers and to present them with fish—fresh fish, barbecued fish, roasted fish, dried fish—so much fish, in fact, that the Spaniards were obliged to ask them to bring no more. Some of the dried fish, however, was loaded onto mules and the travellers were very thankful for it later on when their own supplies were running low.

Costansó's account continues:

The natives not content with making us presents of their eatables, wished, furthermore, to give us a feast, thus manifesting the rivalry and contention between the towns to excel each other in

[33] Costanso. *Narrative*, 43-49.

gifts and festivities, in order to merit our approval and praise. In the afternoon the leaders and caciques of each town came, one after another, adorned according to their custom—painted and decked with feathers, having in their hands some split canes with the motion and the noise of which they marked time for their songs, and the rhythm for the dance, so regularly and so uniformly that there was no discord.

The dancing continued all the afternoon, and we had hard work to rid ourselves of [our visitors]. Finally we sent them away, earnestly recommending them, by means of signs, not to come back during the night to disturb us; but in vain. At nightfall they returned with a large retinue of clowns or jugglers, playing whistles, the noise of which grated upon the ears. It was feared that they would stampede the horses, and, for this reason, the commander, with his officers and some soldiers, went out to receive them. We gave the natives some glass beads, and intimated to them that if they came back to disturb our sleep, they would no longer be our friends and we would give them a bad reception. This was sufficient measure to cause them to leave us in peace for the remainder of the night.[34]

There were several Indian villages at this place and the soldiers named them Mescaltitán, but good Father Crespí "christened them with the name of Santa Margarita de Cortona." It was here that the Fathers of Mission Santa Bárbara later erected a chapel dedicated to St. Michael and the locality became known as the Rancho of San Miguel. It has a place in our story of after-mission years.

The natives of Dos Pueblos and Gaviota entertained the Spaniards as had those of Mescaltitán. Gaviota, Fr. Crespí tells us, was so named by the soldiers because they had killed a gull at that place. They had previously given the name of Carpintería to one village because they had seen natives building a canoe there. At El Cojo they found natives with European beads in their possession, telling of barter with tribes other than those of California.

Beyond El Cojo fewer Indians were encountered but those met were friendly and made gifts to the strangers of such foodstuffs as they had, the Spaniards always reciprocating with gifts of beads or other trinkets. In Price Canyon, north of Pismo, there occurred something of a ceremonial nature which, according to Fr. Crespí, they had not seen practiced by any of the other Indians. Women of the village there spread out mats, and after scattering seeds on them, told the explorers to be seated—a ceremony reminiscent of Pueblo Indian custom.

Natives near Watsonville, not having been warned of the approach of the white men, were terribly frightened when confronted with the spectacle of men accoutered and mounted as were the Spaniards. Sergeant Francisco Ortega, however, was able to quiet their fears and won their confidence by asking for food.

. . , and their women at once set to work to grind seeds, of which they made balls of dough and gave them to the soldiers. The sergeant then gave the Indians some beads and they were very pleased and happy.[35]

[34] Costanso, *Diary*, 43.
[35] Bolton, *Palou's New Cal.*, 2. 195.

A little farther on the company came upon a large village which the inhabitants had burned and abandoned in fear of the advancing white men. By Gazos Creek they discovered a village which for some days, Fr. Crespí says, they had been wishing to find.

> They had already learned of our coming from the explorers [the scouting party sent on ahead]. They welcomed us with demonstrations of pleasure, and immediately gave us some tamales made of seeds, some acorns, and some of other kinds of seeds, as well as a certain kind of honeycomb which some of our party said was bee honey. They brought it very neatly wrapped in leaves of reed grass. Their gift was repaid with beads, which pleased them greatly.
>
> In the middle of the village there was an immense house of spherical form, large enough to hold all the people of the town, and around it there were some little houses of a pyramidal form, very small, well constructed of stakes of pine. Because the large house rose above the others the soldiers called it the village of Casa Grande, but I dedicated it to San Juan Nepomoceno. There is a good arroyo of water here, much pasture, and an abundance of firewood, and not far from the village is a grove of redwoods.[36]

Next day the Spaniards left this village accompanied by two of the natives who went along to act as guides. They camped that night at San Gregorio Creek, near the coast. Here, as Fr. Crespí informs us, they found a good village of friendly Indians, who were fair, well formed and some of them bearded. Not until they came within sight of San Pablo Bay did the explorers experience any hostility. At that place, the advance scouting party reported, they were met by fierce ill-tempered natives who angrily tried to prevent them from going farther.

A year later Lieutenant Pedro Fages, with six soldiers and a muleteer, set out from the then established presidio of Monterey to explore this same region. The party passed through a country overrun by herds of antelopes while around the lagoons and along the streams they saw numerous flocks of geese. Most of the natives were frightened at the sight of the strangers, but close by one lagoon they found, as the lieutenant notes:

> many pleasant and affable heathen, to whom we presented some strings of glass beads. They reciprocated with plumes and geese stuffed with straw, which they employ to catch an infinite number of these birds.[37]

Constansó, writing after Monterey had been discovered and occupied, says of the surrounding country and its native inhabitants:

> To the south of the port, at a distance of two short leagues, there is a wide canyon through which flows the river called the Carmelo, and where the tall grasses and reedlike shrubs in places entirely cover a man on horseback [thus giving] proof of the fertility of the soil. Its products are valuable, inasmuch as they are walnut, hazelnuts, and cherries, just as in Europe, and everywhere are blackberries, roses and yerba buena.

[36] *Ibidem*, 206-207.
[37] *Expedition to San Francisco Bay in 1770. Diary of Pedro Fages*. Publications of the Academy of Pacific Coast History, Vol. 2, No. 3, p. 13.

In the mountains, there are very large white oaks and liveoaks which bear good acorns; pine trees bearing cones and yielding an abundance of pine-nuts; and groves of junipers, cypresses, and various other trees.

The natives of Monterey live in the hills, the nearest about one and one half league from the beach. They come down sometimes and go out fishing in little rafts of reeds. It seems, however, that fishing does not furnish their chief means of subsistence, and they have recourse to it only when hunting has yielded little. Game is very plentiful in the mountains, especially antelopes and deer. These mountaineers are very numerous, extremely gentle and tractable. They never came to visit the Spaniards without bringing them a substantial present of game, which as a rule consisted of two or three deer or antelopes, which they offered without demanding or [even] asking for anything [in return]. Their good disposition has given the missionary fathers well-founded hopes of speedily winning them over to the faith of Christ.[38]

Fishermen, hunters, potters; weavers of feather and fur robes, baskets "of a thousand forms," mats, fish nets, and nets for carrying burdens; skilled workers in bone, stone, wood, and shell; boat builders and traders,—such were the natives of California as the early explorers found them.

Living in primitive surroundings, they satisfied their wants from the products of Mother Nature. Roving wild animals, birds, fish from the ocean, streams and lakes, nuts from pine trees, acorns from the oaks, berries, seeds from chia and a myriad other plants, as well as parts of the plants themselves, furnished them with food. Certain herbs and shrubs yielded medicines for their bodily ills.[39] Their clothing and bedding were derived from skins, bark, and fibrous vegetation. Native pigments, colored roots and bark, shells, and the bright feathers of birds served to satisfy their inherent love for color and their artistic sense of design.

Peoples of the Earth they were with the ability to wrest from Her the means for subsistence and a certain—and perhaps to themselves, sufficient—meed of bodily comfort and well-being. That they had their bad habits and shortcomings, goes without saying. The same is true of all the peoples of this old world.

They, their children, and their children's children, together with Indians living farther inland and others on up the coast beyond San Francisco, in time became neophytes of the Franciscan missions which were built at intervals from San Diego in the south to Sonoma in the north.

[38] Costanso, *Narrative*, 65-67.
[39] Bard, Dr. Cephas L., *A Contribution to the History of Medicine in Southern California*, MS. Annual Address of the Retiring President of the Southern California Medical Society, delivered at San Diego, August 8, 1894.

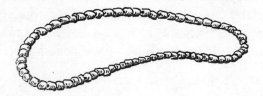

CHAPTER 3

Steps Leading up to the Founding of a Mission
The Ceremony Attending the Mission's Foundation

THERE WERE a number of preliminary steps to be taken in the founding of a mission. It was not simply a matter of two Franciscan Padres finding a site to their liking; setting up a cross; going through the ceremony of founding, and, with the aid of natives, starting to erect the necessary buildings. On the contrary, there were numerous rules and regulations to be observed throughout the entire proceeding. First, the viceroy gave the order or permission to found a mission. Then followed the selection of a suitable site. There were, according to regulations, very definite requirements for a mission's location. There must be a numerous Indian population in the locality and sufficient land for the cultivation of wheat and other crops. Plenty of water for domestic and irrigation purposes was also necessary. And there must be available an abundant supply of timber for building and for firewood.[1]

In the case of the first two missions, San Diego de Alcalá, and San Carlos Borromeo, their sites were chosen by Inspector-General Joseph de Gálvez when he ordered missions founded near the ports of San Diego and Monterey.[2] Both missions were later, with the permission of the viceroy, removed to sites that better filled the requirements. For, besides the necessity for having the viceroy's permission to found a mission, the Padres must also have his consent to its removal to another site should the first one chosen prove unsuitable. In these matters the Padres were not free to act as they saw fit.

When his Excellency, the viceroy, received the glad news of the establishment of the presidio and mission at Monterey he immediately decided, in consultation with the Inspector-General, to have a beginning made of five more missions in Alta California. He accordingly gave orders for the founding of that

[1] Engelhardt, *Miss. & Miss.* 2. 247; *Mission Santa Barbara*, 50.
[2] Engelhardt, *Miss. & Miss.* 2. 3-7.

number and directed that they be established under the names of San Francisco, Santa Clara, San Gabriel Arcángel, San Antonio de Padua, and San Luis Obispo. It was also within the viceroy's province to select the names of the missions. It was left to the Padre Presidente and Captain Rivera to find the most suitable sites.

Later in mission history, exploring parties went out in search of sites. A captain or sergeant usually accompanied one or more of the Padres with a guard of soldiers on these expeditions. A diary was kept of the explorations with full descriptions of the various places examined. This diary was sent to the viceroy usually with recommendations for a certain site.

The location having been approved, the viceroy next requested the guardian of the College of San Fernando to appoint two Padres to take charge of the proposed mission. Then, since the mission must have a church wherein to hold divine services for the conversion of the natives to Christianity, there must be furnished bells, vestments, church ornaments, and sacred vessels for the church and sacristy. For the first nine missions, at least, these goods were, for the most part, taken from the missions of the expelled Jesuit Fathers in Baja California and from their churches in México.[3]

Tools and implements for house and field as well as seeds for the first crops must also be furnished. And, moreover, there must be an allotment of live stock granted to each new establishment. Horses, mules, cattle, sheep, goats, pigs, and even chickens were sent up from Baja California and México for the first nine missions. Those establishments were expected to become self-supporting within a short time and everything was planned toward that end.

With the founding of Santa Bárbara, the tenth mission, a change of policy was determined upon by the Spanish officials in regard to the furnishing of seeds and the initial herd of live stock. For this mission and the succeeding ones, those previously founded were called upon to contribute what they could of the needed supplies.[4] Such aids were considered indispensable for it had long since been well demonstrated that, if the natives were to be Christianized, they must be well-fed and clothed. And there must be the means to accomplish this objective.

Joseph de Gálvez and Fr. Serra had resolved that one thousand pesos were to be given to each new mission to be spent for whatever might be considered necessary for its foundation. A stipend, or an alms, was also to be given annually to each Padre going to Alta California. Both allowances were paid from the Pious

[3] See note 4, Chapter I. this volume. Also Bolton, *Palou's New Cal.*, 2. 308, 309, 311, 312; 3. 26-27, 319, 321, 322, 378,
[4] Engelhardt, *Mission Santa Barbara*, 50.

Fund[5] to the síndico, or procurator, a layman appointed by the college to handle those matters. With the thousand pesos were purchased tools, implements, and goods for house and field. With the friars' stipend the síndico purchased, from a list supplied him by the Padres, gifts of trinkets, beads, and clothing with which to attract the Indians. In later years the Fathers also secured from this allowance additional household and church goods as well as renewal of their own clothing. A sizable portion of the stipend went to pay transportation charges on the supplies ordered.

A guard of five or more soldiers must be provided for the protection of the mission and the missionaries. These men were also expected to assist the Fathers in their endeavors to Christianize and civilize the natives. Last, but not least, blacksmiths and carpenters were necessary to the success of the undertaking. Buildings must be properly erected, tools kept in repair and the natives instructed in their use. A number of these artisans came with the expeditions of 1769. In 1774, Fr. Serra was able to have several more sent up from México with their families.

It will thus be seen that many preparations must needs be made before the actual founding of a mission could take place, for to be unprepared meant nothing short of disaster in a country so far from the source of supply, especially when the transportation of needed supplies was as yet an unsolved problem.

With the site selected and approved and all the necessary monies paid; goods for church, house, and field donated or purchased; missionaries named; guards appointed and workmen secured; live stock, seeds, and provisions provided, all was in time ready to be transported by vessel or mule-back to the chosen location.

There, on the appointed day, was solemnized the ceremony of founding a mission. Being celebrated according to Ritual the actual ceremony itself was, with little variation, the same on each occasion. Sometimes, however, an added or unlooked-for circumstance gave to the function a touch of never-to-be-forgotten splendor. The founding of Mission San Diego was solemnized with perhaps the least magnificence of any. That of Mission San Carlos was attended with all the color and splendor that the presence and dress of the military and civil officials can lend to such occasions. The story of the founding of Mission San Antonio de Padua is one that warms the heart of the romanticist. Three entirely different beginnings were made, yet the simple, solemn ceremony of founding of each was identical.

[5] The "Pious Fund" was created by gifts and donations from wealthy persons to the Jesuit Order for the purpose of establishing and maintaining missions in Baja California. It consisted of monies, estates, and loans to colleges and was administered by the Jesuits.

▲ A CROSS WAS ERECTED and blessed and a shelter for the altar was constructed. (Miniature)

▼ AT FIRST FOR OBVIOUS REASONS the small flocks and herds were kept close at hand. (Miniature)

▲ THE EARLIEST BUILDINGS *were of palisades, or poles set close together in the ground.* (Miniature)

▼ BUILDINGS OF FORKED POLES (de horconería) *walled in with adobes were constructed.* (Miniature)

At San Diego the threat of sickness and death from the dread scurvy hung like a dark, threatening cloud over the Padres, guards, and followers. Portolá with most of the able-bodied men had gone in search of the port of Monterey. Nothing daunted, the zealous Father Serra determined to make a beginning of the first mission in New California on the anniversary of the day on which the Spaniards had, under the standard of the Holy Cross, won a great victory over the Mohammedans. Accordingly, on July 16, 1769, a great cross was made and set in place where the future establishment was to be built. Water was blessed and the cross and surrounding locality sprinkled with it. Within a brushwood shelter there had been placed an altar before which the Padre Presidente sang High Mass and preached a sermon. While the records do not so state, it is to be presumed that the few soldiers who were able to attend assisted by firing salvos from their muskets to take the place of music, even as they had done at the founding of Mission San Fernando de Vellicatá, in Baja California.[6] And, since the incense was lacking, fumes and smoke of the gunpowder served instead.

At Monterey, on June 3rd, 1770, a beginning was made of the presidio of San Carlos and the Mission of San Carlos was founded. An enramada (arbor) had been erected on the shore of Monterey Bay and within it an altar arranged. Drawn up to witness the ceremony, in all military splendor, were Governor Gaspar de Portolá with his officers, red-coated Catalonian Volunteers, leather-jacket soldiers together with the rest of the company that had come up from San Diego in the second search for the elusive port of Monterey; Don Juan Pérez, captain of the *San Antonio* now lying in the harbor; his crew and other members of the sea expedition; Fathers Junípero Serra and Juan Crespí, the diarist. Truly it was a brilliant assemblage!

Bells were suspended from the branches of trees and rung joyously. Thus the celebration began. The *Veni Creator Spiritus* was sung and water blessed. A large cross which had been made was sprinkled with the water, blessed and erected. The royal standard was set up. The whole surroundings and the shore were then sprinkled with holy water to drive away all infernal enemies. Fr. Serra sang High Mass and preached the sermon. The lack of musical instruments was made up for by repeated salutes from the cannon on board the *San Antonio* and volleys from the muskets of the soldiers, gunpowder fumes once more taking the place of incense.[7] The *Salve Regina* was sung and the ceremony concluded with the *Te Deum Laudamus*.

[6] Bolton, *Palou's New Cal.*, 2. 265-268.
[7] *Palou's Life of Serra* (James ed.), 69, 90, 96, 98-99.

The commander, Don Gaspar de Portolá, then proceeded to take formal possession of the land in the name of the Spanish King, Don Carlos III. The royal standard was raised anew and the customary ceremony of pulling up of grass and throwing of stones to the four winds was performed. On this same day Fr. Serra began the new mission under the name of San Carlos Borromeo. He took possession of it in the name of the College of San Fernando and appointed as his companion Fr. Juan Crespí, who had been his pupil in far-off Mallorca.[8]

A year later, for the founding of the mission of San Antonio de Padua, Fr. Serra journeyed from Monterey in company with Fathers Miguel Pieras and Buenaventura Sitjar, whom he had appointed as ministers for that mission. They were accompanied by an escort of seven soldiers who were to serve as guards for the establishment. Three sailors and a number of Christian Indians went along to help with the necessary buildings. Goods for church, house, and field were packed in hampers, bags, and packs and carried mule-back to a spot at the base of the Santa Lucía Mountains. There in a valley thickly covered with oak trees they found what seemed to be a suitable location. The mules were unloaded and bells hung from a branch of a near-by oak tree. Immediately Fr. Serra began ringing the bells and shouting at the top of his voice, "Hear, oh Gentiles, come, oh come, to Holy Church! Come, oh come and receive the Faith of Jesus Christ!" Father Pieras urged him not to tire himself needlessly, saying that there was not within hearing a single pagan soul. But Fr. Serra begged to be allowed to give expression to his feelings, for, he said, he would that the bell might be heard in all the world; at least he would that it might be heard in all that sierra. A large cross was blessed, set up and venerated. Then under a shelter of branches an altar was arranged and Mass celebrated. As he turned from the altar to preach the sermon the Padre Presidente saw a single native who had been attracted to the spot by the ringing of the bell. His joy knew no bounds for this was the first time that a Gentile Indian had been present at the founding of one of the missions. As soon as Mass was finished he began to interest the native by means of little gifts with which he hoped to attract others. And, as Fr. Palóu tells us, this is indeed what took place.[9]

In this manner were the missions of New California begun. Little did Fr. Serra realize that the bell which he had rung in that Valley of the Oaks would echo down through all the pages of California's history. Much less did the native realize that for him and his kin it rang out the old life and rang in a new one fashioned in the Faith and after the ways of those strange white men.

[8] Bolton, *Palou's New Cal.*, 2. 290-293.
[9] *Palou's Life of Serra* (James ed.), 117-118.

CHAPTER 4

Attracting the Indians by Means of Gifts

The Beginnings of the Great Mission Establishments

THE CEREMONY of founding having been concluded, the Fathers turned their attention to the erection of the temporary buildings necessary to the beginning of a mission. In this task they were usually assisted by the soldier guards, the Christian Indians from Baja California and sometimes by sailors loaned to them from the supply vessels.[1] The first missions established near the presidios had the services of blacksmiths and carpenters. A few years later, as has already been noted, other such artisans were sent up from México to assist in the work at the other missions.

With the first buildings started, or even before they were begun, the Padres endeavored by means of gifts and kind treatment to attract the natives. For the Friars' purpose was "to save the souls of the Indians. Everything else was only a means to that end."[2] Now it sometimes happened that the natives had been so frightened by the repeated and terrifying sound of the salutes fired while the ceremony of founding was being celebrated that several days passed before they dared to venture forth to satisfy their curiosity about what had occurred. Curiosity, however, eventually overcame timidity and one by one they came to see what the white strangers were doing.

From the time of Cortés's invasion of México the missionaries had found that the Indians would follow them only when the Padres were able to furnish them with more of the comforts and good things of life than they had enjoyed in their uncivilized state. Therefore the Padres became "fishers of men" using as a lure gifts of beads, trinkets, food, and clothing. Fr. Francisco Pangua, Guardian of the College of San Fernando, called such gifts "the bait and means for spiritual fishing," and declared that without these aids the missionaries "would soon be

[1] Bolton, *Palou's New Cal.*, 2. 315, 318.
[2] Engelhardt, *Miss. & Miss.*, 1. 284.

pounding cold iron." The heathen Indians, he said, "are attracted more by what they receive from the missionaries, than by what is preached to them." But he added, "Once gained in the way indicated they continue this kind of mere material life until they have obtained some knowledge of spiritual things and are grounded in the doctrines of our holy Faith."[3]

And so the Fathers encouraged the natives to approach the site and watch preparations being made for the erection of the necessary structures. Being naturally friendly, the Indians often offered to help with the first buildings,[4] which were erected after a style with which they were quite familiar. Poles, some forked and fashioned from young trees from which the branches had been cut, were set in the ground close together. Usually the whole surface was plastered with mud. The roof was a flat one of poles resting in the forks of the upright posts. Over the rafters was spread a layer of branches covered with earth. Or the roof was finished with a thick layer of tules (bulrushes). The natives always knew where the tules grew thickest and the Padres were careful to see that they were rewarded for any aid given. In this way the Indians' confidence was won and it was not long before they were frequenting the mission outposts in great numbers.

The work, however, did not always proceed without hitch or hindrance. Occasionally a soldier was so careless or forgetful of the purpose for which he had come to California as to greatly wrong one of the natives. In a moment the whole enterprise would be jeopardized. One such incident occurred at the very outset of the establishing of Mission San Gabriel when one of the soldiers assaulted the wife of an Indian chief. The Indians were changed from a friendly, helpful people to a vengeful, threatening mob, and it was some time before the Padres were able to resume peaceful, friendly relations with them.[5]

Still, as a rule, things went fairly smoothly and by means of gifts and kindnesses the natives were at length induced to build their primitive huts, or jacales, within sound of the mission bell which ere long called them to the church for prayers and instruction in the Doctrina. At first this instruction was accomplished with great difficulty due to the Padres' ignorance of the native idioms. Not even the Christian Indians brought up from Baja California were able to understand the languages spoken by these natives. But by associating with them the peninsula Indians were in time able to act as interpreters, and through them the Padres proceeded to prepare the natives for baptism.

[3] Engelhardt, *Miss. & Miss.*, 2. 376, 378-381.
[4] Bolton, *Palou's New Cal.*, 2. 324.
[5] *Ibidem*, 325-326.

Before baptism was administered the Indians were warned that when they had become Christians they would no longer be allowed to roam through the forests, over the hills, and down to the seashore whenever they felt so inclined; they must thenceforth live at the mission. If they left the ranchería (Indian village) they would be followed, brought back, and punished. Moreover, each one must do his or her share of the labor which the running of the community entailed. All must be housed, fed, and clothed—be it with ever so little, and the duties involved were untold.

Long years of experience had taught the missionaries that if the Indian converts were allowed to return to their former homes, they relapsed into their old ways of living and soon forgot all that had been taught them. Also, going away clothed, they often returned as naked as they were when the missionaries first saw them, and it was necessary to furnish them with new clothing. Sometimes, too, they worked great mischief by leading back unfriendly Indians to plunder and steal from the mission stores and herds. Therefore, while the necessity for keeping the Indians held at the missions was regrettable, it was, nevertheless, unavoidable if the purpose of the Fathers' work was to be accomplished. Nor was this rule followed in the missions of Alta California anything new, for it had been proposed as early as 1519 by the Franciscan bishop, the Rt. Rev. Juan de Quevedo, and had been tried out in the Franciscan missions in Texas and México.[6] It was, in fact, the essential feature of what came to be known as the Mission System. As soon, then, as the rites of baptism had been performed the Indian became an active participant in that system, subject to its rules and regulations.

For the purpose of better instruction and more rapid advancement toward the desired goal, the Indian family was divided into three groups and each group housed separately. Thus the married couples with their little children were domiciled in the neophyte Indian village which the Padres persuaded them to erect a hundred yards or so from the first temporary buildings of the mission. The girls of about eight years and upwards, together with the young unmarried women and the widows, were given a room, or apartment, of their own. This room was called the monjerio. Because, until the summer of 1772, there was lacking a Christian woman to care for and instruct the girls and young women, this apartment was at first mainly their sleeping quarters. So much emphasis, however, has been laid on the fact that the monjerio was the girls' sleeping apartment in which they were locked at night to insure their being "secure against any insult"

[6] Engelhardt, *Miss. & Miss.*, 1. 319-324 (Galvez to Lasuen, Nov. 23, 1768), 2.245; *Mission San Luis Obispo*, 38.

that its importance as a training school has been almost forgotten. That the young Indian women and girls were locked in their quarters at night would evoke no comment whatever from one conversant with Spanish customs and practices. For, while the Spanish girls and young women were not locked in their rooms at night, their sleeping apartments had no outside doors, opening only upon the room occupied by their parents.[7] It was then and still is the custom of people of Spanish lands to so guard their daughters.

The fact that the Indian girls were not only locked in at night but were confined to their apartments during the daytime until they had accomplished the tasks allotted them by their Maestras (instructresses, or the women in charge of them); that they took their meals there, amply verifies the contention that the monjerio was far more than a mere sleeping-room. In fact, that student of mission management who fails to see the importance of the women's quarters in the scheme of training and Christianizing the girls and young women, fails also to have a proper understanding of the "Mission System."

It seems well at this point to say something about the soldiers who had been sent to California to guard and protect the missionaries and the missions and to help colonize and hold the new land for His Spanish Majesty, King Carlos III. Far too much has been written and re-written about the evilness of many of those men from whom for the most part the Indian girls must needs be "made secure" in their monjerios. Refutation of this charge, spoken and implied, lies in the fact that the founders of most of California's "first families" were also her first soldiers. Vallejo, Alvarado, Castro, Carrillo, Argüello, Fages, Ortega, Soberanes, de la Guerra, Peralta, Verdugo, Domínguez, Lugo, Pico, López, Estrada, Feliz, Yorba, Estudillo, Pacheco, and many, many others, all were soldiers. As were most of their sons after them. Many of them served as mission guards while others, with rank of corporals, acted as mayordomos for the Padres. That there were evil men among the soldiers cannot be denied. Fr. Font tells of one who was particularly obnoxious to and feared by the Indian women and girls living along the Santa Bárbara Channel. Fr. Serra himself complained about some of those men and while in México, in 1773, secured remedial action against them and their kind.[8] Nevertheless, the writer feels that the mission-day soldiers, as a class, have been much maligned.

In 1772 and 1773, Franciscan Fathers coming up from the missions of the peninsula to those of Alta California brought with them twelve Indian families. In

---

[7] Nordhoff, Charles, *California A Book for Travellers and Settlers*. (Harper & Brothers: New York 1873), 153: Lugo, José del Carmen, "Vida de un Ranchero" (Sanchez translation) published in *Touring Topics*, April, 1930.
[8] Bolton, *Anza's Cal. Exped.*, 4. 252; *Palou's New Cal.*, 3. 14, 33.

1774, the blacksmiths and carpenters sent up from México at the request of Fr. Serra, came with their wives to aid in the work at the new missions.[9] Thereafter, there was no lack of trained women to take charge of the monjerios. Then was that institution able to fulfill its purpose, which was primarily that of a training school. From a simple sleeping-room it came in time to have adjoining work-rooms with a private patio enclosed by high adobe walls. It was, in fact, a girls' school similar in purpose to thousands in existence today. The requirements, it is needless to say, were in those days far different from what they are today. At first the Indian girls were taught simple, homely essentials such as cooking, sew-ing, and keeping themselves neat. After their tasks were finished they were allowed to visit in the Indian village.

The boys and young men slept in their own quarters but they were neither locked in at night nor kept confined to their barracks in the daytime. They were under the especial care of the Padres, and it was from this group that the later musicians, choir-boys, acolytes, bell ringers, and pages, or serving boys were selected. Others under the instruction of Baja California Indians, or other trained workers became blacksmiths, carpenters, farmers, masons, tanners, vaqueros (herdsmen), etc.

Both the monjerio and the barracks were included in those first necessary buildings. These buildings, as they are called in the mission records, were merely rooms erected in a single, continuous row. They included, besides the monjerio and the boys' barracks, the chapel, the Fathers' rooms, a storeroom and some-times a workshop for the carpenter or blacksmith. The guards' quarters usually stood apart from this row but were always so placed as to have in sight the church, the Padres' dwelling and the Indian village.

When permanent buildings were erected this same separation of the members of the Indian families was maintained, for this was an essential feature of mission management. The Padres' greatest hope for the success of their work with the natives lay in the training of the young people. Being young and therefore with-out fixed habits and beliefs, they were easily guided in the way the missionaries would have them go. And, being trained apart from their elders, who found it hard to discard the old ways and customs, they were able more quickly to adapt themselves to new living conditions and duties. The married couples, because of their settled habits, were most difficult to teach. But there were tasks for all in this community of varied requirements and each from the very first had some special work to perform.

[9] *Ibidem*, 52.

From these beginnings, this mere handful of firsts, emerged the great mission establishments of after-years. The Padres' previous experience and expert guidance, together with the aid of artisan instructors and the native Indians' inherent capabilities, made progress and expansion a matter of time only.

▲ Girls from the monjerio *were taught by trained workers to cook, sew, spin, and weave.* (Miniature)

▼ An Indian woman *taking bread from a Spanish or Mexican-type adobe oven.* (Miniature)

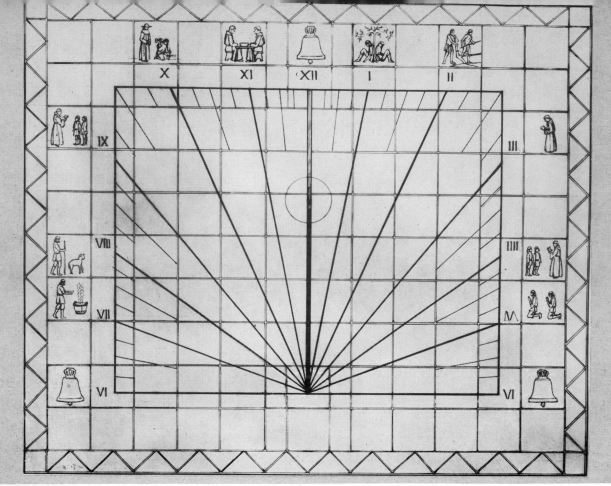

▲ SUNDIAL OF SAN CARLOS *reconstructed according to description given the author.* (COPYRIGHT EDITH WEBB)

▼ AT 11.15, *so the old records tell us, the Padres had their noonday meal.* (Miniature)

CHAPTER **5**

The Part Played by the Mission Bells and Sundials
Regulating the Hours for Work, Rest, and Worship

IN HIS APPEAL for bells for the missions which the viceroy had ordered established when the news of the occupation of Monterey had reached Mexico City, Fr. Serra wrote: "In view of the custom that his Majesty, whom God save, has of giving two bells to each of the missions newly founded, a large and a small one, two are lacking at present for the already founded mission of San Gabriel, two for that of Santa Clara, and two more for that of Our Father San Francisco when it shall be founded. . ."[1]

It is known, however, that the first bells to come to Alta California were brought up from the Jesuit missions of the peninsula.[2] And, there are today, still hanging in belfries of our California missions at least three old bells that once called Indians to prayers and devotions in Jesuit churches of Baja California or México. Two of these are at Mission San Carlos del Carmelo and the other one is at Mission San Diego. Two which most certainly came up with the expeditions of 1769 were, until November, 1926, hanging on a cross-beam supported by two posts, near the little Indian chapel of Santa Isabel in San Diego County. At that time they were stolen and have not as yet been recovered. One of the missing bells bore the date of 1723 and the other that of 1767. The bell at San Diego Mission is dated 1738. One of the two at Mission San Carlos was cast in 1752, in Seville, and bears the Spanish coat of arms; the other bell is dated 1690. The bell with the Spanish coat of arms engraved upon it is the only one at any of our missions that bears any possible proof that it was cast either in the king's foundry or at his expense.[3]

That two bells were allotted to each mission is most significant. These bells,

---

[1] Bolton, *Palou's New Cal.*, 3. 25-26.
[2] *Ibidem*, 1. 53-56, 58, 61; Richman, *California Under Spain and Mexico*, 69.
[3] With exception of the bell which, within recent years, was given by King Alfonso to Mission Santa Clara to replace one destroyed in the fire of Oct. 25, 1926.

it seems, were for different purposes. The missions themselves had a dual purpose—that of administering to the spiritual and also to the temporal needs of the Indians. It is not illogical then to conclude, in the absence of reglamentos to that effect, that one bell, probably the larger one, called to prayers and devotions, while the smaller one sounded the signal for work, for meals and for rest. There were bells for things spiritual and bells for things temporal! Corroboration of this assertion is found in San Antonio's Padres' *informe* of 1773, under the heading of additions to the church: ". . One large bell which the Padre Presidente sent us with a smaller [one] we had that the King Our Ruler gives [and which] they are using for the work in the field."[4] That is, it was being used for calling the workers together to assign to them their various tasks.

In after years some of the missions possessed as many as six or eight bells. These later bells were mostly acquired in trade for mission products, hides, tallow, and grain. They came from México; from Lima, the city of bells; from South Boston and East Medway, Massachusetts; from the Island of Kodiak and from Sitka, Alaska. The bell-casters were Ruelas, Manuel Vargas, Cyrus Alger, George H. Holbrook, and Russians, unnamed save one. There are also a few bells that were probably cast right here in California.

Three or more bells usually hung on a cross-bar, in the church tower, bell wall, or espadaña.[5] One hung near the corporal's, or mayordomo's quarters, and another close by the Fathers' dwelling. These last two were signal, or call-bells, and the manner in which they were rung conveyed to the listening Indian a very definite message.

There are two distinct types of mission bells, exclusive of those used within the church. First, there are the bells whose headstocks consist of four or more canons,[6] ears, or shanks, as they are sometimes called. These bells are hung by passing strips of rawhide or chains through the canons and over the beams of the bell-arches, back and forth until they are securely bound in place. They are known as stationary bells because they do not swing and are rung by causing the clapper, or tongue, to strike the side of the bell with some considerable force. The result is not the happy ringing produced by allowing the bell to swing completely or even partly over while being rung. Nor is the ringing of this type of bell an easy task. For example, a stone of proper shape and size is set in the ground in front of the bell-wall at Mission San Juan Capistrano.[7] Against this stone the

[4] ". . Item una campana grande que nos remitio el P. Presidente que con otra menor que teniamos hacen el juego que da el Rey, N. Sr. para el campo." SBMA.
[5] See Chapter XI for definition of espadaña.
[6] Often erroneously spoken of as a "crown-topped" bell and equally erroneously said to have been the gift of a king.
[7] A similar stone may be seen in old photographs of the bells at Santa Isabel.

bell-ringer sets his foot, braced for strong, sharp pulls on the bell-rope which, being attached to the tongue, brings it clanging against the side of the bell. So strenuous is this performance that when a ceremony of some length is being solemnized, it is often necessary to have one bell-ringer relieve another.

The task of ringing the stationary bells would, in all likelihood, have been given to a man with strong arms and back. It was a work that the Indians loved, that they cherished as an honor. Many of the bell-ringers grew old in its performance and were loath to give the bell-ropes into the hands of another.

Then there are the esquilas, the "glad" bells of the missions. These bells have flat headstocks pierced usually by three or four eyelets, or slots. They are hung suspended from a yoke in which they are secured by bolts passed through the eyelets of the headstock. The yokes, which serve as counter balance for the bells, turn in bearings set in the side-walls of the bell-arches. These bells are fashioned to turn completely over and over, producing a joyous ringing. Today, they are most often found without the picturesque yokes and immovably strapped to the beams of the bell-arches. Consequently, they are no longer rung as esquilas were intended to be, but must be rung in the same manner as the canon-topped bells.[8] So perishes one of the most charming of mission day customs.

Indian boys, young and active, would have rung the esquilas, for, wherever they were properly hung, they were rung by being turned over and over as rapidly as possible. To start them ringing, the boys, standing on the platform back of the bells,[9] placed the palms of their hands against the bell-rims and pushed outward until the tops of the yokes were within reach. Then, grasping the yokes, they gave a mighty downward shove that sent the bells spinning. There was need for care lest the bell catch the ringer and send him hurtling through the arch to the ground below. To prevent such accidents grilles were placed in front of the bell-arches. Evidence of the former existence of such safety device may still be seen in the espadaña of Mission San Antonio. It required considerable practice to keep the esquilas turning. It was an art in which without doubt many of the boys became quite expert. It is from the manner of its ringing that the esquila derived its name: Esquila, meaning hand-bell. It was so named, not because it was held by hand as was the old Town Crier's bell, but because it was *turned by hand.*

Some of the larger esquilas were turned by pulling sharply on ropes which were coiled around both ends of the bell-yokes. (Much as a top is spun except

[8] When La Purísima's espadaña was restored one of that mission's esquilas, long hanging at Santa Inés, was returned and hung in its yoke in one of the bell arches. This bell was rung December 7, 1941, when the church was rededicated.
[9] Such platforms are to be seen at San Diego and La Purísima.

that the one turns on a horizontal and the other on a vertical axis.) The ropes, being fastened to the yokes, were uncoiled and recoiled in the turning of the bells, making it possible to prolong the performance indefinitely.

The esquilas were the bells that were rung on joyous and festive occasions. In Mexico City they were rung hour after hour when news of the re-discovery and occupation of the port of Monterey reached the capital. They were rung when visiting Padres or other visitors of note arrived at a mission, if that establishment possessed esquilas. In 1776, the little bands of workers at the lonely, far-flung missions went wild with joy when Captain Juan Bautista de Anza arrived overland from Sonora with his heroic company of soldier-colonists, settlers, and their families. Destined for the San Francisco presidio and the two missions to be founded near by, they were welcomed ecstatically at each outpost with joyful peals of bells and salvos of musketry. The missionary Fathers came out to meet them, and, conducting them into the church, sang Mass in thanksgiving for their safe arrival.[10] This beautiful custom was kept up throughout the mission period. Many travellers made note of it.[11]

The esquilas were rung when an infant was baptized. When a little one died they were also rung. This was an occasion for rejoicing and the bereaved parents were congratulated, for they now "had an angel in Heaven."[12] Because of these customs the two esquilas at Mission San Juan Capistrano are known throughout the countryside as the "Children's Bells," though they are not now rung as they were in mission days. At this mission, however, many of the old customs of bell-ringing are preserved to this day.[13]

It is not difficult to picture the Indian boys of our California missions racing from wherever they were to answer the signal bells calling them to the ringing of the little swinging bells. Tousle-headed and half-naked, they rejoiced in wildly and joyously spinning them over and over until, becoming exhausted, they were obliged to give way to other boys equally eager to join in the performance.

A few years back the writer with several other persons was standing atop the sacristy at Mission San Gabriel where the old bells are within hands'-reach. The occasion was the re-dedication of the old campo santo (cemetery), and from our vantage point the entire ceremony could be observed. Being interested in the part that the old bells would play, we sought out the bell-ringer. Now that per-

[10] Bolton, *Anza's Cal. Exped.*, 4. 176, 269, 273, 300.

[11] La Pérouse, J. F. G. de, *Voyage autour du monde Paris 1798.* Quoted in Smith, Frances Rand, *The Architectural History of Mission San Carlos Borromeo* (Publication of the California Historical Survey Commission, Berkeley, 1921), 22-23. Hereinafter referred to as *Mission San Carlos;* Robinson, *Life in California*, 123.

[12] *Pioneer Notes from the Diaries of Judge Benjamin Hayes*, edited and published by Marjorie Tisdale Wolcott (The McBride Printing Co.), 122-123. Hereinafter referred to as *Pioneer Notes.*

[13] O'Sullivan, Rev. St. John, *Little Chapters About San Juan Capistrano* (1929 edition), p. 32.

son was a man long accustomed to the ringing of the bells. We stood with him watching the scene below when the signal was given to ring the bells. The man turned to take up the bell-ropes but an eager-eyed, dark-haired boy was before him. Quickly the ropes were gathered into the youth's hands and, with a flickering half-glance at the man, he rang the bells—rang them perfectly. No word was exchanged between the two. Only we three knew that the boy had usurped the role of bell-ringer. There was no occasion for the man to take over, nor did the boy, his eyes glowing triumphantly, relinquish the ropes throughout the entire ceremony. These San Gabriel bells are not esquilas; nevertheless, it was at that time that the writer was able to picture most clearly whole hordes of Indian boys racing across fields and up stairways to take part in the turning over and over of the little "glad" bells of the missions.

That the task of the bell-ringer was an important one is readily seen, for records state that the mission Indians were governed for worship, for labor, for meals, and for sleep by the sound of a bell. The Indians' day began at sunrise when the Angelus bell called them to prayers in the mission church. About an hour later another bell announced breakfast,[14] whereupon each family sent to the community kitchen for its share of the food that had been prepared. After breakfast another ring of the bell sent all who were old enough and able to work to their appointed tasks. There were no laggards in this community. From the small boy who scared birds away from the orchard or straying animals from drying adobes to the little girl who helped prepare the wool for spinning, and the old woman who gathered wood for the kitchen fires, all who were able to work had some special task to perform. In the forenoon and again in mid-afternoon, one of the Padres gathered together all the children over five years of age and instructed them in the Doctrina. Following the morning period with the children, the Padre visited the fields and shops to see that no one was absent from work. Shortly after eleven o'clock the Padres had their noonday meal. From twelve until two o'clock the Indians ate their meal and enjoyed the inevitable siesta. Then back to work they went until about five o'clock, when it was time for prayers and devotions. At six o'clock came the ringing of the Angelus. Supper was then served. For the remainder of the evening until Poor Souls' Bell was rung at eight o'clock, the Indians were free to do as they wished within certain limitations, of course.

Thus it was that day after day, week after week, and year after year, the life of the mission community was regulated by the ringing of a bell. Moreover, not

[14] At San Antonio the Indians had breakfast before going to Mass.

just one but all the missions followed this same routine to such an extent that what was done at one establishment was done at all the others at the same hour. Such were the requirements of the regulations that governed them. The exceptions were the feast days and holidays that were peculiar to the individual missions.

Such regulation, such routine, demanded reliable means for telling the hours. And, in spite of the oft repeated statement that "there were few if any clocks or watches in mission days," it seems quite certain that each mission had at least one such timepiece. For, aside from the need for timepieces for the regulation of the mission community, there existed the rules and regulations imposed upon the Franciscans themselves. The Padres had known nothing but the strict routine of the Rule of their Order since their earliest days of training. It is unreasonable then to think that they would have gone or been sent to a far-distant and unknown field without the necessary means for marking the hours. And, with the reports of early explorers before them, they would have known that our California's days were not all of unmixed sunshine. The sundial, man's first timepiece, would not serve every day. Therefore, clocks were a necessity.

Records inscribed on manuscripts now yellowed with age state that, in 1774, Fr. Serra at Mission San Carlos had an alarm clock. In their first yearly report the Fathers at Mission Santa Clara list among the goods received for the casa: "Un relox de madera con campanitas para horas, y quartas"[15] (a wooden clock with little bells, or chimes, for striking the hours and quarter hours). In answering the question regarding the method observed by the natives in marking the passing of time, the Padres at San Luis Rey state: "The months they calculate according to the moon, and the hours according to the sun. They have never used a calendar. However, the new Christians regulate themselves by the clock of the mission; and for timing their rest, meals, and work, we sound the bell." [16] Captain de Anza, in 1776, reports arriving at Mission San Luis Obispo "just as it was striking half past eleven."[17] The inventories of the missions of San Francisco Solano, Santa Bárbara, and Santa Cruz all list "un relox de sala" (a parlor clock). In the museum at Mission Santa Bárbara are the works of an old wooden clock, which, in all probability, is all that remains of the one mentioned above. Altogether it seems quite certain that each mission had its clock.

It is equally certain that each mission had its sundial. The dial must have been an important item too, for along with the wooden clock which struck the hours

[15] *Informe* 1777. *Santa Bárbara Mission Archives,* hereinafter written SBMA.
[16] Engelhardt, *Mission San Luis Rey,* 30.
[17] Anza's Diary, March 2nd. Bolton, *Anza's Calif. Exped.,* 3. 111.

and quarter hours at Santa Clara, the Fathers listed "una muestra de Sol" (a sundial) which had been purchased for them with funds from the thousand dollars allowed each new mission for goods for house and field.

According to the *memorias*, or invoices of goods, sent in 1771, to the missions of San Diego, San Carlos, San Gabriel, and San Antonio, similar timepieces were ordered for those establishments. The item on San Antonio's list reads: "Un relojito de Sol con su aguja y caja" (A sundial with its style, or gnomon, and box, or case).[18]

These dials were made for the individual mission, each being in a different latitude, for the angle of the gnomon must equal the latitude of the place in which the dial is to be set up. The gnomon is always fixed on the XII o'clock line of a horizontal dial, that line representing the true north and south meridian. The edge of the gnomon is elevated above the face of the dial to an angle equal to the latitude of the place for which it is intended.[19]

Sundials have universal appeal. Their quiet but relentless immutability has impressed man from time unknown. Some of the mission dials were quite picturesque. At San Juan Bautista the dial, believed to be the one that marked the passing hours for the mission Indians, still tirelessly tells the time of day to the passing, curious one. In 1874, the sundial belonging to Santa Cruz stood in the garden of one D. Ricardo Kirby on Mission Street, Santa Cruz. The writer has a water color sketch made of it in that year by Doña Cornelia, daughter of D. Ricardo. Carved in the stone face are these words: "Como la Sombra Huye la Hora" (Like a shadow the hour goes by).

At San Juan Capistrano, the dial most used by Rev. José Mut, in 1866-1886, was the long end of the ridge pole that extended beyond the eaves of that building now used as a souvenir shop. At that time this building had a simple gable end. The dial, of course, was not a horizontal one. Fr. Mut used it in timing the calling of the children of the village to the school which he conducted.

In the museum room of Mission San Luis Obispo is a broken fragment of a dial that once surmounted a column similar to those upon which the corridor roof rests and which stood just in front of the Fathers' dwelling. A traveller of 1850 sketched this dial and a later writer penned a very accurate description of it.[20] The study of the mission sundials is a most interesting one.

The Padre's clock was in the sala and the Indian's in the yard outside where

[18] Copied by Arthur Woodward from originals in *Archivo Nacional*, Mexico City.

[19] Henslow, T. Geoffrey, *Ye Sundial Booke* (London, 1914), 22-26.

[20] *The Santa Fe Trail to California 1849-1852. The Journal and Drawings of H. M. T. Powell*, Grabhorn Press, San Francisco, 1931 (hereinafter referred to as *The Santa Fe Trail*); *Pen Pictures from the Garden of the World* by Yda Addis Storke, 130.

he could observe its changing face. The sundial was something that the Indian could understand and it is the writer's opinion that it was set up mostly for his benefit. For had he not all his life watched the shadow of the rock or pole creep past a given point? Did he not know that when the shadow reached a certain spot on the ground the day was half done? And, therefore, what more simple method was there of teaching him the timing of the bell-ringing than by noting the progress of the shadow of the gnomon as it crept across the face of the dial? When the shadow reached one mark it was time to ring the bell for prayers. When it reached another the bell for work must be rung, and so on until the day was done. Nothing could be simpler—unless it were the sundial that is said to have existed at lovely Mission San Carlos.

Some ten or twelve years ago a friend told the writer this story about the dial that marked the hours for the Indians of that mission. Excavators were at work there in the early 1920's and, while clearing away some debris, they came upon a large flat stone. "There were carvings upon the stone—outlined figures of sheep being tended by Indian shepherds! Incredible! What could it mean?" The workers removed more soil and yet more until a large sundial lay exposed before them.

All around the dial, carved in stone, were objects and figures indicating, apparently, the various duties to be performed by the neophytes at the hour marked by the shadow of the gnomon. For instance, there were carved figures of kneeling Indians calling attention to the hour of prayer; figures of Indians partaking of food—an immense kettle in which it had been cooked indicating the time for breakfast, dinner, and supper. Then there were shown sheep tended by shepherds, workers in shops and fields, reminding the Indians that it was time for work when the shadow touched that spot. All around the dial's face the activities of the day were so noted that all could understand. What had become of the old dial our friend did not know. It was not then at the mission. The stump of the dial's post was later uncovered but that was all.

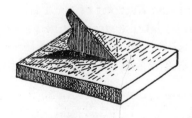

▲ One of the Padres *gathered the children together and heard them recite the* Doctrina. (*Miniature*)

▼ It was the custom *to welcome a visiting Padre with the ringing of the* esquilas. (*Miniature*)

▲ The bells of Santa Isabel (*now lost*), *and the two esquilas at San Juan Capistrano.*

▼ The bells of San Luis Obispo *as they hung in 1936 during the restoration of the espadaña.*

CHAPTER 6

The Interrogatorios *and the Padres'* Respuestas
Indian Food, Dress, Work, and Religious Instruction

THE FIRST years at the missions were filled with trials, hardships, and privations, due in part to the delay in the arrival of supply vessels coming up from México. During the third year particularly the Fathers of the four missions then established found themselves unable to supply their Indian families with sufficient food. The state of affairs was serious. From Mission San Carlos Fr. Serra wrote as follows to Fr. Palóu, his old friend still in Baja California: "The principal supporters of our people are the pagan Indians. Through their sympathy we live as God wills, though the milk from the cows and some vegetables from the garden have been the chief subsistence, but both sources are becoming scarce. However, the long, vexatious delay of fourteen months is coming to an end. News has arrived that the ships are bringing abundant supplies."[1]

In this time of desperate need the neophytes were allowed to take their baskets and go out in search of wild seeds, piñones (pine-nuts) and acorns as they had done in the days before the coming of the Spaniards. Returning, they gave this food to the Fathers to distribute as they pleased. Their offerings, together with bear meat procured by the soldiers in the San Luis Obispo region, tided the little communities of the north over until the supplies from México came. In the south, at Missions San Gabriel and San Diego the Fathers "tightened their cinctures" and sent Fr. Dumetz to Lower California for aid.

Within a few years, however, the missions were harvesting crops of maize, wheat, and other grains. The Indian converts at most of the missions were then fed regularly three hot meals a day.

Fortunately for those interested in the California mission Indians, there are documents extant that are replete with information regarding them. Among

---

[1] Engelhardt, *Mission San Carlos*, 35.

these records are the replies (respuestas) to two series of questions, or interrogatorios, sent to the Padres in the early 1800's. The first *Interrogatorio* came from México and requested information concerning the religious instruction of the Indians, their food, clothing, dwellings, punishment, games, hours allotted them for labor, etc.[2] The second questionnaire was from the Spanish government and was even more comprehensive than the first.[3] The Padres' replies are priceless. Following are translations of some of their answers to the inquiry concerning food given to the Indian neophytes:[4]

There are three meals a day for the neophyte Indians. In the morning they receive the atole [a very rich gruel]. At noon they have pozole, which is composed of a gruel or thick soup of wheat, corn, beans, or horse-beans, and meat for each. In addition they have a pottage, countless kinds of wild seeds, which they prepare in their private homes. At night again they have atole. The sick have their special food in the hospital where the atole of corn tortillas is prepared for them, besides the dish of veal or beef or both together. The cost for each person cannot be calculated, because all eat in community, though I may say that during the year as many as 2,000 cattle are slaughtered for food, and all that is harvested is consumed.

Fr. Luis Antonio Martínez, San Luis Obispo.

The meals of the Indians can not be counted, because it may be said that for them the day is one continuous meal. Even during the night, should they awaken from sleep, they are wont to reach out for something to eat. Their meals at the mission consist of meat, corn, beans, peas, etc. Of these an abundance is given to each neophyte by the missionary Fathers, and they prepare it as suits them best. Besides what the mission gives them they are very fond of what they lived on in paganism, as the meat of deer, rabbits, rats, squirrels, or of any little animal they can catch; while those on the seashore have a craving for whatever the ocean produces.

Fr. Ramón Olbés, Mission Santa Bárbara.

The Indians take no more than one meal a day, inasmuch as when they work they also eat, and at whatever hour of the night they might wake up and remember, they set to eating. At the Mission, there is morning prayer when the sun rises, at which time also holy Mass is said. After sunrise, they are given a ration of atole, and the same is given after the recital of the Doctrina in the evening. At noon the meal consists of pozole made of wheat, corn, peas, and other vegetables. Every week they receive a ration of fresh beef, in sufficient amount, according to the means of the Mission. At this Mission, weekly, sixty, fifty, or at least forty-five head of cattle are slaughtered. In seasons when the cattle are very fat, sixty head are slaughtered twice a week, in order to increase and sell the tallow and thereby procure the necessary goods. The large parts of the meat are taken in carts to the fields and burnt, since there is no one to collect them and there is plenty of fresh meat in the houses. In addition they have in their homes supplies of acorns, chia, seeds, fruits, zacates [herbs], and other various wild eatables, all of which they do not overlook, being very fond of them. They also eat fish, mussels, ducks, geese, cranes, quail, hares, squirrels, rats, and other animals which are to be had in abundance. On account of this hodge-podge of eatables, which they have in their homes and to their being like children who eat at all hours, it is hard to determine how much they eat every day.

Fr. José Señán, Mission San Buenaventura.

The Mission gives them sufficient time so that they have three meals of corn, wheat, beans,

---

[2] Engelhardt, *Miss. & Miss.*, 2. 551-582.
[3] *Ibidem*, 3. 10-11.
[4] All taken from Engelhardt's histories of the various missions. The originals are in SBMA.

and meat a day. Likewise, in their respective seasons is given them an abundance of cheese, milk, melons, peaches, and all other kinds of Spanish fruits peculiar to each season.

Fr. Luis Gil y Taboada. Fr. José María Zalvidea, Mission San Gabriel.

Citing the replies of the other Padres would be a needlessly repetitious procedure, the above covering the main points brought out by all.

The wild seeds and nuts mentioned by the Fathers were gathered by the Indians on those occasions when, for a week or so, they were permitted to roam over the mountains and countryside. The missionaries found at a very early date that, if the neophytes were to be kept from running away, they must be given occasional vacations when they were allowed to return to their former homes and surroundings. This course came to be looked upon as a necessary evil.[5]

Just as they had done in pre-mission days, the neophytes stored their nuts, seeds, and other edibles in large ollas or baskets set in the corners of their houses, or in large basket "granaries" set up outside. Their cooking utensils were their own mortars and pestles, metates and manos, pots and jars, together with earthenware bowls and other utensils furnished them, usually as gifts, by the mission Padres. Their cooking was mainly done over an open fire built between three large stones upon which the pot, jar, or comal was set. In some of the villages there were little adobe cooking places and outdoor ovens for baking bread. Here and there in California one may still find this type of oven.

Jean François Galaup de la Pérouse, French scientific explorer, visited Mission San Carlos. His account[6] of this event provides the following most interesting items regarding the cooking and serving of food for the neophyte Indians:

The Indians as well as the missionaries rise with the sun, go to prayers and mass, which last an hour, and during this time there is cooked in the middle of the square, in three large kettles, barley meal, the grain of which has been roasted previous to being ground; this species of boiled food, which the Indians call *atole*, and of which they are very fond, is seasoned neither with salt or butter, and to us would prove a very insipid mess.

Every cabin sends to take the portion for all its inhabitants in a vessel made of bark; there is not the least confusion nor disorder, and when the coppers are empty, they distribute that which sticks to the bottom to the children who have best retained their lessons of catechism.

The meal continues three quarters of an hour, after which they all return to their labors; in a word everyone is employed in different domestic occupations, and always under the superintendence of one or two of the religious.

At San Juan Bautista there is an interesting architectural detail that is said to have come down from mission days—a turnstile in a doorway that gave entrance to a room where, according to legend, the food was distributed to the Indians. One by one, we are told, the neophytes came through the turnstile into this

---

[5] Engelhardt, *Miss. & Miss.*, 2. 566-567; *Mission Santa Barbara*, 79-80.
[6] Smith, F. R., *Mission San Carlos*, 23.

room and were served. Passing out through another door, each carried his or his family's allotted portion of food. The girls and young women took their meals in the monjerio while the boys and young unmarried men ate in their barracks.[7]

After the first years the girls of the monjerio would have done most of their own cooking, as that art was one of those in which they received instruction.

A search through the Padres' reports and the accounts written by early travellers brings out many interesting facts about the clothing worn by the neophytes. Just as it took many years to approach the desired goal in building the mission structures, so it was with the Indians' apparel. Whatever the Fathers may have brought with them, in 1769, in the way of wearing apparel or goods for clothing to be distributed to the natives as gifts, it could not have been enough to provide even with loin cloths the great number of natives with whom they presently had to deal. And, too, until the missions began trading in hides and tallow, additional goods must needs be paid for with money from the missionaries' allowance upon which so many calls were made. There could not, it seems, have been secured by one means or the other sufficient material to fully clothe the neophytes or the artist who came with La Pérouse would not have represented those of San Carlos as he did. His painting[8] portrays the reception given the French explorer and his companions by the Padres of that mission. It was a great occasion, the welcoming of the first foreign visitors to California and to one of the missions. The governor at Monterey had sent a messenger to apprise the Fathers of the coming of the travellers. In the painting three Indian boys are shown wildly ringing the bells. "The president of the missions," La Pérouse states, "clothed in his cope, the holy water sprinkler in his hand, waited for us at the door of the church, which was illuminated the same as on their greatest festivals; he conducted us to the foot of the high altar, where the *Te Deum* was sung in thanksgiving for the happy success of our voyage."[9] Yet the Indians, who always put on their best clothes for gala occasions, are pictured wearing nothing more than loin cloths or skirts. And this was almost twenty years after the first mission was founded in Alta California.

In 1806, Langsdorff, German surgeon and naturalist, who came to California with the Russian Resánof, visited San Francisco and reported as follows on the dress worn by the neophytes of that mission: "Both sexes go nearly naked, excepting a sort of wrapper around the waist."[10]

[7] Piñedo, Encarnación, "Early Days at Santa Clara," an article appearing in *The Owl*, University of Santa Clara publication, April, 1934. Hereinafter referred to as "Early Days."

[8] Banc., *Hist. of Cal.*, 1. 432-3, note 11. This painting is now hanging in the Escorial, near Madrid, Spain.

[9] Smith, F. R., *Mission San Carlos*, 22-23.

[10] Langsdorff, George H., *Voyages and Travels in Various Parts of the World, during the years 1803, 1804, 1805, 1806, and 1807* (London, 1813), vol. 2, 163. Hereinafter referred to as *Voyages and Travels*.

However, had lack of material for clothing been the sole reason for the neo-phytes' scanty apparel, that obstacle should have been overcome with the set-ting up of looms and the weaving of cloth in the mission workshops. When, in 1814, the Padres penned their replies to the *Interrogatorio* from Spain they re-vealed the fact that many of the Indians were averse to wearing clothes. This was especially true of the older people. The men were particularly disinclined to wear trousers. Too long had they and their fathers before them roamed over the mountain trails and along the seashore clad in little or nothing, to meekly submit to the wearing of clothing that impeded their progress and prevented the unhampered movements of their limbs. In time this objection was overcome as were most of the natives' objections to White Man's ways and customs. But that the apparel of the neophytes was a distressing problem for some of the Padres may be gathered from the following translations of their replies to Question 36, concerning the clothing worn by the neophytes at their respective missions.[11]

Although they are much addicted to nudity, we make every effort to have them go decently covered. The dress which for the present is given for that purpose is the frazada or blanket, a short tunic which we call the *Coton*, and a narrow cloth which serves as covering and which we call the *taparabo* or breechcloth for men. For the women, a blanket, tunic, and a skirt.

> Fr. Luis Gil y Taboada, Fr. José María Zalvidea.

For the present, clothing of the following description is procured: for the men, a blanket, a garment of printed cotton or shirt of wool and "sendal," commonly called breechclout; for the women, a blanket, cotton chemise and woolen skirt; in this way all are clothed somewhat decently. Moreover, we manage to manufacture all wearing apparel. Then, too, the habiliments of the gente de razon[12] are given to some, because they look after the property of the Mission. If all valued wearing apparel much more would be given them, and in a short time we would have them going about as civilized beings. But they (that is the men) are not concerned whether they go about with or without clothing, inasmuch as they gamble away their wearing apparel; nothing is worn out of that which is given them; it is sold, exchanged, gambled or given away, then another gar-ment older or newer is sought. They do, however, enter the church and Fathers' dwelling de-cently apparelled, because otherwise they would be reprimanded. Among the property of the Mission are lambs, not yet a year old, from which sufficient wool is sheared; this the Indians themselves spin and weave and a suit of clothes is given them each year.

> Fr. Juan Amorós, Mission San Carlos.

The male Indians wear the *Cotón*, which is a kind of shirt of wool, the breech cloth, and the majority also wear a blanket. Others on horseback, or who go about the house, such as the al-caldes, or who occupy some position, wear pants, and those who wear pants generally also wear shoes. The Indian women and girls also wear the *Cotón*, a skirt, and a blanket, all these of woolen cloth woven in the Mission.

> Fr. Ramón Abella, Fr. Juan Lucio, San Francisco de Asís.

---

[11] Taken from Engelhardt's local histories of the missions.
[12] *Gente de razón*—people of reason, a term applied to Spanish and Mexican peoples or others not Indian.

The Fathers are solicitous that the neophytes go dressed in a most decent, though humble, manner, the clothes being of a coarse woolen cloth or of sack-cloth. Those who excel in industry, diligence, etc., are given clothes similar to those worn by the white people. They are fond of appearing well dressed: but this is not the case with the old men and old women; for at times it is necessary to have recourse to threats in order to induce them to cover themselves decently and modestly with the clothes that are given them.

Fr. Ramón Olbés, Mission Santa Bárbara.

The men wear a shirt of wool, called Coton; a strip of woolen cloth, with which, instead of pants, they cover themselves and which is called Taparabo; and a blanket. The women wear the same shirt or Coton, a petticoat, and a blanket. All go barefoot.

Fr. Pedro Múnoz, Fr. Joaquín Pasqual Nuez, San Fernando.

The neophytes here go about decently clad. The men wear the woolen shirt or overall with sleeves. It reaches down below the thigh. They also wear the sapeta or taparabo—or breechcloth. In Sonora this is a piece of cloth with which the Indians cover their loins all around. It is of cotton or wool about a yard and a half long and something more than half a yard wide. It measures less long and less wide for the boys. In addition, they wear the blanket. The women wear the chemise, the petticoat of wool and the blanket. All this wearing apparel is made in the weaving rooms of the Mission by the neophytes selected for this kind of manufacture.

Fr. Estevan Tapis, Fr. Francisco X. Uría, Mission Santa Inés.

. . . The vaqueros and principal men wear trousers, stockings, shoes and hats which are sometimes of those made in the country, and sometimes of those made in Mexico. . .

Fr. Felipe Arroyo de la Cuesta, Mission San Juan Bautista.

Those who by their irreprehensible and Christian conduct are of more use to assist me in the interest of the community, I distinguish by giving them pants of soft skin, a jacket of ordinary cloth, and a cotton shirt, when I can procure it, . .

Fr. Luis Martínez, Fr. Antonio Rodríguez, Mission San Luis Obispo.

The words "coarse woolen" and "sack-cloth" are suggestive of heavy, drab material. Heavy and bunglesome it was, but by no means without pattern or color. Speaking of the dress of the Indian women of San Miguel, the Fathers say: "Their outer dress is of wool, either blue, or white and blue, at least mixed black and white (gray)." Blue or white flannel was also worn at San Luis Obispo. Nor was blue the only color employed in dyeing the woolen cloth woven on the mission looms. Yellow, red, green, and purple dyestuffs are also mentioned in the mission records, though they may not all have been used in dyeing cloth for wearing apparel. Red, we know, was so used.

In 1827, Auguste Duhaut-Cilly, a French trader, visited San Luis Rey and afterwards wrote what is perhaps the best account that was ever penned of a fiesta held at one of the missions. He witnessed a bullfight that took place within the inner court, the spectators watching from the ladrillo-latticed veranda which topped the arcade surrounding the patio. A splash of color is introduced into the scene when he describes the dress of the girls of the monjerio. "They were more than two hundred in number," he wrote, "aged from eight to seventeen; their dress was alike, composed of red flannel petticoat and a white shirt. Their black hair, cut off to a length equal to half their height, floated over their shoulders."[13]

Captain Frederick William Beechey, who visited California in 1826-1827, attended Mass at Mission San José and confirms Duhaut-Cilly's description of the girls' and young women's dress. "Before the prayers began," he writes, "there was a procession of the young female Indians, with which I was highly pleased. They were neatly dressed in scarlet petticoats, and white bodices, . . ." [14]

Choris, artist of the Russian scientific expedition sent to California in 1816, left what Kotzebue, captain of the ship "Rurik," said were faithful representations of the costumes worn by the neophytes of San Francisco. Choris' sketches[15] show those Indians with shirt, blanket, and even breechcloth of striped material. Rugs, or blankets, laid on the ground and upon which players of a game of chance are seated, are woven with stripes of a contrasting color. No trousers are to be seen in either of the two sketches produced.

Adding to the color and design of the Indian costumes were the large handkerchiefs that the Padres sometimes ordered as gifts for their Indian charges. Alfred Robinson[16] tells of the Indians asking for "paños colorados" and "abalorios" (red handkerchiefs and beads). Color and ornament has always appealed to the Indian and no one knows this better than does the missionary.

In the instruction of the Indians, in matters both spiritual and temporal, the early Fathers encountered many difficulties. The first was the lack of a common medium of speech. It had been expected that the Christian Indians brought up from the missions of Baja California would serve as interpreters and that through them the Padres would be able to acquire the native idiom. In Alta California, however, many languages, or idioms, were spoken and it was found that none of them was understood by the Baja California Indians. It was only by associating with the natives that the Christian Indians were able to learn the idioms spoken in the various mission localities. Then, too, while they continued to be not only useful but necessary[17] throughout the mission period, interpreters were merely "stop-gaps," so to speak, second only to sign language and the giving of gifts. Furthermore, it had been commanded as much as a century before the advent of these Fathers in this new land, that missionaries in Spanish California must teach the ordinary prayers and catechisms in the language of the natives.[18] If a

---

[13] "Duhaut-Cilly's Account of California" (translation by C. F. Carter of Duhaut-Cilly's *Voyage autour du monde,* etc.), published in 1929, in the *Quarterly of the California Historical Society,* Vol.VIII, nos. 2, 3, 4. Reprinted through the courtesy of the Society. Hereinafter referred to as "Duhaut-Cilly's Account."

[14] Beechey, Capt. F. W., *Narrative of a Voyage to the Pacific and Beerings Strait,* etc. (London 1831 2 vols.), 2. 31.

[15] Mahr, August C., *The Visit of the "Rurik" to San Francisco in 1816.* (Hereinafter referred to as *Visit of the "Rurik"*)

[16] Alfred Robinson came to California, in 1829, on the trading vessel *Brookline,* as agent for the Boston firm of Bryant and Sturgis. He is author of the well known work, *Life in California.*

[17] Necessary because of the constant influx of "gentile" Indians.

[18] Engelhardt, *Miss. & Miss.,* 3. 42-43, 607-611.

missionary were to make himself understood he must master the native dialect.

In his mission in the Sierra Gorda region, Fr. Serra had acquired the Pame language with the aid of a Mexican Indian and had at once set about translating the prayers and catechism into that idiom. He had also directed the other Franciscans to do likewise and their work had been crowned with great success.

As soon, therefore, as the Padre Presidente had secured permission to change the site of Mission San Carlos from Monterey to the one it now occupies on the Carmel River, and while temporary buildings were being erected there, he began studying the language of his future charges. As Fr. Palóu tells us:

Whenever the Indians would come to visit the Venerable Father, and the day rarely passed in which they did not come being attracted either by curosity or by the presents he gave them, the first thing he did was to make the sign of the cross on their bodies with his own hand, and then he made them worship before the Holy Cross. When these sacred ceremonies were finished he would give them some little present, either food which he had ordered made for them of wheat, or boiled corn, with a porridge made from the meal of these grains, or else beads and trinkets, and so he tried to win their favor as far as possible, learning to talk with them in their own language.[19]

When, on May 21, 1771, there arrived at Monterey the ten missionaries who had been sent from the College of San Fernando in Mexico City to take charge of the five new missions which were to be founded along the coast, Fr. Serra detained them long enough to celebrate the feast of Corpus Christi. He then dispatched them to their respective fields of labor, going down himself with Fathers Miguel Pieras and Buenaventura Sitjar to found Mission San Antonio. All these Padres were instructed to learn the language of the natives. As has been noted above, however, there were numerous dialects spoken by the various little tribes, or groups inhabiting the villages that were scattered along the coast and farther over into the interior. There was scarcely a mission whose prospective converts all spoke but one idiom. At Mission San Luis Obispo, it is said, fifteen different dialects were spoken though but one was in common use. Some of the Padres faced a task of tremendous proportions.

Fr. Sitjar applied himself to the task with great zeal and diligence, the result of which Fr. Font describes in the following lines:

Their [the Indians of San Antonio] language is very rough and most difficult to pronounce because it has so many crackling sounds. It has been learned by Father Fray Buenaventura through continual application and hard labor, and he has written the catechism in their language; but since there are no letters to express such barbarous and ridiculous crackling and whistling and guttural sounds, he has made use of the K, and of various accents and figures, whereby the catechism is as difficult to read as to pronounce. But the Indians can already recite in Castilian, and in this language they say the prayers at least once a day.

[19] Palou, *Life of Serra* (James ed.), 124.

▲ The Indian woman's *seed gathering equipment, and mesquite granary at Martínez.*

▼ Acorn leach basket, *and the writer demonstrating the Indian woman's method of gathering seeds.*

▲ INDIAN GRANARIES *filled with mesquite beans or other seeds at Torres, San Diego County.*

▼ INDIAN WOMEN GRINDING CORN *under the protecting roof of the mission corridor.* (Miniature)

I think it would be a most difficult thing to find among heathen anywhere else in the world such a variety of crude and barbarian languages.[20]

Fr. Font's remark about the Indians reciting the prayers in Castilian reminds us of the fact that not only were the Padres commanded to teach in the native tongue but in the Castilian as well. Much is found in their replies to Question 11 of the famous *Interrogatorio* that throws considerable light not only on this subject but also on that of the intelligence and aptness of the Indian pupil. Space does not permit the quoting of all the replies, the following excerpts being chosen because they contain the gist of all and present a well rounded summary of points touched upon by the missionaries regarding the catechism used:[21]

In this Mission we use the short catechism, containing in the Indian language and in Castilian what is absolutely necessary for a Christian to know; at the same time we teach the acts of Faith, Hope, Charity and Contrition. The Indians are taught in both languages the Pater Noster, Ave Maria, the Credo, the Salve, the Ten Commandments of God, the Precepts of the Church, the Sacraments, and the General Confession, or Confiteor.
Fr. Antonio Peyri, Fr. Francisco Suñer, Mission San Luis Rey.

This Mission has the catechisms in the respective idioms of the nations or tribes of which its population is composed; but they are not approved by the Bishops, because not only is it difficult but well nigh impossible for the Bishops to find an interpreter who could revise them; for even composing them the missionaries found it a matter of much labor and patience. Superiors of these Missions, however, have taken pains and time in this grave matter.
Fr. Gil y Taboada, Fr. José María Zalvidea, Mission San Gabriel.

In this Mission, for instance, there are five Indian languages so different from one another as Spanish is different from Mexican. It is into the language of this particular locality the Doctrina Cristiana has been translated. The *gente de razon* call it La Doctrina Chiquita—Little Doctrine.
Fr. Ramón Abella, Fr. Juan Sainz Lucio, Mission San Francisco.

On the subject of the Indian's intelligence, capability, and adaptability much remains in the Padres' *respuestas* that is very enlightening. Regarding the learning of the Spanish language, the following replies are cited:

The generality of the Indians understand to a great extent the Spanish language, and they speak it with sufficient fluency, especially those who were born at the Mission. Those who have had opportunities to deal more with the Spaniards excel, of course.
In the boys born at the Mission and of better instruction, there is noticed much inclination to read and write in Spanish; but for reading and writing in their own idiom little or no inclination has been observed, but we doubt not that with facility they would acquit themselves in the one as in the other language were not paper, pen, etc., lacking.
Fr. Juan Bautista Sancho, Fr. Pedro Cabot, Mission San Antonio.

At the Mission five languages or idioms are spoken. Those who join at the age of thirty and over never learn another language than their own. . . . There is a good number that learn to speak Spanish.
Frs. Abella and Lucio, Mission San Francisco de Asís.

[20] "Font's Complete Diary," Bolton, *Anza's California Exped.*, 4, 279-280.
[21] From Engelhardt's local histories of the missions.

The little boys of the Mission in a few months learn anything, as reading in Spanish or Latin, and learn to read from manuscripts, to sing the plain as well as the figured music.

Fr. Juan Martín. Fr. Juan Cabot. Mission San Miguel.

It is not easy to discuss the means and method that the Indians may have the knowledge of Spanish, because it is most difficult to abandon the native language when there are more that speak the latter than those who speak the foreign language. When the conquest is complete, and some generations shall have passed by, they will be able to speak Spanish well.

Fr. Felipe Arroyo de la Cuesta. Mission San Juan Bautista.

It seems to us that the easiest and simplest way of getting them to devote themselves to speaking and understanding the Castilian tongue is emulation fostered by means of premiums, especially as regards the children. We have had no difficulty in getting them to speak and understand Spanish. For this reason the majority of the neophytes speak either the one or the other language, especially the men. Of those born in the Mission, all speak Castilian.

Fr. Antonio Peyri, Fr. Francisco Suñer, San Luis Rey.

In 1810, Fr. Mariano Payeras penned a letter to Fr. Estevan Tapis, then Father President of the missions. One paragraph of this epistle is so pertinent to the subject under discussion that it is cited herewith:

I believe I have written to your Reverence in these past years, that with the help of interpreters I have compiled a large catechism with the acts of Faith, Hope, and Charity, and another with what is necessary for salvation, a complete confesionario [booklet explaining about confession], and other little things, all in the language of these natives. By dint of effective patience, we succeeded in having nearly all the men learn by heart the large catechism, and the very aged the little one. With the women, because after all they are women [!], teaching the catechism did not proceed so well. Those who already know the said number of prayers in their own language learn it in perfect Castilian, which costs them hard labor, because they are even greater blunderers than I. Many (even aged ones) have made their confession in Lent, and some have received holy Communion.[22]

In later years some of the Padres seem to have grown careless about mastering the native idioms, and, in 1817, we find the comisario-prefecto, Fr. Vicente de Sarría, after paying a canonical visit to all the establishments, issuing a circular which was sent from mission to mission. "He reminds the Fathers that the Third Council of Lima, convoked by Archbishop Toribio in 1583, made it a rule that the Indians should be taught in their own dialect. Hence it is not enough, Fr. Sarría declares, to give instructions in Spanish and say nothing in the language which the Indians understand. They must be taught in the native idiom, even though it were necessary to employ an interpreter."[23]

Touching on the subject of punishments meted out to the Indian neophytes, Question 12 of the viceroy's *Interrogatorio* asks:

Which are the punishments inflicted on the neophytes with distinction of the sex and for what transgressions? Specify whether the Fathers have fetters, chains, stocks, and jails of their own, and whether they avail themselves only of those that are in the guardhouse of the soldiers.

[22] Engelhardt, *Mission La Purisima*, 22. Original preserved in SBMA.
[23] Engelhardt, *Miss. & Miss.*, 3. 42.

In reply Fr. Estevan Tapis wrote:

The punishments which the missionaries of Mission Santa Bárbara employ with the Indians, when we see corrections and reproof without avail, are shackles, the lash and the stocks. There is no lockup at the mission. The women are seldom punished with any of those instruments, save the stocks. This information contradicts that of the comandante [24], for His Honor reports that the men are punished by being put in the calaboose. We assure him that there is none at the mission; for the pozolera [kitchen] cannot be called a calaboose, inasmuch as it is open day and night, and always visited by many Indians; but the stocks are there. The comandante also asserts that the same punishments are inflicted upon the women as upon the men, save the stocks; but we insist that this latter is the most common chastisement. Whence comes this contradiction we shall explain later. For the present we shall describe the manner in which the punishments are meted out. A man, boy or woman either runs away or does not return from the excursion until other neophytes are sent after him. When he is brought back to the mission, he is reproached for the transgression of not complying with the obligation of hearing holy Mass on a day of obligation. He is made to see that he has freely subjected himself to this and other Christian duties, and he is then warned that he will be chastised if he repeats the transgression. He again runs away, and is again brought back. Then he experiences the chastisement of the lash or the stocks. If this is insufficient, as is the case with some, seeing that a warning is useless, he is made to feel the shackles, which he wears for three days while he is kept at work. The same practice is observed with those who are caught in concubinage. With those who steal something of value, or who fight with the danger of doing harm, this order is not observed; for these are first chastised and then made to abhor theft or exhorted to keep the peace. It has been noticed that this is the most successful way of maintaining public and private tranquility.

The stocks in the apartment of the girls and single women are older than the Fathers who report on the mission. As a rule, the transgressions of the women are punished with one, two or three days in the stocks, according to the gravity of the offense; but if they are obstinate in their evil intercourse, or run away, they are chastised by the hand of another woman in the apartment of the women. Sometimes, though exceedingly seldom, the shackles are put on.

Such are the chastisements which we inflict on the Indians in keeping with the judgment with which parents punish their own beloved children. We have begotten the neophytes for Christianity by means of our labors for them, and by means of Baptism in which they received the life of grace. We rear them by means of the Sacraments and by means of the instruction in the maxims of Christian morals. We therefore use the authority which Almighty God concedes to parents for the education of their children, now exhorting, now rebuking, now also chastising when necessity demands it. For these chastisements generally the assistance of the comandante or of the guard is not solicited. Yet it has always been asked when it appeared to us expedient. The Indians feel that they are never chastised without being well convinced of their guilt, and that, by the grace of God, they are never punished because of some ill will the missionary is supposed to have for one or the other, as Goycoechea asserts. Hence it is that the neophytes accept with humility the chastisement and afterwards they remain as affectionate towards the Father as before.[25]

One of the matters upon which Fr. Serra, in 1773, sought a ruling from Viceroy Bucareli and the royal council in Mexico City was the Padres' authority for the chastisement of the neophyte Indians. Evidently the Padres and the members of the military force in Alta California held different opinions on the subject. Therefore, under Point 9 of Fr. Serra's *Representación*, we find the following plea:

---

[24] Comandante Felipe de Goycoechea of the Santa Bárbara presidio.
[25] Engelhardt, *Miss. & Miss.*, 2. 572-574.

Your Excellency should make it known to each officer and to the soldiers that the management, chastisement, and education of the baptized Indians, and those that may be baptized, shall pertain privately to the missionary fathers, except in crimes of blood; and, therefore, that no chastisement or ill-treatment shall be inflicted upon any of them, either by the officer or any of the soldiers, without consulting the missionary father, for this is the immemorial custom of the kingdom since its conquest. It is in complete harmony with the natural law concerning the education of children, and an essential condition for the proper education of the poor neophytes. Therefore, in consequence of these considerations and others that could be accumulated, the illustrious visitor-general so ordered before leaving California, although it has been done very differently there, as a consequence of which very serious evils have resulted. I would like to dilate more on this important matter, and I will do so later if it should be necessary.[26]

Approved and signed by the viceroy and members of the royal council, the decision of that body in regard to this vital point reads:

In respect to the ninth [point], that the management, control, and education of the baptized Indians pertains exclusively to the missionary fathers, it was declared that it ought to be thus in all economic matters, just as a father of a family has charge of his house and of the education and correction of his children, and that the governor of California should be advised to preserve harmonious relations and communication with those missionary fathers.[27]

Obviously the above is not the granting of permission to punish the neophytes but the confirming of the Padres' authority to mete out the punishment. The question as to whether or no the Indians, young and old, should be punished if they were guilty of misdemeanors was not discussed. That they should be was taken for granted. That was, in truth, the custom of the time and had been, as Fr. Serra stated, from time immemorial. Nor was the use of the lash, the stocks, and the shackles confined to the correction of mission Indians. Those implements of punishment were employed in that day among civilized peoples in many parts of the world.

Harrison G. Rogers, secretary to Jedediah Smith, pathfinder and trapper, was at Mission San Gabriel from November 29, 1826, to January 19, 1827.[28] Rogers was a keen observer and his First and Second Journals are replete with informative details concerning this and other phases of mission life.[29]

Indian officials, elected annually by the neophytes themselves, acted as constables and were known as *alcaldes*. One of their duties was to bring before the Padres those of their number who were guilty of disobedience and minor offenses.[30] To them also fell the task of carrying out the sentence imposed by the Padres. The corporal of the guard usually stood by to see that the sentence was properly executed.

[26] Bolton, *Palou's New Cal.* 3. 15.   [27] *Ibidem*, 50.
[28] For the story of Smith's coming to California and his party's stay at Mission San Gabriel, see *The Travels of Jedediah Smith* by Maurice Sullivan.   (The Fine Arts Press, Santa Ana, California, 1934).
[29] *The Ashley-Smith Explorations and Discovery of a Central Route to the Pacific, 1822-1829.* Edited by Harrison C. Dale (The Arthur H. Clark Company 1941), 200, 204, 213. Hereinafter referred to as "Journal."
[30] Indians guilty of serious crimes were taken by soldiers of the mission guard to the presidio of the district in which the mission, to which the offender was attached, was located.

From both military and mission documents, too, it appears that corporals of the guards occasionally did some flogging of the Indians on their own initiative. Thus we find Governor Pablo Vicente de Solá issuing the following regulations:

Whereas it has come to my knowledge that some of the corporals of the guards have become guilty of inhuman treatment, and have arrogated to themselves powers which they cannot have in punishing Indians in their own name with excessive lashes, and I have considered it my duty to put an end to this abuse and to instruct Your Honors for the future to make known and to see that the following directions be carried out in all places in your charge.

1. No guard corporal is authorized to use the lash in his own name on any Christian or pagan Indian, unless the Rev. Missionary Father surrenders the Indian to him or orders him to seize the Indian and specifies the punishment he must apply. In this case he must seize or capture the Indian, inflict the punishment enjoined, and inform me through the next mail.

2. The corporal of the guard shall give a detailed report of every Indian, Christian or Pagan, who has been arrested for some crime committed, to his own presidio commander,[31] in order that through him I may receive it and impose the punishment of which I consider him deserving.

3. In order that no one may allege ignorance of this command, Your Honors will make certified copies, which you will affix in all guard-houses. Know ye also that on this date I transmit a copy to the Rev. Fr. Prefecto of the missions, Fr. Vicente Francisco de Sarría, so that he may notify the religious subject to him for its observance, and that I may be informed of any transgression they may notice. When the comandante of San Diego has appended the acknowledgment of its receipt and circulation he will return the circular to me.[32]

The governor's circular was dated July 20, 1818, yet on February 21, 1824, an uprising of the Indians of Missions La Purísima, Santa Inés, and Santa Bárbara was touched off by the flogging of a La Purísima Indian by order of Corporal Cota of Santa Inés. Discontent, it is said, had long been smouldering in the hearts of the Indians, due to the increasing demands from the soldiery for foodstuffs, clothing, and other articles produced by Indian labor.[33] The revolt was directed solely against the troops. The mission Padres were not molested. The story does not add luster to the military. Bancroft, Engelhardt, and others[34] give details which for lack of space cannot be told in this chapter.

Punishment, in any form, is not a pleasant subject but the story of the mission Indians would be neither complete nor true without its mention.

---

[31] There were presidios at San Diego, Santa Bárbara, Monterey, and San Francisco. Soldiers for the Missions' guards were furnished from those posts.

[32] Sola, "Circular," July 20th, 1818. SBMA; Engelhardt, *Miss. & Miss.*, 3, 39-40.

[33] Due to the Mexican revolution, begun in 1810, the soldiers had received no wages and, unlike the settlers, having nothing to sell or trade for clothing and other goods, were dependent on the missions for those necessities.

[34] Banc., *Hist of Cal.*, 2. 527-537; Engelhardt, *Mission Santa Barbara*, 120-136; *Santa Ines*, 30-35; *La Purísima*, 49-54.

CHAPTER 7

The Padres' Previous Experience in the Sierra Gorda

The Indians are Taught the Various Agricultural Arts

Food supplies had been brought up from Baja California by the expeditions of 1769 and the supply vessels transported more from time to time. It was not, however, the intention of the Spanish government to furnish the missions with food and other provisions for an indefinite time. Indeed, it was expected that, with industry and the careful husbanding of seeds, fruit tree cuttings, cattle, and other live stock allotted them, the missions would become self-supporting by the end of a five-year period.

Accordingly, after the necessary temporary buildings had been erected on the mission site, the Padres turned their attention to the planting of various seeds and grains. Some of the missionaries had had considerable experience in Indian missions before they came to Alta California. For instance, Fr. Cruzado, senior missionary at Mission San Gabriel from 1772 to 1804, had labored for twenty-two years in the missions of the Sierra Gorda in México.[1] Fr. Murguía, early Padre at Mission Santa Clara, had nineteen years' experience in those missions, while Fr. Crespí, beloved disciple of Fr. Serra, had spent sixteen years in that same field. Fr. Paterna, first missionary of Santa Bárbara, had for twenty years directed the affairs of a mission in that region. Fr. Lasuén had served there. Fr. Serra and Fr. Palóu had labored together there for eight years, Fr. Serra being at that time presidente of those missions.

It will be remembered, too, that the viceroy had been much pleased with the methods used in the missions of the Sierra Gorda and it had been decided that the "new missions of Monterey" should be managed in the same way. Those Mexican missions had been guided by instructions formulated by the Rev.

[1] The Sierra Gorda is situated in the southern part of the State of San Luis Potosí and in the northern part of the States of Guanajuato and Querétaro.

Father Pedro Pérez de Mezquía, first president of the College of San Fernando. His "Rules and Regulations for the Spiritual Direction" as well as those for the "Temporal Government" of the missions of the Sierra Gorda region and the regulations which governed those of Alta California were one and the same.

From his experience as a missionary in Texas missions Fr. Mezquía had learned that to gain the desired "spiritual fruitage" the temporal good of the Indians must be secured. "Because if these things were lacking the Indians would not be able to come to the mission nor attend Mass or take part in the daily prayer, for they would be obliged to be scattered abroad in search of food and clothing." He therefore urged the Fathers of the missions to request "tools and other implements necessary to plant crops, as well as cows, oxen and other cattle in order that the fruitage of these things might maintain the mission, as was the custom in the early days of the church."[2]

Acting upon Fr. Mezquía's instructions for the temporal government of the Indians of the Sierra Gorda missions, Fr. Serra and his companions, while serving there, diligently planted and harvested crops; cared for cattle and other live stock and their increase. The Padres themselves superintended the work in the fields until proper persons were found or trained to act as overseers. When crops and live stock had so increased that there was a surplus over and above the missions' needs, the Indians were taught to sell the grain and other products and buy with the proceeds tools, clothing or other needed articles—all under the guidance of the Fathers "who instructed them and prevented them from being cheated."[3]

From the foregoing it will be seen that the Padres who came to Alta California in the first years of the conquest were neither wholly inexperienced in agricultural arts nor in the management of Indians. Moreover, they had brought with them from the peninsula trained Indians who were to aid in the instruction of the natives of Upper California. Then, too, after 1773, when Fr. Serra had journeyed to México to obtain better measures for the success of the undertaking, each establishment was supplied with from four to six young men recruited in México to work in the missions as cowboys, carpenters, farmers, and muleteers. They were also expected to teach their trades to the native Indians.[4] For, aside from furnishing the neophytes with food and clothing lest they be forced to wander in search of those essentials, it was also necessary to train them to

[2] *Palou's Life of Serra* (James ed.), 26.
[3] *Ibidem*, 32.
[4] Bolton, *Palou's New Cal.*, 3. 19, 51.

become self-supporting as had been done in México. Furthermore, the work of Christianizing and civilizing the Indians was inseparable.

Another aid obtained by Fr. Serra, at the time mentioned, was the restoration of the old custom of allowing the Fathers to choose, from the mission guard, a soldier who would act as mayordomo. This official would have charge of the work "and everything else that came up in the duties of the mission and if the soldier conducted himself properly it was usual for him to grow old in that position." "This measure," Fr. Serra writes, "is of great importance for the advancement of the temporal affairs of the missions for the Father cannot attend personally to everything, nor would he know how to direct all the manual work that comes up, for at the monastery they did not teach him this."[5]

If the Padres brought with them from México treatises on agriculture, the fact has not been noted. In 1777, however, there was published in Madrid a book entitled *Agricultura General*. Twenty years later a copy of this work was sent to Padre Fray Antonio Jayme, missionary at La Soledad Mission. This book is now in the Santa Bárbara Mission Archives. It treats of everything that the amateur farmer might wish to know, from the selection of the soil to the storing of the garnered crops, not neglecting to mention the beneficial properties of each. In it is also discussed the care and breeding of animals. Another copy of this work is in the library of the University of Santa Clara. In 1883, Helen Hunt Jackson found in Don Antonio Coronel's library (*Glimpses of California and the Missions*, 197) "a quaint old volume called 'Secrets of Agriculture, Fields and Pastures,' written by a Catholic Father in 1617, reprinted in 1781, . . ." This last book was, in all likelihood, from the library of Mission San Fernando. Listed in the inventory taken, in 1853, of books belonging to La Purísima and Santa Inés is one entitled *Secretos de Agricultura*. Other copies of similar works had probably found places on the shelves of other mission libraries.

From time to time the Spanish government required the missionaries to make out various reports on the condition of the missions and the Indian neophytes. These reports, or *informes*, were made in triplicate, one copy being sent to the governor who passed it on to the viceroy who, in turn, forwarded it to His Majesty, the King of Spain. The second copy was sent to the Fr. Guardian of the College of San Fernando in Mexico City. The third was kept by the Padre Presidente.[6] These documents are most valuable since from them may be gleaned so many facts and intimate details of mission life and management. Not all of the *informes* written by the Padres have come down to us of this day. Many were

[5] *Ibidem*, 20-21.
[6] Engelhardt, *Miss. & Miss.*, 2. 445-446.

▲ THE ADOBE WALL *that once surrounded the garden and orchard of Mission San Fernando.*

▼ OXEN, THE WORK-ANIMALS *of the missions, were used in plowing and harrowing the fields.* (*Miniature*)

▲ A ɴᴇɢʟᴇᴄᴛᴇᴅ ᴄᴀᴄᴛᴜs ʜᴇᴅɢᴇ *at San Antonio de Pala, asistencia of San Luis Rey.*

▼ Eᴀᴄʜ ᴍɪssɪᴏɴ *had a number of carretas for hauling wool, hides, corn, grapes, etc. (Miniature)*

destroyed during the tragic days and years that followed secularization of the missions. Many were burned and scattered during the destruction, in 1857, of the archives of the Franciscan Order at their great convent in Mexico City; others perished in the devastating fire which swept San Francisco following the earthquake of April 18, 1906. It is believed that the copies sent to Seville may still exist.[7] Perhaps some day pages missing from the story of our California missions will be found in old documents filed away in the archives of Grandmother Spain.

Many documents are preserved in the Santa Bárbara Mission Archives. One of these is an *informe* dated at Mission Santa Clara, December 30, 1777, and is signed by Fr. Jph. Ant. Murguía and Fr. Thomás de la Peña.[8] This report is of particular interest to the student of the industrial activities carried on at the old missions, for, along with a short account of the mission's founding, its location, natural advantages, etc., there is given a list of the tools, implements, and utensils provided in that first year for use in the house, kitchen, field, carpenter and harness shops, as well as for the masons. Translated, the list of tools for use in the fields is as follows:

> 2 plowshares and two points.
> 4 crowbars
> 3 dozen hoes
> 1 dozen digging sticks, or Mexican hoes (coas)
> 2 dozen axes (six for carpenters and the rest for cutting down trees)
> 1 dozen machetes for cutting brush
> 1 dozen sickles
> 4 plows with complete equipment

In all probability the tools and implements supplied each new mission varied but little from those listed by the Padres of Santa Clara. These tools were crude and unwieldy as compared with those in use today. Examples of hoes, axes, sickles, spades, saws, and other implements used by the mission Indians are still to be found in some of the mission museums. The plows listed in the Santa Clara report of 1777 were of the type described by Forbes, who wrote in the 1830's:[9]

The plow used, not only in California, but in all other parts of America inhabited by the Spanish race, is of great antiquity—and is also I believe still used in old Spain.[10] It is composed of

---

[7] *Indians of the Rio Grande Valley* by Adolph F. Bandelier & Edgar L. Hewett. Part II. *Documentary History of the Rio Grande Pueblos by Adolph F. Bandelier* (University of New Mexico Press), 118. Hereinafter referred to as *Documentary History.*

[8] As the Padres signed their names.

[9] Forbes, *California: A History of Upper and Lower California* (London 1839), 248-249.

[10] This type of plow is still used in countries of Spanish-speaking peoples. See *National Geographic Magazine*, May, 1916; Nov., 1922; Feb., 1927; May, 1927; Feb., 1929; Jan., 1934; March, 1934; Feb., 1944.

two principal pieces; the one which we shall call the main piece, is formed out of a crooked branch of timber cut from a tree, of such a natural shape as to form this main piece, which constitutes of itself the sole and handle or stilt; it has only one handle, and no mould-board or other contrivance for turning over the furrow, and is therefore only capable of making a simple rut equal on both sides; a share is fitted to the point of the sole, but without any feather, and is the only iron in the construction of the plow. The other piece is the beam, which is of great length so as to reach the yoke of the oxen by which the plow is drawn; this beam is also formed of a natural piece of wood, cut from a tree of the necessary dimensions, and has no dressing except the taking off the bark; it is inserted into the main piece, and connected with it by a small upright piece of wood on which it slides, and is fixed by two wedges: by withdrawing those wedges the beam is elevated or lowered, and by this means the plow is regulated as to depth of furrow, or what plowmen call, giving more or less earth.

The long beam passes between the two oxen like the pole of a carriage or ox-wain, and no chain is required for drawing the plow; a pin is put through the point of the beam which passes before the yoke, and is fixed there by thongs of rawhide. The plowman goes at one side of the plow holding the handle or stilt with his right hand, and managing the goad with his left. There are never more than two oxen used in these plows,[11] and no driver is required; the plowman managing the plow and directing the oxen himself. The manner of yoking the oxen is not as is done in the north of Europe by putting the yoke on the shoulders and fixing it by a wooden collar or bow, round the neck: the yoke is placed on the top of the head close behind the horns, tied firmly to their roots and to the forehead by thongs, so that instead of drawing by the shoulders they draw by the roots of the horns and forehead. When oxen are so bound up they have no freedom to move their heads; they go with their noses turned up and seem in great pain.

Since the plow did no more than make a "rut" in the earth it was necessary to cross and re-cross the field many times to break up the soil. Plowing was commenced after the early rains had softened the ground sufficiently to render it more workable. It seems that every ox and plow that the mission possessed was put to work at the same time and in the same field. The Indians must have enjoyed this work, hard though it was, for through it they had a foretaste of the mastery of animals—an experience entirely new to them. Moreover, it was work that challenged their inherent desire to excel in feats of skill, and it required some considerable skill to steady the plow with one hand, and, by means of the goad held in the other, to guide the slow, lumbering oxen. Then, too, Indians like to work together, as many as possible on the same job at the same time. It seems inevitable that there should have developed no little rivalry between the drivers of the numerous ox-teams, and friendly rivalry was encouraged by the Padres. It produced results.

What a sight it was that met the eyes of Sir James Douglas of the Hudson's Bay Company when, in 1841, he visited the Mission of Santa Clara and watched the neophytes preparing a field for planting. In his *Journal* he declares:

I saw near the Mission of Santa Clara ten of these ploughs at work, drawn by 60 oxen with 10 Indian drivers, all following each other in the same direction, but so irregularly that scarcely two

---

[11] This is an error. See Sir James Douglas's account.

furrows were in parallel line. As they met, crossed and receded according to the vagaries of the cattle.[12]

After the ground was plowed the grain was sown broadcast and was covered by dragging brush or long, heavy logs over the field. The logs, not turning, pushed the soil before them and over the grain. Maize, or Indian corn, was planted in furrows, several seeds being dropped into each hill and covered by foot with loosened dirt. Beans, peas, and lentils were planted in rows and covered in the same manner.

Weed-hooks and hoes were provided for weeding, which was usually done by the men. When men laborers were scarce or busy with other tasks, Indian boys and some of the older women, not able to do heavier work, were assigned to this task.

Gardens and fields were not at first fenced to keep out the live stock but rather the animals were guarded and kept away from the growing crops. As the live stock increased and Indian vaqueros were trained to care for them, the various herds were pastured away from the missions. But at first for obvious reasons everything was kept close at hand. In time orchards, gardens, and vineyards were fenced with adobe walls, cactus hedges, and even ditches, wide and deep enough to keep the cattle from passing over. At one or two missions cattle horns, with skulls attached, were piled high around garden plots or affixed to the tops of low adobe walls enclosing the area.[13] Portions of these walls or hedges may still be seen at some of the old missions, though no cattle horns remain.

When corn, or maize, was ripe it was gathered from the stalks in large Indian-made baskets—the burden-baskets of pre-mission days. When full the baskets were emptied into a carreta (Spanish cart) that stood near by. The carreta has been described by most writers of early California. Edwin Bryant, who came to this state in 1846, says of it:

The carreta is the rudest specimen of wheeled vehicle I have ever seen. The wheels are transverse sections of a log, and are usually about 2½ feet in diameter, and varying in thickness from the center to the rim. The wheels are coupled together by an axletree, into which a tongue is inserted. On the axletree and tongue rests a frame, constructed of square pieces of timber, six or eight feet in length and four or five in breadth, into which are inserted a number of stakes about four feet in length. This framework being covered and floored with raw hides, the carriage is completed.[14]

[12] This excerpt was taken from the article, "From Columbia to California in 1840" (from the *Journal* of Sir James Douglas), appearing in *Quarterly of the California Historical Society*, June, 1929, by permission of the Society. The Douglas *Journal*, a manuscript, is in the Bancroft Library, University of California, Berkeley.

[13] Banc., *Hist. of Cal.*, 1. 725, n. 62; Engelhardt, *Mission San Francisco*, 118; Vallejo, Guadalupe, "Ranch and Mission Days in Alta California," *Century Magazine*, December 1890 (hereinafter referred to as "Ranch and Mission Days"); Mylar, Isaac L., *Early Days at Mission San Juan Bautista*, 20.

[14] Bryant, Edwin, *What I Saw in California* (The Fine Arts Press, Santa Ana, California, 1936), 294-295. Hereinafter referred to as *What I Saw*.

Drawn by two or more oxen the cart, heaped high with corn, was hauled to the mission. Here the maize was usually husked by the Indians and stored on the cob[15] in rooms, or buildings, erected for that purpose. In later years attics, or lofts, were built over the rooms of the main wing of the quadrangle at many of the missions. Most often ventilated by means of small, barred windows, as at Missions San Francisco and San Fernando,[16] these attics furnished ideal store-rooms for corn. At Santa Bárbara ventilation of the loft was secured through an open-work arrangement of ladrillos (floor tiles) set in the upper front wall of the Fathers' house, as the main front row of rooms is usually called. Several early sketches of the mission show this unique detail.[17] Some of these lofts had tiled floors. That of Mission Santa Inés, for instance, was floored with ten-inch-square tiles laid to simulate diamond-shaped ones. At San Fernando, until recently, the attic over that room which forms the entire east end of the Fathers' dwelling, had its ladrillo floor.

Wheat was harvested by hand, Indians in great numbers invading the fields and cutting down the ripened grain with sickles as is done in Peru today.[18] Left heaped in piles over the field, the grain was afterward gathered up, loaded onto carretas, and taken to the mission to be threshed.

Each mission had its circular threshing floor. According to Duhaut-Cilly, Mission Santa Clara's floor was sixty feet in diameter and "entirely enclosed in a palisade"[19] instead of an adobe wall. San Antonio's threshing floor was approximately eighty-five feet in diameter and was paved with smooth round stones. Some of the floors were of "beaten earth" and many, in later times, were paved with ladrillos. An adobe wall was built around the floor. Entrance was had through a gate. After sufficient grain had been piled on the floor, mares[20] from the mission droves were driven in and the gate secured. Perched on top of the wall were numerous howling and gesticulating Indians who, by means of their wild antics, kept the animals moving. At intervals these tormentors dashed in before the mares, making them reverse their motion, thereby plowing up the straw to the very floor. In a short time the grain was threshed and the animals released.

Next came the winnowing of the grain, through which process it was separated from the straw and chaff. As much straw as possible was first removed with

[15] Corn left on the cob kept longer than it did when shelled.
[16] Seen in old photographs taken before a succession of changes were made following the collapse of the old kitchen chimney.
[17] See sketch by Powell in *The Santa Fe Trail*.
[18] *National Geographic Magazine*, Feb., 1927.
[19] An enclosure of poles set close together in the ground.
[20] Duhaut-Cilly says that the mares were used because, being kept only for breeding purposes, it did not matter if their legs were ruined—as they were in this threshing performance.

a wooden fork. Then, using a large wooden shovel, the grain was tossed into the air, the wheat falling to the floor while the chaff, being lighter, was blown to one side by the breeze. Winnowing was done only when there was sufficient breeze to blow the chaff away. After this process was repeated once or twice the grain was stored, until needed, in the mission granary.

Peas, beans, and lentils were piled on the threshing floor and beaten with flails.[21] They were then winnowed and stored away in large leathern bags, or pottery storage jars.

In all this labor the mission Indians were guided by overseers or others previously trained in the various activities connected with agriculture. Step by step they were taught to prepare the soil by plowing, to plant seeds, to cultivate and weed crops, and to harvest and store the products for the daily needs of the community.

In spite of, or perhaps *because* of[22] their crude tools, the missions achieved remarkable success in the agricultural field, as is indicated by the yearly reports of the Padres. Their plow did no more than loosen the top soil, which, by reason of its covering of centuries-old accumulation of plant debris, was rich and fertile. Good crops resulted except, of course, in years of drought. And, despite loss suffered through primitive harvesting methods, the yield was such as to excite comment from many early visitors to California.

From 1783 to 1832 the missions all together harvested 4,137,625 bushels of grain of all kinds.[23] As mere bushels of grain that amount does not impress one greatly, especially in this day and age when thinking is done in terms of billions and hundred billions, but, measured by the various primitive processes through which the result was achieved, the amount was enormous.

Not only did the Indians perform the work in the fields, gardens and orchards of the mission community, but, as in the missions of the Sierra Gorda, those who desired them had gardens of their own to care for. They were encouraged to plant various seeds and cuttings and were allowed to dispose of the produce as they chose.

Robinson writes of gardens at Rancho Las Flores, cattle establishment of Mission San Luis Rey, which "were cultivated by the Indians for their own personal benefit, and in which they were permitted to labor when not required to give their time to the interests of the Mission." According to that writer, "Along

[21] A flail may be seen in the Santa Bárbara Mission museum.
[22] Faulkner, *Plowman's Folly*.
[23] Agricultural reports were first demanded of the Padres in 1783. See Engelhardt, *Miss. & Miss.*, 4. 535, for total amount of various kinds of grain grown at each mission during the 1783-1832 period.

the margin of the river St. Buenaventura are many small gardens belonging to the Indians, where they raise fruit and vegetables, which are taken to town and disposed of. The whale ships that touch at Sta Barbara are from them frequently supplied with provisions."[24] Choris, the artist of the Russian expedition of 1816, says of the Indians of San Francisco: "In their free time, the Indians work in gardens that are given them; they raise therein onions, garlic, canteloupes, watermelons, pumpkins, and fruit trees. The products belong to them and they can dispose of them as they see fit."[25] Mention of Indians' private gardens is also made—though inadvertently—in reports sent to the Spanish government by the mission Padres.

[24] Robinson, *Life in Cal.*, 39-40; 61-62, 93.
[25] Mahr, *Visit of the "Rurik"*, 94-95.

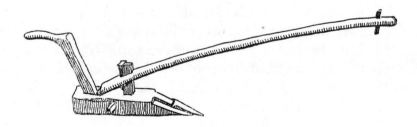

CHAPTER **8**

The Development of the Mission Water Systems
The Indians Build Aqueducts, Dams, and Reservoirs

THE PADRES' first attempts at agriculture did not always meet with success. Indeed, until those pioneers became somewhat acquainted with the vagaries of California's "unusual" climate, its rainy season, and the habits of its rivers and streams, the results of their agricultural ventures were often very disheartening. For example, in the first year at Mission San Diego, a planting of wheat was made along the San Diego River. The rains came, the waters of the river rose, overflowed the banks, and swept away the precious seed. Next year the grain was sown on higher ground but the season was a dry one and the crop was very meager. Moreover, there was no running water in the river except during the rainy season; at other times only pools remained here and there in the riverbed. Consequently, the Fathers applied to the viceroy for permission to remove the mission from its site on "Presidio Hill" above "Old Town," to its present location, about five miles farther up in Mission Valley, where there was more land suited to cultivation and a more dependable water supply.

In granting permission for the removal, Viceroy Bucareli called the Padres' attention to the rules which governed the selection of a mission site. "To prevent a similar calamity in future reductions," he wrote, "Your Reverence ought always to look to the best results for the natives and his majesty, whom God save, with relation to ample and good lands with plenty of good waters, as the matter of first importance in accordance with Law 8, Title 3, Book 6, of the *Recopilación*, which laws every establishment ought to have for the best understanding and government."[1]

The viceroy's letter also brought out the interesting fact, often denied, that

[1] Green, F. E., "The San Diego Old Mission Dam & Irrigation Works" (Tome I, 1769-1825, *Archivo de Las Misiones, Papales Originales*, Bancroft Library). From the Green manuscript in the library of the Junípero Serra Museum, San Diego.

grants of lands and waters were made to the missions by the Spanish government. Moreover, it clearly indicates that the mission property was to be held in trust for the Indians and their children, for that official continued:

> As the objective point in this letter, and for the better comprehension of Your Reverence, His Grace orders a holy trust upon your conscience and also upon the Reverend Fathers of that Mission, to acquire and administer this concession and Royal grant to the water in this arroyo [stream] referred to for the common benefit of all the natives, whether Gentile or converted, who dwell today or in the future in the province of this Mission of San Diego de Alcalá. This concession and fruits also shall be held as to these children and their children and successors for all time forever.

In order that there might be no scarcity of grain during the removal to the new site, the viceroy advised the Padres to begin irrigating the lands by digging small ditches from pools in the bed of the river, "or outside of the bed in wells made by labor in a better chosen place." He suggested that, at a later and more opportune time, the Padres should build a firm dam from which water might be drawn for the future pueblo[2] and agriculture and mills in this community, . . ."

It is difficult to see how water could have been taken from those pools, or wells, in the riverbed without mechanical lifts of some sort and the Padres would hardly have been equipped with the means for erecting such contrivances at that early date. What the missionaries did about the matter seems not to have been recorded.

In 1780, grain was again sown in the lowlands along the riverside, the Indians having previously dug a deep ditch along the field to carry off the flood waters, but a heavy rainfall came and the swirling water overtopped the river banks, greedily ate up the neophytes' ditch, and flooded the planted fields, once more carrying away most of the seed grain. The Indians were at once set to work widening and deepening the protective ditch, but anyone who has seen one of California's rivers on a rampage during the rainy season will realize how futile such measures were.

San Diego's history was for many years one of hardship and struggle—struggle to raise grain in quantities sufficient to support all the converts at the mission. As it was, the missionaries were obliged to allow the majority of the neophytes to live in their native rancherías in the mountains or along the seashore, coming to the mission from time to time for instruction. "In the meantime," Governor Fages reports, "there was a continuous struggle to make the land productive. The missionaries having to deny their neophytes the provisions whilst

[2] Through this letter it will be seen that it was from the very first the intention of the Spanish government that the missions should eventually become Indian pueblos.

▲ THE FILTER, RESERVOIRS, AND RUINS of the water-power gristmill at Mission Santa Bárbara.

▼ FLUME BUILT IN THE TOP of a rock wall to carry water from the reservoir to the garden.

Top: DISTRIBUTION BOX at La Purísima; pool where Indian women washed their clothes at San Luis Rey.
Bottom: Gargoyle through which water spouted; water filter at La Purísima.

the Indians were increasing the acreage, stormed Heaven with ceaseless petitions for rains, whenever their fields needed them, until they succeeded."[3]

Finally, in 1783, Fr. Lasuén writes: "Hence indescribable efforts have been made, though so far with meager success, to plant great stretches of land, to clear and enclose it, to run irrigation ditches, and to perform the other fatiguing labor necessarily connected with such undertaking."[4]

The Padre's words conjure up visions of Indians working through summer's heat, clad only in breechcloth, donning the cotón (the long shirt) as winter's cold came on. Shoeless and hatless, they trudged to their task. Armed with axes and machetes, shovels and hoes, crowbars and pickaxes, they worked to make fit for cultivation land that was encumbered with weeds, rocks, trees and shrubs.

In 1795, the San Diego Fathers found a spring which produced water sufficient for irrigation. In 1797, under their supervision, the Indians built a ditch 1,300 varas[5] long that brought water presumably from the spring to the mission. There is little, however, in the reports of crops harvested to cause one to believe that either the ditch dug in 1797, or the aqueduct of a later period, brought water to the grainfields. Rather, it seems that this life-giving fluid must have been spent on such crops as beans, peas, corn, and various vegetables planted in the gardens, and on the fruit trees in the orchards; the grain, wheat and barley, depending almost entirely on the rainfall.

No other mission was forced, through lack of provisions, to allow its neophytes to live in their native rancherías, yet San Diego's struggle with the irrigation problem was, more or less, typical of that waged at all of the establishments. In a number of instances mission sites were changed to secure better lands and more dependable water supply. Besides San Diego, this was true also of Missions San Juan Capistrano, San Gabriel, San Antonio, and San Carlos. Santa Clara was moved twice on account of floods.

Considering the importance of securing an abundant supply of water for domestic and irrigation purposes, it is a matter of no small wonderment that so little is found recorded about this vital matter. However, from age-old manuscripts, the Padres' *informes*, letters, surveys, and from accounts written by foreign visitors and traders, many bits of information may be gathered. Explanatory details, lacking in the records of one mission, are sometimes found in those of another. Through these data, together with the study of existing ruins of aqueducts,

---

[3] Fages, *Informe General Sobre Misiones.* Bancroft Collection, nos. 6-12. Cited in Engelhardt, *Mission San Diego,* 120-122.
[4] Engelhardt, *Mission San Diego,* 111.
[5] The Mexican vara used in California mission measurements was equal to 33 inches.

dams, reservoirs, and mills a fairly complete understanding of the subject may be acquired.

As in all other lines of mission endeavor, the beginnings of their irrigation systems were very simple. Directed by one of the Padres, an Indian from Baja California, or other overseer, the Indians built a dam of brush, earth, and rocks across a stream and diverted the water into a previously dug, open ditch wherever it was feasible to do so. Unfortunately, many of California's streams and rivers have beds too low for such diversion.

In the case of Mission San Antonio, which, in 1771, had been founded by Fr. Serra on the banks of the river named San Antonio, the Fathers found a year and a half later that their river had run dry and there was not even water for domestic purposes. Accordingly they moved farther up the valley to the spot where that lovely mission, recently rebuilt, stands beside the arroyo which the Padres named San Miguel (now known as Mission Creek). This stream, as Fr. Palóu tells us, flowed with more than a buey[6] of water even in the driest time of the year. From this arroyo, he states, the Padres secured an abundance of water which had been conducted in a ditch dug by the neophytes along the slope of the land to water a field near the mission.[7] According to Governor Fages, the dam which the Indians built was one made temporarily of stones, poles, and brushwood until time and material were available to make it of lime and rocks.[8]

Regarding the situation at Mission San Carlos in 1773, Fr. Palóu reported: "The mission has at this site plenty of good land, although not for irrigation, for the river [the Carmel] runs too low, and in the rainy season it is very rapid and if it is retained by a dam it is sure to carry it away. But, according to what has been observed, seasonal crops can be raised, of wheat as well as corn, by the humidity of the earth and the constant fogs that prevail after the cessation of the rains."[9]

San Gabriel's second and present site was fortunately well supplied with water that came from near-by springs and a ciénega (marsh) in which water from various small streams was wont to collect. Fr. Font, writing in 1776, says: "After dinner I went with Father Sanchez to see the creek from which they had made the acequia [ditch] for this mission of San Gabriel, and with which it has the best of conveniences. For, besides the fact that the acequia is adequate, and passes in front of the house of the fathers and of the little huts of the Christian

---

[6] Buey—Stream as wide as an ox hide?
[7] Bolton, *Palou's New Cal.*, 3. 224-226; *Informe* Mission San Antonio, 1773. SBMA.
[8] *Fages' Description of California*, translated by Herbert Ingram Priestly (University of California Press, 1937), 56-57.
[9] Bolton, *Palou's New Cal.*, 3. 231.

Indians who compose this new mission (who must be some five hundred souls recently converted, counting large and small), it dominates all the plains of the immediate vicinity. . ."[10]

Founded in September, 1772, Mission San Luis Obispo was located on a hill at whose foot ran a stream with a flow of water sufficient not only for domestic use but for the irrigation of a field as well. Near by was another arroyo with water enough to irrigate another field. These two streams, the San Luis and Stenner creeks, were both below the level of the mission buildings. Consequently, for domestic purposes, it was necessary to tap the former stream at a point up near its source in La Cuesta (the Pass), and to conduct the water by dug ditch, or aqueduct, down the slope to the mission premises. Legend says that this work was done by Ignacio Vicente Vallejo[11] in the early years of the mission's existence. And it may well be true that Vallejo did superintend this work for, in 1776, he was employed at San Luis Obispo as carpenter, and the carpenter's trade in those days included many others. Moreover, according to Bancroft, Vallejo was often called upon to oversee such undertakings. But it was, of course, the Indians who did the actual work.

Mission Santa Clara was founded January 12, 1777, "en las vegas del Rio de N. Sra. de Guadalupe" (in the lowlands of the river of Our Lady of Guadalupe). At the end of the first year the Padres reported that there had been built a dam and corresponding ditches, for the benefit of the fields ("Para el beneficio de dhas [dichas] tierras se ha hecho presa, y zanjas correspondientes"). Already there had been planted and harvested corn and beans, and, in the last month of the year two and a quarter fanegas[12] of wheat had been sown. Land had also been prepared for other crops. At this time thirteen converts were living at the mission. Of this number seven were adults. Ten other adults were under instruction, that is, they were being prepared for baptism.[13] All must have worked with a will to have accomplished so much in addition to setting up the first temporary buildings, for, before the land could be planted it had to be cleared of encumbrances, plowed and harrowed. Unfortunately, floods in 1779 compelled the Fathers to remove their mission to another site.

Santa Clara's second site lay a few hundred yards northeast of the spot on which the University of Santa Clara stands today. Excavations made at Campbell and Franklin streets uncovered the cornerstone of the church built in 1781-1784.

[10] Bolton, *Anza's Calif. Exped.*, 4. 177 ("Font's Complete Diary").
[11] Ignacio Vicente was the founder of the Vallejo family in California.
[12] Fanega—Spanish measure for grain equalling 100 pounds.
[13] *Informe*, Mission Santa Clara, 1777. SBMA.

Captain George Vancouver, British navigator and explorer, visited this mission in 1792 and penned the following excellent description of its second location:

> The particular spot which had been selected by the reverend Fathers, for their establishment, did not appear so suitable to their purpose as many other parts of the plain within a little distance of their present buildings, which are erected in a low marshy situation for the sake of being near a run of fine water; notwithstanding that within a few hundred yards they might have built their houses on dry and comfortable eminences.
> The stream of water passes close by the walls of the Fathers' apartments, . ." [14]

A survey made in 1854, by G. Black, C. E., outlines the buildings of both the second and the third sites of Santa Clara Mission. It will be noted that the church and Fathers' dwelling of the former face due west. The stream of water mentioned by Vancouver, therefore, ran along the west side of these buildings, and not at the rear and along the line of the orchard as has been believed. Its source appears to have been springs lying to the southeast and beyond the orchard.

When, in 1782, Fr. Serra founded Mission San Buenaventura, he left Fr. Pedro Cambón there because, "being expert with irrigation," he could supervise the taking of water from the arroyo (the San Buenaventura River) for use at the mission and for irrigating the fields, and, Fr. Palóu tells us, this was soon accomplished. [15] In this instance the laborers were, without doubt, the Christian Indians who had come with Fr. Serra from San Gabriel to help with the erection of the first buildings. Trained workers were often loaned by older establishments to the new ones.

Fr. Cambón was also at San Francisco de Asís during its early days, and in all likelihood, it was he who, in that mission's first year, directed the Indians there in digging the ditch that brought a good stream of water to the site. [16]

Of such dug ditches and temporary dams the irrigation facilities of the missions consisted until 1790-1795, when there were sent up from México, at government expense, a number of artisan-instructors including masons, potters, millmakers, carpenters, and blacksmiths. These men were under four or five year contracts and were expected to teach their trades to both neophyte and white apprentices. Later complications arose over their salaries, but that does not alter the fact that the mission Indians received instruction from those master workmen, some of whom became permanent settlers in the province.

---

[14] Vancouver, Capt. George, *Voyage of Discovery to the North Pacific Ocean, and Round the World. 1790-5* (London, 1798, 3 vols.), 2. 18-19. Hereinafter referred to as *Voyage.*
[15] Bolton, *Palou's New Cal.*, 4. 214; *Palou's Life of Serra* (James ed.), 240.
[16] Bolton, *Palou's New Cal.*, 4. 134.

Immediately after the advent of these artisans, there appear, in the Padres' *informes*, records of structures built of stone and mortar—structures that required the advice and supervision of surveyors and engineers, expert stone masons, and blacksmiths. Churches and water-power gristmills received first attention from the artisans, as will be noted elsewhere.

To present a truer picture of the progress made at various missions, it seems best to note in chronological order the improvements made in the irrigation systems after the coming of the artisans. To avoid confusion, the story of each mission's accomplishments will be carried to its conclusion before taking up that of another.

The first[17] improvement of any great magnitude was made at Santa Clara where, in 1795, a zanja, or trench, half a league long, nine feet wide, and five feet deep was dug[18] by the neophytes to carry water from the Guadalupe River to the mission. This water-course followed the line of the famous "Alameda," the shaded carreta road and walk that connected the pueblo of San José with Mission Santa Clara at its second site.[19] According to an early map, this zanja passed between the pear orchard and the rear wing of the quadrangle of the second site. Apparently it intersected the stream seen by Vancouver and the two were combined to furnish an ample supply of water for all the mission's needs. Surplus water from all sources (there were many springs in the vicinity) joined an ancient water-course that led to a marsh, or ciénega, not far to the north. The marsh was marked by a large grove of sycamore trees.[20]

Then, in 1805, the Padres of San Antonio record the beginning of a ditch to bring more water to their establishment. The following year the construction of a water-power gristmill was noted, and, while the details are meager, the records and archeological remains leave no doubt that the ditch of the preceding year was being built to supply water to turn the millwheel. Also, from available data it seems that this ditch of 1805 was but an improvement of the one dug by the Indians in 1773. That first ditch, or trench, tapped the arroyo of San Miguel and was about a league long.[21] Such, apparently, was the case with the zanja of 1805. But the ditch of 1805, or as it was always designated after that Father's death "the zanja which was begun in the time of the deceased Fr. Sitjar," was, in places, embedded in sandstone cliffs; it crossed side gullies on built-up walls, and ran across more level stretches of land, carrying its water to the mill reservoir. From

[17] That is the first discovered by this writer.
[18] Banc., *Hist. of Cal.*, 1. 725, note 62.
[19] Hall, Frederick, *The History of San Jose*, 83-84.
[20] See Map of Santa Clara Mission in *The Three Churches of Santa Clara Mission* by James A. Colligan, S. J.
[21] *Informe* Mission San Antonio, 1773. SBMA.

the reservoir the water passed in open ditch through the Indian village to within about eighty-seven yards of the mill. Here it entered a masonry flume which conducted it to the mill forebay. At the point of entrance into the flume, if evidence found at other missions holds true here, a water-gate provided the means for shutting off the water from the mill when not needed and diverting it into other channels, of which there undoubtedly were several leading to the tannery or garden or wherever water was needed for other than domestic purposes. One needs little imagination to be able to picture the Indian children gleefully playing in the ditch as the water passed through the ranchería.

Water for the mission establishment itself would, in all probability, have been diverted by gate at the point of entrance into the reservoir, or mill pond, as it is most often called. Should San Antonio ever undergo the excavation that Mission La Purísima did a few years ago its grounds would probably be found honeycombed with a network of water channels, mostly underground.

The ditch begun in 1805 was finished in 1809, but Fr. Sitjar was not there to witness its completion. He passed away September 3, 1808, having spent thirty-six years at this mission. According to Fr. Pedro Cabot, who wrote the account of his death, Fr. Sitjar had, only five days earlier, accompanied "his" Indians to their work as was his custom.[22] Apparently, he was the Padre who looked after the temporal affairs of the mission, while Fr. Pieras and Fr. Cabot after him, attended to the spiritual activities. He probably accompanied the Indians who dug the ditch of 1773, and throughout the following years had visited the shops, the fields, and the ranchos to see how the laborers were progressing. It was by working with "his Indians," or supervising their tasks, that he was able to acquire such perfect knowledge of their speech. Fr. Sitjar's mantle fell upon Fr. Juan Bautista Sancho, who as Fr. Cabot wrote "would be seen at labor in the shops and in the field during the greatest heat and extreme cold weather with the same patience. . . He saw that the neophytes never lacked the spiritual instructions or remained idle."

He was, as Fr. Cabot states, "a declared enemy of all idleness." Of himself, Fr. Sancho declared: "If I must eat, I must work."[23]

In 1824, a noria (a well operated with an endless chain of buckets) was constructed for irrigating the large field. A roof, tiled and upheld by pillars, protected the wheels and other woodwork of the well from the rains and sun. Whether Indians furnished the motive power is not known, but it is not un-

[22] Engelhardt, *Mission San Antonio*, 107-109; Smith, Frances Rand, *The Mission of San Antonio de Padua*, 16-18.
[23] Engelhardt, *Mission San Antonio*, 109-111.

likely that they did, and that this well[24] was similar to the one that Duhaut-Cilly saw at San Luis Rey.

In this same year (1824), the Indians at San Antonio, working under the direction of Fr. Sancho and skilled workmen, constructed a masonry pool or reservoir, five by seven varas in size; made 750 clay pipes for conducting water to the garden, and built two other masonry reservoirs, or pools that were "somewhat large." An indecipherable number of tiles were manufactured, and Fr. Sitjar's zanja, started in 1805, was repaired by building a wall 40 varas long, of which one-fourth or more was of masonry. All this was done in one year.[25] One may readily imagine how busy the neophytes were kept and how many crafts were represented in the construction of the above-noted water-system units. Moreover, this represented one branch only of mission activity. All the various industries incident to the life of the community were carried on as well, and at this time there were but 806 Indians living at the mission and on its various ranchos. This number included men, women, and children.

Like the roof and floor tiles, the clay water-pipes were burned, or fired, in a kiln. They were about twelve inches long, five inches in diameter at the larger end and four inches at the smaller end. A potter taught the making of these water conductors. Among the artisans coming to California in the 1790's, were Mariano Mendoza, tile-maker, and Mariano Tapía, potter.[26] Lozero, a soldier, also taught pottery making at the northern missions.

In laying the clay water-pipes at San Antonio, a trench was first dug and roofing tiles laid in the bottom of it. The pipes were then laid on the tiles, the smaller ends of the pipes fitting into the larger ends of those previously laid. Stones were then set in along the side of the trench to keep the dirt from falling in. Other roofing tiles were placed on top of the pipes. Large flat stones laid across the trench completed the channel.[27]

In 1825, the rainfall was very heavy and the waters of the San Miguel River washed away about 80 varas (220 feet) of wall "of the zanja begun in the time of the deceased Fr. Sitjar." The varas of wall referred to may have been those built-up embankments or walls upon which the zanja was carried across ravines. This had happened before, for this was the history of all mission aqueducts and zanjas. Constant repairs and improvements were needed throughout the years.

It is possible that the Padres had experienced too much trouble with this

---

[24] Norias were also in operation at Santa Clara and San Juan Bautista.
[25] *Informe* Mission San Antonio, 1824. SBMA.
[26] Banc., *Hist. of Cal.*, 1. 615-618, note 29.
[27] Portions of such water-ways have been found at La Purísima, Santa Bárbara, San Gabriel, and San Juan Capistrano. At San Fernando the clay pipes were laid in a bed of mortar and small stones.

ditch. At any rate, in 1827, the Indians constructed another zanja from Met,[28] on the way to Soledad. This new ditch tapped the San Antonio River at a point about three and one-third miles north of the mission. The Padres explained that they had not availed themselves of this source before because of the press of other duties, and, too, because of the difficulty of taking out the water.[29] The new zanja followed the cliffs along the right side of the canyon (going toward the mission) and part of the way ran through rock which was broken into by means of crowbars. Nearing the mission the aqueduct crossed the San Miguel River (Mission Creek) and united with the ditch begun in 1805. The walls built across ravines to carry this new zanja were of masonry, and, as Mr. Lou Hare, County Surveyor of Monterey, found in 1913, "the storm water of the gulches was carried under the walls through masonry culverts with arch rings of flat tile laid on edge in mortar."[30] It has been said that the lack of culverts was responsible for the carrying away by storm waters of many portions of mission aqueducts, but one wonders how many of the old remnants have really been investigated.

In 1913, the owners of the Milpitas Rancho, which includes the land adjoining the old mission on all sides, were anxious to determine if this second zanja would still serve to carry water to the dry fields. At that time Mr. Hare made a complete survey of the old water-course from its intake to its junction with the first ditch and on to the ruins of the old gristmill. The dam built in 1827, across the San Antonio River, he found to be "150 feet long, twelve feet high, three feet at the top and five feet at the base. At one end of the dam is an anchor piece, made of huge rocks and cement, as a protection against storm waters. . . Unfortunately this dam could not be used at the present time to divert the waters into the ditch, for the course of the river and its bed have changed considerably since its construction. The dam now rests sixteen feet above the present river bed and the channel is one hundred and fifty yards away."[31]

Tapping the river about half a mile farther up, the workers of 1913 constructed a corresponding length of ditch to join the one built by the mission Indians. Then after cleaning out the old zanja and rebuilding some washed-out portions, they turned the water into the channel. And, to quote Mr. Paul Parker, who wrote up Lou Hare's findings, "it flowed as merrily as it had done a century be-

---

[28] Met, it appears, was a spot in the canyon where some of the Indians had little gardens, or milpitas—hence (?) the name of the rancho granted in after-secularization days, and which included a vast acreage surrounding the old mission.

[29] *Informe*, Mission San Antonio, 1827. SBMA.

[30] Smith, Frances Rand, *The Mission of San Antonio de Padua*, 74. Hereinafter referred to as *Mission San Antonio*.

[31] *Ibidem*, 70.

MISSION RANCH HOUSES: Top: *Paso del Robles and corridor detail.* Center: *Los Flores; Santa Margarita, rancho of San Luis Obispo, undergoing changes.* Bottom: *Los Ojitos and La Asunción.*

▲ Indian homes at Pauma and Santa Isabel; Pala's campanile and the chapel at Warner's Hot Springs.

▼ The little adobe chapel in which the Indians of Pauma once gathered for worship.

fore, forcing the thirsty lands to bloom again." Mr. Hare "checked up the work of the Padres and found that the grade established by them, even around rocky bluffs, through sandy stretches and across gulches and creeks, could not be improved upon with modern surveying instruments."[32] Obviously, the zanja had been constructed under the supervision of an engineer, or surveyor, or at least someone who had had considerable experience in such undertaking.[33]

One other bit of work accomplished at San Antonio, in 1827, deserves mention for the resourcefulness and practicality displayed in its planning. There was, it seems, too much moisture around the church and Fathers' dwelling. Accordingly a drain was constructed. It began at the Indian village and extended along the front of the mission to beyond the houses of the soldiers of the guard. (The Indian village stood at the right of the church, and in front of the orchard, while the guards' houses were located at the extreme left end of the front wing of the quadrangle.) The drain was about two varas deep. It was made of ladrillos and flagstones. From it came a spring of fine water which the soldiers drank and their wives used for washing clothes. Afterwards, it served to help irrigate the corn planted near by.[34] Water was very precious and every possible use was made of it before it was turned into the fields to irrigate the beans, peas, and other crops.

It would be impossible, in one short chapter, to recount in such detail the construction of all the mission water systems. It would be impossible, also, from the fact that so far as this writer has discovered no Fathers, save those of San Antonio, described in such interesting detail their more advanced work in this field of activity.

In the same year that San Antonio began to improve and enlarge its water-system, San Luis Obispo recorded the building of a water-power gristmill (the second to be constructed at this mission) and a reservoir. The reservoir was built in conjunction with the mill, as at Santa Bárbara. Both were located at the rear of the quadrangle. The reservoir, according to long-time residents of the town, was about sixty feet square, its top being flush with the ground on two or three sides. In after-mission days it was used as a slaughter pen, one sidewall having partly fallen down. Bull fights were also said to have taken place within it. "Billy"

[32] Parker, Paul, "Irrigation in California before the Gringo Came," *San Francisco Chronicle*, September 6, 1914. Quoted in Smith, F. R., *Mission San Antonio*, 69-72.

[33] Alberto Córdoba, engineer, came to California some time in the 1792-1795 period. Bancroft's list of the "Inhabitants of California, 1769-1800" (*Hist. of Cal.*, 1. 732-744) contains a surprising number of mechanics, carpenters, smiths, masons, etc.

[34] "Se ha abierto un zanjon de, 2, varas de ancho y 211 de largo, para quitar la humedad de la Iglesia, y de la casa de los padres que empieza desde la ranchería, hasta mas allá de la Guardᵃ y en lo profundo, que son como, 2, varas ó mas, se ha hecho un caño de ladrillos, y lozas de piedra, y sale de el un ojo de agua hermosa, del que beben los soldados, y lavan alli mismo sus mugeres y en el año entrante, se le hará una pila grande para empozar la agua, y servirá para ayuda del riego del maiz." *Informe*, Mission San Antonio, 1827. SBMA.

Alberts[35] saw one of those fights, which, he said, occurred partly in and partly out of the reservoir. "The reservoir was built up against the hill," he explained, "and the ground in front of it was fenced off for the fight." A portion of the old structure still stands back of houses on Palm Street. Just beyond it, some forty or fifty years ago, were two round tanks, or cisterns, each being about fifteen feet in diameter. Luis Moreno, native of the town,[36] remembers these cisterns as being about six feet deep. His recollection of them dates back to his boyhood days when he used to hide in them on his way home from Sunday school. Just beyond these two auxiliary reservoirs were the mission's tanning vats. Ramón Ybarra, who, in 1936, had been a resident of San Luis Obispo for seventy-eight years, said there was a reservoir near the "Fremont Place" forty or fifty feet long, twenty-five or thirty feet wide, and five or six feet deep. Other long-time residents confirmed the existence of "something of mission construction" at that place which was filled in when the streets were graded in 1874-1875.[37]

In 1806, a masonry reservoir was built at Mission Santa Bárbara. It was 40 varas, or 110 feet, square and 2½ varas (about 7 feet) deep. Constructed of stone and mortar, it still stands at the right (from the front) of the mission. The next year a dam was built, also of stone masonry, or cal y canto. It was thrown across the west fork of the Pedregosa Creek about a mile and a half north of the mission. No mention is made of the aqueduct that was constructed to convey water from the dam to the reservoir built in the previous year.

In 1808, the fountain and lavatory still existing in front of the mission were built "for the benefit of humanity" ("en beneficio de la humanidad"). These three records are the only ones that the writer has been able to find in the *informes* of Santa Bárbara Mission to account for two dams, two reservoirs, a water-power gristmill, a fountain with adjoining lavatory, a filter, and innumerable water channels laid to carry water to the mission establishment, to tanneries, fields, orchards and gardens, and to provide sanitary facilities for the jail and the monjerio.

Fortunately, Duhaut-Cilly visited this mission in March, 1827, and found Fr. Antonio Ripoll completely engrossed "in a water-mill he was having built at the foot of a hill to the right of the mission." The foreign visitor's description leaves no doubt in the reader's mind that he actually saw the mill being built. The reservoir which adjoins the mill was, without question, constructed at the same

---

[35] Mr. Alberts came to San Luis Obispo as a small boy and spent the remaining years of his life there.

[36] Luis Moreno is the grandson of Don Santiago Moreno, administrator of San Luis Obispo in 1850-1855.

[37] The writer made many investigating trips to San Luis Obispo. For information about the old water system she is indebted to Mayor Sinsheimer, Billy Alberts, Neil O'Leary, Luis Moreno, Ramón Ybarra, and E. P. Rogers of the Title Security Office.

time. The dam and aqueduct, bringing water to furnish motive power for the mill, were already finished. "The water," Duhaut-Cilly says, "was brought for more than two leagues [over five miles] by a canal which followed the sides of the mountains, . . ."[38] The work must, therefore, have been started in the preceding year, at least. But there is no mention of these things in the *informes*, though they surely were of vital importance.

The filter,[39] which stands a little to the north of the mill reservoir, served to clarify the water for domestic purposes. Water being conveyed by aqueduct to the mill reservoir was diverted by a gate to the water-course leading to the filter. Charcoal and crushed granite placed in the bottom of the filter acted as clarifier of the water, which, after passing through the filter bed, was carried to the mission grounds in a flume built in the top of a high stone wall. A section of the aqueduct that brought water to the mill may still be seen on the hillside above the mill reservoir. The diversion gate and part of the canal were removed when the Mission Ridge Road was cut through on the hillside, if not before. Part of the wall that once carried water from the filter to the mission remains beside the lower road. The manner of its construction is shown in another remnant of wall standing to the northeast and in front of the cemetery. It is not known how long these various aqueducts continued in use in after-mission days, but one of the first improvements instituted by Fr. J. M. Romo, Guardian of the Santa Bárbara Mission community in 1872, was to have water piped to the kitchen. "Till then the water had to be brought by the brothers from Mission Creek in buckets carried, Chinese fashion, dangling from a yoke on the shoulders."[40]

When Langsdorff visited Mission San José, in 1806, he noted a small rivulet that ran through the garden and preserved a constant moisture.[41] The source of this rivulet was, it seems, the creek that coursed along the north side of the vineyard and the enclosure that adjoined the quarters of the soldiers of the guard. Alfred Robinson mentions a large reservoir in the rear of the quadrangle, pipes carrying water to buildings and gardens, and, in front of the mission, a fountain with conveniences for bathing and for washing clothes.[42] This fountain with its lavatory was probably similar to those constructed at Santa Bárbara and San Buenaventura and was built for the benefit of the Indians whose village faced the church and the Fathers' dwelling. In the daguerreotype taken, in 1853, by J. M. Ford and later copied by C. E. Watkins, a tile-lined water-course is seen in

[38] "Duhaut-Cilly's Account," 160.
[39] Often mistakenly called the Padres' bath house.
[40] Engelhardt, *Mission Santa Barbara*, 416.
[41] Langsdorff, *Voyages and Travels*, 2. 193.
[42] Robinson, *Life in Cal.*, 86.

the street that separated the main buildings from the neophyte ranchería.

Some time prior to 1808 and during the administration of Padre Antonio Jayme, a masonry aqueduct at least five—some say fifteen—miles long was built by the Indians at Mission La Soledad. It tapped the Arroyo Seco near its source. H. M. T. Powell, who, in 1849, answered the call to California's gold fields, rode beside this acequia for five miles before reaching the mission.[43] Presumably this was the stream of water that Mr. B. A. Soberanes and others said formerly ran in front of the mission buildings and that, in season, had large salmon in it.

In April, 1808, the Padres of Mission La Purísima, at its first site on the out-skirts of Lompoc, announced the completion of a zanja that brought water to the establishment from the Salsipuedes Creek.[44] This zanja was over six miles long. During the restoration, in 1935-1941, of the buildings of the second site, this aqueduct was investigated. Parts of its dams, built to impound water in the creek, were located as well as traces of the waterway. These were measured, surveyed, and recorded. Remnants of similar structures were also found in San Miguelito Canyon and records made of the findings.[45]

At the second and present site, to which the mission family repaired as soon as official permission was received after the earthquake of 1812, the Padres had the water collected from three springs and led for more than a mile in tile pipe and open tile-lined aqueduct down Los Berros Canyon to the mission. Distribu-tion boxes and reservoirs were constructed along the way for the diversion of the water into various channels and the storing of it until needed.[46] In 1817, a foun-tain was built for the benefit of the Indians and another near by for the use of the infirmary and for other minor purposes.[47] At a date unrecorded a filter was built for clarifying the water, and two pools, or storage reservoirs, were constructed. These fountains, pools, and reservoirs were all built of ladrillos and were plas-tered over on the inside with a pinkish cement.

In 1937, the aqueduct of 1814 and all its underground appurtenances were un-covered, enabling the visitor to observe the simplicity, ingenuity, and efficiency of the irrigation system that provided water for household purposes, for the Indians' use, and also for the irrigation of the near-by orchard. Used in building the distribution boxes were odd-shaped, ornamental ladrillos, quite foreign to any found in the buildings at the second site. These told of the salvaging of usable

---

[43] Powell, *The Sante Fe Trail*, 220.
[44] Engelhardt, *Mission La Purisima*, 18-19.
[45] Hageman, Frederick C., *An Architectural Study of the Mission La Purisima Concepcion California*, 28.
[46] "Se han fabricado .. , y una huerta ya plantada de quantos arboles se han tenido âmano y para cuyo riego se jun-tan en uno varios ojitos de agua, qᵉ saguando en sus tanques, prometen regarla con abundancia." *Informe* 1814. SBMA.
[47] *Informe*, 1817. SBMA.

materials from the ruined buildings of Misión Vieja (old mission), as the first site was known thereafter. The Padres say that they brought away all church goods, tools, and implements that could be saved from the "horrible earthquake." Having to start all over again at the new site, it was also easier to salvage tiles, clay pipes, ladrillos, and even adobes than it was to make new ones. Time, too, was "of the essence," for the rainy season was not far distant. Therefore, for weeks or months the Indians were kept busy digging out those materials (where it could be done safely), loading them into carretas to be hauled by oxen to the site across the river. Every available man, ox, and cart was set to this task, and the rutted road between the two locations was kept alive with men and teams going for and returning with loads of rescued goods and materials.

For the irrigation of the fields spread out before the mission, the zanja, built by the Indians to carry water to Misión Vieja, was continued across the Santa Inés River. Writing in 1814, the Padres reported that they expected to have the water brought in this channel to within 500 paces of the new establishment. In that year, when this mission was the scene of such great activity, there were but 982 Indian neophytes, young and old, to assist in the re-establishment of the community and to carry on the various industries.

At the Mission of San Luis Rey, in 1808, an adobe wall was erected around two springs near the establishment. According to Lt. C. J. Couts's map[48] and his son Cave's statement, these springs were located to the east of the mission and on the way to Rancho Guajome. Water sufficient for domestic purposes with some to spare for irrigation seems to have been developed from this source. But when the mission was first established, water was secured from a spring in the marsh lying in front of the quadrangle. Reporting in 1827, on the extent of mission property and lands, Fr. Antonio Peyri describes the method employed in obtaining that water: ". . , we established the mission in a short time," he writes, "on a mesa situated near a marsh, the water of which by hauling earth we succeeded little by little in forcing up so that it could be reached. By means of two dams the water was then collected so that it sufficed for the assembled Indians and for irrigating a garden."[49] This was then the only water that they could depend on for the San Luis Rey River, which flows past the mission on the west side, has water in it only during the rainy season.

In 1827, Duhaut-Cilly visited San Luis Rey and found that the marsh lying

[48] Engelhardt, *Mission San Luis Rey*, 257. Lt. Cave Johnson Couts, an U. S. army officer, married Ysidora Bandini' daughter of Juan Bandini of San Diego. Cave J. II was their youngest child, and occupied the ancestral home at Rancho Guajome for many years. He died July 15, 1943.

[49] Engelhardt, *Mission San Luis Rey*, 51.

in front of the mission had been transformed into a garden of great beauty and usefulness. He writes:

Two well-planted gardens furnish an abundance of vegetables and fruits of all kinds. The large comfortable stairway by which one descends into the one to the southeast [the former marsh], remind me of the orangery at Versailles: not that their material was as valuable, or the architecture as splendid; but there was some relation in the arrangement, number, and dimensions of the steps. At the bottom of the stairs are two fine lavers in stucco; one of them is a pond where the Indian women bathe every morning; and the other is used every Saturday for washing clothes. Some of the water is afterward distributed into the garden, where many channels maintain a permanent moisture and coolness. The second garden situated in a higher place, can be watered only by artificial aid: a chain pump, worked by two men, is used twice a day to accomplish this object.[50]

In about 1895, Fr. Peyri's garden was excavated by Fr. J. J. O'Keefe, O.F.M., then in charge of the mission. A somewhat ornamental gate opened upon a stairway which led down to the lavatories and garden described by Duhaut-Cilly. This stairway, Señor Cave Couts said, extended from wall to wall, having a width of about seventy-five feet. The steps were one ladrillo wide with risers of about five inches, the ladrillos being about 15″ square, 2″ thick[51] and were laid in cement. He had, so he told the writer, often ridden his horse down them. He remembered well the stairway and the two gargoyles carved from stone and representing human heads. He recalled seeing water spouting from the mouths of the gargoyles into the pools, or lavers, described by Duhaut-Cilly, but he remembered best of all the delicious peaches that grew on two trees in the garden there. The flood of 1862, which did so much damage in Southern California, Señor Couts said filled Fr. Peyri's garden with many feet of mud. And so it remained until the coming of Fr. O'Keefe.

Once again, perhaps during the floods of 1916, the garden with its lavatories and gargoyles was covered with soil and debris, and, in 1931, it was partially re-excavated. The lavatories were uncovered and one of the gargoyles taken up to the mission to the later regret of the Father Guardian. At this time it was found that the ladrillos which once formed the steps of the stairway had all been removed.

The writer saw the lavatories soon after they were last uncovered and, with the French visitor's account in mind, was able to visualize most vividly scenes that had taken place in that garden times innumerable. Hollows worn in the la-

---

[50] "Duhaut-Cilly's Account," 228.

[51] At no other mission were ladrillos made in such numbers and of such varying sizes. Visiting there in 1937, the writer found the old guardhouse being excavated. She measured ladrillos that had been uncovered and found the following sizes:

6½″ x 10″ x 3″	9″ x 12″ x 3″	11″ x 11″ x 2″
8″ x 15″ x 2″-2½″	9″ x 15″ x 3″	

The church steps were built of ladrillos that were 9″ x 15″ x 2½″. Ladrillos in the baptistry floor are 11″ x 11″.

drillos of the pools furnished mute corroboration of the Frenchman's tale. It had been Fr. Peyri's custom to distribute soap to the Indian women every Saturday. Soon thereafter, the pools were crowded with women doing their weekly wash-ing. This was a sort of holiday with them and they laughed and chattered as they worked. When clean, the clothes were spread out on the bushes and hedge-rows to dry.

In 1808, the mission of San Fernando, then in its eleventh year, reported the construction of a stone masonry dam. Three years later an aqueduct, half a league (1 1/3 miles) in length, was built. A fountain was also constructed ("Se ha echo una fuente de agua ducto de media legua"). In 1813, another fountain ("Una segunda fuente") was erected to receive the overflow of the first one.[52]

Today, at the outskirts of the town of San Fernando—going towards New-hall—one sees, tacked to an old fence, a sign bearing the inscription "Old Mis-sion Wells." Turning to the left off the San Fernando Road and following an obscure little street through a grove of eucalyptus trees, he comes eventually to a square sort of vat-like structure of mission masonry. This bit of construction is known as "the intake." Evidently water from near-by springs or wells was col-lected in this masonry box, or intake reservoir, and diverted into a common ditch leading to the mission. A little farther on, between the mission and the "intake," are to be found the ruins of the dam which was built by the Indians to impound the accumulated waters until released by flood-gate for irrigation or other purposes. A mill is said to have been built beside this dam. Some structure was there, but excavation alone might determine its purpose.

In the park across the road from the Fathers' house at San Fernando Mission are two fine old fountains, presumably the two mentioned above. The one near-est the mission was originally gaily decorated with designs in red and yellow ochre. A white stone dove stood on its brim. In 1922, the second fountain was removed from its original location, some few hundred feet south of the first one, and placed within the park limits. A third fountain, or more properly reservoir, much larger than the other two, stood as late as 1883 just outside the east wing of the quadrangle. All three are shown in the survey made, in 1854, by John C. Cleal, C. E.

At its second site, San Juan Capistrano was located between two streams, the Arroyo de Trabuco and the Arroyo de la Misión Vieja. The latter stream is now known as the San Juan River. From these two sources the mission secured an abundant supply of water by means of zanjas and underground water-ways. In

[52] *Informes*, Mission San Fernando for years 1808, 1811 and 1813. SBMA.

1809, the Fathers report the construction of an aqueduct and arch built of brick masonry for the purpose of bringing water to the mission. During the following year the water-course was continued for a distance of more than 500 varas, or about 1,375 feet.[53]

Some of the older inhabitants of this little mission town say that the arch mentioned in the report of 1809 was built across a barranca (ravine) near the Trabuco Creek to carry water in a flume to the vineyard, the flume ending at a spot in front of the present high school. This arch was torn down and the ladrillos sold in after-mission days. These statements are corroborated by a visitor of 1889, who wrote:

> Even so lately as a quarter of a century ago, there were at Capistrano extensive remains not now visible or known of. The present village is honeycombed with covered masonry aqueducts. Flumes were built across ravines on brick piers, after an ancient and substantial style now unknown. These became quarries for the moderns.[54]

A portion of the zanja that brought water from the San Juan River may still be seen along the left side of the road leading to the San Juan Hot Springs and, since 1932, there have been uncovered in the mission patio numerous masonry channels which in days gone by distributed the water to the various apartments and industrial plants needing it. These water-ways were covered with large, flat, blue stone slabs, gathered by the Indians and hauled, it is said, by ox-cart from what is now known as Dana's Point. Channels have frequently been dug up in the mission settlement, where in days long gone stood the five rows of little tile-roofed, adobe houses that comprised the Indian village.

At San Diego Mission, in 1813, the Padres went six miles up the canyon to find bedrock in the San Diego River upon which to build their dam and commence[55] the aqueduct about which so much has been written. There is little left now to tell of this great undertaking. Storm waters have destroyed part of the dam and carried away most of the aqueduct that the Indian workers toiled so long and so laboriously to complete. Souvenir hunters and others, who have wanted the fourteen-inch-square ladrillos to pave corridors or build chimneys, have carried away almost all of the tiles that formerly lined the aqueduct. Yet the ruins of the dam are well worth a visit and it is interesting to follow the course of the irrigation channel down to where it joined a dug ditch and on to the mission.

[53] Engelhardt, *Mission San Juan Capistrano*, 49.
[54] Steele, James, *Old Californian Days*, 95. Chicago, W. B. Conkey Company, 1893.
[55] In 1816, the Padres report that the laborers were still working on the zanja to bring water to the mission. There seems to be no record of its completion.

▲ It was the duty of the little Indian boys to guard the drying adobe bricks. (Miniature)

▼ Adding another room, or building. Three-cornered windows were often employed. (Miniature)

▲ BUILDING A CORRIDOR of *forked poles as was done in 1780 at Mission San Diego.* (Miniature)

▼ USING THE TWO-HANDLED RIP-SAW. *Indians were taught the use of tools by artisan instructors.* (Miniature)

In 1867, Judge Benjamin Hayes, accompanied by José María Estudillo,[56] visited the old San Diego dam and wrote the description of it that has been copied and re-copied by writers without number. The judge measured the dam and found it to have been originally 244 feet long, 13 feet high, and 13 feet thick. It was built of large blocks of stone. The gateway was 12 feet wide and was faced with square tiles. Twenty-four feet of massive concrete had been torn away by violent torrents, leaving a gap between the left bank (looking downstream) and the standing portion of the dam. "Upon the cement of the wall," writes Judge Hayes, "we made little impression with a crowbar, seemingly as hard as the rocks or brick."[57] His description of the aqueduct reads as follows:

Immediately on the right bank [going downstream], a few feet above the channel, commences the aqueduct by which water was drawn from this grand reservoir. It consists of a single tile about six inches at the bottom, resting upon small stones; on each side, a brick [ladrillo] 18 inches square inclined outward, so as to make a surface of two feet of water, some 12 inches deep; these bricks lined on the inside with cement, and propped on the outside by small rocks solidly cemented. From this point Don José Maria [Estudillo] has carried off all the bricks for a chimney. . . The aqueduct commenced at the dam and ran full three miles through a gorge the most difficult that can be conceived—keeping on the hillsides of the right bank of the river. Sometimes it crossed gulches from ten to fifteen feet wide. In such places a stone foundation was built up high enough to keep the level. The canal in general was simply of cobblestones and a narrow tile laid in cement in the bottom. In the gulches, the rock foundation has with time fallen down or been washed away. Such has been the strength of the cement, this brick canal holds together across the gulch as firmly as if cast-iron pipe, and now and then portions of it hang to the rocky wall at the height often to twenty feet above the bed of the river. . . .

Still I am not inclined to overrate the value of this work. Don Blas Aguilar, who was mayordomo of the mission eleven months in 1831, says that at that time this aqueduct was useless. . . Prior to that time the great dam above had been partially thrown down in a flood.[58]

Evidently this work, which had caused the Padres so much anxiety and the Indians so many years of back-breaking labor, had not been of long lasting benefit. Keeping the mission dams and aqueducts in usable condition required a constant battle with the forces of nature. The first temporary dams were probably rebuilt after each heavy rainfall, and, as has been told in records quoted above, even the aqueducts, walls, and dams of masonry occasionally had to be repaired.

Mr. F. E. Green, engineer of San Diego, who, in the 1930's, made a study of the dam and aqueduct, gives technical details lacking in Judge Hayes's description. Concerning the water-course, he writes:

While the masonry and tile work in this part of the aqueduct were very good, much of it still standing well preserved today, the alignment, location and adherence to grade are quite deficient,

[56] One-time commander of the San Diego presidio.
[57] Hayes, *Pioneer Notes*, 293.
[58] *Ibidem*, 293-296.

and the job is not to be compared with the well finished construction work in the dam.

As a construction job, however, there was over three times the amount of material and labor in the six miles of main aqueduct as there was in the dam, with many more difficulties to over-come. . . The aqueduct was an open ditch for its entire length, and no pipe or syphons were used. In passing boulders, cliffs and overhanging ledges, loose rock walls were built up to grade from available bottom surface. . .

The numerous arroyos entering the river along the course of the aqueduct also were crossed by building a loose rock wall up to grade line, without much deflection of the alignment up the arroyo for the sake of reducing the height of the wall. In this case, these loose rock walls really amounted to rock fill dams, as evidently there were no culverts or storm openings. Several of these walls remain fairly well intact, but with the masonry ditch on top entirely gone through the action of flood water from the arroyos and the crumbling of the top of the walls. One such fill was forty feet in length, nine feet in height, and twelve feet across the top—a good example of a rock fill dam held in place by its own weight.

Evidently there was very little rock removed along the aqueduct grade line for improving the alignment. The aqueduct, therefore, is a succession of sharp curves around obstructing high points, and in many places it also contains many ups and downs. In fact the capacity of the aque-duct was llmited by these curves and uneven grade. . .

The bottom of the masonry ditch originally was built of inverted tile which were 1.7 feet in length, 0.35 feet in depth, and 0.70 feet in width at one end and 0.65 feet at the other end, the larger end being placed down stream. These tile were laid end to end in a bed of three or four inches of mortar, and evidently they were intended to carry water, but in all sections of the ditch examined, these bottom tile had been filled with mortar. In some places they were only partly filled, in other places they were filled to the top, and at one point it was noted that the mortar filling had been poured in two different operations. . . The filling process evidently was resorted to in an attempt to overcome the unevenness of the bottom. . .

The typical cross section of this masonry aqueduct had a depth of one and one-half feet and a top width inside of two feet or a little less. The sides were lined with one row of flat tile placed directly on top of the sides of the inverted bottom tile. In sections of the ditch deeper than one and one-half feet, the side walls contained additional flat tile, laid either vertically or horizontally. The average thickness of the side walls was about six inches, consisting of field cobbles back of the tile liners. These field cobbles did not extend to the bottom of the ditch or under the ditch. The top of each side wall was nicely plastered flush with the ground surface and sometimes peb-bled with small gravel.

. . . A blacksmith shop was maintained for the care of the tools used in the ditch work, as in-dicated by the iron scraps, refuse, etc., found by ranchers at a site on the north bank of the river about two miles above the mission.

In establishing the grade line of the ditch, there probably was no precise level instrument used. In the dirt ditch the grade could have been carried ahead by eye and by flowing water, while in the masonry ditch the bricklayer's plummet level or the carpenter's "A" frame, or the "water-trough" level may have been used. . . .

No part of the dam has failed on account of faulty foundation work or faulty masonry work. . . Much credit therefore is due to the men who built this Mission dam for the careful and uniform manner in which they made their lime and mortar, for the expert care in which they selected the rock, and for the professional manner in which the masonry work was done.[59]

From Mr. Green's account it appears that the San Diego dam was built under the supervision of an engineer and expert stone mason, while the construction of the aqueduct was probably directed by some person less proficient in such

[59] Green, F. E., "The San Diego Old Mission Dam."

work. The laborers, however, were the mission Indians. There were no others.

At an unknown date the Padres of San Buenaventura had a dam built across the river of that same name. About five miles up the Ventura Canyon the water was diverted into an aqueduct which was built along the base of the hills on the east side of the canyon. As at San Antonio, the zanja crossed side ravines and gulches on walls of masonry built up to preserve the grade of the channel. A section of one of these walls remains standing about four miles up the canyon and is well worth investigating. It is about two hundred feet long, six feet thick at the base, fourteen feet high, and is strengthened at intervals by massive masonry buttresses. It is not known whether this wall was provided with culverts for the escape of the storm waters. The water-channel, which is 30″ x 10″ in dimension, is a covered masonry flume built in the top of the wall.

This aqueduct carried the water to the mission grounds where it was diverted into the usual channels. It was apparently in use until 1861-1862 when it was destroyed by floods. A filter, which stands on the hillside at the rear of the mission, supplied the community with clarified water for household use. According to accounts written by visitors, and evidence preserved in early sketches,[60] there was a fountain in the mission patio and another one with adjoining lavatory near the Indian village which stood in front and slightly to the left of the mission church.

Three reservoirs had also been built by the neophytes of this mission. One was at the place which the natives called Mupu but which the Fathers called Santa Paula. The other two were at a distance of one league to the north from the mission. No mention was made in the *informes*[61] of the above works, though it is true that the early reports are missing. The Padres' account-book might have supplied the name of the master workman who supervised the building of the dam, the aqueduct, etc., but it is nonexistent.

Little is left and less to be found recorded of the water systems of the rest of the missions—with one exception. At Santa Inés, third from the last mission to be founded, there remain to this day ruins of some considerable extent of reservoirs, lavatories, and other structures of undetermined use. Directly in front of the mission is a sunken ladrillo-lined enclosure, whose greatest depth at the farther end must be about fifteen feet. Leading down to this end is a ladrillo-paved, inclined walk from fifteen to eighteen feet wide. At the foot of the incline is a

[60] Sketches by Alfred Robinson and H. M. T. Powell.
[61] *Informes* of this mission in the Santa Bárbara Mission Archives begin with the year 1810. The *Libro de Patentes*, which Fr. Engelhardt consulted, and which was then in the mission library, seems to be missing. The *Informes* had been copied into that book.

vat-shaped pool or reservoir. Originally a gargoyle, through which the water issued into the pool, was installed at one end. Ladrillos, slightly sloping toward the sunken cement-lined structure—pool or whatever it may be—fill the space between it and the wall of the enclosure. A sheet-iron roof covers this interesting relic today and a padlock forbids investigation, but old photographs give excellent details of its construction.

Across the river in front of the mission, and built into the sloping hillside, are the ruins of extensive reservoirs of masonry construction. There also may be seen what are probably the remains of the Chapman mill built in 1820, though further investigation is needed to establish its identity.[62]

Lying in front of the site of the former neophyte Indian village at Santa Inés is what remains of a lavatory wherein the Indian women washed their clothes and probably their brown babies too. A gargoyle once ornamented this bit of construction also, and not so many years ago the cement-covered aqueduct, which once carried water to the lavatory, was to be seen crossing the field in front of the village. After the water had served its turn in the laundry pool it flowed on to help irrigate the field beyond. Much of interest might be revealed at this mission by proper investigation and excavation.

When, in 1820-1823, San Gabriel's first water-power gristmill was built, the Padres had a stone dam constructed at the mouth of Wilson Canyon. Water from the stream there was then diverted into an aqueduct built to convey it down to the mill, or "El Molino," as it is always called. After turning the mill-wheel, the water flowed on into the previously mentioned ciénega, and from there was conducted by ditch down to the mission. Then, in 1822-1825, Joseph Chapman, native of Boston, built a New England type mill for the Padres. For the operation of this gristmill he needed a greater volume of water than that provided by the dug ditch. Accordingly a dam was constructed across the lower end of the ciénega. Presumably it was Chapman who directed the Indians in its building as well as in the erection of the water-powered sawmill[63] which stood just beyond the dam. The dam was still standing in 1895 and was examined by Dr. Hiram A. Reid, who states: "The solid stone wall of the dam is from 6 to 7 feet thick, with reinforcing ledges and buttressed flume cheeks on lower side; 10 to 12 feet high at outlet; and 70 paces or over 200 feet entire length at top of wall." By the building of the dam Dr. Reid estimates the area of the lagoon,[64]

---

[62] In 1934, with the kind permission of the present owner, Mr. Thorwald Rasmussen, the writer, her husband, and two friends did considerable investigating and excavation in and around the building.

[63] The sawmill, operated by water, is reported finished in the *Informe* of 1825.

[64] The lake thus formed was afterwards known as "Mission Lake," "Wilson's Lake," "Kewen Lake," and "Lake Vineyard."

which had formed in the marsh, to have been more than doubled, and the water storage increased four or five times in depth.

The stones for this dam, Dr. Reid declares, were collected by the Indians from what was later known as Lincoln Park (now Eastlake Park), and hauled by ox-cart to the ciénega which lay between the mission and "El Molino." "And cement for the work, a sort of water lime, was dug out of the hillside and burned where the Lincoln Park reservoir now stands in the old lime pit."[65]

From the dam the water was let by gate into a channel leading to the sawmill. After serving the sawmill it flowed in open dug ditch down to the mission, where, as occasion demanded, it was again turned by gate into the cement-lined mill race, or other water-course.

The story of the mission irrigation systems deserves more time and space than can be given it in a volume such as this. It is, moreover, one that should have been written long ago by surveyors and engineers. Too much of it is now lost to us forever.

This writer is primarily concerned with the Indians' part in the projects described above, in the various skills they acquired or perfected through the building of dams and aqueducts and in the repairing of them.

Millions of stones, some large and some small, were collected and carted or carried in nets, sometimes from miles away, to the spot where they were needed. Limestone was dug from hillsides and sea-shells were gathered to burn for lime to be used in making mortar. Lime kilns were constructed in batteries of two, one being fired while the other was cooling and being emptied. Then the lime was carried by cart or mule-back to designated places along the aqueduct line. Ladrillos were fashioned, fired in kilns, and carted to the scene of activity. Clay pipes were molded under the direction of a potter and burned in a kiln for use in underground water-ways. Blacksmiths worked constantly to keep the picks, crowbars, and other tools in working order.

When the work was some distance away from the mission, camps were undoubtedly set up and the Indian women with their small children went along to cook for the laborers as well as to help with the lighter tasks involved. A shelter of boughs would have sufficed for temporary residence, for this work would not have continued through the rainy season. Truly those were times of strenuous activity when each was obliged to do his or her share and shirkers were punished. But the results were bountiful harvests, well-filled granaries, busy mills, and plenty of atole and pozole in the great copper kettles.

[65] Reid, Dr. H. A., *History of Pasadena,* 51, 377-378, 394.

CHAPTER 9

Indians Care for the Orchards, Fields, and Viñas

First Grapes at San Juan Capistrano and San Diego

THE PADRES were required to report on the amount of grains of all sorts sown and on the yield of each. They were also required to note the increase in the flocks and herds. This information was faithfully set down in the *informes* compiled annually and signed by the two missionaries in charge of the various missions. The Padres were not, however, obliged to report on the harvest of fruits and vegetables. Consequently, we would know little about the variety or quality of those products were it not for the Fathers' correspondence and the accounts written by visitors, explorers, and traders who came to California in mission days.

Were it not for the latter accounts also we would know even less about the neophytes employed in agricultural labors, their implements, tools, and practices. To the "foreigners" the carreta, the plow, and the manner of yoking the oxen were unusual. Therefore, the visitors described them. All these writers agree that it was the Indians, directed by one of the Padres, a mayordomo, or Indian foreman, who performed the labors not only at the missions but for the people of the pueblos as well. One Padre, we are told, attended to affairs spiritual while the other visited the various workshops and fields to see that work was progressing and that no laborer was absent. This Padre could not, of course, spend all his time with one group of workers; consequently, there was the foreman, often an Indian himself, to direct the work. Men of Spanish or Mexican descent, who were not serving as soldiers, were often hired by the Padres as overseers, gate-keepers, stewards, etc. They had, apparently, no objection to such employment, but, as has been noted in substance by more than one writer of that period, they did no work themselves that could not be accomplished on horseback. The Indians, therefore, were the laborers in the shops and fields.

A description of the fields and orchards together with their products is here-in given to acquaint the reader with the wide experience gained by the neophytes under the direction of the mission Padres, as well as the many agricultural arts in which they became so proficient that in after-mission days many of them were employed as laborers on the extensive ranchos.

Probably the first description of a California vegetable garden was written in March, 1776, by Fr. Pedro Font. With Captain Juan Bautista de Anza and a few soldiers from the company which that officer had brought from Sonora, Fr. Font visited Mission San Carlos. The garden, he tells us, was a stone's throw from the mission.[1] It had been well laid out by Fr. Palóu, who was waiting at San Carlos until everything was in readiness for the founding of the mission that was to be named in honor of St. Francis. In the meantime the Padre spent the whole day in the garden, which was square and bordered all around with alelies already in flower. There were beds of cauliflower, lettuce, artichokes, and other vegetables and herbs than which there were no better in México. The garden was not irrigated because the Fathers had as yet found no way of taking water from the river. However, the plants were watered by hand, a gourdful of water being thrown on each.[2] Water evidently was carried from the Río Carmelo to the garden, perhaps in cowhide buckets similar to that one in the Junípero Serra Museum at Old Town, San Diego, and was ladled out with a gourd.

In 1773, Fr. Serra had reported to the viceroy that a beginning had been made at this mission for a little enclosed garden, but for want of a gardener it made little progress. Fr. Palóu, it seems, filled the want and the garden was now thriving. This mission also had its fields of wheat, barley, beans, chickpeas, peas, and lentils.

In 1777, Fr. Lasuén was stationed at Mission San Diego. In making out the report for that year he mentions the fact that his mission had received from that of San Gabriel a donation of "twenty-four fanegas of wheat, twelve for planting and twelve for our own consumption, also forty fanegas of corn for the Indians, three fanegas of beans, and a large quantity of onions, garlic, tomatoes, and chile for ourselves, one fifth fanega of barley for sowing, . . ." In 1783, that Padre reports gifts from the gardens of both San Gabriel and San Juan Capistrano. Among the products mentioned were a crate of melocotones (peaches), watermelons, and sugar melons.[3]

In 1786, Jean François Galaup de la Pérouse introduced the potato into this

[1] Old pear trees still mark the site of the garden.
[2] Bolton, *Anza's Calif. Exped.*, 4. 303.
[3] Engelhardt, *Mission San Diego*, 95, 112.

state, his gardener giving the missionaries of San Carlos some "perfectly sound" ones which they had brought up from Chile.[4]

When Captain George Vancouver visited California, in 1792-1793, he was entertained by the Fathers at Missions San Francisco, Santa Clara, San Carlos, and San Buenaventura. He was shown through their churches, industrial apartments, granaries, Indian villages, and orchards. In the last he found trees which in season produced peaches, apricots, apples, pears, and figs. The vegetable gardens of the northern missions he considered too small, though "producing several sorts of vegetables in great perfection and abundance."[5]

He was greatly impressed with the buildings of the mission and the arrangements of the gardens and cultivated fields of San Buenaventura. The garden, he wrote, "far exceeded anything of that description I had before met with in these regions, both in respect of the quality, quantity, and variety of its excellent productions, not only indigenous to the country, but appertaining to the temperate as well as torrid zone; not one species having been sown or planted that had not flourished, and yielded its fruit in abundance, and of excellent quality. These have principally consisted of apples, pears, plumbs [sic], figs, oranges, grapes, peaches, and pomegranates, together with the plantain, banana, cocoa nut,[6] sugar cane, indigo, and a great variety of necessary and useful kitchen herbs, plants and roots. All these were flourishing in the greatest health and perfection though separated from the seaside only by two or three fields of corn, that were cultivated within a few yards of the surf. The grounds, however, on which they were produced, were supplied, at the expense of some labor, with a few small streams, which, as occasion required, were conducted to the crops that stood most in need of water."[7]

Two old date palms still overlook the spot where the mission Indians once cultivated the garden and gathered the fruit from the orchard inspected by the English captain. Where they were all located is not known, but, in 1828, Fr. Francisco Xavier Uría reported: "This Mission has ten orchards of fruit trees, besides vegetable gardens. It cultivates vineyards and olive groves, the products from which serve to cover expenses."[8] From which it seems that the Padres exported, or traded for needed articles, wine, olives, and olive oil.

Dr. G. H. von Langsdorff adds to the list of vegetables known to have been grown in the mission gardens. In describing Mission San Francisco, he writes:

---

[4] Banc., *Hist. of Cal.*, 1. 431.
[5] Vancouver, *Voyage*, 2. 20.
[6] That the plantain, banana, and cocoa nut "flourished and yielded fruit in abundance" in California is doubtful.
[7] Vancouver, *Voyage*, 2. 294.
[8] Engelhardt, *Mission San Buenaventura*, 66 (*Libro de Patentes* in the Mission Library).

Top: The ruined pottery kiln at Santa Bárbara. Ruins of the pottery shop still exist. Bottom: Tile molds and a finished tile; C.C.C. boy making tiles at La Purísima.

Left Panel: "SERRA CHURCH" *showing uneven rafter ends; interior of chapel at Pala.* Right Panel: *Pole and bamboo ceilings at San Luis Obispo; San Antonio roof construction.*

"The only things that grow well in the gardens are asparagus, cabbage, and several sorts of salad, onions, and potatoes. In some fields tolerably sheltered from the wind, peas, beans, Turkish corn (maize), and other pulse (legumes) are cultivated, and thrive pretty well." The few fruit trees that had been planted were stunted and scarcely bore any fruit, due to the prevailing northwest winds and the dry, sandy nature of the soil.[9]

Alfred Robinson describes Mission San Gabriel as having several extensive gardens attached to it "where may be found oranges, citrons, limes, apples, pears, peaches, pomegranates, figs, and grapes in abundance."[10] This mission had, according to the inventory of November, 1834, 2,333 fruit trees in nine orchards.

The pomegranate was a great favorite with the Padres, either for its symbolic significance or for its flowers and fruit. It made a wonderfully showy shrub or tree with the whitewashed adobe walls for its background and was often planted by the pillars of the inner court. A row of these trees is said to have been planted along the western side of San Gabriel's orchard and garden. One still grows and blossoms within San Antonio's courtyard.

Guadalupe, daughter of Don José Jesús Vallejo,[11] wrote of the early gardens:

I have often been asked about the old Mission and ranch gardens. They were, I think, more extensive, and contained a greater variety of trees and plants than most persons imagine. . . . I remember that at Mission San Jose we had many varieties of seedling fruits which have now been lost to cultivation. Of pears we had four sorts, one ripening in early summer, one in late summer, and two in autumn and winter. The Spanish names of these pears were the Presidenta, the Bergamota, the Pana, and the Lechera. One of them was as large as a Bartlett, but there are no trees left of it now. The apples, grown from seed, ripened at different seasons, and there were seedling peaches, both early and late. An interesting and popular fruit was that of the Nopal, or prickly pear. This fruit, called tuna, grew on great hedges which protected part of the Mission orchards, and were twenty feet high and ten or twelve feet thick. Those who know how to eat a tuna, peeling it so as to escape the tiny thorns on the skin, find it delicious. The Missions had avenues of fig, olive, and other trees about the buildings besides the orchards. . . The old orchards were pruned and cultivated with much care, . . ."[12]

When the inventory[13] was taken at San José, in 1837, there were growing in the main orchard (Huerta Principal) 784 fruit trees. There were pear, apple, quince (membrillo), fig, olive, and peach trees. Among them were 62 grafted pear and apple trees ("62 Yngertos entre perales y manzanos"). In "Huerta del San Cayetano" were 660 trees of which 100 were small apple and pear trees that had been grafted.

[9] Langsdorff, *Voyages and Travels*, 2. 161-162.
[10] Robinson, *Life in Cal.*, 45, 272.
[11] Administrator of Mission San José after secularization.
[12] Vallejo, Guadalupe, "Ranch and Mission Days," 188-189.
[13] In SBMA.

Sir James Douglas noted in his Journal: "I saw in several gardens that I visited, pear, apple, olive, fig, and peach trees growing luxuriantly. There is also a mongrel fruit grown from the pear or apple stocks grafted on each other, the fruit always bearing the affinity to that of the tree from which the graft is cut."[14]

That the Padres were acquainted with the science of tree-grafting was also attested to by Mr. E. M. Sheridan,[15] long a resident of San Buenaventura, who told the writer that he had seen, in the old orchard of that mission, trees that had been grafted. It naturally follows that the Indians were instructed in that art.

In Libro Tercero (Book Third) of the previously mentioned work, *Agricultura General*, the Padres found instructions not only for grafting but for various other horticultural tasks ranging from the choosing of the proper soil and site for the orchard to the care of the harvested crops. No essential horticultural detail seems to have been omitted from this treatise on the propagation, planting and care of trees. Shade and ornamental trees are considered as well as those bearing fruits and nuts. Frequently emphasis is laid on the best time for performing the various tasks outlined, whether in the full of the moon or in the crescent ("en luna lleña, ó creciente").

As a rule the orchards and gardens were planted quite near the missions and were enclosed by high adobe walls or cactus hedges, for the Padres soon found that, if they were to enjoy bountiful harvests or any harvests whatever, their gardens must be guarded from winged, four-footed, and other marauders. Writing from Mission San Carlos, in 1779, Fr. Serra observes: "Corn has just been shelled, and thus [this?] amounted to little more than fifty fanegas, because horses, cattle, crows, and thieves left us only that much, although God had provided abundantly."[16] At Mission San Diego the Padres add this note to their *informe* of 1783: "This year we have seen it necessary to take the cattle away from the Mission in order to raise grain and fruit there."[17]

During the 1820's the mission gardens seem to have been raided by an unusual number of pests. In 1821, Fr. Ybarra writes to Captain de la Guerra, of the Santa Bárbara presidio, protesting against the actions of the soldier-guards of the San Fernando Mission. "In addition to all these troubles," he declares, "caterpillars have almost consumed the habas (horse-beans), while the locusts have covered the wheat fields, so that from seven fanegas of wheat not so much as a shrub [?]

[14] Douglas, "Journal," 112.
[15] Mr. Sheridan passed away in October, 1941.
[16] Engelhardt, *Mission San Carlos*. 87-88.
[17] Engelhardt, *Mission San Diego*, 113.

remains to tell that wheat had been planted." Two months later he wrote: "I just came from Rancho de San Francisco. Things are as I said. There are only sixty or seventy fanegas. Rabbits and hares and worms have done much damage to the crop."[18]

Reporting on the lands of San Luis Rey Mission, in 1822, Fr. Peyri notes: "It must be observed also that the fields are very much damaged by locusts, squirrels, crows, blackbirds, and other plagues, which can be driven off only by means of many dogs and scarecrows."[19]

At Mission San Juan Capistrano there was set up in the enclosed orchard and vineyard a watchtower of poles with a tule platform on top. The watchman was an Indian whose duty it was to frighten away the birds by making a loud noise on a sort of drum. Indian boys were usually assigned to the task of scaring away or snaring the birds and were given the title of *pajareros*.

It was undoubtedly necessary also to protect the gardens and orchards from raids by the Indians themselves. It would have been strange indeed if they had resisted the temptation to pick the delicious fruit ripening within reach of their hands. Therefore, the walls around those fields were from eight to ten feet high.

Inside the enclosures adobe cottages were erected for the gardeners, who were also the caretakers. At Mission San Gabriel the picturesque, red-tiled, adobe casa of the gardener still stands some distance to the south of the mission church. It has been immortalized by the brush of Charles H. Owens. Photographs, taken in 1905-1909, of the gardener's and vineyardist's houses at Mission San Antonio furnish excellent examples for the study of the construction of those buildings. It is a great pity that they have been allowed to slowly disintegrate.

When the fruit was ripe it was gathered by the Indians, working under the watchful eyes of the caretaker, or mayordomo, and carried in large baskets to the mission. Here it was sorted. Some of the fruit was eaten fresh for dessert. Occasionally a box was sent to one of the Padres' friends, as happened at San Buenaventura when Fr. Señán sent to Captain de la Guerra "two crates of fruit, containing an assortment of pears, apples, and apricots."[20] Sometimes fruit was given to the Indians as an extra treat.

Apples and pears of good keeping quality were laid away on shelves that had previously been covered with a thick layer of straw, and, with moderate care, lasted throughout the winter and sometimes into the late spring. In the early days of Santa Clara College this procedure was followed by the Jesuit Brother,

[18] Engelhardt, *Mission San Fernando*, 39-40. *De la Guerra Papers*.
[19] Engelhardt, *Mission San Luis Rey*, 41.
[20] Engelhardt, *Mission San Buenaventura*, 42.

Ristori, who was very proud of a "species of pear of extraordinary size" which was gathered from trees in the old mission orchard and laid away on a shelf to ripen in the coolness of an adobe room.[21]

According to tradition, at San Juan Capistrano some of the fruit was cut and dried on a flat roof constructed for that especial purpose. And from the rest were concocted all those delicious and toothsome conserves, candied fruits, and jellies that only a Spanish cook can concoct. Under the guidance of their instructresses, the girls and young women of the monjerio learned in time to prepare many of those delicacies.

Very little remains today to tell of the former extent and location of the mission orchards, gardens, and vineyards.[22] Here and there around the old establishments one comes upon an occasional pear or walnut tree. A greater number of the old olive trees exist but even they are fast disappearing. At San Diego, for instance, but three remain in the famous old orchard formerly occupying several acres in the lowland directly in front of the restored buildings. In 1839, this mission had, in fact, in two orchards 467 olive trees "besides various other fruit trees, notably pomegranates."[23] A number of olive trees survive at Santa Bárbara, and at San José those trees still border lots once covered with grapevines. Until 1920, olives were still being produced on trees growing within the adobe-walled enclosure at the left of Mission San Fernando's church. Two fine old palm trees stood guard over them. The palms remain but the wall and the olive trees no longer exist. Several of the old date palms are yet living, and within the grounds of the University of Santa Clara is an old fig tree believed to have been planted in mission days. A few apple trees[24] remain at Santa Cruz, and, until some time after 1850, one continued to grow and bear fruit within the patio of one-time Mission Santa Clara.

At the missions of San Antonio, San Carlos, San Juan Bautista, Santa Inés, and San Juan Capistrano, gnarled and twisted pear trees still burst into bloom and bear odd-shaped fruit as season succeeds season. At La Soledad one lone walnut tree is left; a few more are found at other establishments. Mute reminders, they are, of the orchards once cared for by the Indian neophytes. But the peaches, plums, and apricots, being shorter lived, have disappeared. For many years a peach tree, grown from a pit taken from a mission-day tree, was carefully nurtured in the inner court of Mission San Juan Capistrano. The legend of its

[21] Waddell, John A., "Some Memories of Earlier College Days in Santa Clara," MS, courtesy of Rev. Arthur D. Spearman, S. J.

[22] Some shown in surveys of mission property made in 1854, 1858-1873.

[23] Inspector William Hartnell's report. Engelhardt, *Mission San Diego*, 240.

[24] Apples said to have been planted at the time of Russian occupancy are still bearing fruit in the orchard at Ft. Ross.

having been planted by a sister of Pio Pico provided one of the highlights in the stories told by eccentric old Pat, the guide, and handed down to Juan Aguilar, hijo del país, who succeeded him in that office.

When Mission La Purísima Concepción was rebuilt an effort was made to re-create a mission garden there. Mr. E. D. Rowe, of Lompoc, California, was in charge of that part of the work. With boys from the Civilian Conservation Corps for his helpers, he gathered and planted seeds of such native flowers and herbs as the Padres would have had in their gardens. Then, visiting missions and their former ranchos, he gathered cuttings and seeds from the sad remnants of the old orchards and gardens. The cuttings, taken from pear trees found at the above named missions, he grafted on seedling pear stock. The parent trees he believes were seedlings, but the pear, he says, is one fruit that comes true from seed.

At the old Ortega rancho at Arroyo Hondo on the coast, Mr. Rowe found trees of the "Prunus Kapolin," a cherry,[25] native of México. Seeds from these trees were planted at La Purísima. They grew, were transplanted, and are now bearing fruit. Cuttings were taken from the fig tree at Santa Clara, from pome-granates at San Antonio, and from the grapevines at San Francisquito, one of La Purísima's own ranchos. All these were planted and are producing fruit in abundance.

To represent the peach trees once flourishing in the mission orchards, Mr. Rowe obtained, through the United States Department of Agriculture, seeds from trees planted by Pueblo Indians in the Cañon de Chelly and at Oraibi, in Arizona. Those trees, he was told, could be definitely traced back one hundred years and it was reasonably certain that they descended from seeds planted by the first missionary of 1685. The fruit is small, freestone, its white flesh showing pink on the sunny side, is very juicy and has a good flavor. The Indians of those places dry the fruit on the roofs of their houses. The peach is a short-lived tree, but coming true from seed, it has been perpetuated by those almost unchanging peoples. And so we have in a mission garden today peach tree descendants of old Spanish stock.

The olive trees in the Purísima garden were thirty-year-old trees that were boxed and moved from Los Olivos some thirty-five miles away in the Santa Ynéz Valley. They were started, Mr. Rowe was informed, from cuttings taken from mission trees. The cuttings were pieces about two feet long, one or two inches in diameter, and were planted where they were to grow.

---

[25] Writing about Mission Santa Bárbara, Duhaut-Cilly says: "Banana trees spread their broad leaves between apple and pear trees; and with the ruby of the cherries were mingled the golden apples of the orange trees." "Duhaut-Cilly's Account," 159.

Roses of Castile from the then pathetic ruins of San Antonio, hollyhocks, rues, rosemary, thistles, old fashioned pinks, matilija poppies, pennyroyal, and numerous other herbs, flowers, and shrubs contrive to make this one of the most interesting gardens in California.

According to the report made to Governor Echeandía, in 1827, Mission San Antonio's wheat fields were planted two leagues[26] or more to the south from the mission. Unlike those of most of the other missions, these wheat fields were irrigated. In 1892, the Padres' old irrigation ditch was located by E. J. Cahill, C. E., and found to extend as far as Jolón, a distance of almost seven miles.

From the first the Fathers searched far and wide for locations suitable for various crops. They tried one spot after another. Evidence of this is found in a letter written, in 1779, by Fr. Serra to Fr. Lasuén at San Diego, in which he says, in part: "Even more delighted am I with the fair prospects Your Reverence outlines to me, as also with your perseverance on observing that land was found suitable for wheat and other grain. Thanks be to God. . ."[27]

Thus with the necessity for removing flocks and herds from the immediate vicinity of the mission in order that fruit and vegetables might be raised there, and with the pressing need to find land most suitable for the cultivation of various crops to feed the ever increasing number of neophytes, the mission ranchos, or estancias, came into being.

Best known of these ranchos are Santa Isabel, located in San Diego's "back country"; San Antonio de Pala, Las Flores,[28] and Santa Margarita, estancias of Mission San Luis Rey; San Bernardino, Santa Anita, and La Puente belonging to Mission San Gabriel; San Francisco and Camulos of Mission San Fernando; La Cieneguita, or San Miguel, Dos Pueblos, and San Marcos of Mission Santa Bárbara; Guadalupe, Jalama, and San Francisco of Mission La Purísima; Santa Margarita and San Miguelito of Mission San Luis Obispo; Paso del Robles, La Asunción, Santa Isabel and San Simeón, of Mission San Miguel; Los Ojitos and San Benito of Mission San Antonio; Buena Vista of San Carlos del Carmelo, San Mateo of Mission San Francisco, and Santa Rosa of Mission San Rafael. There were scores of others dotting the landscape from San Diego to San Francisco Solano (now Sonoma). Some of them were at a considerable distance from the parent mission. Mission San Gabriel is said to have had from twelve to fifteen ranchos, the most far-flung one being San Gorgonio (Beaumont).

In time red-tiled adobe quarters for the mayordomo, or overseer, and the

[26] See Chapter II, note 7.
[27] Engelhardt, *Mission San Diego*, 102. Original in SBMA.
[28] Sketched in 1850 by H. M. T. Powell. See illustration.

Indian workers were built on these estancias. Many of the ranch houses were really beautiful, the one at Paso del Robles being particularly picturesque. This building no longer exists, but the one erected at Los Ojitos, to house the Indians in charge of the cattle there, still stands much as it did in mission days though without its roof of red tiles.

Occasionally, when the distance from the mission was too great for the proper attendance at religious services, a chapel was built in connection with the ranch buildings for the benefit of the Indians living there. There were such chapels at Santa Isabel, San Antonio de Pala, Las Flores, San Bernardino, and perhaps at other ranchos in the southern district. Wheat, beans, and corn were grown at the four sites mentioned. At San Bernardino stock raising was also carried on. At La Puente, in 1816, Fr. Zalvidea reported six hundred Indians working in the grain fields. Cattle, horses, and sheep were also kept at this latter place. A chapel was needed there, but whether one was built is not recorded.

At San Miguel (Cieneguitas, Sagslipeel, or Mescaltitán), rancho of Santa Bár-bara Mission, there existed until 1849, at least, an Indian village consisting of an adobe chapel and a number of red-tiled, single-roomed, adobe cottages for the Indians, surrounded by well-cultivated little orchards of fruit trees of many varieties.[29] This was one of Santa Bárbara's main wheat ranchos. Dos Pueblos was another. There were also ranchos where corn and beans were grown.

Santa Margarita de Cortona was Mission San Luis Obispo's principal wheat rancho. Here the Padres had caused to be erected a long building of stone and mortar, with tiled roof, arched doorways, and wide corridors. This structure was divided into a number of apartments for the mayordomo and the Indian workers, as well as for storerooms for the grain. One room was set aside for a chapel and another for the Padre who occasionally came to say Mass and to in-spect the wheat fields. It was while he was on such visit that Fr. Luis Gil y Taboada was taken ill and died at Santa Margarita, December 15, 1833. The grain was being planted at that time.

According to the *informe* of 1822, this estancia was established for the pur-pose of raising grain and also to furnish a retreat for the mission family in case of maritime invasion.[30] In 1818, two vessels from Buenos Aires carrying some three or four hundred insurgents under the command of Hipólite Bouchard had sailed into the port of Monterey. The presidio was attacked, some of the buildings, the

[29] Rogers, David Banks, *Prehistoric Man of the Santa Barbara Coast* (Published by Santa Barbara Museum of Natural History), 19-29 (hereinafter referred to as *Prehistoric Man*).

[30] "Por cuyo motivo se ha tomado la providencia de formar dos Ranchos uno para Trigos en Sta Margarita, en el camino de Monterey, y para formar alguna retirada de la Mision en caso de Inbaciones Maritimas, y otro en la Playa o Puerto, para mais y Frixol. ." SBMA.

orchard, garden, and officers' personal property destroyed. Then, going on down the coast, the rebels raided the Ortega rancho and Mission San Juan Capistrano, though at the latter place they did little or no damage.[31] This invasion, it seems, was still fresh in the memories of the Padres when they built the Santa Margarita ranch house.

At San Miguelito, the second rancho mentioned in the *informe* of 1822, corn and beans were planted and harvested by the neophytes. A chapel for this estancia was approved by the governor but again there seems to be no record of one having been built.

In 1830, Fr. Gil reporting for his mission said: "All the walls of the house at Santa Margarita have been cracked by earthquakes. The ranch and buildings of San Miguelito are destroyed."[32] Edwin Bryant found Santa Margarita still in ruins in 1846. This ranch, with acres added, had been granted to Joaquín Estrada in 1841, and later came into the possession of Gen. P. W. Murphy. This owner, according to Raymundo Pacheco, who was raised on the place, "liked the old building left as it was." But when the present owner took possession in about 1904, the inner walls were removed and a sheet-iron roof put on to provide a storage granary for the produce of the fields. Señor Pacheco told the writer that he had removed the inner walls himself with pick and crowbar, and not with dynamite as had been reported by George Wharton James.[33] Dynamite, he explained, would have destroyed both inner and outer walls. This building has, by the way, been the subject of more fantastic stories than has any other of the old mission ranch houses.

In 1934, the writer examined the site of the buildings of San Miguelito. It lies a few miles inland from the quaint old town of Ávila, named for Miguel Ávila, who, in 1842, received from Governor Alvarado the grant of this valuable piece of property. Nothing remains of the buildings save heaps of adobe soil. A broken tahona millstone lies near the creek that flows by the site.

Another sad reminder of mission days is the little tile-roofed adobe house on the Asunción Rancho about two and one-half miles out from Atascadero. La Asunción was one of Mission San Miguel's wheat farms. In 1812-1813, a house and granary were built there. The little ruined adobe house which still stands beside the winding road is said to have been a two-storied building originally, similar, possibly, to the Los Ojitos or Paso del Robles houses. Here a number of neophyte Indians lived; planted, guarded, and harvested the wheat. There was

[31] Banc. *Hist. of Cal.*, 2. 220-249.
[32] *Informe* 1830. SBMA.
[33] James, George W.. *The Old Franciscan Missions*, 244.

▲ San Francisco Solano (*at Sonoma*) *in the early 1860's. The chapel shown replaced the old church.*

▼ San Francisco de Asís *as it stood ten years after American occupation of California.*

▲ SANTA BÁRBARA *in "about" 1875. Ruins of the ranchería lie beyond the main buildings.*

▼ SAN BUENAVENTURA *from the rear in 1875. The tiled roof of the church has disappeared.*

a spring on the place that provided water to irrigate a garden. Still growing there are one of those twisted pear trees and several grape-stocks of considerable girth, which, as was their custom, the Indians probably planted for their own benefit. It was to this rancho and house that Fr. Juan Moreno asked leave to re-tire during the terrible days that followed the secularization of the missions. He wanted to cultivate the garden "on his own account."

It has often been said that grape cuttings were brought to California by the expeditions of 1769, but there seems to be little corroboration of that statement. At any rate, if they were brought they seem not to have survived. In 1779, how-ever, Fr. Mugártegui penned two letters that tell of the planting of grape cut-tings (sarmientos) and also of the removal of his mission from its first site, Mis-ión Vieja, to its second and present location. In the first letter dated at Mission San Juan Capistrano, March 15, 1779, the Padre writes, in part:

Alabado sea Dios. Luna en Aquario. Nieves a tutiple. P⁰ [pero] para templar la mucha frialdad y condexa del agua se plantaron todos los sarmientos, que con su recomendacion de Vmd. [Vues-tra Merced] nos remitieron de estos paises bajos. Damos las debidas gracias a Dios, a Vmd. a los amantisimos Padres y Hermanos, Bienhechores. El nuevo parage a que nos trasladamos pinta bien. . . [34]

Translated, this passage reads: "God be praised. The moon is in Aquarius. Snow is plentiful, wherefore, until the severe cold moderates and the floods sub-side, the vine cuttings which at your request were sent to us from the lower country [Baja California] have been buried. We give thanks to God, to yourself, and to our benefactors, the beloved Fathers and Brothers. The new place to which we are moving promises well [shows good prospects]."

A month later, April 18, 1779, Fr. Mugártegui writes again to Fr. Serra. His letter, after giving a report of items of lesser importance, ends with this para-graph:

Esta Misión se mudó, y erijió a fundamentis este verano pasado, se ha fabricado una casa de adobe entero para habitación de los padres, una iglesia de medio adobe, una de palizada para el Jato. Los dos corrales respectivos a ganado mayor y menor. Se ha cercado la milpa y echado zanja al arroyo para el riego. [35]

Translated, the above reads: "This mission was moved, and re-established this past summer [1778], there was built entirely of adobe a dwelling for the Fathers, a church of part adobe, a [structure] of palisades for the calves. The two

---

[34] Excerpt from Fr. Engelhardt's copy of the original in the Museo Nacionál, Mexico City. Transcript of same in *Arch. Banc. Lib.*
[35] Copied for this writer by Fr. Maynard Geiger, O.F.M., from the original in the archives in Mexico City.

corrals [are] one for the large live stock and one for the small. The garden is fenced and a ditch from the arroyo finished to irrigate it."

Such were the beginnings at the second site of San Juan Capistrano. There can be little doubt that the grape cuttings mentioned above were set out by the Indian workers within the fenced garden and that they were soon bearing fruit, for the grape produces fruit two years from the planting of the cutting and by the sixth or seventh year has reached maturity.

That San Diego shared in the gift of grape cuttings, sent up in the spring of 1779, is indicated in the following letter written by Fr. Serra to Fr. Lasuén of that mission. Dated at "Misión San Carlos de Monte-Rey," December 8, 1781, the Padre Presidente's letter is a newsy, encouraging one to the Padre whose mission was beset with so many difficulties. After speaking of the dedication of San Diego's new church and Fr. Lasuén's report of a bountiful harvest of grains, Fr. Serra continues: "Tambien deseo que el maiz se haya bien logrado, y que vivan, y fructifiquen los sarmientos, que ya se haya inaguantable esta falta de vino para las Misas. . ."[36] (I hope that the maize is doing well, and that the vine-shoots are living and bearing fruit, for this lack of wine for the Mass is becoming unbearable).

It seems obvious that had vine-shoots been planted in 1769, there need have been no lack of wine twelve years later. Nor does it seem probable that, if vines were already growing in Upper California, Fr. Serra would have requested that cuttings be sent up from the peninsula. Moreover, the Padre Presidente seems to be pinning his hopes for wine on the grapes to be produced from those very cuttings. At San Diego the vine-shoots of 1779 were probably planted in the garden in front of the mission. In 1839, this establishment had three vineyards, one with 5,000 vines, another with 3,600 vines, while the third, planted at Santa Monica (El Cajón), contained 8,000 vines just two years old.[37]

From data gathered from inventories taken when the missions were secularized, and from surveys of mission property, made in 1854-1873, it appears that most of the establishments had vineyards. These ranged in size from one hundred-seventy acres to one acre, the former being at San Gabriel and the latter at Santa Clara Mission. Santa Clara, however, may have had other plots.

A memorandum, made in 1834, of San Gabriel's property listed four vineyards with 163,578 vines. One of these vineyards was called the Viña Madre (Mother Vineyard), probably because it was the mother of all that mission's vineyards

[36] From a photostat copy of the original in SBMA.
[37] This last named is the vineyard which, in 1867, Judge Hayes found in the possession of Don José María Estudillo. It was then "near ruined" but as late as 1863 excellent wine had been made from its grapes. Hayes, *Pioneer Notes*, 292.

and not, as is often said, because it was the first vineyard planted in Alta California.[38] Certainly there is no record to support this claim.

The missions of Santa Bárbara, La Purísima, San Miguel, and San José each had more than one site for growing grapes, though none equaled in size the Viña Madre of San Gabriel. At San José 6,029 vine-stocks were growing in the Huerta Principal and 34 in San Cayetano.

Mission Santa Bárbara's largest vineyard, called San José, covered a plot of about nine acres. It was fenced and within the enclosure was a house for the vineyardist. 2,262 vines were planted there and 100 fruit trees. According to Hawley this vineyard "was located at La Goleta, on the western bank of San José Creek, and nearly a mile north of Hollister Avenue."[39] In two other vineyards, not named, there were 3,695 additional vine-stocks.

San Marcos was an estancia of considerable importance. In 1804, it was stocked with cattle, horses, and sheep. A large vineyard was planted there and a number of buildings erected. These structures included an adobe dwelling for the mayordomo, 55' x 19', with corridor; a kitchen, 11' x 8'; a lagar, or wine-press, 11' square; a bodega, or cellar, of adobe 5' 6" x 22'; a granary of adobe and an adobe dwelling for the Indian workers. This last named building was 30 feet long and 11 feet wide.[40] A chapel of adobe was also built in order that the Padres might celebrate Mass when they came to inspect the rancho. This estancia was eight leagues from the mission and the care of the herds and flocks together with that of the vineyard necessitated the constant employment at that place of some considerable number of Indians. The same was true of most of the large ranchos. The almost obliterated ruins of the San Marcos buildings may still be traced beside the San Marcos Pass road that leads from Santa Bárbara over the hills to Mission Santa Inés and points beyond.

Mission La Purísima's two vineyards were located in the canyon that leads to El Cojo, a place of anchorage for the trading vessels that plied the coastal waters in mission days. Jalama, a vineyard of some seventeen acres, was about eight miles south of the mission; while San Francisco, or San Francisquito as it was sometimes called, was located two miles farther west. The latter covered an area of a little more than five acres. Here the Padres had caused to be built a wine-press and a house for the caretaker. Ruins of the wine-press still stand on top of a slight eminence above the creek that flows through the one-time vineyard. It was from the old vines in this hillside plot, once tended by the mission Indian

[38] Just as San Miguel's largest vineyard was called La Mayor.
[39] Hawley, Walter, *The Early Days of Santa Barbara, California*, 60 (hereinafter referred to as *The Early Days*).
[40] Inventory of Mission Santa Bárbara, 1834. SBMA.

vineyardists, that cuttings were taken for the re-created garden of La Purísima.

San Luis Obispo's vineyard, next in size to San Gabriel's Viña Madre, covered a plot of forty-four and sixty-six-hundredths acres. It lay across the San Luis Creek directly in front of the mission and was enclosed by a stone wall. Inside the wall was a row of large olive trees. And, as was customary, there was, in all probability, a casa for the vineyardist within the enclosure. Though the records do not so state.

A description of the house built, in 1815, at Rancho del Aguage (ranch of the spring) will perhaps serve as an example of those erected for the caretakers at the various viñas. It had, the Fathers of Mission San Miguel report, two rooms and a little parlor. It was built of adobe, roofed with tiles, and was protected from winter's rains and summer's suns by a tile-roofed corridor. This vineyard had an area of twenty-two acres and was located in a canyon three miles northeast of the mission.

At Rancho del Aguage and Santa Isabel, at which latter place there was a small vineyard, 5,500 vines were growing. At both these places a spring provided water for irrigation. At Santa Isabel, too, a house was built for the foreman, or overseer, of the rancho's activities, chief of which was the raising of sheep. Robinson stopped at this estancia where, he writes, "were two large houses and a number of straw huts. Gardens were attached to them, in which a variety of vegetables were cultivated by the Indians, who were there as keepers of eight or ten thousand sheep."[41]

The Padres of Mission La Soledad also chose a canyon for the site of their vineyard. Located about three and one-half miles southwest of the mission buildings, it had for its limits on the north, south, and west the precipitous sides of the canyon which formed a natural boundary for it, and on the east side the narrow gorge which provided entrance to the field. Within this walled-in pocket were twenty and thirty-two-hundredths acres devoted to the raising of grapes.

At harvest time the vineyards were centers of great activity when the luscious purple grapes were picked by the Indians under the vigilant supervision of the overseers. Then piled high on hide-lined carretas, the fragrant fruit was hauled, by slow, lumbering oxen guided and prodded by other Indians, down to the mission. There the juice was extracted and converted into wine as will be told in a subsequent chapter.

As has been noted on another page, the book, *Agricultura General*, now in the Santa Bárbara Mission Archives, belonged to Fr. Antonio Jayme, who labored at

[41] Robinson, *Life in California*, 93.

La Soledad from May, 1796, to February, 1821, when, his active working days done, he retired to Santa Bárbara. There it was that Duhaut-Cilly found him seated on a bench in the lovely front corridor, taking a well-earned rest and being cared for by his fellow Franciscans while awaiting the Summons that "comes to all men."

Libro Segundo (Book Second) of that treatise on agriculture is devoted entirely to the cultivation of the grape. It discusses the subject from the selection of the soil and location of the vineyard, the planting of cuttings, to the harvesting of the grapes, the converting of the grapes into wine and the storing of the wine in a properly built bodega. Pages of the old book show much usage, especially those devoted to the process of wine-making. Needless to say, those neophytes who were selected to care for the vineyards acquired, in time, a pretty thorough knowledge of viniculture.

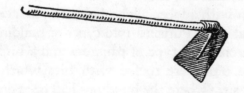

CHAPTER 10

First Temporary Buildings Erected at the Missions

Indians Gain Experience With the Passing of Years

THE FIRST temporary buildings erected on the various mission sites were mostly of palisades, that is, of poles set in the ground close together and usually plastered with mud. The roofs were flat and were covered with grass, tules, or earth. According to the *informes*, Mission Santa Clara's first row of buildings was "de palizada embarrada con techo terrado"[1] (of palisade construction mud-plastered with flat roof). Mission Santa Bárbara's was "cercada de varas, y embarrada con techo de sacate," or "con techo de terrado"[2] (enclosed with poles and mud-plastered with roof of grass, or with flat roof). At the end of 1814, at the second site, the Padres of Mission La Purísima reported: "There have been built such structures as a mission must have temporarily, . . . all of palisades, and roofed with tile, and besides a church of forked poles walled in with adobe, which holds all the people."[3]

It will be noted that at La Purísima two types of building construction were reported, namely, the ordinary type of palisades and a building of forked poles walled in with adobe. All were roofed with tiles which had probably been brought from the first site[4] where the buildings had been destroyed by the earth tremors of December, 1812. The remarkable thing about the use of tiles is not that they were to be had that first year, but that they should have been used to roof palisades. For the mission tiles are very heavy.[5] However, the description of the church built at this site furnishes a clue to the mystery.

---

[1] *Informe*, Mission Santa Clara, 1777. SBMA.

[2] *Informe*, Mission Santa Bárbara, 1787. SBMA.

[3] Se han fabricado provisionalmente quantas piezas necesita una Mision (aunqᵉ con la estrechez qᵉ se dexa entender) todas de palizada, y techadas con texa, y â mas una Yglesia de horconeria cercada con adove qᵉ contiene toda la gente . ." SBMA.

[4] At the present town of Lompoc.

[5] Single tiles from San Carlos, San Antonio, and San Juan Capistrano weighed 10 lbs., 10½ lbs., and 12¼ lbs. respectively.

The forked pole, used to strengthen sidewalls and to carry ridgepoles and rafters, was an architectural detail that was borrowed from México where it still may be found in old religious structures. Excellent examples of its use in early California buildings are found in old photographs of mission ranch houses where the beams, upon which the rafters of the corridors rest, are supported by forked poles in lieu of pillars of adobe or brick. The little tile-roofed adobe cottage that stood beside the path leading up into the canyon beyond Mission San Antonio was protected with a corridor whose roof was so supported. And so, originally, was the corridor roof of the ranch house of Paso del Robles. A photograph,[6] taken probably in the early sixties, shows one of the old forked poles still standing. The missions' first belfries consisted of two forked posts set in the ground with a transverse pole, or crossbar, resting in the forks, the bells hanging suspended from the crossbar. It is quite possible, too, that lack of evidence of corridors, where the present-day excavator would expect to find them along mission buildings, may be due to the fact that the supports were such poles whose destruction left no trace of their former existence.

Before the rebuilding of the present church at La Purísima was begun, considerable excavation was done in the area around the church ruins and the cemetery. Trenches about twenty-five feet apart were dug in both directions. During these operations the workmen, in 1937, came upon three parallel lines of post-holes beginning about fifty feet south of the cemetery. (There was at that time no trace of cemetery wall or other evidence of burial place on the surface of this plot.) These post-holes were about nine feet on center apart each way and were lined with stones. Complete excavations uncovered the remains of an L-shaped structure, the main wing being one hundred seventy-seven feet long and the shorter one forty-five feet. A pinkish cement flooring extended across a portion of the cemetery area, while along the east line of post-holes, as far as the south wall of the cemetery, there was found some evidence of a narrow stone foundation, or "footing," that might have supported a thin wall of adobe bricks. These archeological remains were believed to be those of the first temporary structures erected on this site.

The post-holes, together with the Padres' report of the erection of "una Yglesia de horconería" (a church of forked poles), enable one to reconstruct this L-shaped building quite satisfactorily. Forked poles set in along the sides and tamped with rocks strengthened the side walls and upheld the timbers which

---

[6] Photograph published in *Overland Monthly*, Nov., 1892, accredited to Taber, but was probably made by Watkins, most of whose work later came into the possession of the former.

supported the rafters of the roof. The center line of forked poles carried the ridgepole. Tie beams were probably employed. Notched to fit the timber upheld by the forked poles of the side walls and secured to it, as well as to the center pole, by means of strips of "green" rawhide, tie beams would have added considerably to the strength of the structure. Along the purely palisades portion of this building the spaces between the forked poles of the side and partition walls were filled in with smaller poles stuck in the ground but not tamped with stones. A thick coat of mud plaster was then applied to the walls inside and outside.

But with the church, the framework of forked poles was walled in, or enclosed, by adobes, the poles becoming an integral part of the walls. The forked poles of the center and along the sides carried the entire weight of the tiled roof. This was a much more interesting structure than one of palisades. Nor was this church ever referred to in the original records as being of palisades, but always as "de horconería." Manifestly there was a distinct difference between the construction of the church and that of the rest of the temporary buildings, and, since that difference did not lie in the use of forked poles, it must have existed in the construction of the walls.

In appearance this L-shaped structure would not have been unlike one of regular adobe construction with its mud-plastered palisades, and adobe walled church, the tiled roof extending along the entire length of the building.

In 1940, excavators working in the area now known as the "Forgotten Cemetery" at La Purísima, came upon the remains of other buildings of such primitive construction as those just described. Three rows of stone-lined post-holes identified these former structures as of the 1814 period. There was evidence, however, that told of the remodeling of two of the one-time buildings. These were identified as the infirmaries which the Padres reported as having been repaired in 1815 and rebuilt the following year—one for the men and the other for the women.[7] Adobes from the destroyed buildings of the first site (fábrica vieja) had been used in the reconstruction. Excavators uncovered foundations laid along the line of the outer posts which thereby had become a part of the foundation, side and end walls as the structures rose. The center posts, which undoubtedly were forked, had carried the ridgepoles. Roofs of tile were indicated by pieces of broken tile found in the debris.

These two buildings were in the process of being reconstructed when the

---

[7] "Se fabricaron 50 vª con los materiales ante dichos pª recoger los enfermos, y se compusieron otras tantas de fabrica vieja para enfermeria de Mugeres." *Informe* La Purísima, 1816. SBMA.

▲ Mission San José in 1853. *The frame building shown was built in after-mission days.*

▼ View of the inner court *at San Luis Rey, showing the old chimney and balustrade.*

▲ SAN JUAN BAUTISTA *in about 1865. Note the primitive bell-hanging.*

▼ THE SOUTHWEST CORNER *of San Gabriel's quadrangle, the quarters of the mission guard.*

Second World War set its seal on the project "for the duration." Their completion will be awaited with interest.[8]

Santa Bárbara is the only other mission at which the remains of the first temporary buildings have been uncovered. At that establishment, in the spring of 1901, Brother Bernard had filled in the pond that lay a little beyond the left wing of the quadrangle and toward its farther end. In leveling the ground that was to be used for a garden for the novitiate, he came upon some foundation stones of the "nigger-head" variety. No mortar had been used in these foundations except at the east end where a small portion appeared of an apparently later date. After making measurements of the foundations and consulting the mission records, Fr. Theodore Arentz, O.F.M.,[9] concluded that these were the remains of the "first and original buildings of the mission."

The first buildings, previously described, having been erected at the various missions and the cultivation of the fields begun; water having been led by open ditch to the mission establishments and their fields, the Padres now turned their attention to the building of permanent structures around a central patio, or court. This arrangement of buildings was known as the "quadrangle." The quadrangle is one of the oldest forms of communal building. Erected in ancient times with but one or no entrance from, or exit to, the outside, it formed a citadel of defense against attacking enemies. With the missions it provided not only protection from outside hostile forces, should any appear, but it enabled the Padres, by appointing a gate-keeper, to keep track at all times of the Indians working within the square. For, aside from the doors that opened into the rooms of the Fathers' dwelling, there were only one or two gates, or zaguáns, that gave access to, or egress from, the inner court. The doors of the various shops and other buildings opened upon the patio.

The quadrangle was planned with care. Throughout their experiences in the missions of the Sierra Gorda, Baja California, and elsewhere, the Franciscan friars had learned to place the various buildings in locations most advantageous to their intended use. There was no set rule for the arrangement of these structures, still, throughout it all there was a pattern from which, for some of the buildings, they deviated but slightly. Evidence of this plan is very plain. As Charles Howard Shinn wrote: "They built awhile, and then waited for another season and

[8] The buildings are finished. One has forked poles supporting its ridgepole. A sheathing of cane was laid on the cottonwood rafters and the tiles were laid directly on the cane, as they were in mission days. The floor of this building is of unfired adobe bricks. The second building, intended for use as a museum, was given a tighter roof and floored with adzed redwood planks.

[9] Guardian of Mission Santa Bárbara from January, 1908, to May, 1910; reappointed July, 1912, and served until December, 1916.

built again, yet with regard to the fitness of the plan."[10] The success of some enterprises and the unforeseen need for others naturally created changes in the building arrangements. In time some of the missions even found it necessary to add a second square at the side or in the rear of the first one. And, eventually, structures housing various industries were clustered around outside the quadrangle. But always the Fathers' dwelling occupied the front row of rooms and the monjerio found place in the least disturbed part of the square;[11] the boys' dormitory was sometimes within and sometimes without the main group of buildings; the married population occupied a village near at hand, and the houses of the guards were built with the neophyte Indian village, the church, and the Fathers' dwelling within sight. Where this arrangement did not obtain, it was because the building plan was as yet unfinished, as at La Purísima (second site), or where changes were being made, as at Mission San Fernando.

But, before permanent buildings could be begun, the Indian builders must needs be taught how to make and lay adobe bricks; how to fell trees, saw and hew them into shape for timbers and lumber; how to prepare lime and mix mortar for the foundations, and later how to make tejas (roof tiles) and ladrillos (floor tiles). All this took time and the building program advanced no more rapidly than did the Indian workmen in knowledge and ability. For theirs were the hands that carried out, under the direction of overseers, the projected plans of the Padres.

As most of the early Fathers had already gained some experience in building construction, they were soon able, with the help of trained Indians from Baja California and other experienced workers, to begin to instruct the neophytes in the making of adobes and in other basic arts of the building trade. As has been noted elsewhere, too, missions newly founded sometimes borrowed trained workers from others more firmly established. The lending of both workers and materials was by no means an unusual procedure. Many instances of this custom are found in the Padres' reports.

Fortunately, instruction in the handling of saws, axes, adzes, planes, and other tools used in the preparation of timbers, beams, and boards for use in the new buildings, was usually in the hands of carpenters brought up from México. At some of the missions today, where the original beams and boards have not been replaced with newer ones, marks of the adz wielded by Indian hands may still be seen. They are particularly noticeable on the ceiling beams of San Francisco's

[10] Shinn, C. H., "Mission Bells" in *Overland Monthly*, Jan., 1892.
[11] According to Fr. Lasuén's report of Nov. 12, 1800, the monjerio was moved many times, always seeking better accommodations until they were able to construct the form desired by the Fathers. Smith, F. R., *Mission San Carlos*, 28.

church, on floor boards laid down with wooden pegs at San José, and on attic floor boards at San Fernando.

During the reconstruction of Mission La Purísima, youths of today might have been seen using the adz, the two-handled rip-saw, and other tools as did the mission Indians of long ago. Those who failed to visit that mission while this work was going on missed an education in mission-day building practices, for in order to have the restored buildings as authentic as possible, old methods and tools were used. Moreover, the boys doing the work under the direction of experts were quite as inexperienced as the mission Indians had been. Consequently, an almost exact duplication of effects and finish that mark the handiwork of the Indians was achieved. This was particularly true in the work of smoothing out the plaster on the walls of the adobe buildings. For this operation the neophytes had used round, flat stones that fitted into the palms of their hands. This tool left neither sharp edges nor square corners. Specially made, rounded trowels in the hands of the boys of 1937 produced the same results.

The making of adobes was probably the first step toward permanent building to which the Padres gave their attention. There was plenty of adobe soil to be had for the digging. That at La Purísima had been taken from subsurface material below top soil level. At many places it was not even necessary to go below top soil level. Straw or grass broken into bits, or in later days, taken from the threshing floors, was used for binding material. A trough of suitable proportions was dug in the ground, or one was built of boards, and broken-up adobe soil and straw thrown in. Sufficient water was added to bring the mass to the consistency of a stiff mud. Then Indians, stripped of all clothing save the taparrabo, waded in and trod the mud and straw until the whole was thoroughly mixed.

In the meantime, molds were fashioned usually with a center partition for making two adobes at a time. These molds were mere frames without tops or bottoms. An average size was 11″ x 23″ x 4″ for one adobe and twice that length plus the width of the partition for two. Cleats nailed to the end pieces served for handles.

The molds were wet thoroughly and set on a stretch of dry, level, and well-cleared ground. The prepared mixture was carried to the molds in leathern buckets, poured or shoveled in, tamped down and levelled off. The frame was then lifted and the adobes left to dry, guarded by an Indian boy whose duty it was to see that no roving animals walked on and demolished them. After a number of days in the sun and having been frequently turned, the adobes were "cured" and ready for use. When dry an average adobe brick weighs about sixty pounds.

Early in 1800, Fr. Miguel Lull, Guardian of San Fernando College, sent a series of questions to Fr. Presidente Lasuén regarding the treatment given the Indians, their food, clothing, and other matters relating to their welfare, as has already been noted in another chapter. In reply to the question about the number of hours they were required to work, Fr. Estevan Tapis of Mission Santa Bárbara replied in regard to the making of adobes, that: "Men make the adobes. Nine men will make three hundred and sixty adobes a day, which is forty for each one. The soil is soft and the water is near by. Those who work at this task never labor after eleven o'clock in the morning, and never on Saturdays, nor many times on Fridays, because during the first days of the week they have accomplished the task for the last days, and are then free."[12]

This reply was penned fourteen years after the mission was founded when everything was running smoothly. Without doubt, in the earlier days, when the need for speedy erection of permanent buildings was imperative and before the Indians had become expert at adobe making, the hours were longer and the work more strenuous.

With the stones collected for the foundations, the adobes made, and timbers brought from the mountains or the nearby countryside and prepared for use, it remained to secure lime for mortar for the foundations and for plastering and whitewashing the buildings. Lime kilns were constructed of adobe bricks and, wherever possible, were built against a hillside to permit of easy dumping of limestone, raw lime, or seashells into the kiln from above. Mr. F. E. Green says: "In size and shape these kilns at San Diego Mission are all quite similar, and like the early kilns at other places up and down the coast. A bottle shaped opening was dug in the hillside from seven to fifteen feet in depth and five to eight feet in diameter, with the top and bottom slightly contracted, and sometimes curbed with brick or stones around the top, and rarely all the way to the bottom. . . . The preparation of a kiln for a run required that a full supply of the necessary fuel should be gathered, and also the necessary amount of raw lime material for one firing should be gathered and sorted for culls, and all of this material be brought to the top of the kiln. Then the kiln was filled with alternate layers of fuel and limerock and fired, adding more fuel if necessary to obtain the desired temperature. From two to five days would be required in the burning and cooling process."[13]

In his study of the San Diego dam and water system, Mr. Green located the ruins of eight kilns along the aqueduct line. There are the remains of a kiln in the

[12] Engelhardt, *Miss. & Miss.*, 2. 560.
[13] Green, F. E., "The San Diego Old Mission Dam."

hillside of the garden, made famous by Duhaut-Cilly's description, at San Luis Rey Mission. Ruins of several are to be seen at Rancho del Escorpión, estancia of Mission San Fernando. At the latter place the adobes lining the kilns have become vitreous through the great heat generated in the burning of the lime. Without doubt similar kilns were operated at all the missions for lime was a prerequisite for building. And there were numerous deposits of lime, limestone, or sea-shells within reach of all.

According to the reports of experts who made analyses for Mrs. Frances Rand's use in her book, *The Mission of San Antonio de Padua*, the mortar used in the construction of the diversion dam on Mission Creek was made by burning limestone from deposits in Roblar Valley and then mixing it with clay and river sand. The mortar used for building the intake on the San Antonio River was made by mixing ordinary burnt lime with river sand without the addition of clay. The use of clay, it seems, depended upon either the purity of the lime or the composition of the sand. The Roblar Valley limestone was said to be very pure. This same mixture was, in all probability, used at other missions.

After all the necessary building materials had been procured the neophytes were taught to lay foundations of stone and lime mortar and walls of adobe bricks set in mud mortar (a thin adobe mixture); to install doors, windows, and ceiling beams; to plaster the walls, and finally, to complete the structure with a protecting roof of thatch or earth. The floors in the early buildings were, almost without exception, earthen.

Regarding the process of plastering, it appears that walls exposed to winter's rains and winds were usually protected with a coat of lime plaster, which old Mexican workers say was prepared by mixing three or four parts of lime to one of sand with water. Later, when the mission cactus hedges were thriving, the huge leaf-slabs were cut off, placed in a barrel, chopped up, and, with water added, left to soak for several days. Then the liquid was poured off and used to mix both plaster and whitewash, adding, it is claimed, to the adhesive and water repellent qualities of both.

Two other practices were followed to insure the plaster's adherence to the adobe walls. One was that of pressing pebbles or bits of broken tile into the exposed layers of mud mortar in which the adobe bricks had been laid. This was, of course, done while the mortar was still fresh and soft. The other method employed was that of scoring, or cutting furrows in, the walls. Evidence of this latter practice may be seen in many old mission photographs, particularly those of San Luis Rey and La Purísima.

Interior walls and others not exposed to the ravages of storms were often fin-ished with a mud plaster and then whitewashed. One Mexican worker, versed in the old ways, said that whitewash was sometimes prepared by mixing lime with goat's milk and adding a little salt. Experiments made by the writer proved that the use of milk and salt did indeed produce a soft, smooth whitewash that did not easily rub off. Moreover, it provided an excellent surface for mural decoration.

Tiles were not made until about ten years after the first mission was founded and, contrary to Fr. Palóu, our first historian, the first tiles made in California were not manufactured at Mission San Luis Obispo but at San Antonio. One of the many treasures stored away in the Santa Bárbara Mission Archives is a letter dated at San Carlos, December 8, 1781, and written by Padre Presidente Serra to Fr. Lasuén at San Diego. After congratulating Fr. Lasuén on the dedication of his new church, Fr. Serra remarked: "Hasta aquí vince San Antonio, ymas con su techo de texas [tejas]. Es â todas luces bella Iglesia"[14] (So far San Antonio excels, especially with its roof of tiles. It is in every way a beautiful church.) San Antonio's church had been built in 1779 and, in 1780,[15] was roofed with tiles. Our first tiles, then, were made not later than 1780.

Referring again to Fr. Tapis's report on the amount of labor done by the Indians, we read, in regard to tile making: "Those who make tiles have a certain number to make. Sixteen young men, and at times as many more middle-aged men, with two women who bring the sand and straw, make 500 tiles a day. The troughs with the clay are close by and are always filled. These neophytes accom-plish the task before eleven o'clock in the morning, and always include the task for Saturdays likewise, on which they are then free to make excursions or to rest."[16]

In the making of tiles, as in the making of adobes, wooden molds were used. There is absolutely no truth in the story, often told and written, of the mission tiles having been molded on the Indians' thighs. There were two molds for the tiles, one being a shallow frame without top or bottom and wider at one end than at the other. The other was a rounded mold like a half-piece of log, or tree trunk, giving the tile the desired curve. One end of the mold was shaped smaller than the other, because, when laid on the roof, the larger end of one tile fitted over the smaller end of the other previously laid. In an undated inventory taken

---

[14] Through the courtesy of the Franciscan Fathers at Santa Bárbara, the writer has a photostat copy of this letter in her possession.

[15] San Luis Obispo's third and last fire occurred Nov., 1782, after which, according to Fr. Palóu, the Fathers at that mission began making tiles. For record, with authorities, see Banc., *Hist. of Cal.*, 1. 385, note 26.

[16] Engelhardt, *Miss. & Miss.*, 2. 560-561.

at Mission San Francisco Solano, there are listed two wooden ladrillo molds (2 ladrilleras de madera) and eight tile molds (8 moldes de teja).[17]

The writer witnessed the entire process of tile making, except the firing, at La Purísima, in 1937, when tiles were being made for the restored buildings. Mission-day methods were employed throughout the entire process, except with the mixing of the clay and other ingredients. For that operation, "Yankee ingenuity," it would have been called in bygone days, devised a more speedy and less strenuous method *a la máquina.*

Preparatory to the molding of the tiles, a long bench, or table, had been arranged; the molds, or forms, were wet and a bucket of water set close by for use of the worker, who repeatedly dipped his hands into the water to keep them sufficiently wet for the proper handling and smoothing of the clay. When the clay was of the desired consistency, portions of it were thrown into the flat mold, firmly pressed down and into the corners by hand until the mold was completely filled. Any excess material was scraped off with a piece of board. The mold was then pulled to one end of the table, the form lifted by means of cleats nailed to the end pieces and the unfinished tile urged over the edge of the table onto the semi-cylindrical mold. This was a critical moment for it took some considerable skill to get the clay from the table to the mold without mishap. This feat was accomplished by holding the curved mold just below the edge of the table and turning it slowly as the clay was pushed over and onto it from above. The performance was perfect and the eyes of the youthful worker gleamed with satisfaction.

The mold with the clay on it was next placed back on the table and the tile maker, after once more wetting his hands, pressed the clay upon the mold, smoothed it, and then carefully trimmed its edges. It was now ready for the drying rack. There mold and clay were set—small end first—on a shelf of slats and the wooden form quickly jerked out by means of the handle attached to its larger end. If the clay mixture is of the proper consistency it will retain its curved shape without the form under it. It took many days for these tiles to dry, sometimes as long as a month, depending on the weather, of course. When thoroughly dry they were fired, or burned, in the tile kiln and were then ready for use. None of the mission tile or lime kilns survive intact today, though the ruins of an almost complete one have recently been excavated at Mission San Luis Rey.

Ladrillos are made with a little stiffer, or heavier, mixture of clay than that required for the roof tiles. The mixture for the latter must be pliable for molding

[17] SBMA.

over the curved form, but that for the ladrillos is thrown into a flat mold, tamped in, the frame lifted and the molded clay left to set before it is taken into the drying shed. Most clays need an admixture of sand to prevent cracking or excessive shrinking. Both roof and floor tiles shrink slightly in drying and firing.

Speaking of the tile work at San Juan Capistrano, Rev. St. John O'Sullivan,[18] pastor of that mission from 1910 to 1933, told the writer that all the tiles—the ladrillos used in flooring the corridors and the buildings of the quadrangle, and the tejas which covered all the structures save the stone church—were made and fired on the hillside just north of the mission. The remains of one of the kilns stood there until about 1945. The little valley between the hills derived its name, La Cañada del Orno (the canyon of the oven), from the mission tile kilns.[19]

Those vari-shaded, red roof tiles, handiwork of the neophyte Indians, are one of the most distinctive features of our mission architecture. It is a great pity that more of the original ones are not still in existence, but with the break-up of the mission establishments, buildings quickly fell into disrepair, roofs gave way and many tiles were broken. Many others were appropriated to cover roofs of private and other buildings. Some were shipped to Hawaii. The story is one that does not bring pleasure to those who love the old missions.

Being handmade and imperfectly burned, the old tiles were more or less porous and in time lichens found lodging in their surfaces, giving to the roofs an even greater variation of color. Also, not being machine made, they varied in shape and size, a circumstance that gave to the roofs that uneven look that so delightfully suits the thick adobe walls beneath them.

Another factor that added to the artistic make-up of the roofs of earlier days was the ridgepole. Composed of poles of uneven thickness and overlapping at the joints, it gave to the roof a pleasing, slightly uneven sky line. Then, too, the rafters were often unequal in size, having variously cut, uncut, or crooked ends, and looking as if the length of the pole had been the only consideration. And, moreover, the sheathing of saplings, willows, or long limbs of trees laid crosswise upon and fastened to the rafters with rawhide thongs, further accentuated the unevenness of the tiles when laid upon it. Photographs of the "Serra Church" at San Juan Capistrano taken before the end of 1896, when the Landmarks Club began the work of re-roofing the ancient adobe building, show its uneven ridgepole with a corresponding irregular laying of tiles, and an extraordinary variety of rafter ends and willows of the sheathing that extended beyond the side walls

[18] Shortly before his death the title of Monsignor was bestowed upon him.
[19] See O'Sullivan (Rev. St. John), *Little Chapters About San Juan Capistrano* (1912 booklet).

Top: SIDE DOOR of San Buenaventura's church; door with cat-hole at San Gabriel. Bottom: The sacristy door at San Miguel and the great front door of the church.

HANDIWORK OF THE INDIANS: *Cupboard at San Juan Bautista; bench made at Santa Bárbara; chairs made by the Indians of San Carlos; chairs and lectern fashioned by those of San Juan Bautista.*

of the church. Some time previous to 1896, probably during Fr. Mut's pastorate, a portion of the roof had been repaired, but, fortunately for the study of early mission construction, the major part was left untouched.

When the church was finally restored in 1922-25, Fr. O'Sullivan pleaded unavailingly with the architects to reproduce the original primitive ridgepole and rafter construction. He did insist on having the tiles laid unevenly, going up onto the roof himself to show the workmen how it should be done. There is an inexplicable strangeness in the modern architect's failure at times to see that a restoration should follow as closely as possible the lines and peculiar details of the original building.

In restoring the "Serra Church" the walls of the sanctuary zone were heightened to admit of the installation of a beautiful retable sent from Barcelona, Spain, in 1906, and assigned by the Rt. Rev. John J. Cantwell, Bishop of the diocese,[20] to the San Juan Capistrano Mission, "judging that the restored church would be the most fitting place in the diocese for it." This church is the only one standing in our California in which Fr. Serra officiated. According to Fr. Mugártegui's letter of April 18, 1779, quoted in the preceding chapter, it was begun in the summer of 1778 and before the mission community was moved from the first to the second site. That it underwent changes and enlargement in its early days was evident to anyone who closely examined its walls. And again this was true of most of the early churches. As the mission family increased the first church became too small and was enlarged by adding to its length, unless the Padres were prepared to build a new and larger edifice.

Evidence of early building techniques may be seen in photographs of the missions taken during the period 1850-1880. Little had been done in the way of misguided so-called restoration up to that time and the remaining buildings, though much in need of attention, still bore witness of a charming disregard for sharp edges, square corners, straight lines and other such fetishes of the modern builder. Indeed, it is those very irregularities, the hall-mark of Indian handiwork, together with the lovely vari-colored tiles, that set our old mission buildings apart from all others in California.

One of those early photographs is of that portion of the left wing of Santa Bárbara's quadrangle that joins the front wing, or Fathers' dwelling.[21] The buildings shown are, according to Fr. Theodore's measurements and conclusions, those built in 1787 and roofed with tiles in 1788. They were the first permanent

[20] On Dec. 6, 1936, Bishop John J. Cantwell became the first archbishop of the recently created Archbishopric of Los Angeles.
[21] Photograph probably by Watkins, reproduced in Engelhardt, *Misson Santa Barbara*, 329.

buildings and marked the beginning of the quadrangle. Built for the mission soldiers of the guard, available building records place them next to the "Serra
Church" of Capistrano in point of age.

Writing about them in 1905, Fr. Theodore says: "The outside walls and some
of the partition walls are still extant and the rooms are being used as class rooms.
One being used as a laundry. In the year 1896 a second story of frame was built
over them which until 1901 was used as College, from 1901-1905 as novitiate—
and since as clericat."[22]

Spurred on by Brother Bernard's finding, in 1901, of the remains of the temporary buildings erected at this mission, Fr. Theodore began a serious study of
the old mission buildings. He took measurements of all those still in existence
and of the ruins of others of which any trace could be found. He prepared a Map
and on it made note of their location "with great care and exactitude." What
became of the Father's finished map, if indeed it ever were finished, is not known.
A rough preliminary sketch alone remains. However, Fr. Theodore's measurements of the old buildings and the ruins of others, together with his sketch and
other available historical data[23] provide the most complete picture to be had of
any of the mission establishments. It will, therefore, best serve the purpose of
this chapter to follow the story of the building of the Santa Bárbara establishment.

Because this mission faces southeast there have always been conflicting desig-
nations of the various wings of the quadrangle with regard to their relation to
the points of the compass. To avoid confusion it seems best to speak of the front
row of buildings as the Fathers' dwelling; the row adjoining it on the right, as
the church wing; the one on the left, as the left wing; and the one in the rear,
as the rear wing.

The year that saw the houses of the mission guard finished (1788) witnessed
also the enlargement of the temporary chapel. In 1789, a church, a granary, and
an apartment for the young Indian women and girls over nine years of age were
built. Two other quarters were also erected, one for the chickens and one for a
jail. All were built of adobe. The jail and chicken house were built outside the
quadrangle.

The church of 1789 was 30 varas long and 6 varas wide, or 83' x 17'. The
granary was 31 varas long and 7 varas wide, or 85' x 19', while the young women's

[22] Arentz, Fr. Theodore, *Chronicle of the Franciscans or Friars Minor at Santa Barbara, California*. MS. unfinished.
In SBMA.

[23] *Informes* Santa Bárbara, 1787-1832; *Inventario* 1834; sketches by Robinson, H.M.T. Powell, Wm. Rich Hutton,
Vischer; photos by Watkins, Houseworth, et al; Survey of 1854 ("Alemany Plat"), Survey of 1862 (U. S. Govt.)
W. A. Hawley's survey of about 1895; personal investigations of the writer.

apartment was 12 varas long and 7 varas wide, or 33′ x 19′. From evidence which appears in later building reports the monjerio was built in the church wing at the end adjoining the rear wing of the quadrangle. The granary was built adjoining the monjerio in the church wing. These two buildings were of the same width.[24] It does not appear that the church constructed this year was more than a temporary one. It was built too hastily, and the Indian workers were not yet sufficiently skilled to erect an edifice that would satisfy the Padres as a permanent church. It was, it seems certain, built outside the square. Indeed, one writer[25] who, in 1894, with the assistance of an engineer, made surveys of all the buildings and ruins of the old mission, declares that the church of 1789 stood a short distance from the south corner of the quadrangle, a part of its foundation showing near the fountain.[26]

In 1790, the rear row of rooms of the Fathers' dwelling, now standing, was built. This row included, besides two rooms each for the two Padres, a refectory, kitchen, toilet, harness room, passage-way, a room for firewood, jail, molendería (room in which grain was ground), and a room for the women. The latter was, perhaps, a room where the young women and girls worked at tasks assigned them until their own quarters were more complete. Or it may be that women from the village were assembled there and instructed in various useful duties. It is referred to in the records merely as "casa para Mugeres" (house for women). The entire row was built of adobes, plastered with mortar and roofed with tiles. Besides these buildings, a granary 12 varas long and 7 varas wide, or 33′ x 19′, was constructed. A pozolera, or kitchen where the pozole was cooked, was also built. Both were of adobe, plastered with mortar, and roofed with tiles.

In 1791, a guardhouse and three rooms for keeping the tools and implements of the carpenter shop and field were built adjoining those previously erected for the soldiers in the left wing of the quadrangle. These buildings were all 6 varas, or 17′ wide.

During the next year two corrals were built, one for the large live stock and one for the small. Evidently, as at the other missions, the Padres found that live stock running loose were a menace to both gardens and buildings. The animals were, of course, corralled at night only. By day they were herded by vaqueros and pastores (shepherds).

In February, 1793, Fr. Antonio Paterna died. Co-founder of the mission and its senior missionary until his death, he had, as Fr. Presidente Lasuén wrote to

[24] An important factor in determining the former location of buildings.
[25] Hawley, W. A., *The Early Days*, 51.
[26] As late as 1915 the writer saw such evidence of former building at that spot.

the Fr. Guardian of the San Fernando College: " . . conducted himself like a good old man and always labored like a robust young man until his death, distinguishing himself in the estimation and sight of all by a zealous discharge of his ministry."[27] His was the hand that had guided the affairs of Mission Santa Bárbara throughout its first difficult years. He was, apparently, laid to rest in the new church reported built this year, though at the time of his death it was far from being completed, since it was not dedicated until March 19, 1794.

This was the church that was destined to stand in the quadrangle. That it had been planned by Fr. Paterna is obvious. It was a building 45 varas long and 9¼ varas wide, or 124' x 25'. The adjoining sacristy was 9¼ varas long and 5 varas wide, or 25' x 14'. Both church and sacristy were roofed with tiles and plastered with mortar inside and outside. It had six side altars. The portico in front of the church was of ladrillos and was roofed with tiles.[28] As the Padres of 1796 remarked in a special *Nota*: "Though the church of this mission is of adobe it is very becoming. It was completed in the year 1794."[29]

Fr. Estevan Tapis, one of the Padre musicians of the missions, assumed Fr. Paterna's task and the building of the quadrangle continued.

In 1794, another adobe granary was built. It was 26 varas long and 7 varas wide, or 72' x 19', and was, it seems, erected in the front row of the rear wing adjoining the carreta entrance. A weavery, or building for the looms, 18 varas long and 7 varas wide, or 50' x 19', was constructed. It had its own patio which was 10 varas wide and 18 varas long, or 28' x 50'. Here was the perfect set-up for the monjerio. Nowhere else at Santa Bárbara could it have been located except at the junction of the church and rear wings. With the monjerio at the end of the church wing, adjoining the weavery built in the rear wing of the quadrangle, and having a walled-in patio for their own private use, the quarters for the young unmarried women and girls were almost complete. One indisputable proof of the location of the monjerio in that spot is the drain which was traced from that corner diagonally across the main patio to the opposite corner and on to the orchard in front and to the left of the mission buildings. Such were the sanitary facilities afforded places of confinement at that time. And these drains are undeniable evidence of the former existence of women's work rooms, monjerios, and sometimes of jails. They have been found at San Juan Capistrano, San Gabriel, Santa Bárbara, San Antonio and La Purísima, though at the latter

[27] Engelhardt, *Mission Santa Barbara*, 68, 359-363.
[28] *Informe*, 1793, under Fábricas: "Se ha fabricado una Iglesia de adove de 45 vˢ de largo, y 9 y quarta de ancho. Una sacristia de adoves de 9 vˢ y quarta de largo, y 5 de ancho: ambas piezas estan techadas de teja, y embarradas de mescla por dentro y fuera. Un portico al frontis de la Iglesia de ladrillo, y techado de lo mismo, y de teja." SBMA.
[29] Engelhardt, *Mission Santa Barbara*, 64.

mission proper identification of this detail was not made during the recent reconstruction.

Concerning the monjerio Fr. Tapis reported in 1800: "At Santa Bárbara it is floored with brick, at Purísima [first site] with boards. It has a large window high up for light and ventilation. They have all the conveniences for the night. There is a fire kept there at night and a candle is always burning."[30]

In 1794, a wall was built around the cemetery, or campo santo, which was 45 varas long and 16 varas wide, or 124′ x 44′. The wall was capped with tiles. It will be observed that the cemetery was exactly the same length as the church of 1793, and less than twice as wide. The mission cemeteries were always incomprehensibly small. As a consequence, in time they all became very much overcrowded.

In this same year a corral was built for the lambs. It was 62 varas square and 3 varas high, or 171′ x 171′ x 8′, built of adobes and topped with tiles. Adobe walls were always so protected, otherwise they soon disintegrated.

In 1795, the roofs of most of the buildings of the mission square were renovated. The rafters and beams of cottonwood and sycamore, having nearly all rotted, were replaced with new ones of pine. Moreover, four small rooms (quartitos) were added to the Fathers' dwelling. Their combined length was 25 varas, or 69′. Each was 3 varas, or 8′ wide. Two of these rooms served as bedrooms and two as studies. For the most part, the record says, they were of mortar, stone and ladrillo. The partition walls were probably of adobe. Fr. Theodore believed that these four rooms were added to the row previously built for the Fathers, and that they began the second, or front, row of rooms at the end nearest the church, "as only the front walls are of stone and mortar."

In 1796, the roofs of six more buildings were renewed, new beams and rafters replacing the old that "through shaking" were threatening ruin (que por concomidos amenazaban ruina"). A corridor 3 varas wide and 45 varas long was erected to protect the wall (of the Fathers' dwelling) facing the presidio. Its pillars were of ladrillo and mortar and it was roofed with tiles. Another corridor was built in the patio of the weavery.[31] It was 3 varas (8′) wide and 18 varas (50′) long. Its pillars were of adobe and its roof was tiled. And moreover, at the two extreme ends of the corridor were built two adobe rooms 3 varas wide and 6 varas long. According to the inventory taken in 1834, these two rooms served

---

[30] Engelhardt, *Miss. & Miss.*, 2. 558.

[31] "Se hizo otro corredor de 3 varas de ancho, y 18 de largo con pilares de adoves, y techado de teja, en el patio del telar: y tambien se hacieron en los dos extremos del corredor dos quartitos de adoves de 3 varas de ancho, y 6 de largo." SBMA.

as dispensa (pantry) and cocina (kitchen). And now the quarters for the Indian girls and young women were really complete. Built adjoining the weavery where many of them worked at weaving and spinning wool, with patio and corridor for outdoor workrooms, comfort, and enjoyment, this monjerio was similar to many built at other missions. An oven and cooking places were constructed in the cocina or out in the patio, for cooking was one of the arts taught the young Indian girls. At Missions San José and San Gabriel the monjerio patio contained a pool for bathing. Trees were sometimes planted within their walls. The monjerios were indeed something more than mere sleeping apartments.

In 1797, there were built at Santa Bárbara three granaries each 25 varas, or 69′, long; one building 6 varas long which served as an entrance to two of the granaries; one 10 varas long for a leather workers' shop and another of the same dimensions for a chicken-house. All were 6 varas wide, constructed of adobes, plastered on the outside with mortar and roofed with tiles. And, moreover, they were built to form a distinct square to which entrance was had through the old one of the missions ("y aunqᵉ forman un quadro distinto, se entra a el por el antiguo de la Misión"). These buildings were added to those already standing in the left wing, and, extending beyond the rear wing of the quadrangle, formed the left wing of the second square.

Nineteen adobe houses were built during the next year for that number of neophyte families. Each house was 4 varas (11′) wide and 6½ varas (18′) long. Each had a door and window which closed, was plastered on the outside with mortar, whitewashed on the inside and roofed with tiles. There was also erected a wall 3 varas (8′) high and 1200 varas (3,300′) in circumference. It was capped with tiles and surrounded the garden, orchard, and vineyard. Accordingly, up to this time it had been the duty of Indian boys to keep chance roving live stock away from the fruit and vegetables.

In 1799, a large granary 45 varas (124′) long and 6½ varas wide was erected. It was built of adobes, plastered inside and out with mortar, and was roofed with tiles. This storeroom apparently occupied the entire length of the rear wing of the second square.

Next year the neophyte village was enlarged by the addition of thirty-one little houses, in all respects the same as the ones previously built. Besides these, three rows of corridors were constructed along the buildings of the main inner square of the mission. Pillars of ladrillo laid in mortar supported the tiled roofs. The floors were to be paved with ladrillos.

In 1801, thirty-one more houses were erected in the neophyte village for as many Indian families—that is, husband and wife and the smaller children. These houses were laid out in rows with little streets or alleys between them. And then another house was built, presumably for the gardener. It was 21 varas (58') long and 6 varas (17') wide, and contained a bedroom, parlor, kitchen, and chicken-house. It was plastered with mortar, a corridor was added and the roof tiled. This building stood just inside the garden wall, in that corner nearest the main buildings.

Another row of thirty-one adobe houses was erected for the married neo-phytes, in 1802, and the village was enclosed on three sides with an adobe wall eight feet high. A house for the mayordomo was also built. It was 18 varas (50') long and 6 varas wide and was divided into kitchen, parlor, and bedroom. Adjoining the house of the mayordomo, who was probably one of the soldier guards,[32] there was constructed a building 20 varas (55') long and 6 varas wide, with five troughs, or vats, of ladrillo, for tanning hides. Both the mayordomo's casa and the tannery were provided with corridors. And lastly, there were con-structed five buildings for various purposes necessary to the mission. The total length of these five structures was 40 varas (100'). All were 6 varas wide. They were erected within the second square, probably forming its right wing. The mayordomo's house, with the adjoining tannery, was built outside the quad-rangle, slightly in front and a little to the right of the church building. Early photographs show both.

During the year 1803 forty-eight adobe houses were added to those of the Indian village. This year, too, a church was built in the ranchería called San Miguel, which was two leagues distant from the mission. The church was 22 varas long and 9 varas wide, including walls, or 61' x 25'.

In the next year thirty-seven additional houses were added to the habitations erected for the neophyte families. Moreover, a large patio was constructed for the Indians' various needs.

In 1805, two large buildings were erected for granaries, and another of the same dimensions for lumber. The dimensions, however, were not given. With the construction of these three buildings the second square was complete. Clus-tered around this second patio were the mission's workshops. Here, according to the inventory, were the soap and tallow works, the house of the mill for grinding grain or corn,[33] the olive mill, blacksmith shop, leather and carpenter shops, as well as a building for housing carretas, of which this mission then had six.

---

[32] In 1800, two soldiers constituted the mission guard. One was employed by the Fathers as mayordomo. Engelhardt *Mission Santa Barbara*, 72.

[33] A tahona, or mill that was turned by a mule or burro, usually the latter.

In 1806, the reservoir described in Chapter VIII was constructed, and, during the following year, four houses were built for the soldiers of the guard, while eighteen houses were added to those of the Indian village. A corridor was erected along one side of the soldiers' houses, and, while the records do not so state, a patio, or enclosed yard was probably added, as was customary, for the convenience of the soldiers' wives. Ovens built of adobe and cooking places of ladrillos, similar to those uncovered at San Juan Capistrano and San Gabriel, were set up in the patio. Such was the ultimate arrangement in the construction of the quarters for the guards. These buildings were located in front of the church but at a distance of 150 varas. There they stood with the Indian village, the Fathers' dwelling, the church, and the jail in full view. This jail was also erected in 1807,[34] the one built in 1789 having, in all probability, been taken over for some other purpose.

The new jail was constructed of stone and mortar and stands today bereft of its roof of tiles and heavy oaken door, by the side of the "Alameda Padre Serra," the first road that leads past the mission church to the right and on up the hill. It is 14' 6" wide and 15' long. Its side walls are 5' 7" high, while from the floor to the ridge the height is 8' 6". Its one window is 10" x 21" in size and its doorway 3' x 6'. The window had no lintel, the opening extending to the top of the side wall. The lintel and sill of the door are both stone slabs. These, however, may not be original as the jail was once repaired. The floor was apparently paved with ladrillos, one discovered near the doorway measuring 9" x 16". Flume openings in the end walls are about 7" x 12". This flume provided the sanitary facilities for the building. Comparatively speaking, this was a small and low structure but jails were not built for comfort and it is very doubtful if any more commodious could have been found anywhere along the mission trail.

In 1808, besides the fountain and lavatory previously described, a pottery shop (alfarería) was constructed. According to the inventory of 1834, this building was 20 varas (55') long, 6 varas (17') wide, and contained three rooms having two (outside?) doors and three windows. Tiles, clay pipes for water conductors, pottery jars, and other utensils were made here. Near by stood two kilns, one for firing tiles and one for pottery. One of these kilns, existed until the road that passes the jail was built. It may be seen in an early photograph said to have been taken by Houseworth. Remnants of the walls of the pottery factory still stand near the lower reservoir, and in the mission museum is a tall jar that may have been manufactured in the old alfarería.

[34] Banc., *Hist. of Cal.*, 2. 120.

During 1809, additions were made to that part of the Fathers' house that faces the ocean. The walls were of masonry and the roof was flat.[35] The roof of the Fathers' dwelling at Santa Bárbara underwent as many changes as did that of San Gabriel's church. At this time (1809) the back row of rooms, built in 1790, was covered with a gabled roof of tiles.

In 1810, work on the Fathers' house and guest rooms was continued. During the following year it was finished with a corridor of stone arches along its entire length. Work was also commenced on the fachada of the church, a description of which was to be given when the work was finished.[36]

But the earth tremors of December, 1812, badly damaged this church and other buildings of the establishment. After a thorough examination the church was declared unsafe and the Padres decided to build another as soon as permission was obtained from the government. In the meantime, some other building must, of necessity, have been used as a house of worship. If the church was deemed unsafe the Padres certainly did not continue to use it. It is this writer's opinion that the church of 1789 was still standing, in use perhaps as a granary, and that it was put in order and used until the new edifice was finished in 1820. Permission to build a new church was received in 1815 and work on it was commenced immediately. Meanwhile, the old building had been taken down. A similar procedure was followed at the other missions visited by the earthquake of 1812. At San Gabriel a granary was built adjoining another one to serve until their church was repaired. At San Juan Capistrano the Padres reopened the "Serra Church," and at Santa Inés a temporary church, which afterwards served as a commissariat, was used until the new and present church was finished in 1817. At San Buenaventura a temporary church was used until the repairs on theirs were completed in 1814. The earth tremors of 1812 destroyed or damaged mission buildings from San Juan Capistrano in the south to La Purísima in the Santa Bárbara presidial district. They did not damage missions all along the line.

The church begun at Santa Bárbara in 1815 and finished in 1820 was apparently built on the site of the one erected in 1793. It was a larger and finer building than the preceding one and stands today, faithfully restored after the earthquake of 1925, the most beautiful of all our mission churches. But the story of its construction belongs to another chapter.

In 1816, a row of buildings was erected to provide a granary, a harness, or leather shop, and rooms to house the implements and tools used in the fields.

---

[35] "Se ha aumentado pr la parte qe mira a la mar la habitn [habitación] los pe Minitros [Ministeros] con pared de cal, y canto, y techo de azotea." SBMA.

[36] ". . ; y se ha comenzado el frontispicio de la Sta Yglesia, . . " SBMA.

Evidently the structures built, in 1791, for such purposes had become inservice-able through the earthquakes of 1812, or, for some other reason a new arrange-ment seemed advisable. In this same year considerable repairing of old buildings was done and a gabled roof constructed to cover both rows of the Fathers' dwell-ing. It must have been at this time and before the buildings were roofed that the attic with its ventilation system of ladrillo lattice work was built over the front row of buildings, or rooms. Now at last the Padres' dwelling was complete. Begun in 1790, it was finished in 1816. Many of the partition walls appear to have been removed before the inventory was taken in 1834.

No other building construction is reported at this mission until 1827, when Duhaut-Cilly, visiting Santa Bárbara, describes the erection of a water-power gristmill at the foot of the hill to the right of the mission.

Besides most of the above mentioned buildings, the inventory lists a wine cel-lar (bodega),[37] a shoe shop, and six hornos, which name was applied to both ovens and kilns alike. Two ovens were for the bakery, two kilns for lime, one for the alfarería and the other for the tejería (tile factory). Then, too, there was the threshing floor, which was paved with ladrillos and enclosed by an adobe wall with gate.

The lime kilns were set up southwest of the mission buildings just beyond the site of the temporary structures of 1787. The threshing floor was a little farther to the west and near the extreme end of the long left wing.

During the years of the mission period some of the buildings erected were either remodeled, enlarged, or taken down as necessity demanded. The granary constructed in 1789, for instance, must have been removed when the church of 1815-1820 was built, if indeed it had not been taken down in part at least when the church of 1793 was erected. When Fr. Tapis made his report in 1800, the monjerio had been enlarged by five varas, or fourteen feet in length. It is almost certain too that the first temporary buildings were repaired or rebuilt and later used as a weavery, just as those at La Purísima were remodeled to serve as infirm-aries for the invalid Indian men and women.

The story of the buildings existing at Santa Bárbara in 1834, however, is told in the inventory taken that year and the structures described formed two squares with an extending left wing. Grouped around these main buildings were the neophyte village of one hundred eighty-three (cienta ochenta y tres)[38] little red-tiled, whitewashed adobe houses; the dwellings for the gardener, the soldiers of

---

[37] The wine press was not mentioned, but according to Hawley (*opus cit.*, 60), at Viña Arroyo, located one mile north of the mission there was "an adobe building where the tools were kept and the vintage taken."
[38] Some of the dwellings had been destroyed during the insurrection of 1824.

the guard, and the mayordomo. There were the tannery, the jail, the pottery, the mill with the two reservoirs, the filter, aqueducts carried atop stone walls, and the fountain with its adjoining lavatory.

It is a story of great accomplishment on the part of the Padres and artisan instructors, but most of all on the part of the neophyte Indians who, through the work carried on year after year, became each after his trade, skilled adobe, tile, and pottery makers; carpenters and blacksmiths; plasterers and stone masons; wall decorators, etc. But it is not a story of buildings that sprang up like mushrooms in the night. Santa Bárbara's establishment was forty years in the building. Forty years of making adobes and tiles; of felling trees and hauling logs, or dragging them by ox-team from the canyons; of sawing and hewing them into shape for use. Forty years of gathering limestone and sea-shells and preparing lime; of gathering and carrying stones for foundations and later for walls, for reservoirs, for the mill, the jail, and the church. Year after year adding a few buildings here and a few there until an almost complete community was established. That is the way most of our missions were built.[39]

And in the meantime work was going on in all the other branches of mission industry. Other Indians not engaged in the building activities guarded the horses, cattle, and sheep; tended the fields, orchards, and vineyards, or performed the hundred and one other tasks involved in the running of the establishment. None but the sick and the infirm were excepted.

[39] At its third site, Santa Clara's entire quadrangle (church included) together with the adjoining guardhouse, soldiers' workshop, jail, and six houses for the guards were all built in 1822-1825. But by this time the Indians were well trained in building crafts.

CHAPTER **11**

Mexican Artisans Teach the Indians Various Trades

Architectural Details Tell of Indian's Progress

I N SEPTEMBER, 1790, Governor Fages, at the request of the Padres, informed the Spanish officials in México that fifty-one artisans, besides teachers, millers, and a surveyor were needed in Alta California.[1] Up to this time no buildings other than those of very simple construction had been erected. No corridors with pillars or arches of ladrillo or stone had been constructed; no dams of masonary, mills, stone aqueducts, or fountains. There were no bell towers, or espadañas, the mission bells being hung suspended from crossbars laid in the forks of upright posts.

There was need of expert masons to erect the stone churches planned at San Carlos, Santa Bárbara, San Juan Capistrano, San Gabriel, and San Buenaventura. Those Fathers who had seen magnificent stone churches rise under their direction in the Sierra Gorda region had naturally visualized something beyond mere adobe structures for their houses of worship in this new land. It was this dream that drove Frs. Serra and Crespí at San Carlos to lay the plans for the present stone church and to have quarried and hauled to that mission site stone for its building as early as 1781. They had had the services of artisans in the Sierra Gorda and they needed them here. Therefore, until those experts came they made no attempt to set up other than simple adobe buildings, plastered and whitewashed inside and outside, and roofed with tiles. The buildings of Pala before they fell into ruin, and without the campanile, might well serve as an example of the mission establishments of 1790. Indeed it was said of Pala that all it lacked of being a mission was having a Padre to attend it.

The San Diego church built in 1780 served until it was replaced by a larger one some twenty years later. It is described as being 30 varas long, 5½ varas

[1] Engelhardt, *Miss. & Miss.*, 2. 535.

wide and high, or 83' x 15' x 15', inside measurement. Its walls were three feet thick, its beams were of pine and its rafters of cottonwood. Poles of alder or rough boarding covered the rafters. Tules were laid upon the poles or boarding. Earth covered the tules. A sacristy was added whose length equaled the width of the church, which indicates that it was built adjoining the rear of the church. The sacristy had one window and the church had four. All were protected on the outside by grilles of cedar wood, and were equipped on the inside with shutters of planed boards. Both the side and the front doors of the church were provided with locks. And, "along the entire length of the church and sacristy, on the north or Gospel side, lay the cemetery which was ten varas, or twentyeight feet wide. The corridor that extended along the church and sacristy on the south or Epistle side in the courtyard was two and a quarter varas, or about seven feet, wide. Instead of stone pillars, posts of oak served as supports of the roof."[2]

At Mission San Carlos there is little to be learned about the church that replaced the first temporary one, but it seems certain that an adobe building was erected during Fr. Serra's lifetime.[3] Governor Fages' report of 1787 bears out this assumption, for, in reporting on the churches of the missions then in existence, he noted that San Francisco, like San Buenaventura and Santa Bárbara, had a church that barely supplied the need. The churches of the other missions, he wrote, were of adobe.[4]

At Mission San Antonio the church of 1779-1780, of which Fr. Serra had said "Es todas luces bella Iglesia," and which had a roof of tiles, stood until the new one of 1810-1813 was finished. It was 47 varas long, 9 varas wide (129' x 25'), inside measurement, and 9 varas high. The walls were one and one-half adobe thick. Apparently the length of the church included that of the sacristy also.

When San Francisco was founded Don Fernando Quirós, commander of the packet *San Carlos*, sent the ship's carpenter and a number of sailors to aid the Padres in constructing the necessary mission buildings. Timber was cut and a church eighteen varas long was built of wood covered with clay. It was finished with a roof of tules. The ship's carpenter made doors and an altar table for it. Behind the altar was the sacristy.[5]

[2] Engelhardt, *Mission San Diego*, 106-107.
[3] In a manuscript written July 1st, 1784, shortly before his death, Fr. Serra lists, among buildings then existing at Mission San Carlos, "An adobe church, forty by eight varas, with thatched roof." This report was found by Rev. Maynard Geiger, O.F.M., in the *Archivo General y Publico de la Nación* in Mexico City. Its translation in full appears in the *Academy Scrapbook* (The Academy of California Church History publication), July-August, 1950.
[4] Fages, *Informe General Sobre Misiones*, nos. 25-31. Cal. Arch., Bancroft Collection. Quoted in Engelhardt, *Mission San Francisco*, 109.
[5] Bolton, *Palou's New Cal.*, 4. 132-4.

On April 25, 1782, Fr. Francisco Palóu blessed and laid the first stone for a new church. This building was not finished until 1791. In the meantime Captain José Joaquín Moraga, Anza's capable aide, died and on July 15, 1785, was buried "in the old church." That this old church was none other than the one built in 1776, with the assistance of Captain Quirós, is another assumption that may be gathered from Fages' report of 1787. For, by listing the church of San Francisco with those of Santa Bárbara and San Buenaventura as "un suplemento de Iglesia" while the others were of adobe, he indicates another type of construction. The church of 1776, probably built of redwood, given a roof of boards and kept in repair, may easily have lasted until 1791 when the church begun in 1782 was completed.

That no church other than that of 1782-1791 was built at this mission after Moraga's death, in 1785, is indicated by the fact that immediately after the new one was dedicated his remains were transferred with ceremony befitting his rank "from the old church to the new one."[6]

In mission days it was customary upon the completion and dedication of a new church, to transfer to it the remains of any Padre who had been buried in the one previously built, in the event, of course, of a change of building site. This ceremony was always attended with great solemnity and a record of the proceedings inscribed in the *Libro de Difuntos* (Book of the Dead). Captain Moraga, because of his importance in San Francisco presidial and mission affairs, was accorded this honor.

Of the other mission churches standing in 1790, Santa Bárbara's temporary church of 1789 has already been described, as has the "Serra Church" of San Juan Capistrano.

In 1781, at Santa Clara's second site, Fr. Serra, assisted by Frs. Crespí, Peña, and Murguía, laid the cornerstone of a new church. On May 15-16, 1784, this church was blessed and dedicated, Fr. Serra being Celebrant and assisted by Frs. Palóu and Thomás de la Peña. The account of the laying of the cornerstone as well as that of the blessing and dedication of the church is in the Baptismal Register now at the University of Santa Clara. To Fr. Murguía, who for nineteen years had toiled in the missions of the Sierra Gorda, México,[7] is given the credit for the building of this church. That he actually assisted in its construction seems certain. Unhappily, as the record of his burial in the *Libro de Difuntos* states, he died four days before it was dedicated. This was the church seen and

[6] Engelhardt, *Mission San Francisco*. 106, 117.
[7] Where he had directed the building of a magnificent stone church.

described by Vancouver, but it was not, as is sometimes stated, the one shown in early photographs of Santa Clara. The following description of it is found in the old Baptismal Register:

The church walls are one vara and a half thick, of adobe, on stone foundations, supported by buttresses one vara thicker. Its dimensions inside are eight varas high, forty and one-half long, and nine varas wide. The sacristy, which is in the rear of the chancel, has the same height and thickness of the walls as the church; its length is equal to the width of the church, and its width is six varas. A portico measuring five varas extends, as regards the roof, along the entire length of the building. In the church and the sacristy there is a flat ceiling of wooden beams on brackets with a planking of wood of alerche, commonly called redwood. Above this flat ceiling there is a pavement of adobe flags, and above all there is a slanting roof well adapted for drainage. The brackets extend beyond the walls, as also the thatch of the roof, to protect the walls from rains, which are very abundant. The main door and the cloister door, or side door, each have two leaves, are made of cedar and redwood respectively and each is provided with a lock. The two doors of the sacristy are of the same material [redwood], each having one leaf, and provided with locks. The church is whitewashed inside and outside. The walls inside are painted with a border above and below. The entire chancel and a great part of the ceiling are also painted. The whole floor is a pavement of adobe flags.[8]

This was the largest and most pretentious church erected up to this time and it continued in use until 1818, when it was so badly damaged by an earthquake as to be rendered inserviceable.[9] A temporary church was built in 1818-1819 and a few years later an entirely new establishment was set up on the third site.[10]

The ceiling of Santa Clara's church as described above was quite an improvement over primitive ones still to be seen at San Juan Capistrano and San Luis Obispo. In the pantry at the former mission are the remnants of a ceiling of poles or handhewn rafters upon which tules are laid, secured with rawhide thongs, and then plastered. In some of the rooms, ladrillos, seven by fourteen inches in size, were laid on two-by-three inch joists which in turn rested on beams (vigas) which spanned the ceilings. At San Luis Obispo, in the old sacristy, is an interesting ceiling of bamboo (carrizo) covered with tule, and, it is said, with a coat of brea on top of the tule. The ceiling of the old zaguán (cart entrance), adjoining the sacristy and now serving as the room for arranging the flowers for the altar, is equally ancient. It is composed of saplings, perhaps of the elderberry bush or tree, tied together with hempen twine[11] and plastered over. When, in

---

[8] From *The Three Churches of Santa Clara Mission* by James A. Colligan, S.J.

[9] *Nota Historica*. Ynventario Gral. de la Yglesia de Ntra Madre Santa Clara . . . en 21 de Marzo de 1851.

[10] *Informes*, 1818, 1819, 1822-1825. SBMA.

[11] Fr. Serra, reporting Feb. 5, 1775, on the state of the Mission of San Carlos, listed under *Additions to House and Field*," . . twelve pounds of twisted twine, made of agave fibre."

During the recent work of repair, change, and addition carried on at this mission, the ancient bamboo ceiling was taken down, and new beams and ceiling set in the old sacristy. Then some of the saplings were removed from the ceiling of the zaguán, and a few of the bamboo poles laid in their place.

1920, fire destroyed the roof of the present church, a great variety of primitive ceilings and roofs were uncovered.

In a shed at Los Ojitos, rancho of San Antonio, is a ceiling like that of the zaguán at San Luis Obispo, while the original ceiling of the ranch house itself is of wild bamboo. This latter is seen from the loft above.

In many of the early mission buildings there were no ceilings at all, as at Pala, where one looked up and saw a network of beams, ridgepole and rafters of saplings with sheathing of willows or branches of trees, the tiles on top showing in between. In this chapel, beams laid in the side walls spanned the building. Trusses surmounting the beams upheld the ridgepole, while upright poles set in along the center of the floor supported the beams. In 1902-1903, when the Landmarks Club did its restoration work at Pala, the center poles were removed and the primitive sheathing of willows replaced with scantlings.

As the churches were always the most elaborate and best constructed of the buildings in the quadrangle, the description of Mission Santa Clara's church of 1781-1784, will give the reader a fairly good idea of the type of structures erected before the coming of the artisans in 1790-1795. Of the number of master workmen requested by Governor Fages about twenty were sent to California "chiefly in 1792 and 1795," according to Bancroft.[12] A few had come earlier. Some of the artisans were distributed among the missions and presidios while others, like the weavers, traveled from one mission to the next instructing the neophytes. Their contracts were for four or five years. A carpenter was expected to teach his trade to twelve Indians within four years.

Almost at once work was begun on the chapel for the royal presidio at Monterey and on the church at Mission San Carlos. Both the presidio at Monterey and the mission at Carmel were dedicated to St. Charles (San Carlos) of Borromeo and that fact has been the cause of much misunderstanding regarding the former. The chapel built at Monterey in 1793 was never a mission church. It was erected for the benefit of the governor, the officers and soldiers of the presidio and their families, just as the "Plaza Church" at Los Angeles was built for the settlers of the pueblo. Both were for many years served by priests from near-by missions through the good will of the Fathers only. Neither were asistencias nor stations of the missions, no more than were the churches of the presidios of

[12] Their names were: Santiago Ruiz, Manuel D. (E?) Ruiz, Toribio Ruiz, Salvador Rivera, and Pedro Alcántara, masons; Mariano Tapia, potter; Cayetano Lopez, mill-maker; José A. Ramirez, and Salvador Véjar, carpenters; Miguel Sangrador, tanner and shoe-maker; Joaquin Avalos, tanner; Mariano Tapinto and Joaquin Botello, tailors; Pedro Gonzales García, José Arroya, and José F. Arriola, blacksmiths; Antonio Dom. Henriques and Mariano José Mendoza, weavers; Manuel Muñoz, ribbon maker; José de los Reyes and Antonio Hernandez, saddlers. Banc. *Hist of Cal.*, 1, 615, n. 29; 684, n. 15.

Santa Bárbara and San Diego, and that of the Pueblo of San José. Rightfully the Spanish government should have furnished chaplains for both presidios and peublos.

Since the chapel at Monterey was a government building, an architectural plan of the proposed edifice was drawn and sent to México for approval.[13] This plan consisted of a drawing of the fachada of the present church and belfry only. At least that is all that remains of it. It was returned to Monterey with the statement that the proposed building, as drawn, would be too tall and narrow and should be widened out. In passing it may be well to state that the belfry attached to this chapel, as originally built, was an espadaña, not a torre (tower) as it stands today. This change was made in the 1890's. The original, it may be added, was much more picturesque than the present belfry.

Manuel Estevan Ruíz, master mason and stone-cutter who came to California in 1791, supervised the construction of both the chapel of the royal presidio and the church of Mission San Carlos. In 1793-4, several San Carlos Indians were instructed in stone cutting and brick laying.[14]

There can be little doubt that Frs. Serra and Crespí planned the building of the San Carlos church still standing at Carmel. For, when in his last illness he realized that death was imminent, Fr. Serra said to Fr. Palóu: "I wish you to bury me in the church next to Fr. Juan Crespí, for the present, and when the stone church is built you may place me where you will."[15] Three years previously he had written to Fr. Lasuén at San Diego saying that they hoped soon to begin work on the new church "for which some stone has already been brought from the quarry." Needless to point out that the building must already have been designed.

The belief, prevalent among students of Mission San Carlos history, that the location of the church in which Frs. Crespí and Serra were buried was the same as that of the present church, is strengthened by the fact that no record has been found of the transfer of those Padres' remains from the old church to the new. And the officiating Padres never failed to make note, in at least one Register and sometimes two, of the ceremony which always attended this event.

As was done at other missions, when the Padres did not wish to have the location of the church changed, a temporary building was probably constructed elsewhere in or near the quadrangle. The old church was then taken down and the new one of stone erected on the same site. Its cornerstone was laid July 7, 1793,

[13] Found by Rev. Maynard Geiger, O.F.M., while searching through the archives in Mexico City for documents and letters relating to Fr. Serra.
[14] Banc., *Hist. of Cal.*, 1. 617.
[15] *Palou's Life of Serra* (James ed.), 270.

with the ceremony prescribed by the Roman Catholic Ritual. The church was blessed and dedicated in September, 1797.

There is much about the San Carlos Mission church that reminds one of the little churches found in small towns around Mexico City. And it will be remembered that, after being recalled from the Sierra Gorda missions to work among the Apaches of the San Saba River region, Fr. Serra spent several years at the College of San Fernando before being sent to Baja California in 1767. While at the college he conducted numerous missions in many of the provinces and dioceses around Mexico City where he had every opportunity of seeing churches that in many details resemble those built later in Alta California.[16]

Comparing the mission church with that of the near-by presidio, one is compelled to admit that the latter with its carved stone niches, pilasters, and other embellishments, shows far greater evidence of the work of a master stone mason. The handmade appearance of the mission church with its towers of widely differing design, "its star window that seems to have been blown out of shape in some wintry wind, and all its lines hardened again in the sunshine of the long, long summer,"[17] bespeak the work of the neophyte Indians, directed of course by the master mason and stone cutter. There is, however, much in the stone carving at San Carlos that denotes the touch of the master hand. But the bulk of the work is Indian and proclaims the neophytes' advancement in the building arts.

Some time after the mission church was finished certain changes were made in both belfries. The arches in the south tower were shortened. Originally they extended to the cornice below, as does the south arch today, and may have been so fashioned to hold two bells each, one above the other. At one time, it is said, grilles guarded the bell arches as in Mexican churches. These grilles, however, were not of iron, according to Harry Downie,[18] who found in the walls of the south arch evidence of the former existence of a wooden railing. An iron cross surmounted the remate of the tower and the four windows of the Fathers' dwelling were equipped with iron gratings. The forging of handwrought iron was one of the arts taught the mission Indians by the artisan blacksmiths.

After many years of neglect and vandalism, during which time practically everything movable was carried away; after suffering for fifty years the indignity of an alien roof, the church of the Mission of San Carlos Borromeo del Carmelo is at last coming into its own. Its ancient ceiling, constructed in the form of a catenary arch, has been restored as well as its low gabled roof of many hued

[16] See—*Catalogo de Construcciones Religiosas Del Estado De Hidalgo*, vols. I. and II.
[17] Stoddard (Charles W.), *Footprints of the Padres*, 155.
[18] Native of San Francisco, artist of many trades, long identified with mission restoration work.

tiles. Its interior has been re-decorated and its sacred pictures re-hung. Within its sanctuary, and in accordance with his expressed wish, lie the mortal remains of the mission's founder, Padre Presidente Junípero Serra, beside those of his missionary companion, Fr. Juan Crespí. And never again will its walls be allowed to crumble, for, due to the crusade for the canonization of the first Presidente of our missions, San Carlos has become a shrine for pilgrims from the ends of the earth.

Outside, one by one the buildings of the quadrangle are slowly emerging from the adobe mounds into which they had fallen and soon, it is hoped, the four wings of the old compound will once more be complete. Erected to meet the needs of the day, they will not, of course, be exact reproductions of the buildings of long ago. But they will be built in keeping with the spirit and traditions of the past, and more than that one cannot ask. Throughout this long period of reconstruction Harry Downie has been the guiding genius. San Carlos, the loveliest of them all, is indeed coming into its own.

Mission La Soledad's church, of which not a trace remains above ground today, was built in 1791 and enlarged in 1805. Throughout its history it suffered much on account of floods. This mission has been given scant attention by the various writers of mission history, few going beyond quoting Robinson's description of it as "the gloomiest, bleakest, and most abject spot in all California" and someone else's remark about its "never having got beyond the adobe stage."

Seeking facts about the old church of 1791 this writer, in 1931 and later, interviewed several members of the Soberanes family, one of the oldest in California, José María Soberanes having come with the expedition of 1769. His great-grandson, Mr. Ben A. ("Benito") Soberanes, of Salinas, California, made several trips to the ruins of Mission Soledad with the writer. There, with surveys and photographs to guide him, the old gentleman pointed out the former location of many structures of which not a trace remains today. He remembered that the old church building blocked the right end of the corridor which extended along the front of the Fathers' dwelling. As a boy of eight or ten years he visited his cousins who at that time were living in the old mission and he remembered running with them up and down the corridor. The church, he said, formed a wind-break for it. He told of "going up something" in the old church where he saw "an old musical instrument—something like a harp." He had, of course, climbed up into the choir-loft which, in mission churches, is built over the front entrance. The front of the church, he said, stood until about 1863, at least.

J. Ross Browne visited this mission in the summer of 1849 and made a very interesting sketch of the old church.[19] In his drawing the curved pediment of the fachada is surmounted by what is presumably the outline of a belfry of the espadaña type, similar to many to be found today on some Mexican churches.

It was, it seems, the sanctuary end of the church that fell into ruin in 1832. The sacristy, which adjoined the church at the rear, and the church itself were both damaged by excessive rains or floods in 1824. The church was repaired and strengthened that same year and the sacristy in the year following. Then, in 1832, Fr. Vicente Francisco de Sarría, alone at Soledad, reported the building of a temporary, or "provisional" church, the other one having tumbled down.[20] This provisional church was the little chapel whose ruins stand today at the left and in front of the crumbling walls of the Fathers' dwelling.

The church of 1791 stood at the right of the Padres' apartments and between them and the houses of the soldiers of the guard. Within the confines of its foundations lie the remains of Fr. Florencio Ibañez and Governor José Joaquín Arrillaga—their graves unmarked.

In the southern part of the state, building construction requiring the services of architects and expert stone masons began, apparently, as soon as the artisans arrived. José Antonio Ramírez, carpenter and mason, is known to have assisted in the building of the churches at Santa Bárbara, San Gabriel, and San Luis Rey.[21] He was master architect for the "Plaza Church" and, in 1811, is found at La Purísima engaged in making stone troughs, vats, wash-tubs, and drinking fonts. In the Account Book of Mission Santa Bárbara his name appears in the records for the years 1795, 1800-1802, 1817-1819. He probably served first at San Gabriel.

It is not known just when San Gabriel's church of stone and mortar was begun, but, in 1795, Fr. Presidente Lasuén reported that it had been raised to half its intended height. By 1801, its vaulted roof was finished but had become cracked and the Padres were wondering if it would not be necessary to take it down and replace it with a roof of timbers. However, the cracks were repaired and the church was blessed in 1804. Unfortunately, this same year a severe earthquake caused more cracks to appear and an "intelligent mason" judged it best to take the roof down and substitute a gabled one covered with tiles. Finally, in

[19] See *A Dangerous Journey*, wherein Browne tells a humorous story of his visit to the old mission.

[20] *Informe*, 1824. "En las Fabricas se ha reparado y compuesto la Santa Yglesia y lo restante lo mejor qᵉ se ha podido." *Informe*, 1825. "En las Fabricas, se ha hecho la sacristia qᵉ el año pasado la tumbo el agua, y se ha reparado lo restante . . ."

Informe, 1832. "Se ha echo una Yglesia provisional i bastante decente para el culto Divino por haberse caydo la otra." SBMA.

[21] "Duhaut-Cilly's Account," 227. In San Luis Rey's *Libro de Patentes*, now in SBMA, is an account of the laying of the cornerstone of San Luis Rey's present church. In that document José Antonio Ramírez is named architect and superintendent of its construction.

1808, the vaulted roof, threatening ruin, was taken down and replaced with a flat roof covered with mortar and ladrillos.[22] Evidently this flat roof did not withstand the earthquake shocks of December, 1812, for the long-promised roof of timbers and tiles appeared on San Gabriel's church sometime before 1830. Both Alfred Robinson and William Rich Hutton, paymaster's clerk to the United States volunteer forces sent to occupy California in 1846, sketched this building. Hutton's sketch shows a tiled roof, hipped at both ends, with a lantern over the sanctuary.[23] His drawing makes Robinson's[24] more understandable.

San Gabriel's belfry, about which there has been so much speculation, was destroyed by the tremors of 1812. Had the Padres' report of this disaster been properly translated there need have been no doubt of the campanario's form. The record reads: "Dicho terremoto ó temblor maltrato la yglesia vastante y a la espadaña la hizo muchas rasaduras y por ultimo cayo el remate de ella con su beleta."[25] (This earthquake, or temblor, damaged the church greatly, made many cracks in the espadaña and finally the finial with its weather vane fell down.)

The campanarios, or belfries, of our California missions may be divided into three classes or types, namely: the two upright posts with crossbar; the espadaña, for which term there is no equivalent in the English language; and the tower (torre). The espadaña is defined in the *Enciclopedia Universal Ilustrada* as —"Campanario de una sola pared en la que se abren una o varias arcadas en uno o dos órdenes" (Belfry of only one wall, in which one or more arches are cut open in one or two levels). The *Diccionario de la Lengua Española* gives the following definition: "Espadaña—Campanario de una sola pared, en la que están abiertas los huecos para colocar las campanas" (Belfry of only one wall, in which openings are found to hang the bells).

In making out their reports, the Padres never confused the term torre with that of espadaña, or vice versa. Both and all bellhouses may properly be called belfries, or, in the Spanish tongue, campanarios. There were towers at San Luis Rey, San Juan Capistrano (stone church), San Fernando, San Buenaventura, Santa Bárbara, San Carlos, Santa Cruz (after 1831), Santa Clara, and San José.[26] At San Juan Bautista, San Miguel, San Rafael, and San Francisco Solano the bells were hung from that most primitive of all belfries—two upright posts with

---

[22] *Informe*, 1808. Lib. Mission San Gabriel.
[23] *California 1847-1852. Drawings by William Rich Hutton* (Huntington Library Publication, 1942), Pl. 41 (hereinafter referred to as *California Drawings*).
[24] Robinson, *Life in Cal.*
[25] *Informe*, 1812. SBMA.
[26] For fear of earthquake damage the Fathers at San José shortened their tower until it was on the level of the church loft. *Inventario San José año de 1837*. SBMA.

crossbar.[27] The rest of the mission campanarios were, according to Mexican and Spanish definitions of yesterday and today, all espadañas, regardless of their arrangement.

At San Antonio de Pala, station of Mission San Luis Rey, a campanile was erected, but that is unique.[28]

Returning to the San Gabriel Padres' report of the earthquake disaster of 1812, one is struck with the strangeness of having a finial surmounted by a weather vane. The cross over a sphere, symbolizing the triumph of Christianity over the world, crowns many belfries the world over, but not a weather vane. Believing that the two must have been combined, the writer began a search for precedent for such unusual arrangement. This was found in abundance in Baxter's splendid work on Mexican architecture.[29] There, pictured on church towers in Celaya, Puebla, Querétaro, Guanajuato, Tlaxcala, and other towns were crosses with weather vanes affixed to them below the cross-arms. Thus we have another architectural detail borrowed from México.[30]

A study of the architectural remains of San Gabriel's espadaña, especially in conjunction with details of the restored campanario at Mission San Diego, convinces one that the lower portion of the structure contained but one chamber. It is the writer's belief that the present belfry is a copy of the upper stages of the original one, except for the upper right-hand arch which gives every evidence of having been added later.[31] This espadaña, then, would have had much the same appearance as that one at San Diego, except for its ornamentation and the stairway which at the latter mission leads directly to the bells. At San Gabriel the bell-ringers mounted the stairs built on the other side of the church and passed through the choir loft to the belfry beyond, as they did for so many years at San Luis Rey.

Since there were some fine examples of hand-wrought iron work at San Gabriel, one would expect to find ornamental iron grilles protecting the two lower bell arches in which esquilas were usually hung. And this mission had its little "glad" bells, one of which has but recently been returned, its date and inscription chiseled off, but still bearing evidence of being one of the bells seen by Fr. Serra at San Blas in 1772.[32]

[27] An early picture of Santa Isabel, San Diego County, shows the crossbar laid in two forked posts, as they probably all were at first.

[28] It is to be regretted that when Rancho San Bernardino was reconstructed a replica of this campanile was erected there.

[29] Baxter, Sylvester, *Spanish Colonial Architecture in Mexico*, J. B. Millet Publisher, Boston, 10 vols.

[30] Early sketches reveal the fact that iron crosses with weather vanes attached also crowned towers at San Diego and Santa Clara.

[31] See reproduction of Deppe's painting of Mission San Gabriel executed in May, 1832, for confirmation of this belief.

[32] Bolton, *Palou's New Cal.*, 3. 1, 25-26.

At Santa Cruz a church was begun in February, 1793. It was about one hundred twelve feet long, thirty feet wide, and twenty-five feet high. "The foundation walls to the height of three feet were of stone, the front was of masonry and the rest of adobes." The church was finished and blessed May 10, 1794.[33]

In 1811, it was roofed with tiles and two years later was given a floor. In 1814, an espadaña was built for the protection of the bells ("Se a levantado una Espadaña para resguardo de las Campanas"). In September, 1825, there began a series of earth tremors that were still being experienced on December 31, when poor Padre Luis Gil wrote his annual report. The church was threatened with ruin and the house of the Fathers had suffered cracks. There was no prospect of rebuilding due to the scarcity of workers. The number of Indian neophytes at the mission at that time was four hundred twenty-nine, men, women, and children—the well and the sick.[34]

This mission's story for the next seven years is one of struggle to repair and strengthen the damaged buildings. Walls around the cemetery and garden were rebuilt, the Fathers' house and its corridors reroofed. In 1831, a large pilaster (pilastrón) was built to serve as a buttress against the left front corner of the church. A campanario was set up, possibly for the purpose of supporting the other corner. This campanario, according to the *informe* of 1840, was a torre. In 1832, a buttress of stone was built on the cemetery side of the church which was in a ruinous condition.

In 1840, an "abundance of waters" (tidal wave?) destroyed the tower. There is in the Padre's report no mention of the earthquake which Bancroft says preceded the tidal wave, or flood. Two of the bells hanging in the tower were broken.[35] Ernest Massey, visiting Santa Cruz in 1850, wrote in his Diary: "Today the church is in ruins. Only the nave, dilapidated both outside and in, is still standing; it is still used for holding services. The tower has fallen, and the bells, fastened to a few crude beams, are lying in the debris."[36]

On the morning of January 9, 1857, an earthquake, which, it is claimed by one writer,[37] was felt from the northern Sacramento Valley to the Bay of San Diego, destroyed the much buffeted and battered church of Santa Cruz. A por-

[33] Banc., *Hist. of Cal.*, 1. 496.
[34] *Informes* 1811-1814. SBMA.
Informe 1825. "Pᵒ esta vigente la ruina qᵉ amenaza dicha Yglesia; y es terrible se realice, si viene un temblor violente, y fuerte entre los varios suaves, qᵉ han menudeado desde el Septbre pasado a esta epoca; y no es posible reedificarse qᵉ la carencia de brazos, . . ." SBMA.
[35] *Informe* 1840. "La Yglesia en el presente año ha tenido el demerito de qᵉ la torre se ha venido al suelo por la abundancia de agua, como tambien por lo falto del piso en qᵉ se fundo, y repicando las campanas se rompieron dos. SBMA.
[36] "Diary of Ernest de Massey," translated by Marguerite Eyer Wilbur and published in *Quarterly of California Historical Society*, Vol. V. 1926.
[37] Torchiana, H. A. van Coenen, Litt. D., LL. D., *Mission of Santa Cruz*, 390.

tion of the building was later repaired with boards and used as a stable for horses and storage place for hay.

Of the entire establishment, which was quite extensive, nothing remains to-day save two adobe houses formerly occupied by members of the escolta (soldier guard), and one old residence that stands beside the Catholic church.[38] In 1931, a smaller replica of the mission church and rooms of the Fathers' dwelling was erected on ground adjoining the former compound.

In about 1793, the Fathers of Mission San Buenaventura began the building of the present church. Whether they had the services of expert workmen, other than the Indians, is not known. Since this building was, in part at least, constructed of masonry, it is probable that they did. It was completed in 1809 and, on September 9th of that year, was blessed with the prescribed solemn ceremonies. On the 10th, the first High Mass was sung, and on the following day the remains of Fr. Vicente de Santa María, who died July 16, 1806, were removed from the old church to the new one after a vigil and a holy Mass for his soul had been sung.

In 1810-1811, the altars were gilded and the ceiling decorated.

On December 8, 1812, began a series of earthquake shocks that lasted until February of the next year. The church of San Buenaventura, completed but three years previously, suffered greatly from the tremors. There were three horrible shocks, according to the Padres; the top of the fachada was shaken about three varas out of plumb; a considerable aperture was made in the presbytery, and the tower was left inserviceable and they were going to take it down.[39]

The several succeeding years were spent in repairing and rebuilding the damaged buildings. At length, in 1819, Fr. Mariano Payeras, Commissary Prefect, reported to the College of San Fernando and the Mexican Government that the church and sacristy of San Buenaventura, as well as the chapel dedicated to Saint Michael, had been placed in such condition that, "since it was all done by the neophytes under the direction of the missionaries and at little cost, it was worthy of the praise of God."[40]

Earthquake shocks, particularly those of 1800, 1808, and 1812, were the cause of some peculiar details, otherwise not understandable, in California mission

---

[38] *Ibidem*, 8.

[39] *Informe* 1812. "Han padecido bastante de resultas de tres horribles temblores, o terremotos, en q⁵ nos parecio se venia abajo la mision. La Ýglesia tiene como tres varas de lo mas superior del frontis algo desplomado, y en la pared testera del Presbiterio una abertura considerable. Esta pared debe hacerse de nuevo; lo demas admite composicion, y confiamos, q⁵ con contra cimientos de piedra, y cal, y fuertes estrivos, quede en estado de mayor firmeza, q⁵ tenia antes. La torre ha quedado inservible, y vamos á derribarla." SBMA.

[40] Engelhardt, *Mission San Buenaventura*, 42-43.

architecture. At San Buenaventura, following the destructive tremors of 1812, the Padres built the huge buttress that stands at the left of the church entrance. They rebuilt the tower, overlapping its front wall on the church fachada to form a buttress at that corner. In making those changes, however, they destroyed and rendered meaningless the structural decorations of the frontispiece. Could the heavy buttress on the left and the overlapping wall of the tower on the right be taken away, San Buenaventura's church, as the mission Indians originally built it, would stand revealed. It is the overlapping, spoken of above, that gives the bell chambers the appearance of being off center.

Since about 1870, the fachada of this church has undergone a number of changes which, though slight in each instance, have added to the alteration of the original design. That which contributed most to its loss of character was, perhaps, the removal of its broad front steps, somewhat similar to those at Santa Bárbara. Its tiled roof had been destroyed by the earthquake of 1857 and was replaced with one of shingles, as seen in all the early photographs of this mission.

In all likelihood, it was because of the earthquake of 1812 that the two huge buttresses, seen today, were built against the front of San Diego's adobe church erected in 1808-1813. Though the tremors did no damage in the south beyond San Juan Capistrano.[41] At a later time, perhaps, the space between these buttresses was roofed over, forming a portico to the church. The portico roof was tiled and three arched doorways were built giving entrance to the atrium.[42] Still later, when the United States troops occupied the building, those arched entrances were squared, a door and four windows installed, and the portico was divided to serve as offices. Many early photographs show this latter arrangement.

At San Luis Rey, in 1926, an upper portion of the lower chamber of the east tower fell away, carrying with it part of the two upper stages of the belfry and a bell. This same thing had happened about twenty-five years previously. In repairing the damage the Fathers of 1926 found that the stairway, or lower chamber of the tower, was packed solidly with adobes. The vaulted brick ceiling of this room had never been finished, leading the excavators to believe that it had never been used, but, for fear of earthquake damage, had been filled in while the church was under construction, in 1811-1815. In the meantime, access to the belfry had been gained by way of the long stairway leading up to the left tower and

[41] 1812, Dec. 31. "The churches of this jurisdiction [San Gabriel and San Juan Capistrano] have been destroyed by a great earthquake of Dec. 8 of this year—those of San Diego, the new and the old alike, did not suffer at all, and the new church will be finished this year." Francisco Ma. Ruíz Comandante, Presidio, San Diego. *St. Pap. Miss.*, IV. 24. Courtesy of California State Historical Association.

[42] See sketches by H. M. T. Powell, *The Santa Fe Trail;* H. C. Pratt in Bartlett, *Personal Narrative;* W. R. Blake, *U. S. Government Survey, 1853.*

on through the choir loft. The Fathers believe that it was this adobe, packed in so solidly and which expanded when damp, that caused the damage on both occasions mentioned.[43]

At Mission San José the church, shown in the daguerreotype of 1853, was finished in 1809. In the inventory of 1842 note was made of the fact that its tower had not been continued for fear of earthquakes. On the contrary it had been shortened until it was on the level of the church loft. Here four medium sized bells were arranged.[44] The earthquake shocks which caused the San José Padres to abandon their plan for building a tall tower were those which shook the San Francisco district in June and July of 1808. They were said to have been the most severe that ever visited that section of the state.[45] San José's church was completely destroyed by the earthquake of 1868. The present church is said to have been built on the foundations of the earlier one. Nothing else remains of this once great establishment save a few rooms of the Fathers' dwelling and one or two buildings across the street which are believed to have been part of the Indian village. A photograph of the early 1860's shows a number of these little adobe houses still standing, their tiled roofs intact.

At Mission San Juan Capistrano, on March 2, 1797, the first stone was laid for a church that was to surpass any yet built in Alta California. The roof was to be vaulted like the sky, and to be constructed of concrete. The building was to measure 53 varas in length, and 10 varas in width, or 146' x 27' 6", inside measurement. The vestry on the epistle side was to be 28' x 19'. A tower and baptistry were included in the plan.[46] Evidently a chamber in the tower was to serve for the latter since no other provision appears to have been made for it.

This was the great stone church whose ruins still stand as a monument to its planners and builders, Frs. Fuster and Santiago, Isidro Aguilar, maestro albañil (master mason), and the Indians. That there had not been a sufficient number of master masons and architects among the artisans coming in 1790-1795, is evident from the fact that the Padres of San Juan Capistrano were obliged to appeal to Governor Arrillaga to secure one for them to superintend the building of their proposed church. Finally, Isidro Aguilar, of Culiacán, was induced to undertake the task.

The stones used in building this great church, Fr. O'Sullivan learned from the

---

[43] Information given by Fr. Dominic Gallardo, O.F.M.
[44] *Inventario* 1842. "Por temor de los terremotos qᵉ ha solido haber no se continuó la torre antes bien se minoró el cubo de alla hasta ponerselo al nivel del desván del techo de Yglesia y se colocaron asi 4 campanas medianas, a las qᵉ debe agregarse una chiquita qᵉ actualmenᵉ sirve en la guardia." SBMA.
[45] Banc., *Hist. of Cal.*, 2. 129.
[46] Engelhardt, *Mission San Juan Capistrano*, 28-29; *Informe*, Dec. 31, 1797. SBMA.

"old people" of the village,[47] were brought from Misión Vieja (the first site), and from the rocky point near the ocean, now called San Juan Point. They were unhewn and of irregular size and shape. Consequently, the services of an expert stone mason were required to insure the safety and durability of the building.

The church was built in the form of a Latin cross. Its vaulted ceiling was constructed in a series of domes—one over the sanctuary, three over the transept, and three over the nave beyond the transept. A lantern,[48] said by the "old people" to have been constructed of large, square ladrillos, was set in the center dome over the transept. In 1850, H. M. T. Powell sketched this mission.[49] Apparently four, at least, of the seven domes of the ceiling were intact at that time. The lantern is shown in Powell's sketch.

The transept was, floored with diamond-shaped brick tiles, but the nave, perhaps because the church was never fully finished, never had other than an earthen floor.

The bell tower is said to have been so high that it could be seen ten miles away, while the sound of the bells carried even farther. This tower stood at the right of the church near the front entrance.[50] Judging from the arches, pilasters, cornices, capitals and the carved stone doorways the fachada of the church must have been quite ornate. Steps, similar to those of Santa Bárbara's church, led up to the main door.

In 1803, Padre Presidente Lasuén reported in his *Notas* that work on the church of San Juan Capistrano had come to a standstill due to the death of the master mason, Isidro Aguilar.[51] There seems to be no record of another artisan having been secured to take his place, but it is extremely unlikely that work on that church would have been continued without one.

Capistrano's church was finished in 1806, and, on September 7th of that year, was blessed by Padre Presidente Tapis; assisted by the resident Fathers and others from the missions of San Gabriel, Santa Bárbara, San Fernando, and San Luis Rey. There assisted also Governor José Joaquín de Arrillaga, officers, and soldiers from the presidios of San Diego and Santa Bárbara. Spanish people and neophytes from neighboring missions joined in the celebration. It was indeed a great occasion. An account of the three-day ceremony is found in the mission's

---

[47] As soon as Fr. O'Sullivan arrived at this mission he began the study of the Spanish language, and the gathering of facts and legends about the old mission. To that end he always carried in his pocket a notebook in which to jot down words and information.

[48] The mission churches were semi-dark and the lantern was designed to throw light upon the altar.

[49] Powell, *The Santa Fe Trail*, 206.

[50] In 1937 the foundations of the tower were uncovered by workers under the direction of Rev. Arthur J. Hutchinson.

[51] "La (Iglesia) de San Juan Capistrano ha pasado porque murió el Maestro Albañil, y se hacen diligencias para conseguir otro que la concluya." Lasuen *Notas*. Ar. S. B. XII, 69. Courtesy of State Historical Association.

old *Baptismal Register*, under Baptism 2,723. Written into this record is the Padres' statement that the stone church had been "constructed by the neophytes at the cost of supplication and labors." Nine years in the building, it had been in use just six years and three months when it was destroyed by the earthquake of 1812.

There was considerable iron work done at San Juan Capistrano, and some of it still exists. The iron altar rail from the old stone church now serves in the choir loft of the "Serra Church," while here and there in the old buildings are hinges, locks, and bolts that tell of the Indians' work in the shops. Iron nails from one-half inch to fourteen inches in length were made in the mission blacksmith shops. Iron for this work, as well as steel and carbon to work it with, was sent up from México in the earlier years. In later years much of this metal was secured from Russian and other traders in exchange for mission products. But as early as 1777, Mission San Diego, in her years of scanty crops, repaid gifts of various foodstuffs from San Gabriel and San Juan Capistrano with iron, steel, and carbon. Trained laborers were sent along "to work it into whatever should be desired."[52] These trained laborers were, in all probability, Indians from Baja California missions. Apparently plow points, nails, and simple tools were made in those early years; the forging of grilles, crosses, locks, and ornamental pieces awaited the coming of the master workers.

According to Bancroft,[53] the church still standing at San Luis Obispo was built before 1793, in which year a portico was added to its front. It was a simple adobe structure of ample proportions with sacristy adjoining it in the rear. Presumably the portico was of the same form as the present one but of that one cannot be certain for, in 1830, the earthquake which destroyed rancho San Miguelito and damaged Santa Margarita, brought disaster to the mission as well. Some of the buildings were badly damaged and the front of the church had to be taken down because it threatened to fall. In 1831, the espadaña was repaired. During the next year, however, it was destroyed by excessive rains and was rebuilt of stone masonry.[54] This latter was the espadaña seen in the Watkins photographs of 1765-75 and in sketches of even earlier dates. When built, in 1832, it was, apparently, not bonded, or tied in, with the front wall of the church and, in consequence of the earthquake of 1868, cracked away from that building.

In an effort to save the portico, the heavy tiles were taken from its roof. Not-

[52] Engelhardt, *Mission San Diego*, 95.
[53] Banc., *Hist. of Cal.*, 1. 690.
[54] *Informe*, 1832. " . . y la Espadaña de que se hablo el año pasado, la derribaron las aguas, p^r la que este año se a echo de Cali-Canto ó Mescla y Piedra." SBMA.

withstanding this precaution, it became necessary within a few years to raze the structure. At that time the church and Fathers' casa entered upon one of the worst phases of so-called restoration that has ever been inflicted upon any of the old historic establishments. Both buildings were boarded over with tongue-and-groove siding, while the bells were hung in a steeple-like belfry that was perched atop the roof that covered the stairway to the choir loft. Fortunately, in 1934, there came to San Luis Obispo a young priest[55] who tore off the offending boards, rebuilt the portico, and restored the mission to some measure of its former dignified appearance. Unfortunately, the successive grading of the street in front of the buildings has destroyed the original setting, for which there is no cure save a return to the former street level. This same thing happened to a lesser degree at San Francisco. One often wonders what the old Padres would say could they return and see what has been done to their churches, dwellings, and other buildings, in the name of progress and expediency.

At San Antonio the pathetic ruins of the church, built in 1810-1813, stood until 1948, a silent rebuke to all California. As late as 1889, the Fathers' house and the church were in fairly good condition and, given a little attention, the original buildings might easily have been standing today, although the earthquake of 1906 did considerable damage here. In 1889 the roofs needed new ridgepoles and rafters but the walls seemed to be intact save those of the far end of the front wing.

Two photographers, O. H. Knight and W. B. Tyler, visited the mission that year and left us general views, one rare picture of the inner quadrangle, and another of the interior of the church. This building was evidently just as Fr. Ambris[56] had left it; religious services were still being held there. The altar, statues, paintings, confessionals, pulpit and all the necessary paraphernalia were in place. To get the picture of the interior, Mr. Knight broke into the church, which was locked up at the time. For months, an informant told the writer, there was talk of prosecuting the trespasser.

The ceiling, which was one of this church's interesting features, is shown in Knight's photograph. It was a compromise between a flat and an arched one and extended over the sanctuary and nave. Perhaps the Padres profited by the disasters which had overtaken the vaulted ceilings of masonry constructed at other missions and decided to build one of planks, with sides slightly inclined and top

[55] Rev. John Harnett, who passed away July 3, 1939.
[56] Rev. Doroteo Ambris was stationed at Monterey, in 1846, from which place he visited San Antonio. Becoming resident pastor of the mission in 1851, he remained there until his death in 1882. A Mexican priest, he was greatly loved by his parishioners, many of whom were Indians. He was buried in the mission church.

flat. A cornice which supported the slanting joists of the ceiling was built into the walls at about three-fourths their height from the floor. The floor, according to the inventory of 1842,[57] was "de mescla y ladrillo bien bruñido" (of mortar and ladrillo well burnished). However, in the recent restoration of the church, workers found no indication of the employment of ladrillos in the construction of the floor. It was merely "de mescla bien bruñido."

As first constructed, this church had a severely plain fachada like that of San Miguel. In 1821, eight years after the building was reported finished, an arch was built to the portico of the church. The fachada of this arched vestibule serves also for that of the church, and is truly the best built and most interesting part of the church if not of the entire establishment as it once stood. Constructed of ladrillos, some plain and some molded for ornamentation, its lower half is pierced by three arched entranceways. Its beautiful gabled pediment, carrying a central bell arch flanked on either side by a small tower-like belfry, forms an espadaña that is one of the most pleasing to be found anywhere. Three bells hung in those arches in 1889. Long ropes attached to their clappers trailed on the ground in front of the entrance. Iron fittings, still embedded in the walls beside each arch, tell of grilles which formerly protected the bells and gave added adornment to the espadaña. These grilles were probably removed after secularization and before Fr. Ambris came to the mission, since they do not appear in any of the early photographs.[58]

It is said that a heavy oaken, two-leaved door of many panels, similar to two still at San Juan Capistrano, but having a leaf-like decoration carved in each corner, once hung in the front doorway of the church. It disappeared after 1893 as did the mission bells.[59]

Between the fachada and the church proper is the arched vestibule built in 1821. This is an unique bit of construction. It, the fachada, the wine cellar (bodega), and the arches of the corridor which extended along the front of the Fathers' house all give evidence of the work or supervision of a master mason. As do the funnel-shaped forebay and wheel chamber of the water-power gristmill.

At this mission both willows and cane (carrizo) were used for sheathing in the construction of the roofs. Tied together in sheets, very much as bamboo shades are fashioned, they were laid on and fastened to the rafters with rawhide thongs to form a bed for the tiles. Photographs taken in the 1890's show this detail

[57] Inventory of April 23, 1842. Archives of Monterey-Fresno Diocese.
[58] The grilles were restored in 1948-1949.
[59] Until this time Richard Díaz had been caretaker for the Milpitas Rancho. When he left there was no one to look after the mission property and, piece by piece, everything movable was carried away. Fortunately Mr. Díaz took the statues with him for safe keeping, returning them to the Franciscans when they were repossessed of Mission San Miguel.

very clearly, the rafters having broken and the tiles fallen, leaving the sheathing exposed.

That San Francisco's present church, built in 1782-1791, may also have been finished with a fachada that was devoid of ornamentation is a distinct possibility. Just when the structural elements now adorning it were added is not known. It seems quite unlikely, in view of the scarcity of expert masons at the time the church was finished, and especially in view of later *informes*, that this fachada should have been constructed as early as 1791, when the church was dedicated. Moreover, it is a matter of record that the mission churches were not necessarily entirely finished when they were blessed and dedicated. According to the Padres' reports a portion of San Francisco's church was roofed with tiles in 1794, and four years later "work on the church was continued so as to close up the quadrangle." At Santa Bárbara, it will be remembered, work was commenced in 1810 on the frontispiece of the church built in 1793. The church of Santa Cruz was blessed and dedicated in 1794 yet it was not until 1811 that it was roofed with tiles and its fachada constructed ("Se a [ha] techado la Yglesia de texa, se a [ha] hecho el frontis de la Yglesia desde al cimiento, . .''),[60] and not until 1813 that it was floored. Other such instances might be cited.

A sketch of 1816[61] depicts a portion of San Francisco's church with a fachada somewhat similar to the one seen today, though without the balcony above the entrance. Captain William Smythe's sketch[62] of 1826 shows the front wall devoid of ornamentation. And the well-known, much-copied photograph "taken by an Englishman returning from the Orient in about 1856,"[63] portrays it as it stands today. These discrepancies need not disturb the student of the development of mission architecture. The sketches mentioned are, in all probability, both fairly reliable delineations of the church building at the time each was drawn. Other details of the sketches are too nearly accurate[64] to be ignored as corroboration of this belief. The desire for change on the part of the Padres, or the rebuilding of the fachada because of damage inflicted on it by earthquake or excessive rains might easily explain the absence or presence, of ornamental elements, on different occasions.

In the Smythe sketch the mission church is portrayed as a long barn-like edifice with a lean-to structure built along its entire left side. Proof of the former

---

[60] *Informe*, 1811. SBMA.
[61] Sketch by Louis Choris, who came with the Kotzebue expedition.
[62] Smythe came with Capt. Beechey in 1826. Sketch published in Forbes, *California*.
[63] So identified by C. E. Watkins, pioneer photographer.
[64] Though it is very doubtful that an eaveless roof, such as is shown in the Choris sketch, ever topped a California mission.

existence of this lean-to is found in many photographs taken of this side wall. It is known to have been divided into three rooms, the first at the front being the baptistry. Harry Downie remembers seeing decorations in color on this section of the church's outer wall. The mortuary chapel occupied the center room and stood where the tall monument now marks the grave of Don Luis Antonio Argüello, California's first governor of the Mexican regime. This chapel was entered through the doorway that now serves as the baptistry. The end room was used as a sacristy. Confessionals built into the wall of the church are a feature found at this mission only. A doorway converted to such use was formerly found at San Miguel, but this was not, it seems, its original purpose.

Built-in cupboards and closets were found at a number of the missions. Some of them had doors hinged at the bottom and, when let down, served as tables.[65] Excellent examples of the cupboards are to be found today at San Luis Obispo and in the room now used as the museum at San Juan Capistrano; their doors are identical in design. At San Gabriel, doors of clothes' presses built into the sacristy walls are similarly designed and ornamented.

San Juan Bautista's church, which was built in 1803-1818, has the distinction of being the widest of all California mission churches and also of being the only one having three naves. The two side naves are separated from the main one by a series of arches. Needless to say, such construction called for the services of a master workman, though none is mentioned in the Padres' records. The pillars which support the arches of the side naves are three feet by three feet six inches in size and are built of ladrillos. They stand twelve feet apart. Curiously enough the space between all the pillars, save two on each side near the sanctuary, are filled in solidly with adobe bricks. This circumstance has been variously explained by numerous writers. The truth is, apparently, that when the quake of 1808 shook the region, the Fathers became alarmed for the safety of the church and filled in the arches with adobes.

This filling-in saved the church from total destruction during the earth tremors of 1906 when the pillars supporting the arches, and the walls above them were badly damaged and portions of the outer walls of the side naves were destroyed.

The present bell tower[66] at this mission is entirely foreign to mission architecture. It was built sometime after 1865, it is said, to make the task of bell-

---

[65] Robinson, *Life in Cal.*, 48; Bolton, *Anza's Calif. Exped.*, 4. 241.

[66] In 1949-1950, under the direction of Harry Downie, this tower was taken down. One of the bells was hung as it was in the days of the Padres, and numerous alien features, including the plank ceiling, were removed from the church interior.

ringing easier for the Father, who, for lack of helpers was often obliged to perform that duty himself. Originally, the bells hung suspended from a crossbar supported by two posts that stood a little to the right and in front of the church.

San Carlos and Santa Bárbara have, without doubt, the most beautiful settings of any of our California missions, the former with the blue of the ocean and distant Point Lobos for its background and Santa Bárbara with the serene and eternal hills beyond it. As one approaches the latter from Los Olivos Street in the late afternoon of a mellow California day, it seems that there could be no fairer sight on earth than this beautiful old mission. The stone church with its fachada of classic design, its red-tiled roof, and twin towers stand out strikingly against the purpling green of the mountains. The fachada, so different from that of any of the other missions, was patterned after a design found in an old book in the mission library. This book, *Architectura de M. Vitruvio Polion*, was translated from the Latin into the Spanish language and published in Madrid in the year 1787. It contains much besides architecture that may have been very helpful to the Padres.

The story of the destruction of Santa Bárbara's church of 1793-1794 has already been told in the preceding chapter. The present church was begun in 1815 and finished in 1820. Due to the ill health of Fr. Francisco Suñer, senior missionary at this mission, Fr. Antonio Ripoll was in charge of the building activities from 1815 to 1827. He it was who directed the building of the church, having as supervisor of construction the master mason and carpenter, José Antonio Ramírez.

The new church was dedicated September 10, 1820. A description of the solemn ceremonies, the feasting and merry-making that marked this celebration is reserved for another chapter. In their *informe* of that year the Padres describe their church in the following words: "The dimensions of the new church are: Length, including walls 60 varas; width including walls 14 varas; from floor to ceiling 10 varas. Work was carried on during the years 1818 and 19 with such effect that on the tenth day of Sept., 1820, the church was finished and blessed. The walls are of large cubes of cut sandstone, and nearly six feet through, nevertheless they were further strengthened by heavy solid stone buttresses at each angle and at sections along the sides. Without doubt it is the strongest mission church building in California. One tower[67] of two stories held six bells, three of which were stationary, the others with yoke. In a niche in the frontispiece, sup-

---

[67] The second tower was not built until sometime after 1827 but before 1841, as will be seen from the accounts written by Duhaut-Cilly, Dana, and De Mofras.

ported by six columns, is a statue of our Patroness Santa Bárbara, cut from the best stone found here and painted. The apex and angles of the frontispiece are adorned with stone statutes, representing respectively the three theological virtues, Faith, Hope, and Charity. The interior is neatly finished, the walls are plastered, the columns and cornice frescoed, the ceiling lathed, hard finished and ornamented with designs from Vitruvius, cut from cedar and painted. The floor of red cement made from oil and lime is hard and finely polished. The altars are neatly ornamented with fine crucifixes and statues in wood."[68]

The baptistry was built adjoining the church to the right of the entrance. During the restoration following the earthquake of 1925, it was removed to the lower chamber of the bell tower on the right. Originally this bell tower had been built solidly of stone.

The corridors which were built along the front row of buildings at all the missions and along those surrounding the inner square, or patio, of most if not all of them, contributed much to the good appearance of the establishments as well as to the comfort of the inhabitants. They also protected the adobe walls from rains and furnished outdoor workrooms for the Indians. They were built with sufficient variety of form and manner of construction to make them one of the most interesting features of mission architecture.

At San Luis Rey, where tile making was carried to the nth degree, the long arcaded corridor in front of the Fathers' dwelling and those once extending along the four sides of the great inner court were topped with a ladrillo-latticed balustrade and must have presented an imposing sight. There, and at San Juan Capistrano and Santa Inés only, were arcaded corridors built within the patio. At all the other missions the roofs of the corridors surrounding the inner court rested on pillars of adobes or ladrillos, or on wooden posts. Wooden posts, probably redwood, were favored by most of the northern missions.

In 1801-1802, the Padres at San Juan Capistrano caused to be built arcaded corridors totaling 222 varas (619 feet) in length. It is not stated where these flat-roofed and ladrillo-floored walks were erected but presumably it was along the front of the Fathers' apartments and the buildings facing the inner court. This mission's patio was at first only 127′ 4″ deep, exclusive of corridors. Proof of this statement is found in photographs taken before the "Serra Church" was restored, and in the spring of an arch still existing in the wall of a ruined room of the west wing of the quadrangle.

At San Gabriel, in 1804, a corridor was erected along the buildings of the

[68] O'Keefe, Fr. J. J., *The Buildings and Churches of the Mission of Santa Barbara*, 21.

main wing. These rooms included those intended for the Fathers' use, a granary, weaving room, carpentershop, pantry, and storeroom. They measured 125 varas (344 feet) in length and 13 varas (36 feet) in width.[69] This double row of build-ings extended from the sacristy of the present church to the building on the cor-ner of Mission Road and Santa Anita Street. Along its entire length stretched the above mentioned tile-roofed and brick-paved corridor giving added beauty and dignity to the whitewashed adobe buildings. The pillars which upheld the roof were substantially built of ladrillos laid in mortar. The houses for the sol-diers of the guard stood at the extreme southwest end of the row. In about 1865, Carleton E. Watkins made a photograph[70] of what remained of the sol-diers' quarters together with a portion of the west wing of the mission quad-rangle. The three remaining pillars of the front corridor are shown in this photo-graph, as are two huge gate posts of hewn timber. Frank Hannon, whose family came to San Gabriel in 1869, remembered the old gate posts which marked the former entrance to the inner court.

Watkins also made a photograph which, looking toward the west, included the last pillar, the street (now Mission Road), and little adobe houses of the village. The course of the open zanja which carried water to the Chapman mill is definitely marked in this picture. Coming east on Mission Road, the water-course turns abruptly at what is now Santa Anita Street and runs southward to join the masonry flume, part of which is still to be seen in the lot at the left of the Souvenir Shop. Both photographs mentioned above have been identified by several long-time residents of the little town.

The mission Indian village, according to Hugo Reid, consisted of four rows of double houses separated by three streets. The houses were of adobe and the roofs were tiled. The village is shown in Deppe's painting executed on the spot in 1832. This painting, long sought by the writer, is now preserved in the Santa Bárbara Mission Archives.

The arcade of the Fathers' casa at San Fernando was originally protected by a flat roof of planks covered with ladrillos. This building has undergone many changes. Begun in 1810, it was rearranged and renovated in 1819. In 1820, a flight of stairs was added to it and, in 1821, it was heightened and reroofed.[71] At this time, apparently, the roof of the building was extended over the corri-dor. The original height of the house is well defined in old photographs. The

---

[69] *Informe, Mission San Gabriel,* 1804. SBMA.

[70] Identified by a photograph found in the State Library, at Sacramento, and labeled "Old Adobe at Mission San Gabriel." No. 4448 Watkins New Series. According to Charles B. Turrill, Watkins' New Series included copies of the best of his earlier photographs.

[71] *Informes* of 1819, 1820, 1821. SBMA.

attic, or upper story, gained by the increase in height, provided a storeroom for corn and other products.

In 1822, the Padres announced the completion of this building. ("Se a [ha] concluido toda la fabrica de la casa de los PP⁵. y demas quartos inmediatos").[72] It had been twelve years in the building.

Old doors, window shutters, and ornamental wrought-iron grilles add to the interest of the building, but its unique feature is a small bell arch, constructed of ladrillos and mortar, that rises from the corridor roof at the extreme west end of the long structure. Bells, in mission days, hung in the tower or other bell-hanging attached to or near the church, one hung in front of the Padres' quarters, and another by the guardhouse. At San Fernando, the Padres occupied the center and eastern end of the building and their signal or call-bell would have hung suspended from a corridor beam near the sala or the Father Superior's room. The bell hanging in the arch at the western end of the building must, then, have been the corporal's.

There are six rooms in that part of the structure that are admirably suited to the housing of the escolta (the soldiers of the guard). They are definitely cut off from the rest of the rooms. The bell hung over what the writer believes was the corporal's quarters; soldiers occupied the three rooms at the back. Doors formerly gave entrance to both the front and back room at the west end of the building.[73] They, with the doors and windows in the south and north walls, provided ample means for observation in every direction. And that was one of the essential features of the guardhouse.

According to legend, the houses of the guards were located directly in front of San Fernando's church, but that arrangement probably existed during that period when the Padres had their living quarters in the wing adjoining the church tower, and before the Indian village was moved farther to the southwest of the establishment.

Outstanding among the pillared corridors of the missions is that of the Fathers' house at La Purísima. Restoration of this building and the beautiful chamfered pillars of the corridor, under the direction of Staff Architect Frederick C. Hageman, leaves little to be desired. The fluted corners of the pillars were produced by the use of specially molded ladrillos.

Round pillars supported the roof of the front corridor at San Luis Obispo.[74]

[72] *Informe* of 1822. SBMA.
[73] These doorways are now filled in, but they were open as late as 1912, when the writer examined the old building.
[74] At San Fernando there were two round pillars in front of the main entrance of the Fathers' house at its first location.

During the work of "modernizing" the old mission, in the 1880's, the loggia was removed. It was restored, in 1935, under Fr. Harnett's direction, but its pillars are not quite so sturdy as the original ones. That, however, is a matter that might possibly be remedied.

At Santa Clara, San José, San Francisco de Asís, San Rafael, and San Francisco Solano corridor roofs were, apparently, supported by pillars of wood.

The construction of the arcade of the Fathers' casa at San Antonio is said to have been the most nearly perfect of all. Contrary to what has been written about this mission, there were no arcaded corridors within the quadrangle. In 1815, the Padres report that to two sides of the patio formed by the four wings were attached two corridors with pillars of adobe, and partly of brick laid in mortar. In 1816, the two sides of the patio, which remained without corridors, were likewise protected; the pillars, however, were all of brick laid in mortar.[75] Tyler's photographs of 1889 show the roofs of the front and back corridors of the inner court resting directly on the pillars.

A custom that was followed in mission days, and one that helps to identify certain buildings, was that of adding corridors to the houses of the mayordomos and the soldiers of the guards. Moreover, those officials were given yards in which to set up ovens or other desired structures.

Other details that belong to the era of the master workers are the wonderful old chimneys of the pozoleras (kitchens) and the fountains with adjoining lavatories. Of the chimneys, San Juan Capistrano's alone remains and it is a most artistic and sound bit of construction. A photograph of 1876 shows the chimney at San Luis Rey to be in an excellent state of preservation. Other pictures taken, in all probability, at the same time give good details of its design. H. M. T. Powell indicates, in his sketches, chimneys at San Diego, San Luis Rey, San Juan Capistrano, and San Juan Bautista. Powell's sketches were not always complete because they were usually hastily drawn while he was "passing by" the missions on his way to the gold fields. But he never added a detail that wasn't there, so his drawings may be relied on. San Fernando's chimney stood until about 1870. Its cavernous top was protected with a tiled roof, openings at either end furnishing proper ventilation and outlet for smoke. Precedent for these chimneys is found in Grandmother Spain.

Few of the original fountains remain. There are two lavatories buried be-

---

[75] *Informe* 1815. ". . De los quatro liensos del patio se han echo do dos corredores con sus pilares de adove, y parte de ladrillo con mescla: . ."

Informe 1816. ". . Se han echo los 2 corredores del patio que quedaron sin hacer el año pasado, con sus pilares de ladrillo, y mescla. . ." SBMA.

neath the mud and debris at San Luis Rey and one fountain is found in what is called the Peyri courtyard. Formerly three fountains, or storage basins, stood in this patio. Two original fountains exist at San Fernando and one at Santa Bárbara. The fountain and lavatory built for the benefit of the Indians at San Buenaventura, those at San Francisco, Santa Cruz, San José, and other missions have disappeared entirely. At La Purísima one of the original lavatories was repaired and two fountains rebuilt.[76] It is known that there was a fountain in the patio of San Antonio. Two faithful old parishioners[77] marked its former location for Brother James (Hance), one-time, self-appointed guardian of the mission ruins.

These architectural details—the fountains, chimneys, and arches, the fluted columns, the wrought iron work and stone carvings, the molded ornamental tiles and other similar advanced works—have come down to us as symbols of the era that followed those first pioneer years, when the Padres were forced to consider only the essentials. They tell better than any written word of the progress made by the Indian workers, the builders of our missions.

[76] The three fountains at San Juan Capistrano were built during Fr. St. John O'Sullivan's pastorate. The fountain in front of San Luis Rey and that one in the forecourt at San Carlos were constructed within comparatively recent times. San Gabriel's fountain was built in 1941, under the direction of Fr. Raymond Catalán.
[77] José Antonio Gomez (Spaniard) and his Indian wife.

CHAPTER 12

Primitive Mills Used by our California Indians

Constructing and Operating the Mission Gristmills

ACCORDING TO the *Encyclopaedia Britannica*, "the ancestor of the millstone was apparently a rounded stone about the size of a man's fist, with which grain or nuts were pounded and crushed into rude meal. These stones were generally of hard sandstone and were evidently used against another stone, which by dint of continual hammering was broken into hollows."[1] Such was indeed the beginning of the mortar and pestle used by primitive peoples the world over. But the writer has always cherished the imagery of old Og-of-the-sore-tooth being the inventor of this first gristmill. Old and lame he sat day by day beside his cave and, seeking a less painful way of cracking his nuts than by crushing them between his teeth, he laid one on the boulder beside him and struck it with a small stone held in his right hand. Delighted with the result, he repeated this performance every day thereafter. In time the boulder was hollowed out and eventually it became necessary for Og to use a longer stone to reach the bottom of the hollow. And thus the mortar and pestle came into being.

After the mortar and pestle, according to men learned in these matters, came the metate, saddle stone, or mealing stone, as it is variously called in different parts of the world. In New Mexican pueblos and ancient cliff dwellings the metates were smooth stone slabs which were set at a slight tilt and securely mortared in bins, usually in a battery of three. Indian girls knelt behind the bins and ground the grain on the slabs by means of long, square-edged stones which were laid crosswise on the slab and thrust forward and back. Castañeda, who entered New Mexico in 1540, described the operation thus:

Where they grind the meal, it is an apartment or closet with a trough and three stones are fast-

[1] *Encyclopaedia Britannica* (Eleventh Edition), X. 548.

ened by mortar [mud] where three women enter, each one [goes] to her stone, one crushes, another grinds, and the third grinds it still finer. Before they enter, they bare their feet at the door, fasten their hair, shake their clothes, and cover their heads. While they grind, there is a man seated at the door who plays on a bagpipe and they grind to the measure [rhythm] of the sound and sing at three voices.[2]

An apartment similar to the above with metates set in a bin may still be seen in a cliff dwelling known as Cliff Palace, in Mesa Verde National Park, Colorado. With Castañeda's description in mind it is not difficult to conjure up the scene so vividly described by that explorer.

The Navajo Indians use this same type of metate today. It is not, however, set in mortar as was the Pueblo stone. Instead, a sheepskin is laid on the ground skin side up, the grinding slab is set on the skin and held at the proper slant by means of a wedge-shaped stone placed under its upper end. The Indian girl kneels behind the stone and grinds the corn, using a long, square-edged mano, or hand stone, as did the Pueblo girls of Castañeda's time, the corn meal falling onto the sheepskin instead of being caught in a bin. The depression worn in this metate shows plainly the type of mano used. This mano was employed by the California Indians, particularly those of the southern part of the State, to whom it may have come from the Pueblo Indians or from México.

Another type of hand stone used by our Indians was an oval-shaped one that fitted into the palm of the hand and was employed with a circular motion. As with the type described above, the women knelt behind the metate at its upraised end and ground the seeds on its surface, using, however, a circular motion with the oval-shaped mano instead of the forward and back thrusting motion employed with the long, square-edged one. The latter mano required the use of both hands; the former, of but one.

Metates upon which the oval-shaped mano had been employed came, in time, to have elliptical cavities in their surfaces. The two types are easily distinguishable. Both were used by the California Indians and are to be found in numerous museums and relic rooms.

According to orderly procedure in milling operations, the metate should have been followed by the quern which has been called the direct ancestor of the millstone. But the quern as such was not known in California.[3] It came into use after 1800 in the form of the tahona and will be described later.

Milling devices in California apparently followed no book of rules. "The mor-

---

[2] Bandelier, *Documentary History*, 175.
[3] There is a quern at the Junípero Serra Museum, on Presidio Hill, North San Diego, brought in from another state or country.

tar," Dr. A. L. Kroeber notes,[4] "is found practically everywhere in California." There are mortars of wood and of stone. There are single mortars of various sizes, some left rough and unfinished on the outside and some beautifully finished and ornamented, according to their intended use. And, there are, especially in the central and southern part of the state, community stones with from ten to thirty mortar holes in their surfaces. Examples of these latter may be found near Santa Isabel, in San Diego County; one near Hemet in Riverside County; in Yosemite National Park, and in numerous other places where oak trees abound. Writing in 1918, Dr. Merriam says:

These ancient grinding mills in hard granite rock are common on the middle and lower slopes of the Sierra Nevada of California and some of them have as many as 20 or 30 mortar holes. The pestles are large and heavy with smoothly rounded striking ends and are held in both hands; . . When pounding acorns, several women usually work together, sitting at neighboring holes and singing in rhythm with the strokes of the pestles.[5]

"The metate or grinding slab," Dr. Kroeber notes, "seems to have come in about as the mortar went out of use."[6] Such was the opinion of those who had studied the question up to the years 1925-1927. At that time David Banks Rogers, of the Santa Bárbara Museum of Natural History, headed the work of excavating ancient Indian village sites along the Santa Bárbara Channel. During those investigations it was determined that two different peoples had occupied that region before the Canaliños, the Indians seen and described by Cabrillo in 1542, and again by the expeditionary forces of 1769.

The first inhabitants Mr. Rogers calls the "Oak Grove People," and the second the "Hunting People." Then came the Canaliños. Among the artifacts left by the Oak Grove People were "massive uncouth metates, or mealing stones, interspersed with numerous manos or handstones." In describing the metates, Mr. Rogers writes: "All are cumbersome and heavy. Occasionally some of the unusually large size are found, and we sometimes find rather small specimens, but the large majority conform very closely to one size. The dimensions are approximately as follows: eighteen inches in length, fourteen inches in breadth, five to six inches in height. The manos are rather more uniform in size, since they had to conform to the grasp of the miller's hand. An average size would be about five inches in length, three and one-half inches in breadth, and two inches in thickness."

"The cavity in the metate is very uniform in shape and size, being restricted

[4] Kroeber, *Handbook*, 926.
[5] Merriam, Dr. C. Hart, "The Acorn, a possibly Neglected Source of Food." *Nat Geog.*, August, 1918.
[6] Kroeber, *Handbook*, 926.

to the sweep of the hand when the miller is in a stooping posture. This produced in nearly every instance, either an elliptical or an oval depression, about thirteen inches long by nine inches wide, the depth depending upon the length of time the mill had been in use."

". . . Near the very close of this epoch crude mortars and pestles that have been used from the first as such, are occasionally found, but this people [Oak Grove] continued to depend largely upon the metate to the very end of their existence. The metate then drops from use, never again to function in this region until re-introduced, in a different form by the Mexicans of recent times."[7]

Added to Mr. Rogers' findings are those made in 1938 at Borax "Lake" near Clear Lake, California, by a party working under the direction of Mark R. Harrington, Curator of the Southwest Museum at Los Angeles. There, were uncovered two ancient metates that experts say are more than 10,000 years old. One grinding stone, "a crude two-faced metate," was found in place at fifty-six inches below surface, and the other, "a crude thin slab of stone with a shallow grinding cavity on one side," was found in place at four feet seven inches. The depressions in these metates were elliptical, showing that an oval-shaped mano had been employed in grinding the seeds. A mortar and pestle were also uncovered at this site, but they were considered of much more recent origin.[8]

As has already been noted in Costansó's account, the explorers of 1769 found the Indians of the Santa Bárbara Channel grinding seeds "in mills or stone mortars," the commonly accepted first mill.

As the missions were founded and the Indians persuaded to build their huts near those establishments, they undoubtedly took with them their utensils and other belongings. Never, it seems, did they part with their mortars and pestles, their metates, and manos, their comales, carrying nets, burden baskets, seed-beaters, water-bottles, storage jars and baskets, and other useful and beautiful articles. In fact, it is known from record, correspondence, and diary that those utensils and tools played their part in mission-day Indian life. Especially was this true during those first lean years when, as the Padres write, the Indians took their burden baskets and other necessary equipment and went into the hills to gather seeds to keep the little communities from starving. This happened not once but many times. Moreover, the Indians' native utensils for the gathering, storing, and preparation of articles of food, fitted very well into the industrial life of the missions.

---

[7] Rogers, *Prehistoric Man*, 351-352. See also Preface, xvii; pp. 342-419.
[8] See "The Folsom Man in California"; "Pre-Folsom Man in California" and "The Age of the Borax Lake Finds," by M. R. Harrington, in *The Masterkey*, July, Sept., 1938, and Nov., 1939. Southwest Museum Publications.

With the coming of the Spaniards there appeared in California a third type of metate, the Mexican three-legged one. Among those goods which were sent, in 1777, to supply the new mission of Santa Clara were six metates with their hand stones ("Seis metates con sus manos, los quatros comprados, y dos limosna").[9] These manos were the long square-edged ones. This type of mill as well as the native one seems to have continued in use throughout the mission period. As did the mortar and pestle. Very good examples of the three-legged metate are to be found in the Bowers Memorial Museum, at Santa Ana, and in the mission museums at Santa Bárbara, San Miguel, and Sonoma.

The next type of mill to be operated in California was the one presented, in 1786, to the Fathers of San Carlos del Carmelo by the Frenchman, M. de Langle, who, with La Pérouse, was making a tour of the world in the interest of science. Anchoring their vessels in the Bay of Monterey, the explorers visited the near-by mission. M. de Langle was so impressed with the tediousness of the Indian women's task of grinding grain on the metate that he gave the missionaries his own mill, by means of which "four women would in one day perform the work of a hundred."[10] This mill, according to Guadalupe Vallejo, was an iron one.[11] Little has been said about it and it has been generally thought that it was discarded. This assumption, however, may be erroneous. In the inventory, taken in 1834, at Mission Santa Bárbara, three iron mills are listed. One was good and of a large size ("1 bueno grande de Fierro de molino"). What these mills were intended to grind is not stated. It may have been chocolate or coffee and it may have been corn or grain. Unfortunately, they seem to have disappeared completely.

With mortars and pestles, metates and manos, and with M. de Langle's iron mill, the Indian women ground the grain and corn for the various mission families until 1796, when the first water-power gristmill to be erected in California was built at Mission Santa Cruz. Artisans necessary for this undertaking had come to California in 1790-1795. Bancroft says: "In March [year not given] artisans were sent to build the mill and instruct the natives. In August a smith and miller were sent to start the mill . . A house for the mill was also built and four millstones were ordered made at Santa Cruz for San Carlos.[12] In the autumn of 1796 the mill began to run but was damaged by the rains of December."[13] It is said that Vancouver gave this mission $1,000 with which to build its mill be-

[9] *Informe de Mision de Santa Clara*, 1777. SBMA.
[10] Banc., *Hist. of Cal.*, 1. 431.
[11] Vallejo, Guadalupe, "Ranch and Mission Days."
[12] Torchiana, *Mission Santa Cruz*, 194, says: "Flour mill stones were ordered made for Santa Cruz at San Carlos." That is more logical since the master stone cutters were then busily engaged at the latter mission.
[13] Banc. *Hist of Cal.*, 1. 496-7.

sides leaving on the shore $505 worth of iron-ware.[14] Erected probably on the banks of the San Lorenzo River, no trace of this mission's mill remains though Guadalupe Vallejo, writing in 1890, refers to it as being "very picturesque."

A miller, a smith, and a carpenter of the king's artisans were sent to San Luis Obispo, in 1794, to build a water-power mill and instruct the Indians. The mill was finished early in 1798 and was the second to be built in California.[15] It was constructed by the San Luis Creek on the spot where the "White House" now stands. Its ruins were uncovered in 1869 when San Luis Obispo's first brick building was erected. Neil O'Leary, who built the "White House" in "about 1912," says that at that time one millstone was still lying by the creek. This old mill, he told the writer, "had a fine stone floor." This was the mill seen by Duflot de Mofras when he visited the mission in 1841, and of which he said: "In front of the buildings runs the little stream San Luis which affords water power for a fine mill, and serves to irrigate extensive gardens, vineyards, and orchards."[16]

As was noted in Chapter VIII, another water-power mill was built at this mission in 1805. The water which furnished its motive power came from a reservoir constructed at the same time. Both stood at the rear of the quadrangle. The ruins of these structures have never been excavated, though portions of their masonry walls are still visible.

California's fourth water-power gristmill was built, in 1806, at Mission San Antonio. To provide power for its operation, water had been taken out from the stream now known as Mission Creek and brought in an open masonry aqueduct to the reservoir lying just east of the mission orchard. There it was stored until needed, when it was let, by means of a gate, into a ditch which crossed through the Indian village and joined a masonry channel, or race, which led to a funnel-shaped forebay built at one side of the mill. This mill house was two-storied, the lower chamber housing the wheel and the upper one the millstones and a store-room. The water entered the wheel room through a clay pipe, inserted at the bottom of the forebay, and spouted against the buckets, or vanes, of the wheel causing it to revolve. The upper stone, or runner, turned with the wheel. This operation will be explained more fully in describing the mill at Santa Bárbara.

The funnel-shaped forebay still exists at San Antonio, though slightly damaged; the wheel-chamber yet stands as does a portion of an adobe wall of the mill-room above. It would not be too difficult a task to restore the whole structure, thus furnishing an excellent example of a mission water-power mill built under

[14] *Ibidem*, 512, note 20, 526.
[15] Banc., *Hist. of Cal.*, 1. 690.
[16] Engelhardt, *Mission San Luis Obispo*, 141.

the direction of Spanish artisans. Unless damage has been done it within recent years, the aqueduct carrying water to the mill is still serviceable.

This writer has found no record of a water-power gristmill having been built at Santa Clara. However, Vancouver was shown "a ponderous black stone which was to be used for building and for millstones as soon as any one could be found capable of working it."[17] That a mill of some sort was eventually built at this mission is attested to by the fact that, in 1924, a millstone, declared to have come from Santa Clara, was found set in the lawn in front of the De Young Museum, in Golden Gate Park, San Francisco.

Mission San José's water-power mill was built in 1820, and stood beside the creek that bordered the mission establishment on the left. The building is listed in the inventory of 1837 as being eight varas square and housing a mill whose wheel was seven feet (7 pies) in diameter. Attached to the mill, or at least as part of the arrangement, a dwelling seven varas by six varas in size had been erected for the miller.[18]

According to an elderly German resident, Mr. Joseph Sunderer, who came to San José before 1868, the mill building was not damaged by the earthquake of that year, but continued in use for a number of years thereafter, furnishing a bakery established in the little settlement with sufficient flour to carry on a flourishing business. After the earthquake, Mr. Sunderer told the writer, the road to the mill was paved with broken tiles from the mission buildings.

A water-power mill was built at Santa Inés also in 1820. This mill was to grind both wheat and maize (Indian corn).[19] Clearly this was the mill built under the direction of Joseph Chapman, the Yankee from Boston, who, as a member[20] of Bouchard's pirate gang, had been taken prisoner by the military at Monterey. Set to work at Mission Santa Inés in 1820-1821,[21] he engineered the erection of a gristmill for the mission Padres. Being a New Englander, he naturally designed a New England type mill. The fact that this mill would grind both corn and wheat differentiates it from the Spanish type mill which was not adjustable for the grinding of different grists.

In September of 1821, Chapman was ordered by Governor Solá "to build a mill at S. Gabriel like that he had built at Sta Inés."[22] In the meantime another

---

[17] Vancouver, *Voyage*, II. 35.

[18] "1 pieza que contiene un molino de agua util de 8 varas en cuadro, una habitacion para el molinero de 7 varas largo 6 de ancho ambas con pared de adove, cubierta de teja, el molino con rodesno de 7 pies de diametro con todas uts [útiles] necesarios." SBMA.

[19] ". . , y se ha hecho un Molino de agua razonable, pª [para] moler trigo, Maiz etc. cuya fabrica es de cal y piedra, tiene 7 varas de largo y 5 v. de ancho y techado con texa." SBMA.

[20] According to his own statement, Chapman was shanghaied by Bouchard.

[21] Banc., *Hist of Cal.*, 2. 568, note 27.

[22] *Ibidem.*

gristmill had been started, in 1820, at San Gabriel. There has been much need-less controversy over this mission's two mills—the one known as "El Molino," still standing in San Marino, though remodeled for a residence, and the other, until 1941, in ruins just south of the mission church and across the railroad tracks.

It has been claimed by many writers and others that "El Molino" was built "about 1810" and was damaged by the earthquake of 1812. But the San Gabriel Mission *informes* do not record the building of any water-power gristmill until 1820, when the Padres report the beginning of two mills, one of water-power for grinding flour and the other for making oil.[23] In 1823, they report the completion of a mill for grinding wheat.[24] And, in 1825, another mill for grinding grain and one for sawing wood are reported completed. Both were water-powered.[25]

It is certain that Chapman could not have built the mill begun in 1820, since he was at that time constructing one for the Padres of Santa Inés. Nor would he have erected a mill of Spanish design. "El Molino" has long been known to have been of Spanish construction and, according to testimony taken in 1894, while many who knew the facts about the old mill were yet living, was built under the direction of Claudio López, famous mayordomo of that mission.[26]

San Gabriel records do not state when the second mill was begun but it seems evident that Chapman could not have started its construction until sometime late in 1822, at least. To begin with, its building involved the erection of a stone dam at the lower end of a ciénega (tule bog) that lay between "El Molino" and the mission,[27] as well as the setting up of a sawmill. Moreover, at this time Chapman appears to have been kept very busy with personal and other affairs such as being baptized at San Buenaventura June 24, 1822, marrying, during that same year, Guadalupe Ortega at Santa Inés, to say nothing of helping to get out timbers for the church of the pueblo of Los Angeles. Ay de mí, qué hombre! As a matter of fact, he was very ingenious, as Bancroft tells us, and soon became a great favorite with the Padres, for whom he performed many difficult tasks, and from whom, as Harrison Rogers naïvely states, he got many favors in return.[28]

Writing about Chapman, Robinson notes that "from his long residence [in California] he had acquired a mongrel language; English, Spanish, and Indian be-

[23] *Informe*, 1820. "Se han comenzada dos molinos, una de agua para [h]arina, y otro para aseite [aceite] y ambas estan adelantados."
[24] *Informe* 1823. "Se concluyó tambien un molino para moler trigo."
[25] *Informe*, 1825. "Se concluyó un molino de mies, y otro para serrar madera, los dos de agua."
The above records were copied from originals in SBMA.
[26] Reid, Dr. Hiram A., *History of Pasadena*, 43, 50-51.
[27] Water from near-by canyons had from time immemorial been collecting at this spot and had formed a lagoon there. After El Molino was built water from its wheel was allowed to flow into the pond, later known as Wilson Lake.
[28] Rogers, Harrison, "Journal," 213, 214, 215.

ing so intermingled in his speech, that it was difficult to understand him. . . Father Sanchez of St. [San] Gabriel used to say that Chapman could get more work out of the Indians in his unintelligible tongue than all the mayordomos put together."[29] And it was the Indians, working under Chapman's direction, who actually built the dam, the sawmill, and the mill.

In 1827, Duhaut-Cilly visited Mission Santa Bárbara and watched Fr. Antonio Ripoll direct workers in the building of a gristmill, the ruins of which still stand with its adjoining reservoir. This mill and all others previously mentioned, save the two built under the supervision of Joseph Chapman, the Bostonian, were of typical Spanish construction. And, bearing in mind Spain's reputation for clinging to methods and customs centuries old, the writer believes that a description of a typical mill will, with slight variations, serve for all.

There is still left in the ruins of the mill at Santa Bárbara much that helps to explain its operation. In 1937, several of the Franciscan Fathers at the mission made a rather complete investigation of the ancient water system. At that time the mill ruins were excavated; the floor of the wheel-chamber was cleared of debris and swept clean. Measurements were made and photographs taken. Through the courtesy of Fr. Eric O'Brien and Fr. Maynard Geiger, the writer was given access to those records.

The findings of these Fathers then, together with the writer's own investigations, measurements, etc.; Duhaut-Cilly's account of the mill[30] and its description in the inventory of 1834;[31] William Rich Hutton's sketch of the "Santa Bárbara Mission Water Works in 1847";[32] the description, in the inventory of 1837, of Mission San José's molino de agua;[33] the Sandham sketch of the water-wheel in the ruined wheel-chamber at Mission San Antonio;[34] Dr. Hiram Reid's description of "El Molino" at San Marino; the writer's personal investigation of a Spanish type gristmill over one hundred years old and still in operation in New Mexico;[35] the study of millstones in mission museums and elsewhere—these form the basis for the following reconstruction of an old water-power mill that once ground grain to feed the mission neophytes.

There is so much of interest in Duhaut-Cilly's description that it seems best to quote it in full:

The project completely engrossing him [Padre Ripoll] at this time was a water-mill he was hav-

[29] Robinson, *Life in Cal.*, 111-112.
[30] Duhaut-Cilly, "Account," 160-161.
[31] SBMA.
[32] Hutton, Wm. Rich, *California Drawings*, Pl. XIV.
[33] SBMA.
[34] Jackson, H. H., *Glimpses of California and the Missions*, 32.
[35] See Illustration, "A Spanish mill in New Mexico."

ing built at the foot of a hill to the right of the mission. The water brought for more than two leagues by a canal following the sides of the mountains, was to fall from a height of about twenty feet upon the buckets of a wheel.[36] The fall of this motive power was not vertical; it worked at an angle of about 35 degrees; the wheel also, instead of being vertical, was horizontal; it was a full circle, upon whose plane were arranged, like spokes, a sort of large, slightly concave spoons, which were to receive one after another, the impulse and transmit the movement.

At first glance I was surprised that the padre, a man of judgment, should have preferred to have the fall inclined, when it was so easy for him, in cutting a hill to a steeper slope, to make it much more powerful; for without being a hydro-statistician, I readily perceived that his motive power lost the more of its force, the farther was it inclined from the vertical. But before expressing my opinion, reflection brought me back to the inventor's idea; and I believed that I saw that whatever motive power he lost at first, he gained it from another side, in avoiding the friction from two sets of cog-wheels, since the turning grindstones would be fixed upon the axle of the wheel.

Another objection also can be made, in regard to the speed of rotation; for in this plan it is the same for both wheel and grindstone, while in our ordinary combination, the speed of the grind-stone increases in the relation of the radius of the wheel to the radius of the axle-hub. Besides, Fray Antonio's workmen being little skilled in mechanics, he avoided many imperfections by simplifying the machinery, and I had no doubt of the complete success of the undertaking. I brought to his attention, however, the fact that the quality of the stone he used for his grind-stones, being made from the same stone was not suitable; because being entirely composed of almost homogeneous parts, and of equal hardness, it would grow smooth too quickly.

According to the inventory, taken seven years after Duhaut-Cilly's visit, the mill was of stone masonry. It was twelve varas[37] square, its roof was of tile, and its floor half ladrillos and half wood. It had one door and two windows. The windows were in that end of the building that faces the mission, while the door pierced the south wall and had perhaps a stone step or two leading up to it. It was a two-storied structure rather curiously arranged. The lower floor was divided in two by a masonry wall. On the north side of this wall was the wheel-chamber, a narrow stone-walled channel with slightly concave, stone-paved floor. The space on the other side of the stone wall was dirt-filled to the floor of the second story.

Heavy oaken beams spanned the wheel-chamber at two different levels and rested upon the earth fill of the other half of the lower floor. The beams crossing the eastern end of the wheel-room were embedded in the north wall at a height of 5′ 10″ above the floor level. There were four of these beams set 5′, 4′ 4″, and 6′ 8″ apart. The beams spanning the western half of the wheel-room were seven in number, one foot square, and set three feet apart. They lay a little short of four feet above floor level. Consequently, the west half of the second story was lower than the east half. Seven steps of masonry construction led down, from near the junction of the two floor levels, into the wheel-chamber.

Planks laid on the beams described above formed the floor of the upper story.

[36] Duhaut-Cilly errs here. The water did not fall from such height.
[37] See Chapter VIII, note 5.

Ladrillos were laid on half of the floor. The mill wheel stood in the east end of the channel with the millstones directly above it on the upper floor.

The mill reservoir, in which water was stored for the operation of the mill, is a many-sided masonry structure which was paved with ladrillos and plastered with the pinkish cement found on most mission reservoirs, fountains, and other structures pertaining to the water systems. The mill adjoins it on the west and their combined walls make one of nine feet in thickness. Piercing this wall at the reservoir floor level is the penstock through which the impounded water escaped to turn the wheel in the adjoining chamber.

The penstock is the work of a stone mason,[38] its walls and ceiling being fashioned of cut stone slabs, its floor of ladrillos. At the inlet the sluiceway is 6' high and 4' wide. It was fitted with a gate which was raised and lowered as needed, the gate sliding in grooves cut in stone buttresses set at each side of the opening. The sluiceway is 8' 10" long and terminates in a stone block about 2' square and 6½" thick. A circular opening 18½" in diameter on the inner side and 17" on the mill side is cut through the center of the stone. A clay pipe, specially molded, was inserted in the circular opening and through it the water spouted at an angle of about 35 degrees from the horizontal against the buckets, or vanes of the wheel. The spouting stream of water struck the vanes with considerable force, causing the wheel to revolve.[39] The outlet from the wheel-chamber is a vertical rectangular opening, 9" x 17" in size, cut through the west wall at about 12" above the floor level. Three one-inch iron bars are set in the opening.

The millwheel, probably about six feet in diameter, was of very simple construction. If built like that one at San Antonio, it was composed of two wooden circles, or rims—one large and one small—several spokes, and a number of vanes, buckets, or as Duhaut-Cilly describes them, "slightly concave spoons." There was no hub as we know it. The short spokes were mortised directly into the shaft. The other ends of the spokes were attached to or mortised into the small, inner circle. The vanes were tenoned and mortised in between the inner circle and the outer rim. They were set at a slant to receive the full force of the spouting water. The wooden rims were about nine inches deep and three inches thick.

The shaft, or spindle, by means of which both the wheel and the upper stone,

---

[38] Possibly José Antonio Ramírez, though probably an Indian. There is no reason to suppose that the Indians who were capable of doing the fine stone work to be seen in our museums today were not equally capable, under instruction, of fashioning the stone parts of a mill. Duhaut-Cilly, it will be remembered, mentioned no artisan assisting Fr. Ripoll.

[39] Most of the water-power mills of that day were quite low powered. Mr. Paul Dalidet, of San Luis Obispo, says that his grandfather's mill built beside the San Luis Creek in after-mission days, did not grind more than a barrel of flour a day.

or runner, were turned, was a wooden one either square, octagonal, or round with iron fittings at each end. Its lower end was fitted with a rounded pintle, or toe, which turned in a bearing, or step, hollowed out to accommodate it. This step—usually a stone block eight or ten inches high and twenty to twenty-four inches square—was set on the floor of the wheel-chamber. Since the floor of the Santa Bárbara wheel-chamber was concave, the step there was of necessity cut to fits its concavity.

The top end of the shaft terminated in an iron rod which passed through the vertical bearing set in the ceiling of the wheel-room and extended on up through the eye (center hole) of the lower millstone seated on a base built up for it on the floor directly above the millwheel. The upper rounded end of the rod, or cock-head, fitted into a recessed rynd, or cockeye, having two extending flanges.[40] The rynd was of iron and was secured to the iron rod by bolt. The extending flanges fitted into depressions cut into the upper millstone on its under surface, and supported it at just the proper distance above the lower stone. The flanges lay level with the face of the stone. The running-stone was kept in place by its own weight and was driven by the flanges. The lower, or bed stone, was stationary.

The cockhead and cockeye, or cup-like portion of the rynd into which the cockhead fitted, extended up into the eye of the upper stone but did not fill its space; channels between the flanges were left open for the flow of grain from the hopper to the grinding spaces between the two stones.

As indicated above and contrary to widespread belief, the upper stone did not rest on the bed stone. Had it done so the stones would have bound, become clogged, and the heavy, rotating stone would have been almost impossible to move. Instead, the runner was balanced upon the supporting flanges at the carefully calculated distance above the bed stone for the grinding of either corn or wheat. It seems certain that the mission mills were not capable of adjustment for the grinding of both grains.

The foundation, or base, upon which the bed stone was seated, was constructed of "rammed earth" or of adobe bricks laid in mud mortar. It was a structure about four feet square, knee-high, and was built around a core of molded ladrillos or stone blocks having a circular opening cut through their centers for the passage of the iron rod of the shaft. Upon this base, in a thick layer of mud mortar, the bed stone was laid, the eye of the stone being directly in line

[40] At the University of Santa Clara (built on the old mission grounds) there is a millstone showing the use of a four-flanged rynd. Jesuit Fathers, however, believe that the stone came from a mill built in about 1870 on the site of the present Science Building.

with the bore of the stone blocks. The millstone was leveled in the bed of mud.

The shaft was then aligned. This could have been accomplished by dropping a plumb line down from the exact center of the eye of the bed stone to the bearing, or step, in the wheel-channel below, and in which the shaft turned. Any necessary adjustment would have been made by moving the step.

A wooden curb was set in around the top of the millstone base, forming a bin for the collection of the meal or flour discharged from the grinding stones. The base, top and sides were then covered with a smooth cement or mud plaster, the surface being worked while wet to the smoothness of glass.[41] With the mill in New Mexico this glass-like plaster was carried up to the top surface of the bed stone. Flour falling over the edge of the bed stone was periodically gathered up from the bin and emptied into bags or large earthen jars to be stored until needed.

A bush, consisting of a hollow iron tube, was fitted in the eye of the bed stone and set by means of wooden wedges driven in between the tube and the stone. A copper or iron plate covered the wedges on top and fitted nicely around the spindle. Under this plate hempen twine, or other cord, was wound around the neck of the spindle to prevent dust and grain from entering the shaft housing. The bush plate lay a little below the level of the surface of the bed stone.

The neck of the spindle was greased with oil, tallow, or lard. This was probably accomplished by raising the runner from its position on the flanges of the rynd by means of block and tackle attached to overhead beams, removing the bush plate, and pouring oil or grease onto the cord around the spindle neck. The plate was then replaced and the stone let down. When it became necessary to make repairs on the millwheel, it was also raised by means of block and tackle. There is, in fact, nothing in the history of these mills to indicate that either stones or wheels were raised or lowered by any other mechanical device. Nothing, in fact, seems to have been added to the working parts of the mission mills that was not absolutely necessary to their operation.

The toe of the shaft of the Santa Bárbara mill required no lubrication as the step in which it turned was constantly immersed in water, the lower edge of the wheel-channel's outlet being about a foot above floor level, as has been previously noted.

It is not possible to determine, at this late date, if the bearing on the floor of Mission San Antonio's wheel-chamber was so kept covered with water. The outlet end of the wheel-channel there has been non-existent since 1882, at least. It

---

[41] This was accomplished, while the plaster was still wet, by smoothing with a small stone constantly dipped in water just as potters, using the old "pat and anvil" method, smooth their pottery.

is quite possible that this wheel-room was always open. It was merely an arched channel in the basement, or lower story, of the mill and may have terminated in a large, open-arched doorway.[42] At any rate the keeping of standing water in the wheel-room would not have been necessary since the spouting and splashing of water upon the open wheel would have kept the bearing wet. And again, the bearing may have been seated *in* the floor; in which event water would have flowed over it while the mill was in operation. This, apparently, was the case at "El Molino."[43] It is such minor differences that make the study of these old mills so fascinating.

It is in San Antonio's wheel-room that we see evidence of the Spanish version of the "bridge-tree." Those who have investigated this mill will remember that a continuous arched recess is let into the walls and ceiling of the wheel-channel.[44] At one time heavy oaken timbers filled this recess, coming together at the top to hold securely in place the vertical stone bearing through which the wheelshaft passed to the grinding room above. This bearing kept the shaft in its proper upright position. There was a similar arrangement in the wheel-chamber of San Gabriel's Spanish mill.[45]

A description of these water-power mills would not be complete without further mention of the hopper and the millstones, from which so much may be learned about the operation of the mills.

If one were to search the world over he would not find a hopper more in keeping with mission mill construction than is the one found hanging in that aforementioned mill-room in New Mexico. About three feet square at the top, it hung like an inverted pyramid a little to one side and above the millstones. Corn, emptied into the hopper, spilled its way through an opening at the bottom point, into a small wooden flume attached to the hopper just under its outlet. The flume, in turn, emptied into an improvised funnel set in the eye of the upper stone. The flow of corn was controlled by an ingeniously devised contrivance. A stick of wood, having a small bola-like stone attached to one end, was suspended over the millstone by means of leather thongs and a wire. The stone attached to the stick rested against the arm of a support for the flume. The other end of the stick touched the upper millstone. As the millstone revolved the stick bounced and the stone attached to its upper end tapped the flume, inducing the flow of corn from hopper to flume and on into the funnel of the feeding hole. As the speed of

[42] See Reid, *opus cit.*, 392, for sketch of "El Molino" showing arched doorways, once open.
[43] But not at Santa Bárbara where Franciscan Fathers, in 1937, found no trace of bearing and the floor undisturbed.
[44] See Sandam's sketch.
[45] Reid, *opus cit.*, 393. Dr. Reid errs, however, in stating that the timbers were to support the waterwheel.

the millstone was increased so was the bouncing of the stick, and the tapping of the stone against the flume; the knocking of the flume against the hopper was accelerated, thereby increasing the flow of corn to the grinding space between the two stones. A true hopper it is and others of its kind may well have hung suspended from beams or rafters over the millstones in California mission mills.

The millstones used in mission days were mostly of granite or volcanic rock. Using the stone cutters' tools sent up from México, Indians were taught to fashion them. Some of these stones are still to be found along the old Camino Real. Some have served as doorsteps and horse-blocks. In the cemetery at Pacific Grove, on the Monterey peninsula, two are found set up as headstones. At Mission Santa Inés one is wedged under the base of a corridor pillar to keep it from toppling over, while another lies half-buried in the debris and crumbled walls of the one-time temporary church. At San Antonio two discarded stones became community mortar stones for after-mission-day Indians. Some are in mission and other museums. In size, those in existence today range from 2½' to 3' 9" in diameter and from 7" to about 12" in thickness. There were stones for the water-power mills and stones for the tahonas (mills run by animal power), each type bearing its peculiar identifying mark.

The runner, or upper stone, of the mission water-power mill has cut in its under surface a depression into which the flanges of the rynd fitted. This depression begins at the margin of the eye and extends toward the outer edge of the stone. The eye of this type of stone is usually 5" in diameter. Grain or corn was fed through the eye.

The eye of the tahona stone is much smaller than that of the water-power millstone. There is no depression for extending flanges, the tahona stone being driven differently. Grain was not fed through the eye, the feeding hole being cut through the stone at a little distance from the center.

The running stones and a few of the bed stones were "dressed." That is, grooves were cut in the faces of the stones. These grooves are known as "furrows" and the spaces between the furrows are called "lands." The lands are the true grinding surfaces. According to Prof. B. W. Dedrick, formerly instructor in milling at Pennsylvania State College and author of a book on that subject:

The furrows answer a threefold purpose—that of distribution, ventilation and cutting or breaking, or preparatory grinding, . . Were there no furrows in a stone, it would crush to some extent and discharge readily enough, owing to centrifugal motion, if the stones were kept at considerable distance apart, as in the breaking of corn into four or five pieces; but in letting the stone approach near enough to grind fine, as into meal, while, owing to centrifugal motion, the stone would still have a tendency to discharge in a feeble manner, it would soon crowd and clog, especially near the eye where the centrifugal motion is about one third that at the skirt [outer edge]. The ultimate result would be that, in attempting to grind, the crowding at the eye or in the bosom would tend to lift the stone, overcoming the pressure of the buhr, creating great fric-tional resistance, heat and moisture and "pasting" the stone.

One has only to let the furrow in a stone become so worn down as to be almost obliterated to note the difference, in the work and capacity of a buhr. Compare the difference, when a stone is freshly and nicely furrowed, grinding cool, with increased capacity and less power, with one whose furrows are almost out, grinding hot, uneven, and consuming or wasting power, and that with greatly decreased capacity, and we note the importance of the furrow, and can appreciate its threefold purpose and duty. . .

The greatest skill in milling in those days was the ability of the miller to keep his stones in order, and he who could not do so was a failure. It took three or four years' practice and experi-ence to become a miller, and a greater part of his time was devoted to the stone, acquiring skill in dressing and handling it.[46]

The mission water-power mills seem to have fallen into disuse at a very early period.[47] This was probably due to the fact that the skilled Indian workers left the missions during the upheaval that followed their secularization. And while there were, in all probability, several Spanish stonecutters, capable of caring for stones, still in California, it is not likely that they would have been employed at the missions during those chaotic days. And so the millstones were neglected, in time the wheels ceased to turn and eventually fell to pieces. Today there is left naught but dry aqueducts and empty reservoirs, ruins, and outer walls of buildings, and one mill remodeled to serve as a residence, to remind us of the rushing, splashing water, the creaking and groaning millwheels. Gone are the busy Indians who felled the trees, hauled and hewed the logs; collected the stones and made the ladrillos and tiles; built the mills and reservoirs and laid the aqueducts to carry water to them; fed and tended the grinding stones; scooped up, sacked and stored the grist.

The tahonas were of much more simple construction than the water-power mills and one would, therefore, have expected to find them set up before the latter. Such, however, was not the case in California, where the building of water-power mills is recorded first. It would appear that all the missions, even those which had mills powered by water, possessed one or more tahonas. These may have been auxiliary mills or they may have been for grinding different grists. Mission San Antonio, for example, after having built a water-power mill in 1806, built a horse-power mill for grinding wheat in 1810.[48] San Francisco is reported by visitors of 1816 to have had two mills operated by mules.[49] Mis-

---

[46] Dedrick, Prof. B. W., *Practical Milling*, 263, 264-5.

[47] Santa Bárbara's mill, built in 1827, was, according to Hutton's sketch, roofless in 1847. Legend tells us that San Gabriel's Spanish type mill, "El Molino," was abandoned at a very early date. The reason for its abandonment is, however, erroneously ascribed to earthquake. San José alone seems to have survived the years of neglect and appro-priation that followed secularization of the missions.

[48] *Informe*, 1810, under *Fabricas*—". . ; se ha echo una ataona [sic] para moler trigo; . . " SBMA.

[49] Mahr, *Visit of the "Rurik"*, 95.

sion San Gabriel's first mill was a tahona, built in 1815.[50] At Santa Cruz, where the first water-power mill was built, a tahona was set up in 1816.[51] At Mission Santa Bárbara a tahona continued in use to a time within the memory of a living Padre. It stood in that little room just beyond the one where souvenirs are now sold, though in mission days it was housed in a room of the second square. A lower tahona stone which probably came from this mill stands in the front corridor near the bell tower.

As previously noted, among the gristmills known to man there is one called the quern, which is said to be the "direct ancestor of the mill-stones." There is a quern in the Junípero Serra Museum in "Old Town," San Diego. This mill is a miniature tahona, or perhaps one should say that the tahona is an enlarged quern. The quern is turned by hand and the tahona by mule or burro; the base and lower stone of the quern is in one piece, while the base of the tahona is built up from the floor or ground and the bed stone is seated upon it. Both operate on the same principle as did the old Roman mills found in the ruins of ancient Pompeii.

In setting up a tahona, a foundation was erected similar to that constructed for the stones of the water-power mill. As a rule it was located in one of the buildings of the quadrangle. The tahona foundation, however, was built up solidly, having no provision for the housing of a shaft. The bed stone was placed upon it and leveled in a bed of mortar. Some of the tahona bed stones have under surfaces that are uncut and irregular, providing, perhaps, better holding qualities when set in the mortar.

A pivot, or round-topped iron rod, was fitted or cemented into the eye of the bed stone. A bearing of iron or very hard wood was seated in and completely blocked the eye of the running stone. The pivot in the eye of the bed stone fitted into the bearing in the eye of the runner. The runner was balanced and turned on this pivot, and was held by it at just the proper distance above the bed stone for the grinding of the chosen grist.

Corn or wheat was fed through a feeding hole cut through the stone a little to one side of the center. A hopper-funnel, set in the feeding hole, was filled with grain which escaped from it through the feeding channel to the grinding surfaces of the stones. A bin was provided as with the water-power gristmills for the collection of the grist as it was discharged from the stones. A sweep was secured to lugs set in the top surface of the runner and a blindfolded burro or mule was harnessed to the sweep. Indian youths tended these mills, keeping the

[50] *Informe* . . *Mision San Gabriel*. . *1815*, under *Fabricas*: "Se han construido 2 piesas de adove techadas con texas, una destinada para molino de 18 var⁸ y 3 quartas de largo, y 9 var⁸ y 1 quarta de ancho; . . ." SBMA.

[51] *Informe del estado* . . . *Sta Cruz* . .*1816*. " . . Se ha hecho 1 molino o rastra." SBMA.

hopper filled and the burro prodded on his dizzy way around and around the mill, turning the stone and grinding the grain to feed the large mission family.

The two mills built by Joseph Chapman, or rather under his direction, at the missions of Santa Inés and San Gabriel were harbingers of things to come with the influx of "foreigners" from other parts of the world. For Chapman's mills were definitely of the New England type, and consequently definitely un-Spanish. His mill at San Gabriel stood about two hundred feet south of the mission church in what was known for many years as the "Bishop's Garden." Its ruins were twice excavated to determine its type of construction and mode of operation—first in 1894, by Dr. Hiram A. Reid and again, in 1934, for this writer[52] in the interest of her proposed book on primitive gristmills of California. At the latter date the ruins were entirely cleared of forty years' accumulation of debris; photographs were taken and measurements made. It was definitely established that this mill had been motivated by an undershot wheel, estimated to have been approximately 13' 6" in diameter; that the motion of the waterwheel, rotating on a horizontal axis, was converted to that of the millstones rotating on a vertical axis, by means of wooden cogged gears. The gear room stood at the right of the inflow end of the masonry wheel-chamber. The millstones were set up on the floor above the gear room.

A masonry flume 6' wide and 2' 6" deep conveyed the water to the mill where it shot down an inclined sluiceway to turn the noisy, creaking wooden wheel confined in a masonry channel 4' wide. There is little doubt that the sawmill, constructed at the same time as the gristmill, furnished lumber for the wheel, the shaft, and the wooden gears. Restored, this gristmill would have been of great historic interest and educational value, but it was torn out by a "bulldozer," in 1941, to make way for a street in a new subdivision! And no one in the settlement raised a hand to stay its demolition.

Rounding out the story of the mission mills is one "molino de viento" (windmill).[53] No details are available except that at La Purísima Concepción Misión one "Ferencio Ruíz agreed by contract to build a windmill and began work December 25, 1822."[54] In a near-by canyon there stands a huge column built of rock and mortar, which, it is believed, may have been part of that mill. Perhaps

---

[52] The party, working under the direction of J. M. Miller, architectural supervisor of the restoration of the San Diego Mission church, included Mr. Elmer King, teacher at the Fremont High School, Los Angeles, with a number of boys from his Pioneer Club, H. P. Webb and the writer.

[53] Langsdorff, *Voyages and Travels*, 2. 169, notes the absence of windmills in California. "When we consider," he writes, "that there is no country in the world where windmills are more numerous than in Spain, it seems incomprehensible why these very useful machines have never been introduced here. . ."

[54] Translation of the original record found in the Account Book of Mission La Purísima now in the library of Mission Santa Inés.

some day excavators will add substance to that belief. They may find, too, that the windmill was not built to motivate a gristmill. There is much in mission ruins to remind us of Steele's words:

"One can only regret for the thousandth time, that the secrets of the dead, and what the dead leave behind them, can never be told."

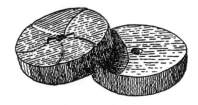

CHAPTER **13**

Cattle and Other Live Stock Sent up From México

Indian Vaqueros; Horses: Cattle and Sheep Brands

BECAUSE THERE was not time to send to the mainland for the supplies needed for the expeditions of 1769, Inspector-General Joseph de Gálvez had ordered Captain Don Fernando de Rivera to take from the old missions of the peninsula whatever could be spared in the way of cattle, horses, mules, equipment, and foodstuffs. Rivera had accordingly traveled from Loreto in the south to Santa María de Los Angeles in the north, taking one hundred-forty mules, forty-six horses (including six mares), two donkeys (burros), besides some considerable number of horses and mules from the government manadas (droves) at Loreto. The latter Fr. Palóu had been unable to count, that being the affair of the governor. The captain left receipts for what he had taken from the missions. The live stock and equipment, the Inspector-General had decided were to be paid for in kind. From Mission San Borja, about one hundred miles southeast of Vellicatá, Rivera had taken two hundred head of cattle, most of them cows with their calves.[1]

One fifth of the cattle were set aside and branded for the mission founded by the Franciscans at Vellicatá, Baja California. Of the remaining number four were killed and their meat "jerked" for the expeditionary forces. The rest of the cattle, being in an unfit condition for further traveling, were left at Vellicatá to recuperate, and until the success of the undertaking was more assured.[2]

In February, 1770, after the unsuccessful attempt had been made to locate the port of Monterey, Governor Portolá sent Captain Rivera to bring up the provisions and cattle remaining at Mission San Fernando de Vellicatá. Rivera arrived at San Diego in July bringing a herd which consisted of one hundred twenty-three full grown animals, mostly cows, and forty-one young ones, male

[1] Bolton, *Palou's New Cal.*, 1. 46, 50-52; 2. 31.
[2] *Palou's Life of Serra* (James ed.), 70; Costanso, *Narrative*, 21.

and female.[3] These were the first cattle to reach Alta California of which definite record was made. The *San Carlos*, first of the supply vessels to leave La Paz, had set sail January 9, 1769, having in its hold six live cattle and hens that were intended for the sick and for breeding.[4] Whether any of these animals survived the trip is not stated.

The cattle brought up by Rivera were intended to furnish a start for the three proposed missions of San Diego, San Carlos, and San Buenaventura. It was expected that other missions founded later would receive a like allotment. Fr. Rafael Verger, guardian of the San Fernando College, had been most insistent on this point. In their work in the missions of the Sierra Gorda region the Franciscans had been given a start of cows, oxen and "other cattle" and their labors in that field had been most successful. Writing to Fr. Francisco Palóu, who had remained in Baja California as president of those missions after Fr. Serra and others had gone on to San Diego, Fr. Verger had said: " . . , and I hope that everything will be arranged, and the new missions will have the same system as we had in the Sierra Gorda, with which it will be possible to work with pleasure, in the hope of reaping much fruit, . . "[5]

The Father Guardian considered the stocking of the new missions with various domestic animals of such vital importance that when, in April, 1772, the Franciscans agreed to relinquish the missions of Baja California to Fathers of the Dominican Order, it was with the stipulation that those old establishments should furnish the new ones with a start of live stock. Furthermore, on several occasions, he called the viceroy's attention to this clause in the agreement.[6] He also compiled a list of domestic animals to be taken from the old missions nearest the frontier of Baja California. The list included horses, cattle, burros, sheep, and goats, male and female.[7]

But the cattle of Fr. Verger's requisition never came to Alta California. Whether or not the horses and burros did is a question. A small number of sheep and goats were purchased by the missions of San Diego and San Gabriel and, in September, 1772, Fr. Dumetz of the former establishment brought up those animals together with some much needed provisions that had been left at Vellicatá.[8] Hogs, which probably came by ship, were distributed four to each of the first nine missions.[9] From Santa Clara's *informe* of 1777, it appears that each was

[3] Bolton, *Palou's New Cal.*, 2. 261, 263-4, 304.
[4] Banc., *Hist of Cal.*, 1. 128-9, note 6.
[5] Bolton, *Palou's New Cal.*, 1. 253.
[6] Bolton, *Palou's New Cal.*, 1. 239, 250-251.
[7] *Ibidem*, 254.
[8] *Ibidem*, 272; 2. 356, 364.
[9] *Ibidem*, 3. 233.

also stocked with a small number of chickens, for that mission reported having twenty hens and three cocks (20 gallinas con 3 gallos).[10]

When, after the presidio and mission had been founded at Monterey, Viceroy de Croix decided to have five more missions established, he seems to have sent up from the peninsula missions about twenty additional head of cattle and sixty mules. A redistribution of the live stock originally intended for San Diego, San Carlos, and San Buenaventura appears to have been made at this time. According to Palóu, in 1771, each mission was allotted eighteen head of cattle, large and small, and four swine. Until San Buenaventura should be founded that mission's live stock were held at San Gabriel. Santa Clara's and San Francisco's animals were in the possession of Don Pedro Fages, military commander of California.[11]

On August 30, 1773, Fr. Palóu arrived at San Diego with all save two of the Franciscan Fathers who had remained in Baja California until the missions of that region had been delivered by inventory to the Fathers of the Dominican Order. Acting as president in the absence of Fr. Serra, who was then in México, Palóu compiled a report on the state of the first five missions founded. He made a list of the stock then in possession of those establishments.[12] By adding to this list the number of animals being held for San Buenaventura with their increase, and an estimated like number for each of the missions of Santa Clara and San Francisco, one arrives at a fairly close estimate of the total count of domestic animals under mission management or set aside for those missions at the end of 1773. According to this reckoning, there were approximately 319 head of cattle, 94 sheep, 67 goats, 168 swine, 4 burros, 73 horses, and 83 mules, male and female, guarded by Indian or other vaqueros.

While in México, in 1773, Fr. Serra had asked Viceroy Bucareli for a gift of 100 mules much needed for the missions. These animals were taken from Sonora and sent by sea to Loreto to be driven by land to the new establishments in Upper California. Eleven died on the voyage across the gulf, leaving only eighty-nine. When these mules arrived in New California is not stated, but it was after Fr. Palóu's report was made. Of the eighty-nine, Fr. Serra received some "forty-odd," the rest having been appropriated by Don Fernando de Rivera, who, in 1774, had succeeded Don Pedro Fages as military commander.[13]

Fr. Serra had also purchased from private individuals in southern Baja California about thirty cows with their calves and thirteen brood mares. To this lot

[10] In SBMA.
[11] Bolton, *Palou's New Cal.*, 3. 211-240. Fr. Font tells us that each mission was given one bull and nine cows.
[12] Bolton, *Palou's New Cal.*, 3. 240.
[13] *Ibidem*, Chapter VIII.

had been added nine mules and six horses given as alms by benefactors. In 1777, after many delays, these animals arrived at Monterey. The mares were given to the new missions of Santa Clara and San Francisco, while the cows were kept for the first establishment needing that assistance.[14]

The story of the difficulties encountered by the Franciscans in securing live stock for their new missions is told by Palóu in his *Noticias.*[15] Finally, not being able to secure from the missions of Old California more animals than those collected by Rivera in 1769-1770, and the few sent up in July, 1771, they appealed to the viceroy for aid. His Excellency told them that should they cancel their agreement with the Dominican Fathers there would be no lack of cattle for the missions of Monterey. With the coming of Juan Bautista de Anza, in 1776,[16] this promise was fulfilled in so far as the missions already founded or proposed were concerned.

Captain de Anza left the royal presidio of San Miguel de Horcasitas in Sonora, México, September 29, 1775, and arrived at Mission San Gabriel January 4, 1776. He brought with him a party of 242 persons, consisting of soldiers and settlers with their families, recruited for the most part in Sinaloa and Culiacán and destined for the protection and settlement of the port of San Francisco and the two missions to be established in its vicinity. The party began the journey with 695 horses and mules, including 30 mares, colts, and burros. 325 beeves were taken along to furnish provisions for the expedition on the way, the remaining number to be used as stock cattle for New California. Individuals brought an additional thirty head. But the way was long, weary and hazardous. Some of the animals were stolen by the Indians, some perished for lack of water, while others died of exhaustion and exposure to the unaccustomed rigors of winter storms.

Going by way of Yuma across the Colorado River and desert sand dunes, the weary colonists, their beasts of burden and their cattle experienced hardships undreamed of today. Penetrating into the northern frontier of Baja California they passed Signal Mountain and entered what is now Imperial County, camping near sites known today as Plaster City and Harper's Well. It was in Old California and our present-day Imperial Valley that they encountered bitterly cold winds and snow storms. Diarists say that snow blanketed the country from Yuma to their camp San Sebastián (Harper's Well). Cattle, mules, and horses were lost or abandoned on the way.

---

[14] Bolton, *Palou's New Cal.*, 3. 346, 381-2.
[15] *Ibidem*, 1. 282-3, 284-290; 3. 309, 311-313, 381-2.
[16] In 1774, Anza had made a trial trip seeking a land route from Sonora to Monterey. He was accompanied by Fr. Francisco Garcés, missionary from San Xavier del Bac, and Fr. Juan Díaz, missionary of Caborca.

Traveling always to the left of the San Jacinto Mountains, Anza led his little band of pioneers up Borrego Valley to Coyote Canyon, through the Puerto de San Carlos (Pass of San Carlos),[17] into the San Jacinto Valley and on to a camp on the Santa Ana River, finally reaching Mission San Gabriel at its second and present site. Anza did not, Dr. Bolton points out, cross the mountains by way of the San Gorgonio Pass.[18]

The cattle that Anza brought to New California were of the same breed as those sent up from the peninsula, for the Jesuit Fathers had stocked their missions with cattle from Sonora.

When Anza returned to México he took with him twenty-nine persons and a considerable number of horses and mules. Several diarists recount the experiences of this expedition; one historical narrative, and an intriguing historical novel have been written about it.[19] All should be read by anyone who desires a better understanding of the beginnings of our California.

Whatever the number of animals the coming of this expedition may have added to the stock already here, it seems to have made little difference to the mission herds and droves. It does appear, however, to have ended the flow (?) of live stock from México, in so far as those establishments were concerned. When Santa Bárbara was founded on December 4, 1786, all those missions previously started and in good running order were obliged to contribute stock and seeds for the new community.[20] This same procedure was followed with all others founded thereafter. The California missions were now "on their own" in this respect.

A rather pathetic little incident is recorded by Fr. Font, chaplain of the Anza expedition. At San Luis Obispo, he was requested by Fr. Domingo Juncosa, who was retiring because of ill health, to see if he could bring it about that more sheep, goats, and horses be brought to that mission. He spoke on behalf of his companion, Fr. José Caveller. "And he concludes by complaining," Fr. Font writes, "of the little effort which his College of San Fernando has made to solicit these things from the viceroy, because the Fathers, being comfortable in México, neither feel nor realize the need suffered by those poor friars, etc., . . "[21] Truly those first years were hard and tried the soul of more than one good old Padre. Mother México and comfort were very far away and here in this new land near-

---

[17] A tablet marking this pass was set up by the Historic Landmarks Committee, Native Sons of the Golden West. Dr. Bolton identifies Anza's camp site, a quarter of a mile from the pass, as being now marked by Fred Clark's corral.
[18] For maps of routes taken by Anza, see Bolton, *Anza's Cal. Exped.*, 1. opp. pp. 120, 152. See also "Tracing the Trails" in *ibidem*, 3. Preface.
[19] Bolton, *Anza's Calif. Exped.*, volumes 1, 2, 3, and 4; Morrow (Honore), *Beyond the Blue Sierra*.
[20] Engelhardt, *Miss. & Miss.*, 2. 434; *Mission Santa Barbara*, 50.
[21] Bolton, *Anza's Cal. Exped.*, 4. 395.

starvation often stared them in the face. Privations were always with them, and they did not always know what was going on behind the scenes.

In order that the mission flocks and herds might increase more rapidly, no domestic animals, especially females, were allowed to be slaughtered for a number of years, except, of course, in case of dire necessity. By the end of 1783, ten years after Fr. Palóu's report was sent to Viceroy Bucareli, eight of the nine missions then founded counted all together 3,717 head of cattle, 3,458 sheep, 1,857 goats, 299 swine, 693 horses and 124 mules.[22] Santa Clara's live stock, as reported by Bancroft, was divided into two classes, large and small. Of the former, which included cattle, horses, and mules, there were 400. The latter numbered 554.[23]

Besides their experience in the raising and management of live stock gained in the Mexican missions, it is quite possible that the Padres had, after 1777, the benefit of the instructions and advice found in the book *Agricultura General*. Libro Quinto of that work treats of the breeding and care of domestic animals, fowls and even bees. One discourse deals with the raising of horses and mules. The relative merits of mules and oxen are discussed. These pages in the book at Santa Bárbara have been turned and consulted many times, as the smudges on them attest.

It is, for the time, a truly comprehensive work, special attention being given to the phase of the moon most propitious for performing various tasks ("por menguantes, y crecientes de Luna, diciendo qué obras se han de hacer en creciente, y quales en menguante").

But the California missions never had the vast herds of domestic animals accredited to them by some writers. The greatest recorded number in each class at any of the establishments in any one year was as follows: 27,500 cattle at San Luis Rey, in 1832; 28,913 sheep at San Luis Rey, in 1828; 1,380 goats at San Gabriel, in 1785; 763 swine at San Diego, in 1791; 4,652 horses at La Purísima, in 1814; 442 mules at La Purísima, in 1813.[24]

However, in their annual report on the state, or condition, of their various missions, the Padres recorded only the number of cattle in their herds at the end of the year, or probably those counted in the late summer or early fall rodeo (when the stock was rounded-up and the calves branded and counted), with, perhaps, a subtraction of the number killed weekly for food since that event. For in their *informes*, they say—"There are [hay] so many heads of cattle, horses,

[22] Taken from tables in Engelhardt's mission histories.
[23] Banc., *Hist. of Cal.*, 1. 477.
[24] From table in Engelhardt, *Miss. & Miss.*, 4. 531.

etc." For instance, in 1813, the Santa Clara Padres report that of cattle, "Hay entre todo 6,120 cabezas, . . " (There are all together 6,120 head); of sheep, "Hay 10,000 entre chico y grande, . . " (There are 10,000 head small and large); of horses, "Hay entre todo 1,000 cabezas, . . " (There are all together 1,000 head).[25]

The Padres were recording the number of each class of live stock existing on December 31, 1813. This left unaccounted for a large number of cattle herded and cared for by the Indian vaqueros. For during the year many were slaughtered for hides, tallow, and food. As was noted in Chapter VI, the Padres of San Buenaventura state that "60, 50, or at least 45 head of cattle" were slaughtered weekly and, when the cattle were very fat, 60 head were killed twice a week.

At San Juan Bautista, Padre de la Cuesta noted in his account book the slaughter of 2,603 cattle in the twelve months beginning June 3, 1820, and ending May 30, 1821. During the next year 2,699 were killed for food.[26]

In 1826, Duhaut-Cilly found that the Padres at Santa Clara were having slaughtered 150 cattle weekly, while at San Francisco, Langsdorff, in commenting on the enormous amount of food consumed by the Indians, claims that between 40 and 50 oxen were killed every week for the community.[27] De Mofras remarks that as a usual thing one-third of the live stock was killed annually.[28]

The Spanish cattle of mission days are generally described as being "leggy" and slim-bodied with long curving horns and sloping hind quarters. John Bidwell, writing in 1841, said they were very large.[29] Bryant declared: "The horned cattle of California which I have thus far seen, are the largest and handsomest in shape which I ever saw. There is certainly no breed in the United States equaling them in size."[30] Duflot de Mofras wrote: "The cattle are large, exceedingly strong and agile, and produce excellent meat. Cows raised in green pasturage give an abundant supply of milk rich in quality and suitable for making cheese."[31]

They were, it seems, large when compared with other cattle of that period, but small according to present-day standards. Writing, in about 1861, about his large fat steers, Abel Stearns said that they would weigh from six to eight hundred pounds.[32]

[25] From original in SBMA.
[26] Engelhardt, *Mission San Juan Bautista* 32-33.
[27] Langsdorff, *Voyages and Travels*, 2. 160.
[28] Mofras, Eugene Duflot de, *Travels on the Pacific Coast* (Wilbur translation. Santa Ana Fine Arts Press), 1. 261. Hereinafter to be referred to as *Travels*.
[29] Bidwell, John, *A Journey to California* (John Henry Nash Printer, 1937), 39.
[30] Bryant, *What I Saw*, 284.
[31] Mofras, *Travels*, 1. 252.
[32] Cleland, Robert G., *The Cattle on a Thousand Hills*, 84, n. 25.

Frequent mention is made of "black cattle," particularly in the Santa Bárbara Mission records. But black, so used, may not refer to the color of the cattle, "black cattle" being the designation given those destined to be slaughtered as opposed to those kept for dairy purposes. However, Stephen Ríos,[33] worker on the historic San Marcos Rancho, remembers some mission stock cattle that were black with very white horns. "They were beautiful cattle," he told the writer. Some, he said, were "blue" (black and white with the hairs so mixed as to give a blue effect);[34] some were red with white feet, broad white stripe down the back, and a white tail. These latter were called "line-backs," and in this description one can readily recognize the cattle seen by Harrison Rogers.[35] Two "line-backs" were secured from San Miguel, the last of that mission's stock, and brought by Stephen Ríos's father to Lompoc.

Mr. Rowe, previously mentioned in connection with La Purísima's recreated garden, says that, in 1904, when he first came to Santa Bárbara there were still long-horned, mission cattle on the San Marcos range. They had, he says, enormous horns, sloping hind quarters, and were not very large animals. He is sure that there was some red in their coloring. Some were dun-colored. A number of these cattle later escaped into the back country and were finally hunted out and shot.

Duhaut-Cilly, riding to San Luis Rey, stopped at the top of a slight hill to view the mission and the valley spread out before him. The scene, he says, was "enlivened by great herds which could as yet be seen only as white and red spots."

Then there were spotted cattle, red, black, and tan with white spots, as early sketches[36] and bottoms on old mission chairs testify.

The mission cattle, the Texas Longhorns, and the cattle of early New Mexico, Arizona, and all other regions overrun by the Spanish conquerors and colonizers, were all descendants from the same Spanish stock. All, it seems, were more or less ferocious looking and half-wild.[37] From centuries of inbreeding they deteriorated and developed, in certain regions, very definite characteristics such as the famous long horns (particularly the type that measured six feet and more straight across), formerly adorning the heads of cattle of the Texas range, and

[33] Stephen, grandson of Petronillo Ríos, who, in 1846, made joint purchase with William Reed of Mission San Miguel. Petronillo built the old adobe house standing near the old mission.
[34] This writer, in October, 1947, saw a "blue" cow feeding in a field lying between San Luis Obispo and Morro Bay. The animal could not have been described otherwise than as "blue."
[35] Rogers, Harrison, "Journal," 194.
[36] Smythe's sketch entitled "Californian throwing the lasso," first published in Beechy, *Narrative of a Voyage to the Pacific*. 1831.
[37] Nordhoff, *opus cit.*, 209.

from which they derived their name.[38] In early sketches and written accounts the horns of the California mission cattle are described as long and curving.

As noted elsewhere, after the herds had increased somewhat and the Indian neophytes had been sufficiently trained in their care, the cattle, horses, and sheep were removed to sites where there was good pasturage and water. Some of the more famous cattle ranches were Las Flores and San Jacinto of Mission San Luis Rey; San Bernardino of Mission San Gabriel; Rancho de Piru, "in the cañon of the Secpé," belonging to San Buenaventura; San Marcos Rancho, property of Santa Bárbara; Guadalupe, of Mission La Purísima; and Los Ojitos, rancho of Mission San Antonio.

On these ranchos the Indians, working under a majordomo, guarded the cattle, rounded-up, branded, counted, slaughtered, skinned them and pegged their hides out to dry. They cut from the carcasses the wanted portions of lean meat and fats and sent them piled high in carretas to the missions. At the time of the matanzas there was an enormous waste of meat, for in those few months when the cattle were slaughtered mainly for their hides and tallow it was impossible to use or preserve all the edible portions.[39]

Duhaut-Cilly wrote that "the favorable season for buying hides and tallow did not commence until the month of May, the time when the cattle are killed to extract from them the most profit; . . ."[40] Sir James Douglas says: "The slaughtering season begins about the middle of June and lasts nearly three months, during which all the trading vessels are on the move and have their agents out in all directions selling goods and receiving payments. This is in short the most busy period of the year, when all is bustle and animation."[41]

Sir James Douglas's observations were written in 1841 and after the missions had been secularized, but the same conditions had prevailed in mission days and one can well imagine the stir and excitement that ran high throughout those months of harvest. From the gathering of the grain; the picking of the grapes; the round-up, branding, and slaughtering of the cattle; the shearing of the sheep; with all the tasks attending those operations, the missions were indeed beehives of industry.

Robinson visited Guadalupe Rancho and found the Indians busy at their annual matanza, or cattle killing. Describing the scene, he writes: "Numbers of the poor animals lay stretched upon the ground, already slaughtered; others just

[38] See page "From old Longhorn family album" in Jo Mora's book, *Trail Dust and Saddle Leather*.

[39] A *Sojourn in California* by The King's Orphan. The Travels and Sketches of G. M. Waseurtz af Sandels, a Swedish gentleman who visited California in 1842-1843. Grabhorn Press, Copyright 1945 by The Society of California Pioneers, 52 (hereinafter referred to as *Sojourn in California*).

[40] "Duhaut-Cilly's Account," 143.

[41] Douglas, "Journal."

suffering under the knife of the butcher, whilst, in a spacious enclosure, hundreds were crowded for selection. The vaqueros, mounted on splendid horses and stationed at its entrance, performed by far the most important part of the labor. When the mayordomo pointed out the animal to be seized, instantly a lasso whirled through the air, and fell with dextrous precision upon the horns of the ill-fated beast. The horse, accustomed to the motion, turned as the lasso descended, and dragged him to slaughter. Another lasso was thrown, which entrapped his hind leg, and threw him prostrate on the ground. In this position he was dispatched, and the horseman returned for another. Sometimes it happened that one would escape and make off for the fields, pursued by the vaqueros, who, as they rode in full chase, swung their lassos above their heads, and threw them upon the animal's horns and neck, giving their well-trained horses a sudden check, which brought him tumbling to the earth; or some one of the more expert would seize him by the tail, and putting spurs to his horse, urge him suddenly forward, overthrowing the bull in this manner."[42]

The round-up, or rodeo, spoken of before, was a gathering together of all the stock at the various ranchos. Strays were separated from the others and the calves were counted and branded. Spanish and Mexican laws, or regulations, set a specified date for this task. Wherefore the Fathers of Mission San Diego, in

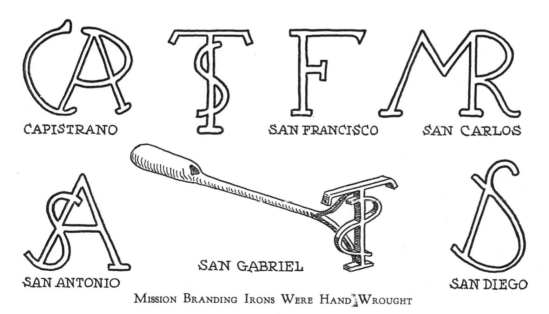

CAPISTRANO   SAN FRANCISCO   SAN CARLOS

SAN ANTONIO   SAN GABRIEL   SAN DIEGO

MISSION BRANDING IRONS WERE HAND-WROUGHT

[42] Robinson, *Life in Cal.*, 95-96; see also pp. 113-114, for his description of Indians catching a bear for a bull and bear fight.

SANTA CRUZ   STA. BARBARA   SANTA INÉS   SAN MIGUEL

STA. CLARA   S. BUENAVENTURA   LA PURÍSIMA   S. FERNANDO

THESE BRANDS WERE USED FROM THE VERY FIRST

replying to the territorial government's request for a statement on the extent of that mission's lands, appended the following: "Nota.—In Article First of the Bando it is said that in the jurisdiction of Santa Barbara and San Diego the time for branding the cattle will be in the months of March, April, and May. I have to say that in the Rancho de San Bernardo the branding can be done in these months; but in the Rancho of Valle de San José[43] it will not be practicable to brand until the months of August and September, because the weather is very cold and the cattle may not be ready until summer. Therefore I supplicate that permission be granted to do the branding in this Rancho during the two months of August and September.

"The stamp and shape of the iron are enclosed.

"In witness whereof I sign at Mission San Diego on the eighteenth of December, 1827.—Fr. Fernando Martín, Fr. Vicente Pasqual Oliva."[44]

Each mission had its hierro, or fierro (brand), and señal (ear mark). These brands were used from the very first, as was noted at Vellicatá. Some of the old branding irons still exist in mission museums, and furnish good examples of iron wrought by experts. One is always told that they were fashioned in the mission blacksmith shops, and doubtless many were in later days, but the first were sent up from México and were designed from patterns supplied by the Padres. In

[43] Later known as Warner's Ranch. See Hill, Joseph J., *The History of Warner's Ranch and Its Environs*, 29. Hereinafter referred to as *History of Warner's Ranch*.
[44] Engelhardt, *Mission San Diego*, 224 (*California Archives, St. Pap. Mis.* vi, pp. 178-180).

a *memoria* covering a requisition for supplies for Mission San Gabriel in 1771, there appears the following item: "Un hierro para marcar, y señalar ganado con la figura siguiente"[45] (An iron for branding and marking the cattle with the following design). In the San Buenaventura *memoria* for 1800 two dozen irons for branding lambs are listed.

Calves were both branded and ear-marked. The branding iron was heated in a fire and applied to the calf's flank. An identifying piece was clipped from the animal's ear, and, to keep tally, was dropped into an open bag. At the close of the day these grisly bits were counted to determine the number branded. Sometimes knots were tied in a string or notches cut in a stick for the same purpose. Horses were also branded and sheep ear-marked.

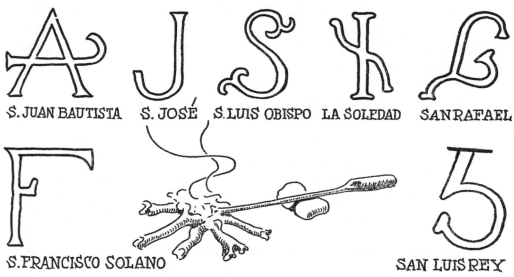

S. JUAN BAUTISTA   S. JOSÉ   S. LUIS OBISPO   LA SOLEDAD   SAN RAFAEL

S. FRANCISCO SOLANO   SAN LUIS REY

EACH MISSION HAD ITS OWN BRAND

Cows from the mission herds furnished the communities with milk, butter and cheese. Early in 1774, when the supply ship from México was delayed there was great distress at San Carlos and the presidio of Monterey. Fr. Palóu, still at that mission during Serra's absence, writes: "The worst kind of a famine that was ever endured in the regions about Monterey visited us. For eight months milk was the manna for all from the comandante and the Fathers down to the least individual; and I shared it with the rest. Thanks be to God! However, all are in good health. At this mission of San Carlos for thirty-seven days we were without a tortilla or as much as a crumb of bread. The meals consisted of a gruel

[45] Copied by Arthur Woodward from the original in the *Archivo Nacional*, México.

made of garvanzos or beans ground to a flour with which milk was mixed. In the morning a little coffee took the place of chocolate."[46]

Anza, who was at San Carlos in April, 1774, found provisions so scanty that there was nothing but milk and herbs without bread or anything else to offer him; not even a small cake of chocolate remained. He was so impressed by the "infelicities and misery" suffered by the people of the region that he wrote in his diary: "In view of these trials and their long continuation, I cannot find words adequate to praise the merit of the friars, the commander, and the troops for remaining in these places."[47]

But milk, together with seeds, herbs, and whatever could be gathered by the Indians, tided the little band over until the supply ship finally arrived.

Forbes speaks very slightingly of the butter and cheese made in Upper California. But it is quite possible that he was not fully informed on the subject, since he did not gather his information firsthand but relied on correspondents and visitors to México.[48]

Fr. Font at San Gabriel, in 1776, writes: "The cows which they have are very fat and they give much and rich milk, with which they make cheese and very good butter. . ."[49]

Robinson describes the lunch prepared for him and his companion at the direction of Fr. Peyri of San Luis Rey. It was, he says, "wrapped up in a nice white napkin, which, opening, was spread out on the grass and exposed to view the following: One boiled chicken, one smoked beef tongue, half a dozen hard boiled eggs, a loaf of bread, a small cheese, and a bottle of wine and a little paper of salt and pepper."[50]

Speaking of the various foods eaten by the Californians, Duhaut-Cilly notes: " . . Their table is, in general, very simple, and the meat of the ox, or rather of the cow, for they prefer this, is the entire expense of their cuisine. . . Cheese is much to their taste; they manufacture several kinds; but their cows give little milk."[51]

None of these writers would have hesitated to say that the cheese was bad or inferior had such been the case. It was not, of course, such cheese as we have today.

From the mission herds were selected the steers that were yoked and broken

[46] Engelhardt, *Mission San Carlos*, 41-2.
[47] Bolton, *Anza's Calif. Exped.*, 2. 107.
[48] Banc., *Hist. of Cal.*, 4. 150-2; 3. 176, note 60.
[49] Bolton, *Anza's Calif. Exped.*, 4. 177.
[50] Robinson, *Life in Cal.*, 269; Rogers, H., *Journal*, 195, 196, 201.
[51] "Duhaut-Cilly's Account " 312.

to pull the plows and haul the heavily laden carretas. They were the work animals of the field. The yoke, as noted in Forbes' description of the plow, was fastened, by means of rawhide thongs, to the animals' horns and rested on the backs of their heads. The tongue of the plow or carreta was attached directly to the yoke, the full weight and pull of the load being borne by the heads and horns of the oxen.

Capítulo V., Libro Primero of *Agricultura General* deals with the subject of plowing with oxen ("Del Arar con bueyes"). Incidentally, the author defends the practice, followed in Spain, of yoking the oxen by the heads, or horns. The animals there are large, he says, and have great strength in their heads. However, in France or Italy, where the oxen are small and have little, thin horns, it is more common to yoke them by the necks—but not in Castile, nor Andalusia, nor Estramadura.

The mission horses, mules, and burros were, like the cattle, descendants from stock introduced into México by the Spaniards. Fortunately, a description was written of the animals brought to that country, in 1517, by Cortés and his followers. There were sixteen horses and mares in the lot. Their colors and markings are variously described as chestnut, light chestnut, light chestnut with three white stockings, sorrel, parched sorrel, gray, dark gray, dappled (gray) with stockings on fore-feet, dappled (almost black), and one very good dark horse.[52] Horses were very scarce in those days and he who had one was considered quite wealthy.

Two hundred-fifty years later descendants from those horses, or from later importations from the same original stock, were gathered together by Captain Rivera for the exploring expeditions of 1769. Like the cattle, they were taken by the Spanish conquistadores into every region invaded by that race. They were small, fast animals capable of remarkable endurance. Trained to the nth degree, the horse and vaquero were a superb pair, as indicated in Robinson's description of the matanza at Guadalupe. Most writers of those days tell of the accomplishments of both riders and horses.

The palomino, not the "golden horse" of today, but still the palomino, was found in the mission droves. Guadalupe Vallejo writes: " . . fast and beautiful horses were never more prized in any country than in California, and each young man [of the pioneer families] had his favorites. A kind of mustang, that is now seldom or never seen on the Pacific coast, was a peculiar light cream-colored horse, with silver-white mane and tail. Such an animal, of speed and bottom,

[52] Diaz del Castillo, Bernal, *The True History of the Conquest of Mexico, 1517-1521* (Maudslay translation 1928), 84-85.

often sold for more than a horse of any other color. Other much admired colors were dapple-gray and chestnut."[53]

William Rich Hutton, paymaster's clerk and surveyor who came to California in 1847, wrote to his uncle: "I have two horses now, or, rather, a mare and a horse, the latter a beautiful little yellow bay, pacer, and good for a lady to pasear [ride] or a vaquero to lazo a steer."[54]

It is said that the Spanish-Californian employed some two hundred words, many of which have no equivalent in English, in describing the exact shade of color and markings of the horses in his manada.[55]

Edwin Bryant noted: "The horses are not as large as the breeds of the United States, but in point of symmetrical proportions and in capacity for endurance, they are fully equal to our best breeds."[56]

Such were the horses ridden by the military, by members of the pioneer families, by vaqueros, and sometimes by the Padres, though it is said that they preferred mules, especially white ones. The mule, being the more humble animal because of his male parent, the burro, was regarded as a more suitable mount for the follower of St. Francis than was the horse. In order to fulfill an ancient prophecy, Christ himself, meek and lowly, had ridden a donkey into Jerusalem. Moreover, back in the time of Ferdinand and Isabella, when laws were passed to encourage the breeding of horses "which had suffered greatly from the preference very generally given by the Spaniards to mules," it was ordered that no person in the kingdom should be allowed to own a mule, unless he owned a horse also; and no one but ecclesiastics and women should be allowed to use a mule in the saddle.[57] This law, which may still have been in effect when Serra and his companions sailed away from Cadiz, may also have had something to do with the Padres' preference for mules.

In the 1780's Governor Fages objected to the neophytes being allowed to ride horses, "the policy of the government being opposed to this, in the fear that like the Apaches the Californians might become skillful warriors." The Padres admitted the danger involved in furnishing the Indians with mounts but could not see how they could do otherwise, since the neophytes were the only ones available to serve as vaqueros and that the work could be done only on horseback. The objections were repeated at later times but the Padres always met them

---

[53] Vallejo, Guadalupe, "Ranch and Mission Days," 189.

[54] Hutton, Wm. Rich, *Glances at California, 1847-1853* (Huntington Library Publication, 1942), p. 53.

[55] Cleland, *opus cit.*, 78-79.

[56] Bryant, *What I Saw*, 284.

[57] Prescott, Wm. H., *History of the Reign of Ferdinand and Isabella* (Phillips, Sampson, and Co., Boston, 1856), 11th Ed. Vol. II,. 340-1.

▲ INDIANS OPERATING THE TAHONA, *a Spanish gristmill. (Miniature)* (COPYRIGHT EDITH WEBB)

▼ LOWER TAHONA STONE AT SAN MIGUEL; *a quern at the Junípero Serra Museum, San Diego.*

Top: WATER-POWER GRISTMILL *still in use at Villanueva, New Mexico.* (COPYRIGHT EDITH WEBB) Bottom: *Upper water-power millstone at Santa Bárbara; millwheel formerly at San Antonio.*

with the query—the soldiers did not want to act as vaqueros and "how else can the vaqueros' work of the missions be done?"[58] For the time the subject seems to have been dropped.[59] In the meantime, the Indian vaqueros had, by all accounts, become quite as expert as the much-lauded Californians in the handling of horses.

The first mission rancho came into being, in 1774, when the Padres of San Diego built a corral for mares and horses in a place which they called Rancho de San Luis. This estancia was one league from the mission. In 1783, their cattle were also pastured there. San Antonio's mares and their young were kept at a site on the coast ten and one-half leagues south of the mission; the horses were herded with those of the guard in the canyon beyond the mission. San Francisco's ranchos for horses were El Potrero and San Bruno. The former is described by Robinson as a large enclosure, the walls of which "were of loose stones, piled up to the height of about four feet." San Bruno lay at a distance of four leagues to the south of the mission. Each mission had its estancias for horses and for mares and their young, and often more than one where living quarters—adobe houses with tiled roofs—were built for the foreman and the Indian vaqueros. Here the horses were "broken" for riding in all its deviations.[60] Horses were never used for work in the fields nor for hauling. Such labor was performed by the oxen. Mules were the pack animals. Mares were never ridden. A comparatively small number of burros were also found in the mission droves. It is believed that, in most instances, these were the animals that furnished the motive power for the tahonas.

In 1773, Fr. Palóu had counted sixty-four sheep at San Diego and thirty at San Gabriel. These "cabezas de lana" (literally heads of wool), as the Padres called them, had been purchased by them "with warrants of the soldiers, which they turned over to those two missions for what they owed."[61] They were brought up to New California by Fr. Dumetz in the late summer of 1772. Goats and sheep together then numbered 166 head. There were neither sheep nor goats at any of the other missions in New California until 1777, when Santa Clara reported having "Viente cabezas de lana" [20 head of sheep], "Dies y siete de Pelo" [17 of goats], and "Quatro zerdas" [4 swine]. San Antonio's sheep [58 head] were acquired in 1778. Mission San Carlos, San Luis Obispo, and San Francisco, ap-

---

[58] Banc., *Hist. of Cal.*, 1. 404-5, 583; 2. 162; Engelhardt, *Miss. & Miss.*, 2. 425.
[59] It was revived in 1818 when Gov. Solá issued orders that only a certain number of neophytes be allowed to ride. Banc., *Hist. of Cal.*, 2. 405.
[60] See Mora, Jo, *Trail Dust and Saddle Leather*, 67-124, for methods of horse "breaking."
[61] Bolton, *Palou's New Cal.*, 1. 272.

parently, did not secure their flocks until 1783,[62] when the Padres of those establishments reported having 220, 900, and 183 head of sheep respectively. Whether those animals were obtained by purchase or gift is not known.

In 1777, Mission San Diego had repaid San Juan Capistrano for aid received in time of need with ten head of sheep and eleven goats besides twenty pounds of iron and sixteen pounds of steel with sufficient carbon to work the metals.[63] By 1783, San Juan Capistrano's flock had increased to 305 head. The goats numbered 830 and the pigs 40. At this time San Gabriel reported 1,300 cabezas de lana. San Diego had only 300 head. But San Gabriel was situated in a fertile, well-watered valley, while San Diego had to contend with numerous set-backs and difficulties before proper fields and pastures were found and proven. San Buenaventura was founded in 1782 and a year later possessed a flock of 41 sheep.

From these small beginnings grew the mission flocks from which were taken wool, skins, and tallow, products which helped to clothe and sustain the mission family. It is said that the flesh of the sheep was not much eaten, there being such a bountiful supply of beef. And, that may be true. On the other hand, so much that is untrue has been written about mission-day habits and customs that one becomes skeptical. When Anza with his company reached San Gabriel, in January, 1776, the Padres killed "three or four wethers which they had. Their flesh was especially good," Fr. Font writes, "and I do not remember having eaten fatter or finer mutton. They also have a few hens."[64] Good old Father Font has supplied us with many an interesting and informative detail. His mention of the three or four wethers disproves Forbes' statement that the mission flocks consisted only of ewes and rams "without any wethers, which are the most valuable stock." "The mutton, . . ," he continues, "is therefore bad."[65]

Edwin Bryant, one of our most reliable writers of early after-mission days, was a member of Fremont's party who, in December, 1846, feasted on mutton at Mission San Miguel and found it "of excellent quality."[66]

Some of the most notable sheep ranchos were San Mateo of San Francisco, Buena Vista of San Carlos, San Benito of San Antonio, Paso del Robles and Santa Isabel of San Miguel, Rancho del Refugio of Santa Bárbara, Buena Vista and Agua Hedionda of San Luis Rey. San Juan Bautista had five or six, or more ranchos for sheep where, in 1828, 10,500 head were maintained. San Buenaventura had four estancias where sheep grazed. At the first, one league above the

[62] At least none were reported at those missions before that date. See Engelhardt's tables of statistics.
[63] Engelhardt, *Mission San Diego*, 95.
[64] Bolton, *Anza's Calif. Exped.*, 4. 177.
[65] Forbes, *California*, 279.
[66] Bryant, *What I Saw*, 352.

river of the mission, six neophytes lived with their wives. At the second, three-fourths of a league farther on, nine neophytes and nine children were living. At the third rancho, which was three leagues from the preceding one, fourteen neophytes, old and young, made their home. The location of the fourth estancia was not given. Without doubt houses for the shepherds, or *pastores*, and their families were built on each of those ranchos, for, as the report reads—the neophytes "live," or "make their homes there."[67] It will be noted that there is no mention of overseer of another race in the Padres' report. The Indians were in complete charge of the herds of sheep. This fact bespeaks their trustworthiness.

Robinson describes Rancho San Mateo, of the San Francisco district, as being "situated in the midst of a small wood. The building, occupied by the mayordomo and servants, is spacious and covered with burnt tiles."[68] The ranch house of Buena Vista, belonging to Mission San Carlos, stood across the river at the site now called "Spreckles" near Salinas. Traces of the walls built to guard the sheep at San Benito may still be seen across the Salinas River bridge at San Lucas, about half a mile west of the highway. There is something very thrilling about the finding of such reminders of days gone by. Only adobe walls, yet once again "A knowledge of history makes the whole landscape alive."

In the work of guarding the live stock, particularly the sheep, dogs played a very important part. Mission records of 1817 speak of shepherd dogs. Nor were dogs unknown to the California Indians before the coming of the Spaniards. The remains of dogs have been found in ancient cemeteries on Santa Cruz Island, which circumstance, it is thought, goes far to prove that the dog's existence on the California coast dates back quite as far as does the Indian's.[69] Fr. Crespí, in writing to Fr. Palóu, under date of February 6, 1770, says: "The Indians have many dogs."[70] These native dogs together with those that may have been brought to New California by the Spaniards, the Indians of the Peninsula, or by traders who came later to bargain for hides and tallow, had become a numerous and curious breed by 1834, when Richard Henry Dana saw them. In speaking of the population of the beach of San Diego, he writes:

"... I ought, perhaps, to except the dogs, for they were an important part of our settlement. Some of the first vessels brought dogs out with them, who, for convenience, were left ashore, and there multiplied, until they came to be a great people. When I was on the beach, the average number was about forty... The father of the colony, old Sachem, so called from the ship in which he was brought out, died while I was there, full of years, and was honorably buried...

[67] Engelhardt, *Mission San Buenaventura*, 66.
[68] Robinson, *Life in Cal.*, 70.
[69] Rogers, *Prehistoric Man*, 320, 448-449.
[70] Bolton, *Palou's New Cal.*, 4. 285.

A smaller dog, belonging to us, once attacked a coyote single, and was considerably worsted, and might, perhaps, have been killed, had we not come to his assistance. We had, however, one dog which gave them a good deal of trouble and many hard runs. He was a fine, tall fellow, and united strength and agility better than any dog I have ever seen. He was born at the Islands, his father being an English mastiff and his mother a greyhound. He had the high head, long legs, narrow body, and springing gait of the latter, and the heavy jaw, thick jowls, and strong fore-quarters of the mastiff. When he was brought to San Diego an English sailor said that he looked, about the face, like the Duke of Wellington, whom he had once seen at the tower; and indeed, there was something about him which resembled the portraits of the Duke. From this time he was christened "Welly," and became the favorite and bully of the beach. He always led the dogs by several yards in the chase, and killed two coyotes at different times in single combats. We often had fine sport with these fellows. A quick, sharp bark from a coyote, and in an instant every dog was at the height of his speed. A few minutes made up for an unfair start, and gave each dog his right place. Welly, at the head, seemed almost to skim over the bushes, and after him came Fanny, Feliciana, Childers, and the other fleet ones,—the spaniels and terriers; and then behind, followed the heavy corps,—bull-dogs, &c., for we had every breed. . . " [71]

Such were the dogs that helped guard the drying adobes and ladrillos, the fields and orchards, and, particularly, the horses, cattle, and sheep. That they were most valuable to the vaqueros and herdsmen is readily gathered from Dana's account, for the live stock, especially the young, were preyed upon by coyotes, mountain lions, and other wild animals which prowled about the pastures. Moreover, wherever there are Indians, there are always dogs, their faithful and trusted companions.

The hogs that were brought up from Baja California for the new missions originally came from China by way of the Philippine galleons. In this new land they thrived especially well where there was an abundant harvest of acorns to feed upon. These animals furnished the necessary lard without which the Spanish cook is completely lost. Surplus fats were utilized in soap making. The hams and shoulders were hung on huge wooden pegs or giant iron spikes, set high up in the cavernous flues of the kitchen chimneys, and smoked to a turn. Let no one say that the flesh of this animal was not eaten, for sausages [72] and smoked hams were considered great delicacies. Included among the many articles sent to the missions, in 1773, as an alms by his Excellency, Viceroy Bucareli, were 10 boxes of hams weighing 60 arrobas [73] net, and 3 barrels of lard. [74] And, in fitting out the Anza expedition of 1775-1776, Juan José Echeveste, a government official, had included in the officers' mess for the table of Anza and the chaplain, Fr. Font, (though contrary to their wishes it is said), a box of hams weighing 175 pounds, and 25 pounds of sausage, along with a number of other delicacies. [75]

[71] Dana, *Two Years Before the Mast*, 186, 192-3.
[72] Listed in San Buenaventura's *memoria* for 1797 is 1 geringa (sausage stuffer).
[73] One arroba, Spanish measure, equals twenty-five pounds.
[74] Bolton, *Palou's New Cal.*, 3. 123.
[75] Bolton, *Anza's Cal. Exped.*, 1. 223.

To complete the roster of domestic animals, note should be made of the mission cats. The first mention of these animals in Alta California was probably made by Fr. Font, who tells us that when he and Anza with others of the 1775-1776 company were returning to México, they were asked by the Fathers of San Carlos to deliver, on their way down the coast, two cats to each of the missions of San Gabriel and San Diego. The Padres of those establishments had urgent need of cats since both missions and the country around them were overrun with mice. So there was work even for the mission cats. Reminders of their existence in those days are found today in the cat-holes cut in some of the original doors at San Gabriel, San Fernando, San Juan Bautista, and Santa Inés.

It is known that chickens were raised at the missions and myriads of doves of many colors. Hugo Reid tells us that at that locality now known as El Monte, the Padres of San Gabriel had their turkey farm, which they called San Francisquito. And, if there be truth in Helen Hunt Jackson's story of the parade of fowls managed by Fr. Martínez' neophytes at San Luis Obispo for the benefit of "General Moreno" and his bride, then there were chickens of many colors, ducks, and geese in the mission barnyards.[76]

At San Fernando a dove-cote, remindful of those in the cone dwellings of the troglodytes of Asia Minor,[77] was built in the rear wall of the sacristy, an occasional adobe brick being removed to provide nesting places for the pigeons. An early photograph shows this architectural feature that is at once interesting and expressive of the resourcefulness and ingenuity of the Padres. This cote has recently been restored.

The building of dove-cotes is also discussed in the book, *Agricultura General.*

[76] Jackson (Helen), *Ramona*, 1. 35-6. (Monterey edition, 2 vols.)
[77] *National Geographic*, April, 1919.

CHAPTER 14

Hides and Tallow, the Chief Sources of Revenue

Indian Tanners, Makers of Shoes, Soap, and Candles

CATTLE RAISING was the missions' greatest industry. And the ramifications of this activity were very numerous, reaching into the farthest corner of mission life. Many, many Indians were employed in the various labors entailed, from the herding and guarding of the cattle to the round up, branding, and slaughter of the animals and the eventual disposal of the numerous parts of their carcasses.

La matanza (the slaughtering season) was perhaps the busiest time of all at the old missions, for following in its wake were tasks that must be attended to at once or the fruits of months of labor would be lost. Robinson's description of the Indian vaqueros lassoing and throwing cattle to be slaughtered at Guadalupe, cattle rancho of La Purísima, has been cited in the previous chapter.

As soon as the animal was dispatched by the butcher, its carcass was drawn a little to one side of the slaughtering place and the hide removed by skinners who, with the passing of time, had become quite expert. The hide was handed to other Indian workers who cut small holes in it around near the edge, stuck wooden pegs in the holes, and staked it out on the ground to dry. Properly staked, hides dried without shrinking. They were then taken up, folded lengthwise down the middle, skin side out, and carted or carried to the mission, where they were stored away for later use in the tannery or for barter with merchant vessels which plied the coastal waters.

When disposed of to traders, the hides were taken from the mission store-houses and transported to the beach or embarcadero (landing place) in oxcarts, by pack-mules, or on the heads of Indians. At San José, Guadalupe Vallejo says: "But often in winter, there being no roads across the valley, each separate hide was doubled across the middle and placed on the head of an Indian. Long files of

Indians, each carrying a hide in this manner, could be seen trotting over the un-fenced level land through the wild mustard to the embarcadero,[1] and in a few weeks the whole cargo would thus be delivered. . . "[2]

A similar scene was enacted at every port of call in California. From Mission San Francisco over the sand hills to the bay, came some such procession or one of pack-mules and carretas loaded with hides, the screeching and groaning of the cart wheels and the yells of the Indian drivers and muleteers announcing the coming of the burden-carriers long before they could be seen. To the port of Monterey hides from the missions of San Carlos, San Juan Bautista, and La Sole-dad were so transported. At what is now known as Ávila, trading vessels stopped to pick up hides and tallow sent from San Miguel and San Luis Obispo. La Purísima sent its produce over the hills, on past its two ranchos of Jalama and San Francisquito, to the anchorage at El Cojo.[3] Stops were also made at Santa Cruz, Santa Bárbara, San Buenaventura, San Pedro, San Juan Capistrano and San Diego. To those anchorages came long lines of Indians on foot, Indians urg-ing on pack-mules and oxen drawing carretas, all bearing hides and tallow taken from mission cattle to be exchanged for articles most needed at the establish-ments. Getting away from the crowded towns and cities of today one can readily vizualize this phase of Indian activity by following the road that leads from Lom-poc (Mission La Purísima's first site) to El Cojo on the coast. Or by going from San Antonio over the hills to San Simeón.

Richard Henry Dana has described the treatment given the hides before they were loaded onto the vessels bound for Boston. "The first thing," he wrote, "is to put them in soak. This is done by carrying them down at low tide, and making them fast, in small piles, by ropes, and letting the tide come up and cover them. Every day we put in soak twenty-five for each man, which, with us, made a hundred and fifty. There they lie forty-eight hours, when they are taken out, and rolled up, in wheel barrows, and thrown into the vats. These vats contain brine, made very strong,—being sea-water, with great quantities of salt thrown in. This pickles the hides, and in this they lie forty-eight hours; the use of the sea-water, into which they are first put, being merely to soften and clean them. From these vats they are taken and lie on a platform for twenty-four hours, and then are spread upon the ground, and carefully stretched and staked out, with the skin up, that they may dry smooth. After they had been staked, and while

---

[1] Hides purchased from the missions of Santa Clara and San José were carried to the embarcadero (Alviso) located on a stream which emptied into the Bay of San Francisco. A launch was used in transporting them from the point of collection to the bay.

[2] Vallejo, Guadalupe, "Ranch and Mission Days," 187.

[3] El Cojo (the lame one), so named by the soldiers of 1769 because the chief of the ranchería at that place was lame.

yet wet and soft, we used to go upon them with our knives, and carefully cut off all the bad parts,—the pieces of meat and fat, which would corrupt and infect the whole if stowed away in a vessel for many months, the large flippers, the ears, and all other parts which would prevent close stowage. This was the most difficult part of our duty, as it required much skill to take off everything that ought to come off, and not to cut or injure the hide. It was also a long process, as six of us had to clean a hundred and fifty, most of which required a great deal to be done to them, as the Spaniards are very careless in skinning their cattle. Then, too, as we cleaned while they were staked out, we were obliged to kneel down upon them, which always gives beginners the back-ache. . ."

"This cleaning must be got through with before noon, for by that time the hides get too dry. After the sun has been upon them a few hours, they are carefully gone over with scrapers, to get off all the grease which the sun brings out. This being done the stakes are pulled up, and the hides carefully doubled, with the hair side out, and left to dry. About the middle of the afternoon they are turned over, for the other side to dry, and at sundown piled up and covered over. The next day they are spread out and opened up again, and at night, if fully dry, are thrown over a long horizontal pole, five at a time and beaten with flails. This takes all the dust from them. Then, having been salted, scraped, cleaned, dried, and beaten, they are stowed away in the house.[4] Here ends their history, except that they are taken out again when the vessel is ready to go home, beaten, stowed away on board, carried to Boston, tanned, made into shoes and other articles for which leather is used, and many of them, very probably, in the end, brought back again to California in the shape of shoes, and worn out in the pursuit of other bullocks, or in the curing of other hides."[5]

This writer has found no description of the treatment given "green" hides destined for the mission tanneries. Still, it does not appear that they were more than staked out, dried in the sun, taken up, folded lengthwise down the middle, skin side out, and stored in the mission warehouses until wanted. Doubtless many of the hides used at the missions came from cattle slaughtered weekly to feed the mission family.

However, as it was vitally necessary that the bits of flesh and fat, still adhering to the skin side, be removed and the hides be cured by soaking them in salt water,[6] if they were to be kept for any considerable length of time before being tanned, it does not seem likely that those steps were long delayed. For the pen-

[4] The "hidehouse" on the beach at San Diego.
[5] Dana, *Two Years Before the Mast*, 187-9.
[6] Or by being sprinkled with dry salt when they were first staked out to dry.

▲ The San Diego Mission dam *built by Indian workmen and destroyed by excessive floods.*

▼ Penstock of Santa Bárbara's gristmill; *flume which carried water to San Antonio's mill.*

▲ Ruins of Chapman's *New England*-type mill at San Gabriel after excavation in March, 1934.

▼ "El Molino," San Gabriel's *Spanish*-type water-power gristmill at San Marino.

alty of such neglect would have been a lot of spoiled hides. That hides were pre-served by the use of salt is indicated by the inventory drawn up on July 14th, 1839, at Mission Santa Bárbara by Inspector Hartnell. Therein mention is made of "29 hides of cattle, 7 hides of cattle salted in the tannery, 6 other hides in the tannery, . ."[7]

Before beginning the process of tanning, lime was prepared, oak bark ground, or crushed, and a sufficient supply of water assured. Some considerable quantity of the latter was needed and its lack severely hampered the tanning industry at some of the missions, especially during the dry season. For instance, at Santa Bárbara, in 1800, Fr. Tapis, in explaining the reason for that mission's asking a higher price for hides than that indicated in the official price list, wrote: "The reason is that more profit is made from them by using them for saddles, sacks, etc. . . In addition we have two other reasons. One is that bark and water are scarce and sometimes very far away, which fact increases the cost of manufac-ture. The other is that the corporal of the guard is paid $150 a year so that he may as an expert manage the tannery."[8] This report was written before Santa Bár-bara had built its first dam on Mission Creek and constructed the reservoir men-tioned in the chapter on mission water systems.

Lime used in the tannery was burned in the mission lime kilns and then slaked. A good description of the method employed in slaking lime is found in an old book written in 1876.[9] The author remarks: "Lime for the tanner's use should always be unslaked, or in the 'stone.' When it is supplied fresh from the kiln, as it should be at frequent intervals, it should be kept in a dry and confined apartment, where neither moisture nor air can reach it. This lime should be 'slaked' with even more care for the tanner than is exercised by the mason and finisher."

"Half a hogshead placed near the lime vat it is proposed to replenish; for a pack of 120 to 140 sides[10] thrown in, say, one bushel of lime; dampen it by pour-ing on one or two pails of water and cover with a thick canvas; a few moments will suffice to absorb the water, and considerable heat will be produced; add water gently, several times rather than 'drown' the lime by an over supply at any one time, and be sure and not allow it to 'burn' for want of water. The hogs-head should be kept covered until slaking is completed. When the reaction is over the tub may be filled with water and thoroughly stirred; after settling, the

[7] Engelhardt, *Mission Santa Barbara*, 227.
[8] Engelhardt, *Miss. & Miss.*, 2. 575.
[9] Schultz, Jackson S., *Leather Manufacture*. 1876, N. Y., 31.
[10] The two halves of a hide.

liquid or soluble portion should be poured off into the vat, leaving all grit, dirt and unslaked lime lumps in the hogshead. Nothing but pure lime water should ever be allowed to go into the vat; this will not only render frequent 'cleaning out' unnecessary, but will save the edge of the fleshing knife, and shorten the time required in subsequent operations."

Just so lime has been slaked for centuries past.

Oak bark,[11] which was the chief tanning agent used in the mission tanneries, was gathered by the Indians from far and near, carted or carried to the mission, and ground or pulverized in the same mill that was used for crushing the olives. This mill consisted of a round stone about three feet in diameter and from eight to twelve inches thick, its edge being slanted to fit the bottom of the saucer or bowl-shaped well, or pit, in which it turned. The stone was affixed to an up-right pole which turned in bearings set in the center of the pit and in a horizontal beam above. This horizontal timber was supported by two upright posts, some-times forked. The mill was usually turned by a blindfolded mule or donkey harnessed to a sweep. Indians threw chunks of bark into the well of the mill, diligently prodded the mule along the never ending path, removed the pulver-ized or crushed product, and repeated the performance until the required amount was ground.

The tannery, with its several vats, was usually located at some convenient spot to which the water might be led after having served a turn elsewhere. At Santa Bárbara, San Luis Obispo, and San Antonio, for example, the tanneries were constructed just beyond the water-power gristmills.[12] The remains of tanks or vats, and the foundations of what probably was the drying and storage room still remain beside the ruins of the mill at San Antonio.

In all likelihood, the first tanning vats constructed at the missions were more or less crudely wrought of handhewn planks. The earliest mention of vats, found by this writer, was made by Fr. Lasuén at San Diego when, in 1783, he reported to Fr. Serra on the finishing of his mission's quadrangle. Outside the square, he wrote, was a tank which had been built shortly before that time for tanning hides.[13] Tanning, then, at this mission was begun as early as 1781. San Diego's cattle, in 1780, numbered 250.

Mention of tanks or vats of brick and mortar, or of stone and mortar, does not appear in the mission records (though it must always be remembered that many

---

[11] Chestnut oak, the best for tanning, grows near Santa Cruz; sumac, another tanning agent, is found growing to some extent in San Diego County. See Banc., *Hist. of Cal.*, 7. 71, 91.

[12] The vats at San Luis Obispo were built beyond the mission's second water-power mill which was constructed at the rear of the square.

[13] Fr. Lasúen's report dated May 10, 1783, covered the years 1781-1782. Engelhardt, *Mission San Diego*, 109-110.

of those documents are missing today) until after the coming of the artisans. Santa Bárbara's five vats were built in 1802; four of San Antonio's six were constructed in 1808, and San Gabriel's four in 1809. Of all those built for tanning hides at the twenty-one missions, San Antonio's and San Gabriel's alone remain, though there are still at Santa Bárbara what may have been two "lay-away" vats, or tanks, not mentioned in the mission records. A few years ago some restoration work was done on those at San Gabriel; those at San Antonio remain untouched and should be left so, though protected by a roof supported by pillars as they were in mission days.

Beginning the process of tanning, the hides were taken from the storehouse and put to soak in water. Those handled by Dana and his co-workers were, he said, "nearly as stiff as boards." Accordingly, it took much time to soften them and many changes of water to wash away all traces of the salt with which some of them had been "cured." At this time, too, the adhering bits of flesh and fat were scraped from the skin side. This accomplished, the hides were put through what is known as the liming process, being placed in vats containing water into which had been poured the requisite amount of liquid drawn from the barrel of slaked lime previously prepared. After remaining in this solution for three or four days, they were taken out and the hair, loosened in the liming,[14] was easily removed.

Having been "dehaired" and scraped clean, the hides were next washed and re-washed to remove the lime. When thoroughly cleansed they were ready for the tanning vat. It is not known whether these hides were first put through a number of progressively stronger tanning solutions. The vats at San Gabriel seem to indicate that such was the case at that mission, at least, for there the four tanks—really one large one having two low division walls with another smaller and deeper vat at the end—are so constructed that the tanning liquid flowed from one vat over into the next. Ordinarily, however, in those days, the following practice obtained: First, the bottom of a vat, which was large enough to permit the spreading out of a whole hide, was sprinkled with pulverized or crushed oak bark and a hide laid upon it. Another layer of bark was sprinkled over this and another hide laid on top of that, and so on until the deep vat, or tank, was sufficiently filled. Water was then poured over the pack and the hides left in the solution for from three to six months or even longer, though during that period they were usually repacked several times in fresh water and bark.

The two masonry vats, still standing just beyond the aqueduct wall at the

---

[14] The hair was not only loosened in the liming process, but the hide was made temporarily more porous and susceptible to the action of the tanning liquids.

right of Mission Santa Bárbara's church, would have served admirably for this purpose, though excavation alone could tell if they might have been so used. Such structures were known as "lay-away" vats.

Taken from the lay-away vats, the hides were once more subjected to repeated washings in order that all sediment and bark might be removed from their surfaces. While still in a moist condition, oil, grease, or tallow was rubbed into them in an effort to replace the natural oil lost in the process of tanning, and to render the leather more flexible. Afterwards, they were hung in a room where they would dry neither too quickly nor too slowly. The adobe buildings of the missions were ideal for this purpose, small barred windows permitting the air to circulate freely throughout the rooms. The drying-room was a necessary part of the tannery, and at Santa Bárbara and San Antonio, at least, adjoined the tanning vats.

When thoroughly dry, the hides were ready for the leather shop where, under the instruction of expert workers, they were converted by the Indians into sacks, saddles, shoes, bridle-reins, lazos, and other needed articles.

From the fact that a tank for tanning was erected at San Diego in the early 1780's, it is evident that there were then at the missions persons who understood something, at least, of the art. It has been said that among those first soldiers sent to California there were those who had been chosen because they were masters of useful trades. Certain it is that some of them, particularly the corporals and sergeants, later became mayordomos and managed the carpenter shop, blacksmith shop, weavery, soap-factory, tannery, etc. Thus Fr. Lasuén, in October, 1800, mentions the fact that Sergeant Ortega, while at Mission Santa Bárbara had taught two Indians to make shoes.[15] This officer was later stationed at San Buenaventura, where he doubtless instructed other Indians in the same craft. Throughout the mission records there are names of soldiers of the mission guards who taught the neophytes various trades.

In 1790-1795, there came to California along with the other artisans, two tanners and two saddlers. The names of the first were Joaquín Ávalos and Miguel Sangrador. The saddlers were Antonio Hernández and Juan María Hernández. Miguel Sangrador, master shoemaker and tanner, was sent to Mission Santa Clara, where, in 1792, two thousand hides were tanned.[16] However, this artisan's career was short lived, as he died at that mission in 1794.

Not all the hides taken from the mission cattle for home consumption were tanned. Some were cured by being sprinkled with salt when they were first staked

[15] Engelhardt, *Miss. & Miss.*, 2. 569.
[16] Banc., *Hist of Cal.*, 1. 615, 725.

out to dry at the time the animal was killed. Hides so treated were used without benefit of tanning, to cover cot and bed-frames, to re-bottom chairs, and as flooring for the carretas. They were converted into bags for tallow; buckets were made from them[17] and they were nailed to door frames in place of boards, as at San José Mission, where all the habitations of the neophyte Indians are described as having puertas de cuero (doors of hide).[18]

Robinson speaks of journeying to Rancho de las Pulgas (located between Santa Clara and San Mateo), "where they found a small adobe building with no windows, and in place of the ordinary wooden door a dried bullock's hide was substituted, which was the case as a general thing, in nearly all the ranchos on the coast, . . The bullock's hide was used almost universally in lieu of the old-fashioned bed-sacking, being nailed to the bedstead frame, and served every purpose for which it was intended, and was very comfortable to sleep upon."[19]

"The products were rude," another writer remarks, "but they served and when anything was wanting they supplied it with rawhide, and if in haste, with the hair on and wet with the natural juices of the animal it covered. This singular material found a place everywhere. Every coupling or cross-beam was bound with it, the handle of everything was tied on with it, and the stock of every old blunderbuss in the province was wrapped with it. It never came loose. Old doors are swinging yet [1889] whose rawhide hinges began to bend half a century ago. Rawhide was to every Californian second nature."[20]

At the time Steele wrote his interesting little sketches, much rawhide (untanned skin) might have been seen so used at a number of the old missions. The timbers of San Francisco's roof are still fastened together with strips of rawhide that were applied in a "green" state, that is, when the hide was freshly taken from the slaughtered animal. Bells were fastened to the bell-cote beams with such thongs. When the earthquake of June, 1925, shook the Santa Bárbara mission buildings, it was rawhide that kept one of the old bells from being hurtled to the ground below. Until within recent years many rawhide strips clung tenaciously to the beams and rafters in the loft of the Fathers' dwelling at San Fernando.

Rawhide, softened by manipulation and the rubbing in of tallow, was used in making bridle-reins, reatas (lazos, or lariats). For the reins the hair was sometimes left on. The old Indian bell-ringer at San Juan Capistrano, familiarly known as "Acú," was an expert at such work. Visiting that mission, in about 1915, the

---

[17] A hide bucket, taken from the well at Mission San Diego, is to be found at the Junípero Serra Museum in North San Diego.
[18] Inventory Mission San José, 1837. SBMA.
[19] Robinson, *Life in Cal.*, 282.
[20] Steele, *Old Californian Days*, 116-117.

writer saw him working at the west end of the front row of buildings. Seated on a hide spread out on the ground, he was cutting a narrow strip from the edge of the hide, going around and around the skin until he reached the center. Fr. O'Sullivan explained that the Indian was making some reins for an old customer. Later in the day Acú, having tied the ends of several strands of the rawhide to a small tree trunk, was busily engaged in braiding the reins. Each strand was wound on a sort of bobbin and secured with a string tied around the middle, only a short length being left free for braiding. Reatas are made after this same fashion. It is said that the reateros (makers of reatas) must be true masters of their craft, for the lazo must work as smoothly as horses and riders do. Descendants of Sergeant Ortega, who taught shoe making to Santa Bárbara neophytes, are today noted for their reata braiding.

Truly there were many uses for the hides taken from the mission cattle. The Indians were also taught to tan deer hides and sheep skins, the former being much used in making the leather jackets worn by the soldiers. The uppers of shoes were also fashioned from deerskins. In the Santa Bárbara inventory previously mentioned, besides the cattle hides, there were listed 29 sheepskins, 40 pieces of parchment, and 42 undressed sheepskins.

The "hide and tallow trade" carried on in mission days has been the theme of many a printed article. Dana's and Robinson's books are standard works on the subject. According to Bancroft, "Not a trading vessel proper touched on the coast before 1800, though there had been some considerable exchange of goods for meat and vegetables on several occasions between the Californians and such vessels as arrived for purposes other than commercial. . . The Spanish laws strictly forbade all trade not only with foreign vessels and for foreign goods, but with Spanish vessels and for Spanish-American goods except the regular transports and articles brought by them."[21]

Nevertheless, following the publication, in 1798, of the accounts written by La Pérouse and Vancouver of their visits to California, trading vessels in increasing numbers began prowling up and down the coast. There were English, Yankee, Russian, and French vessels. The Spanish officials were kept in an almost perpetual state of fear and excitement lest one of those nations represented should attempt to take over the country. Smugglers appeared and some of them, by one means or another, managed to dispose of their merchandise in return for otter skins, California's first lure to traders. Little by little under one pretext or another, and despite restrictions, regulations, and excessive tariff, trading ves-

---

[21] Banc., *Hist. of Cal.*, 1. 624.

sels began disposing of their cargoes to the mission Padres in exchange for hides, tallow, sheepskins, soap, grain, and other produce.

"Though Spanish commercial regulations forbidding trade with foreign vessels were not relaxed, necessity, as Solá[22] reported to the viceroy and for which he was not reprimanded, drove the provincial authorities to purchase every cargo for which they could pay with mission produce. The governor, however, insisted on the collection of duties on exports and imports according to a tariff which, it seems, had been devised to meet the needs of California. Otherwise there was practically no obstacle thrown in the way of trade after 1816."[23]

Marking the beginning of active trading with vessels from Lima, Peru, are six old bells hanging in the belfries of Santa Bárbara, Santa Inés, La Purísima, and San Luis Obispo. These bells are dated 1818 and the place of casting is identified by the maker's name, Vargas, or by that of the city, Lima, or both. In 1822, both the governor and the Fr. Prefecto[24] Mariano Payeras entered into a contract with the English firm of John Begg and Co., of Lima, whose representatives in California were William Edward Paty Hartnell[25] and Hugh McCulloch. "By the terms of this contract Begg and Co. were bound to send at least one vessel each year, to touch at each harbor or roadstead, to take all the hides offered, and at least 25,000 arrobas or 312 tons of tallow, and to pay either in money or in such goods as might be desired. Each mission was free to ratify the contract or not, but the ratification must be for a full period of three years, and exclusive of other traders so far as Hartnell and Co. could take the mission produce."[26]

Another firm which later came in for a large share of the mission trade was that of Bryant Sturgis, et al, of Boston, Massachusetts. Alfred Robinson came to California as agent for this company, while Richard Henry Dana, Jr., an undergraduate at Harvard, took passage on one of their vessels, the brig *Pilgrim*, as a member of the crew. Robinson has described the trade room on board the vessel "which had been fitted up with shelves and counters, resembling in appearance a country variety store."[27] But it remained for Sir William Douglas to add one or two interesting items which explain the *modus operandi* of those traders. "With these three vessels [the *Alerte*, the *California*, and the *Monsoon*], they [Bryant and Sturgis] do all their business, alternately employing them in trans-

---

[22] Pablo Vicente de Solá was governor of California in 1815-1822.
[23] Banc., *Hist. of Cal.*, 2. 419; Engelhardt, *Miss. & Miss.*, 3. 82.
[24] The office of comisario-prefecto was created in July, 1812. The prefecto was "a kind of permanent visitor-general." *Ibidem*, 4.
[25] In later years Hartnell became Inspector-General of the missions.
[26] Banc., *Hist. of Cal.*, 2. 475-476.
[27] Robinson, *Life in Cal.*, 33.

porting goods from America, managing coast trade, and carrying the produce out of the country. They are fitted up with large trading rooms, having shelves for the reception of goods, and the necessary weights and measures. Two active supercargoes acquainted with the language and country are placed in each vessel, who on the moment of their arrival in port, ride out into the country with their Books of Samples, and call from house to house, according to a list they carry in their possession to display their samples, and procure orders for goods, which on their return to the ship, they forward and receive payment in killing season."[28]

From these vessels and others, the missions obtained in exchange for mission products—principally hides, tallow, and soap—a variety of goods too great to enumerate here. Items copied from pages in the W. E. P. Hartnell Sales Book[29] include the following: 30 bundles of beads, 9 dozen shears for various purposes, 1 sack of rice, 1 arroba of card wire, 3 dozen spoons, one-half dozen knives and forks, 1 arroba of indigo, 8 barrels, 170 pounds of iron, one-half dozen shovels, 6 dozen bass strings, 1 dozen handkerchiefs, 10½ varas of coating, 50 sickles, 50 sheep shears, 4 violins, 1 arroba cotton wick [for candles], 3 violins, 1 flute, 10 dozen handkerchiefs and 212 pounds of copper, 6 dozen crosses, 6 dozen rosaries, 6 Saints [paintings or statues], numerous pieces of cloth for wearing apparel, etc.

The beads were probably intended for the Indians, as gifts from the Padres. As were, perhaps, some of the handkerchiefs. The coming of the trading vessel was, it seems, looked forward to with joyful anticipation by Padres and neophytes alike.

Returning to the slaughtering place—as soon as the bullock's hide was removed by the skinners, other Indians attacked the carcass, cutting away the various wanted portions. Long strips of the lean meat were cut from the sides and back to be converted into "jerky," or carne seca (dried meat). Huge chunks of lean parts were set aside for immediate consumption by the members of the mission community. There was, as one Padre said, plenty of meat for all. Suet, the hard fat about the kidneys and loins, and other fatty portions were cut from the carcass, piled into a carreta and sent to the mission along with the lean parts and the tongue. Occasionally the bullock's head was included for barbecuing.

The remaining portions of the slaughtered animal were left, apparently, for the numerous dogs that hung around every mission and ranch house, the vultures, the bears, and other wild animals that prowled over the countryside.

[28] Douglas, "Journal."
[29] This book was the property of Mr. B. A. Soberanes of Salinas, California. Copy of the above items was obtained through the courtesy of Rev. A. D. Spearman, S. J.

▲ Bringing wood *for the mission fires—one of the tasks allotted old Indian women.* (Miniature)

▼ Tallow and soap works *at San Gabriel. An enormous amount of wood was required for their operation.*

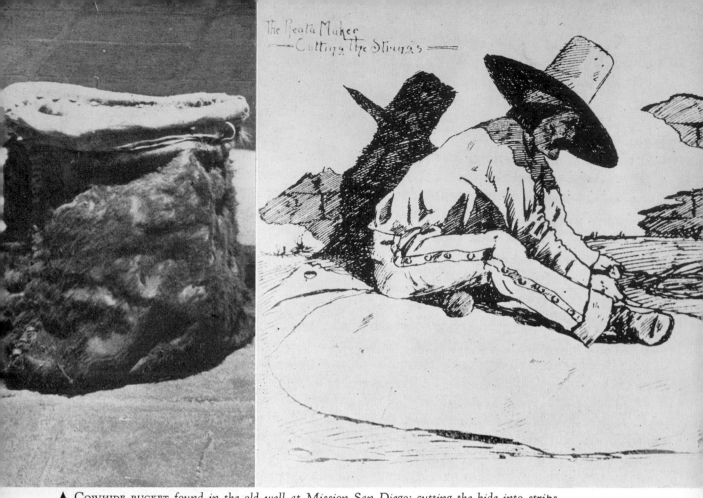

The Reata Maker
— Cutting the Strings —

▲ Cowhide bucket *found in the old well at Mission San Diego; cutting the hide into strips.*

▼ The tanning vats *at San Gabriel, some of the very few left in ruins or otherwise at the missions.*

Though Fr. José Señán at San Buenaventura reported that the large parts of the meat were taken in carts to the fields and burned. Enough, however, of the car-casses remained to cause early visitors to speak of the terrible stench that arose from the slaughtering places. And the waste was enormous, for lack of time, but chiefly for lack of knowledge of ways and means of utilizing the discarded parts. The horns with the skull attached were sometimes gathered up and affixed to adobe walls to keep out marauders.

Arriving at the mission the carretas were unloaded, the lean meat going to the kitchen, or pozolera, and the fats to the tallow and soap works. The lean strips were dipped in brine and hung like stockings on a line to dry. When thoroughly "cured" the "jerky" was stored away in an attic, or loft, to be used when fresh meat was not easily obtainable. The Spanish people were very fond of carne seca, or tassajo, and served it in a variety of savory dishes.[30] The tongues were smoked and stored, or hung rather, for future use. It is said that the old kitchen chimneys were studded with huge iron spikes from which were hung hams, tongues, and other meats to be smoked. Some of those nails may still be seen in the walls of the old chimney at San Juan Capistrano.

Dr. Wood describes the roasting of a bullock's head. It "was deposited in a hole dug in the ground, and surrounded by hot stones that it might cook for our breakfast in the morning. The following morning, after breakfasting on the roasted bullock's head, which all thought a delicious repast, we started for Monterey, . . ."[31]

We may be sure that many an ox head was so barbecued by Spaniards and Indians alike. It was a mode of cooking familiar to both. Just so had the natives cooked the green asparagus-like stalk of the yucca and the bud of the joshua tree, before the coming of the white man.

The fats taken to the mission were separated, the suet being set aside to be converted into tallow for candle making; the other fatty portions were "tried out," rendered, or melted, and used in making soap.

It is impossible now to determine whether or not all the missions had such soap and tallow vats as may yet be seen, though in a ruinous or incomplete con-dition, at San Gabriel, San Juan Capistrano, San Fernando, and La Purísima. Those at San Luis Obispo were possibly quite similar and seem to have stood in that row of adobe buildings that formerly lined the right, or north, side of what is now called Chorro Street. At least Luis Moreno's father told him that when

---

[30] Packman, Ana Begue, *Leather Dollars*, 64; *Early California Hospitality*, 116.
[31] Wood, W. Maxwell, *Wandering Sketches of South America, Polynesia, California, etc.*, 284.

Francisco Estevan Quintana built the brick store for the Schwarz Brothers[32] some "smelters" were uncovered along that line. They were located at that spot where the entrance to E. M. Payne's Plumbing Shop now is. Those at Santa Bárbara were constructed in the second square built at the rear of the main quadrangle and had a yard attached to them.

A study of the remains of the vats mentioned above reveals the fact that they were not inclosed within four walls, but were usually protected by a roof upheld by pillars of adobe, brick, stone, or wood. Sunken wells in the masonry surrounding vats at San Gabriel clearly indicate the use of huge oaken timbers, similar to those two which once flanked the gateway giving entrance to the mission's patio through the front row of buildings. At San Juan Capistrano the vats were built under a lean-to roof extending along the outer side of the west wing as far as that building which projects into what was formerly the vineyard. This roof was upheld by pillars of ladrillos laid in mortar.

The vats at San Juan Capistrano were ideally placed in that the land suddenly gives way at this point leaving a space for furnaces, or fire-boxes, under the cone-shaped masonry vats above. As before noted, this was a favorite building practice of the Padres. Remembering the terrific heat that was generated in the process of trying out fats in those huge cauldrons, one realizes that the soap factory must of necessity have been a building with one or more open sides.

At the missions where vats similar to those described above had not been constructed, the tallow and other fats were rendered in large iron kettles, or cauldrons, upheld by large boulders.[33] Between the boulders was a space for the fire. These kettles, it is said, were obtained from whaling vessels, and had been used for trying out whale oil.

Thinking of the fires that must be kept burning under the huge vats and kettles, one pictures the wood gatherers going and coming in a continuous stream— old women with burden baskets, or carrying-nets on their backs; old men in carretas pulled by oxen; little children to pick up the smaller pieces. All who could be spared were kept busy at this time for the fires must be kept burning until all the suet and fats were "tried out." More able-bodied workers cut and hauled logs to be sawn into proper lengths for feeding the furnaces.

The suet, or sebo en rama (literally, tallow in the rough), was separated from the more greasy and softer fats and rendered into tallow. The tallow was put in casks or in hide bags and set away in storerooms or underground storage vaults, the hide bags having been whitewashed to keep out insects. At San Fernando,

---

[32] Where the Blackstone Hotel now stands.
[33] See drawing by Wm. Rich Hutton, *California 1847-1852*, Plate XXXV. "Trying out Tallow, Monterey."

Robinson said, the tallow was "laid down in large, arched, stone vaults of suffi-cient capacity to contain several cargoes." Nordhoff corroborates this state-ment.[34] It is hoped that when the contemplated reconstruction of this mission's quadrangle takes place the old vaults may be relocated and preserved.

Immense quantities of tallow were stored at all the missions. In 1801, at San Juan Capistrano, for example, 12,500 pounds of that product were destroyed by fire. Evidently it had been stored in one of the rooms of the quadrangle as 600 fanegas of corn, and 1,000 bushels of wheat were also burned.[35] Within recent years there has been uncovered at this mission a large underground storage vault, or cellar, in the area beyond the west wing. It is impossible to say definitely what its purpose was, but it would have made an admirable storage vault for tallow, which needed to be kept cool. It would have served equally well as a cellar, or bodega, for wine. Had it been used for either purpose, steps would have led down into its depths. That no steps were found when the vault was excavated need occasion no surprise, for steps were often built against walls and not incorporated into them. The stair descending into the mill reservoir at Santa Bárbara is an example of this practice. Such steps are very apt to fall and become disintegrated, especially if constructed of adobes from which the customary ladrillo tread has been removed.

Part of the tallow was reserved for trade; part was used in making the innumer-able candles necessary to mission life. That the large rooms and shops with their few windows were poorly lighted is apparent. And candles were the main means of illumination in those days. One may rightly surmise then, that in the shoe shops, carpenter shops, weaveries, etc., where light was essential to good workmanship, many candles were kept burning many days of the year. For, as has been previously pointed out, California does have her days of fog and clouded skies. Perhaps, as Dr. Wood noted at San Juan Bautista when he witnessed a dance given in the sala of the mission, the candles were "set in tin sconces" hung up all around on the walls of the room.[36] In the ruined walls of Mission La Sole-dad there still remain at each side of the main doorway, also flanking the win-dows, and beside a built-in cupboard, small niches cut in the adobe walls where candles were probably set.

Records tell us, too, that on days of great occasions the mission church and other buildings were illuminated on the outside. The rooftops, the corridors, and

[34] Robinson, *Life in Cal.*, 48; Nordhoff, *California*, 243-244.
[35] Prov. St. Pap. Ben. Mil. XXIX. 13. Rodríguez to Arrillaga, April 16, 1801. Copy courtesy of California State Historical Assn.
[36] Wood, *opus cit.*, 268.

even the belfries were lighted up. As this could have been accomplished only with candles, the number used can scarcely be estimated. When Santa Bárbara's church was dedicated September 10th, 1820, a three-day celebration took place. At the conclusion of the religious ceremonies held in the church, the people passed out into the space in front of the mission buildings. "Then in succession," Fr. Francisco Suñar reports, "were illuminated the (azoteas) housetops, the corridors, and the tower, . . " [37] Candles, hundreds of them, were lighted almost simultaneously to create the desired effect! It is regrettable that the Padre did not say how this was accomplished.

The candle factory was undoubtedly a very busy place. The writer is indebted to Mr. B. A. Soberanes for the following description of the method of candle making employed, as he remembered it, in 1860. "I was," he writes, "seven years old then. It was customary at my Father's ranch, in the summer to slaughter 8 or 10 head of beef cattle to make jerkey and lard. The kidney tallow [suet] was saved for candle making. This tallow was rendered, strained in a burlap sack and put away until fall when the cool weather would set in. Then candle making would be put in operation. The candle wicks which were cut off about 16 inches long, were hung on a cross stick, or sticks, and the ends brought together to the length of 8 inches and about three inches apart. The tallow was heated to luke warm degree. Then the dipping would begin and kept up until you would get the candle the size you would prefer. We also used molds, the wicks run through the bottom of the molds and knots ties at the bottom to keep the tallow from running out of the molds. A vessel of water was used to cool them off, and in removing them from the molds we would cut off the knot at the bottom and raise out the candles. The molds would then be ready for another batch. This will give you a fair idea of candle making in early days. . . "[38]

There can be little doubt that these same methods were employed in the mission candle shops. Some of the old molds still exist in various museums and perhaps in some private homes. Juan Aguilar of San Juan Capistrano had some fine specimens of them.

In 1821, Innocente García, a soldier of the Monterey Company, and a soapmaker by trade, became mayordomo at San Juan Bautista. That he taught soapmaking to the neophytes there seems obvious, for it was the custom of the Padres to secure men for that office who were able to teach some trade to the Indians. He was hired at eight pesos a month, one fanega and four almudes of corn,

[37] Engelhardt, *Mission Santa Barbara*, 109. See full account of this celebration in Chapter XIX, this volume.
[38] Correspondence B. A. Soberanes, March 21, 1932.

three almudes of beans, one almud[39] of garvanzos, twenty tallow candles, one peso, four reales worth of soap, and one head of cattle. In addition he was allowed an Indian servant.[40]

Mention of other instructors in the art of soapmaking might be found in other Padres' account books, but the process was so simple that the Indians from the Baja California missions were probably well acquainted with it and able from the first to act as instructors.

For making soap the greasier fats were used—"scrap fats" from cattle, hogs, or other animals. Goat tallow may have been included. These fats were rendered as the tallow for candles had been, strained, and stored until needed. Soapmaking was probably done in the cooler months too, though not during the rainy season because of the necessity of keeping the firewood dry. Wood ashes taken from the furnaces under soap or tallow vats were leached in large kettles or tall masonry tanks and the resultant liquid, containing sodium and potassium carbonates, used in the manufacture of soap.[41]

The melted fat, together with a sufficient amount of the above liquid, was placed in a vat or kettle and boiled for the required length of time. The mass was then allowed to cool somewhat and the soft soap, which floats on top of the water, was skimmed off and poured into a mold to set. When the soap had become sufficiently solid it was cut into bars or pieces of the desired size. These bars were then laid away on shelves, turned occasionally, until they were thoroughly dry, or cured, when they were ready for use.

At San Gabriel there remain, beside the tallow vats, two tall masonry tanks and a long, vat-like structure which quite possibly served respectively for leaches for ashes, and as a cooling and molding vat for the soap. If the buildings back of the front row are ever restored, this writer sincerely hopes that the soap vats and adjoining structures will be left untouched. For they are much more intelligible in their present state than they are likely to be if added to or rebuilt, since no similar structures that might serve as examples, or patterns, for reconstruction, appear to exist. And "reconstruction," or "restoration," that is not authentic is a most deplorable tampering with history.

---

[39] An almud according to Engelhardt, *Miss. & Miss.*, 2. 103, "is the 12th part of a fanega, which is equal to about a hundred-weight."

[40] Engelhardt, *Mission San Juan Bautista*, 34.

[41] Duflot de Mofras reported that at Mission San Diego soap was manufactured from soda obtained by burning seaweed gathered along the shore. At San Juan Capistrano, he said, carbonate of potash that rose to the surface of the ground was used in soap making. See Mofras, *Travels*, 1. 175, 180. Bryant, *What I Saw*, 410, says that he was shown by William Foxen a caustic soda which he had obtained by burning a shrub or plant found growing in the Tulare valley. The resultant ash Foxen used in the manufacture of soap.

These carbonates were probably added to the liquid obtained by leaching wood ashes to increase its efficiency.

CHAPTER **15**

Indian Weavers of Rabbit-Skin and Feather Robes

Indians Learn to Spin and Weave Wool into Cloth

Weaving is a process of interlacing objects long, slender, and flexible (most commonly vegetal or animal fibers), to make a single fabric. It is a process begun by the birds in their nest building and continued by primitive man in his rude clothing and basketry. It was adapted to the simple hand loom by peoples of rudimentary civilization, and finally in our modern era, to the power loom. Weaving spans human history from beginning to end." So wrote Charles Avery Amsden in his fascinating book, *Navaho Weaving*.[1]

Before the coming of the Spanish conquerors the Indians of California had learned to weave mats of bark, rushes, yucca fibers, and grass; nets from vegetal fibers that looked like raw hemp, for catching fish, and nets for carrying loads. They had woven baskets from rushes, grasses, withes, or twigs, splints, roots, stems of maiden-hair fern, or whatever textile the region afforded. Their baskets, to which, as Costansó noted, they gave "a thousand forms," were their household utensils. They ranged in size from the small trinket basket to the granary[2] for storing acorns or seeds. Some were plain, while others were ornamented with designs in brown, black, or red, usually the natural colors of the material used. Some were decorated with the nodding black plumes of quails or the gay scarlet feathers of the woodpeckers' scalps. Hanging pendants of bits of mother-of-pearl and shells were woven into others.

The natives had also learned to weave blankets of fur and of feathers. These blankets, or robes, in the one material or the other, are found to have constituted part of the clothing or bedding of the prehistoric Indians of the cliff dwellings of Colorado, New Mexico, and Arizona, as well as that of the Pueblo

---

[1] Published in 1934 by the Fine Arts Press, Santa Ana, California, in cooperation with the Southwest Museum.
[2] See James, George W., *Indian Basketry*, pp. 105, 168, for storage basket nine feet nine inches in circumference and three feet deep.

Indians of the Southwest and of our own California natives. Spanish explorers of 1769 found the latter wearing such robes. Waseurtz, in 1843, bartered with Indians of the Feather River region for some of their beautiful feather robes and, as he states, slept very well in them.[3]

Dr. Kroeber describes the weaving of the fur robes as follows:

The skins were cut into strips a half-inch wide or more, which were left uncured. As they dried they curled or twisted on themselves, leaving the soft hair everywhere exposed. The strips were then knotted into a long furry line. This was wound back and forth between two stakes to form a vertical plane of horizontal warps. Into this continuous double weft [?], two lines of the same material were twisted alternately up and down, and knitted to the outermost warp on each turn. The completed blanket was thick, soft, and warm, while the hide strips gave it great durability.

In the Sacramento Valley water birds are more numerous than rabbits, and the blankets were usually of feathers. The manufacture was identical except that the more fragile bird skin was first twisted with a string.[4]

Evidently fur and feather robes were woven on what might be called a "fixed-warp" frame, that is, one to which both ends of the warp were fastened and drawn taut. This was an advance over the "free-warp" frame upon which mats were woven, for on those frames the lower ends of the warp strings hung loose and the weaving was done from the top down. Nevertheless, the technique of fashioning not only the mats and baskets, but even the robes, falls under the classification of "finger-weaving,"[5] because the warp strings, or ribs in the case of the twined baskets, were manipulated by the fingers instead of the healds, or heddles, of the true loom. In "finger-weaving" the weft, or woof, was drawn over and under one warp string at a time. Whereas, in weaving on a true loom, the heddles—each controlling a set of alternate warp strings[6]—when moved by pressing on the pedals, separate the two sets of strings and open up a passage-way, or "shed," through which the woof is shuttled in one unhindered motion from one side of the loom to the other. The batten is then pulled sharply toward the weaver, striking home the threads of the woof. Another movement of the pedals and the position of the warp strings is changed, the lower ones now be-

---

[3] Waseurtz, *Sojourn in California*, 68.

[4] Kroeber, *Handbook*, 414-416.

There are on display in the Peabody Museum at Harvard University, Cambridge, Massachusetts, four feather robes woven by California Indians. They are, according to data received from the museum, "of loosely woven stout cords having feathers, principally of the mallard duck, caught into or wrapped around the strands [of the cords] before weaving." In size the four robes measure 50"x60", 47"x55", 46"x44", and 44"x60". The colors, with one exception, are black, white, and buff. Specimen No. 98240, shown in illustration, is decorated with red dots formed with the scalp locks of woodpeckers.

[5] For information on mat and basket weaving the reader is referred to Kroeber, James, and Amsden.

[6] One heddle controlling the odd-numbered strings, 1,3,5, and so on, while the other heddle governs the even-numbered ones.

coming the upper and vice versa. In changing their positions the alternate warps lock in the strand of yarn or other material just passed through, and form a new shed for the next one.

But the true loom was not known to the natives of California nor had they any knowledge of the weaving of cotton or wool before the coming of the Span-ish people.

In August, 1773, Fr. Palóu came up from Old California with five other Franciscans[7] destined to manage three new missions yet to be founded. He brought along ten families of Christian Indians and eleven single men from the former Jesuit missions of the peninsula. These Indians were intended to help the Padres in their work of instructing the natives of New California. Twenty-five families were to have come and there were many more who wanted to accompany the Fathers. However, upon hearing that the supply ship, the *San Carlos*, had broken her rudder and must return to San Blas for repairs, Fr. Palóu decided that it would be unwise to take too many Indians with him since they would but increase the number to be fed in that new land where rations were already short. He accordingly chose, as he says, "those who were willing to go voluntarily, *and seemed most suitable to me for the purpose*" (the italics are this writer's), and loaded the pack-mules, that others would have ridden, with corn and beans for the distressed missions of Monterey.[8]

Arriving at San Diego, Palóu proceeded to leave at that mission one of the families in order that the Indian wife might teach the women there to spin and weave wool.[9] For they were already getting wool from the sheep that Fr. Dumetz had brought up in the previous autumn. Nothing is said about a loom, but the Indian husband or some other person was undoubtedly at hand to con-struct one. The most essential parts of a loom had probably been brought up from Baja California, leaving only the framework to be constructed. It is obvious that Fr. Palóu would not have left a woman to teach weaving without a loom. And, having chosen a weaver from one of the peninsula missions, he would naturally have also brought along an Indian capable of setting up a loom. The Padres who knew these Indians and their capabilities had been present when the selections were made. And the missionaries leaving Old California knew that, to Christian-ize and civilize the natives of the new field to which they were going, food and clothing must be provided for them. Being practical and experienced men they naturally chose those workers who would most speedily advance the cause.

---

[7] These were Frs. Lasúen, Murguía, Amurrio, Prestamero, and Fuster.
[8] Bolton, *Palou's New Cal.*, 1. 263, 282-283, 291-297.
[9] *Ibidem*, 304-305.

Top: FEATHER ROBE WOVEN by Maidu Indian of California. See Chapter XV, note 4 for description. Bottom: Washoe Indian weaving rabbit skin robe; Baja California Indian women wearing feather robes.

Top: Spanish looms operated by *Mexicans of Oaxaca. Mission looms were so fashioned. Bottom: Cloth woven on mission loom; spinning wheel reconstructed at San Miguel.*

Shortly after 1701, when he arrived in Baja California, the Jesuit Father, Juan de Ugarte, had introduced weaving to the neophytes of his mission, San Xavier Viggè. This energetic and resourceful priest showed the Indians how to shear the sheep secured from Sonora, how to card the wool, spin, and weave it. He also made the spinning wheels and looms. Then, not content with the instruction that he could give the neophytes himself, he sent to Tepic for a good weaver to teach them that they might become more skillful in the art. This master worker remained in Baja California for a long time and doubtless taught his trade to the Indians of other missions besides those of San Xavier.[10]

Cotton was grown and woven at five of those Jesuit establishments, while woolen blankets were manufactured at several of them.[11] And some of the Franciscan Padres who later came to Alta California had served for four and one-half years in those former Jesuit missions. They surely gained some knowledge of the art of weaving there. Both Frs. Palóu and Murguía had labored at San Xavier, the cradle of the art of true loom weaving in the Californias. Moreover, one of the unmarried Indians who accompanied Palóu, in 1773, came from Mission San José de Comundú, while others were taken from San Francisco de Borja, where Fr. Lasuén had been stationed.

Wherefore, we may safely say that the art of weaving was brought to New California from the peninsula, and, that in the Indian woman trained in a mission of Baja California and left at San Diego to teach the native women there to weave, we have our first mission-day, loom-weaving instructor. It is a pity that her name was not recorded.

With the women of the Christian Indian families coming in 1773, and those of the two who had accompanied Fr. Dumetz when he returned with the sheep and much needed provisions,[12] the Padres now had guardians and instructors for the girls and young women of the monjerios. And, since the spinning and weaving of the wool was for the most part done by the Indian women, the weavery almost invariably adjoined the monjerio, although there are occasional references to Indian men weaving blankets.

While the sheep purchased from the missions of the peninsula or sent up from Sonora were all Spanish stock, it appears that the breed was not of the best. The wool, by most accounts,[13] was coarse. Specimens of cloth woven on mission

[10] *The History of [Lower] California* by Don Francisco Javier Clavigero, S. J. (Translated from the Italian and edited by Sara E. Lake and A. A. Gray), 188.
[11] Bolton, *Palou's New Cal.*, 1. 172-213. The five missions were San Francisco de Borja, San José de Comundú, Purísima de Cadegomó, San Xavier, and San Ignacio.
[12] *Ibidem*, 3. 20; Engelhardt, *Mission San Diego*, 43.
[13] Bryant, *What I Saw*, 286, 352; Austin, Mary, *The Flock*, 7; Bidwell, John, *A Journey to California* (John Henry Nash Printer), 39.

looms and found with other relics on the Island of San Clemente testify to the truth of these reports. At San Francisco only is fine wool spoken of. Langsdorff, who visited the mission in 1806, wrote: "The wool of the sheep here is very fine and extremely good, but the implements and looms appeared of a very moderate kind, and as the ecclesiastics are the sole [?] instructors of these people, who themselves know very little about the matter, scarcely even understanding the fulling,[14] the cloth is of very ordinary quality."[15]

Bancroft tells us that San Francisco's sheep were of Merino stock, Spain's best.[16] How this mission alone was able to secure such sheep is not explained.

Many writers have wondered why Spain, with the best wool-producing sheep in the world, should have sent to her colonies animals of an inferior breed. Forbes remarks: "Perhaps the propagation of the merinos, like the grape,[17] was discouraged or prohibited in the Americas, in order, as was the policy of the mother country, to give the monopoly to the flocks of Estramadura, as well as to the vineyards of Catalonia. It is extraordinary, however, that some one should not have introduced into any of those vast countries a better breed, even in the time of the Spanish government; and still more extraordinary, that since the revolutions which have removed all obstacles, no amelioration of this breed has taken place. There are large flocks of sheep in Chile; immense herds on the table lands of Mexico which abundantly supply the capital with mutton; and myriads scattered over the middle or southern republics, all of which, as well as those of California, are of the same breed, and their wool invariably exceedingly coarse. . . ."[18]

In this connection it might be well to note that De Mofras reported (1840-1842) that rams from Scotland had been imported by the English to improve the breed.[19]

There were white sheep and there were black ones in the mission flocks. In 1796, the Fathers at San Juan Capistrano sent to the presidio of Santa Bárbara 2,600 pounds of white wool and 500 pounds of black wool. Dr. Hiram Reid says that at San Gabriel the black and white wools "were cleaned and spun separately, then mixed in the weaving, making salt-and-pepper cloth, and sometimes black and white barred or striped goods, etc."[20]

Weaving was another industry that the Padres were not required to include

---

[14] Fulling is a process by which woolen goods are cleansed, shrunk, and felted, making the cloth stronger and firmer.
[15] Langsdorff, *Voyages and Travels*, 2. 159.
[16] Banc., *Hist. of Cal.*, 1. 713, n. 38.
[17] Blackmar, *Spanish Institutions of the Southwest*, 297.
[18] Forbes, *California*, 277-278.
[19] De Mofras, *Travels*, 1. 259.
[20] Reid, *History of Pasadena*, 350.

in their annual reports, and accordingly, until 1792, little was known of the progress made in this field of endeavor. La Pérouse, visiting Mission San Carlos in 1786, makes mention of the fact that the use of the mill which M. de Langle gave to the Padres would enable four Indian women in a day to perform the work of a hundred and leave time to spin the wool of their sheep, and to manufacture coarse stuffs. From this statement it is evident that woolen cloth was being woven at this mission at that time.

In 1792, Captain George Vancouver visited Mission San Francisco. He was shown over the grounds and through the shops within the quadrangle. "One large room," he wrote, "was occupied by manufacturers of a coarse sort of blanketting made from wool produced in the neighborhood. The looms though rudely wrought, were tolerably well contrived, and, had been made by Indians under the immediate direction and superintendence of the fathers; who by the same assiduity, had carried the manufacture thus far into execution. The produce resulting from their manufactory is wholly applied to the clothing of the converted Indians. I saw some of the cloth, which was by no means despicable, and, had it received the advantage of fulling, would have been very decent sort of clothing."

"The preparation of the wool, as well as the spinning and weaving of it, was, I understand, performed by unmarried women and female children, who were all resident within the square; and were in a state of conversion to the Roman Catholic persuasion. Besides manufacturing the wool, they are also instructed in a variety of necessary, useful, and beneficial employments, until they marry which is greatly encouraged; when they retire from the tuition of the fathers to the hut of their husband. By these means it is expected that their doctrines will be firmly established, and rapidly propagated; and the trouble that they now have with their present untaught flock will be hereafter recompensed, by having fewer prejudices to combat in the rising generation. . . "[21]

At Mission Santa Clara also, Vancouver was hospitably received and conducted through the various buildings of the quadrangle. There he found that "apartments within the square in which the priests resided were appropriated to a number of young female Indians; and the like reasons were given as at St. Francisco, for their being so selected and educated. Their occupations were the same, though some of their woolen manufactures surpassed those we had before seen, and wanted only the operation of fulling, with which the fathers were unacquainted, to make them very decent blankets. . . "[22]

[21] Vancouver, *Voyage*, 2. 11-12.
[22] *Ibidem.*, 2. 19.

Among the artisans who reached California in 1790-1795, were two weaving instructors, Antonio Domingo Henríquez (sometimes spelled Enríquez) and Mariano José Mendoza. Henríquez, who had an Indian wife, started at Mission San Diego and taught carding, spinning, and weaving at all the missions of the south as far as San Luis Obispo. He also made spinning wheels, warping frames, looms, combs, and all the tools of the art save those for carding. He taught the weaving of both woolen and cotton cloth.[23]

In 1796, Mariano Mendoza was sent from Monterey to San Juan Capistrano to teach his trade to the neophytes, though it appears that Henríquez had been there before him. But Mendoza had a reputation for weaving wide goods, being known as a "tejedor de ancho." Bancroft notes: "If he neglected his business, he should be chained at night, for he was under contract with the government at thirty dollars a month. A loom was set up and other apparatus of a rude nature, with which by the aid of natives coarse fabrics and blankets were woven."[24] Mendoza's wife taught the Indian girls to spin. Captain Grájera of the San Diego company declared that the carpenter Gutiérrez was the only man who could put up the looms.[25] It must be remembered, however, that looms had undoubtedly been set up and Indians taught to card, spin, and weave some twenty years before this time.

From the various accounts of early writers and visitors to the missions there has arisen the belief that there were many weavers at work on the mission looms. This belief, however, does not coincide with recorded facts. For instance, sixty weavers were reported to be engaged in weaving at Santa Bárbara, in 1800,[26] but it is apparent that all the processes involved in the weaving industry must have been meant since but four looms were recorded in that mission's inventory of 1834. At the same time eighteen spinning wheels, forty-six pairs of cards, and one warping rack (urdidor) were counted. San Gabriel's spinning wheels were not listed in the memorandum made at the time of secularization, but its *four* looms were. At San Diego six looms, two of which were useless, sixteen spinning wheels, twelve pairs of cards, and three combs—two for flax and one for blankets—were listed by the appraisers. Mentioned in San Fernando's inventory of April 29, 1843, are three looms, eight pairs of cards, and ten spinning wheels. Mission San Carlos, in 1835, possessed four large looms with equipment (that is, battens, heddles, harness, treadles, etc.), one small one, seven spinning

[23] Engelhardt, *Mission San Luis Obispo*, 40-41.
[24] Banc., *Hist. of Cal.*, 1. 658.
[25] *Ibidem*, 658, note 31.
[26] Engelhardt, *Mission Santa Barbara*, 72; Rogers, Harrison, "Journal," 205-206.

wheels, and six pairs of cards. In 1816, the Padres of La Purísima added to their equipment two looms for the new weaving (the weaving of wider cloth?). San José, one of the most flourishing of the missions at the time of secularization, counted six looms, forty-one spinning wheels, and one warping frame.[27] It will thus be seen that the number of weaving machines at the various missions was surprisingly small.

But these looms were rude and cumbersome. One at Tierra Azul, New Mexico, stood approximately 7' x 7' x 7' in size. It was a handmade loom, sadly neglected, but had been operated until about 1932 by a Spanish weaver, Don Eologio Gallegos. At the time this writer examined it (1938) the machine had, so the son of the weaver said, stood for a century. Though it was more crude, it had been in its day, in every essential respect, a duplicate of looms used until within recent years by weavers of Oaxaca, México.[28] In all likelihood one would find today this same type of loom still in operation in that interesting town of many handicrafts.

It will readily be seen that a loom of the above given dimensions would have required at least 11' x 11' of floor space to allow room for the sleying of the warp, for making adjustments and repairs. That the looms were ever moved is doubtful. Santa Bárbara, then, with its weavery of 50' x 19' would have had none too much room for its four looms, for, besides those machines, there were warping racks, reel winders, and other necessary paraphernalia which also occupied considerable space. The size of San José's weavery was not given in the inventory; San Luis Obispo's, however, was 15 varas by 7 varas, or 41' x 19'. The dimensions of San Fernando's first room for weaving were 8 varas by 6 varas, or 22' x 17'. It was later replaced by another (dimensions not given) built in connection with the apartments of the girls and unmarried women.[29]

The dimensions of San Juan Capistrano's spinnery, or hilandería, were 16 varas by 6 varas, or 44' x 17', while the one at Santa Cruz measured 15½ varas by 7 varas, or 43' x 19'. The latter was equipped with a garret, or loft, for storing wool, and had one door and two windows. Its floor and roof were both tiled.[30] That but two windows provided entrance for the sunlight to this large room seems incredible, but many candles were used in the workshops, and fortunately, the spinning wheels could easily be moved from one location to another. Certain it is that much of the carding and spinning was done in the mon-

---

[27] Items taken from the inventories preserved in the SBMA.

[28] See illustration "Weavers of Oaxaca," reproduced from the *National Geographic Magazine*, May, 1927, through the courtesy of the publishers.

[29] *Informe* Santa Bárbara, 1794. SBMA; Engelhardt, *Mission San Luis Obispo*, 43; and *Mission San Fernando*, 15.

[30] Engelhardt, *Mission San Juan Capistrano*, 28; Inventory Mission Santa Cruz, 1835.

jerio patios. At San Luis Rey there is a small, low chair said to have been used in the spinnery of Santa Clara. Its back legs show that it has been dragged from one place to another.

Mention has been made by some writers of the use of teasels (thistles) for carding wool. Charles Avery Amsden presents an illustration of three types of wool cards.[31] The first is an American card with fiber bristles; the second, a later American variety with steel teeth; and the third, a "Spanish type" card composed of thistle burs clamped in a frame. One who has done carding, however, would be extremely loath to use this last named type, and would do so only if compelled to through absolute inability to procure the regular variety. It does not appear that the California Missions should ever have needed to resort to the use of thistles.

A partial check of the *memorias*, now in the library of Mission San Buenaventura,[32] reveals the fact that, in the years 1791-1802, sixty-six pairs of wool cards were imported. Three pairs were for carding a second time. Under the date of 1800 there is listed "Un peine para teger manta ancha, y otro para manta angosta, con lissos [lizos] correspondientes" (One reed[33] for weaving, or regulating the weaving of, a wide blanket and another for a narrow one with corresponding heddles). From this record it is evident that the Mission Padres were able to procure loom parts as well as cards from México. In 1797, two spinning wheels were ordered.

The shears with which the sheep were shorn were handmade of steel. They, too, were imported, as were the shears for cutting cloth.

The preparation of the wool for weaving required the attention of quite a number of Indians. The sheep were probably sheared at the ranchos where they were herded, and the wool carried to the mission in carretas drawn by oxen. Arriving there, the fleeces were examined and burs, sticks, thorns, or whatever might have become entangled in the wool removed. The little Indian children helped with this task. Then came the washing and drying of the fleece. The washing was done in large copper kettles, or cauldrons, with generous applications of mission-made soap. If the wool was to be dyed it was necessary to have all the grease removed, or the dye would not "take" well. The cleansed wool was spread out on bushes to dry. After being thoroughly dried it was carded, or

---

[31] Amsden, *Navaho Weaving*, Plate 10.

[32] The pages in this book containing the *memorias* from the beginning of the mission to the year 1790 have been crudely cut out and are missing.

[33] The weaver's reed is a contrivance in the loom consisting of a series of wires in an upright frame set between the opposite sides of the batten, or beater. It is used both to keep the warp threads properly spaced and to pound the weft threads in place.

straightened, to expedite the spinning of it into yarn. How fine a yarn the Indian women eventually learned to produce cannot be told today. The specimens of mission Indian weaving found on the Island of San Clemente, and preserved in the Los Angeles County Museum, show no fine yarn. But, in 1820, Captain José de la Guerra wrote to the governor that in the five missions under the juris-diction of the Santa Bárbara presidio, "the branches of industry are the usual ones of weaving [spinning?] wool which is then manufactured into blankets, coarse cloth, finer cloth and sombreros."[34] In producing the finer cloth the wool was, of necessity, carded and recarded, then spun and respun until a yarn of the desired fineness was obtained.

At San Juan Capistrano, in 1797, Mariano Mendoza, with the help of the Indians, wove baize, woolen blankets, mixed cotton and woolen cloth, a carpet for the church, and thirty yards of white flannel. Flax was also spun and woven at this time.[35] Cotton goods were woven at a number of the missions. Cotton was grown in California to some extent, at least; that produced at Mission San Diego was declared by de Mofras to have been of a superior quality.[36] In all probability, however, most of the raw material was brought up by supply ves-sels from San Blas. 800 yards of cotton cloth were woven on the Santa Bárbara Mission looms, in 1800, besides 700 yards of breech cloth.[37] Since the breech cloths, or taparrabos, were usually about half a yard wide the cloth was probably woven in just that width. This article of clothing was usually wrapped around the loins and secured at the waist with a leather thong. It is so pictured by a number of visitors to California.[38]

In 1795, hemp seed was distributed by Governor Borica to a number of the missions, and, in 1808, Santa Bárbara gathered a crop of 211 arrobas, or 5,275, pounds of the product.[39] It is significant in this connection that one of San Miguel's ranchos was named Cañamo (hemp field). Some of the Indians' cloth-ing was made from this textile, though the material as it was then produced must have been very harsh and irritating. A hemp carder, relic of mission days, is in the museum room of San Juan Bautista. An examination of this tool will convince anyone that carding hemp was indeed a man's-size job.

But the bulk of weaving done at the missions was of woolen blankets, half-blankets, mangas (ponchos) for the shepherds, loin cloth material, loosely woven

[34] Engelhardt, *Mission Santa Barbara*, 115.
[35] Engelhardt, *Mission San Juan Capistrano*, 33-36.
[36] De Mofras, *Travels*, 1. 172.
[37] Engelhardt, *Mission Santa Barbara*, 72.
[38] See—Dana, *Two Years Before the Mast*, 96, for description of Indian clothing.
[39] Engelhardt, *Mission Santa Barbara*, 90.

woolens for clothing the Indians, and a coarse sort of serge (sayal Franciscano) from which the gray habits were made for some of the Padres.

Some of the material was white, some black and white—perhaps striped—some a "bluish color" according to the Padres' reports. Encarnación Piñedo says that white blankets with yellow stripes were woven at Santa Clara. The yellow, she says, was obtained from wild flowers.[40] Most of the dyestuffs were imported. These consisted of brazil-wood, campeche, or log-wood, zacatascal (a weed that no one seems to be able to identify), indigo, and palo amarillo, or yellow-wood. All these dyes are listed in the *memorias*. When Santa Bárbara's inventory was taken there were found among its supplies on hand: "3 arrobas de Palo Amarillo para tinte. 4 dichas de id. Bracil. 2 dichas de id. de Campeche," or, translated, 75 pounds of yellow-wood for dyeing, 100 pounds of brazil-wood, and 50 pounds of campeche. Indigo, also ordered by the arroba, is found in numerous invoices. These same dyes are used today by the Indian weavers of Guatemala.[41]

Brazil-wood and campeche were delivered to New Mexican weavers in "billets two feet long," and indigo "in great lumps."[42] And they were probably shipped to California in like shape.

Some native dyes may have been used. Mountain mahogany, for example, produces a rich, reddish-brown color, and there are in this state numerous other plants and shrubs that could have been utilized in dye-making. From the flowers of the rabbit brush, found in the foothill and desert regions of California, yellow dyes, ranging from a pale tint to gold and even to an olive green, may be obtained. The Indians of Arizona and New Mexico secure yellows from this plant, but it does not appear that our California natives had any great knowledge of dyes before the coming of the missionaries.

Descriptions of the Indians' clothing, as given by the explorers of 1769, indicate very little use of dyestuffs. Rather the natives seem to have supplied the lack of color in their costumes with decorations of colored stones, shells, and the brilliant feathers of birds. The men's clothing was quite negligible, consisting in fair weather of nothing more than a sort of netted belt tied around the waist, the net seeming to serve as a pocket in which to carry various objects rather than as an article of clothing. In colder weather they wore fur capes, or cloaks, or whole skins of animals around their shoulders. The women's skirts, consisting of a front and back apron secured about the waist, were of tules, shredded bark, vegetal cords in their natural colors, or the skins of animals, tanned or untanned.

[40] Piñedo, Encarnación, "Early Days."
[41] *National Geographic Magazine*, October, 1947, p. 562.
[42] Amsden, *opus cit.*, 89-90.

Top: Jar in the Santa Bárbara Mission *museum; wine presses and cellar at San Antonio.* Bottom: *Wine presses at San Juan Capistrano; Acú bringing the "first fruits" to the Father.*

▲ THE OLIVE MILL. *Olives were crushed before being placed in press.* (Miniature) (COPYRIGHT EDITH WEBB)

▼ OLIVE PRESS AT SAN DIEGO *in about 1885; restored press at the Junípero Serra Museum, San Diego.*

Fages wrote of the Indian women of the San Luis Obispo region wearing cloaks or skirts which were stained a "handsome red." The women near the mission of Carmelo, he noted, wore "a short apron of red and white cords twisted and worked as closely as possible, which extends to the knee."[43] Whether the red of the cord was the natural color of the material used Fages does not state. Incidentally, the cords being "twisted and worked as closely as possible" indicates some sort of weaving. Costansó also spoke of a "close-woven netted fabric" being worn by the women of the San Diego region.

In their basketry the Indians, as a rule, used naturally colored fibers or roots of trees in forming their ornamental designs. Fages, too, speaks of this practice. "The women," he wrote, "weave nearly all their baskets, pitchers, trays, and jars for various uses, inter-weaving with the reeds or willows, or embroidering upon them, long, flexible, fibrous roots, which keep their natural color, white, black, or red. They also do the same with shells, and small stones of the same three colors for decorating their cloaks and embroidering their headgear."[44]

The red found in some baskets was obtained from the long red roots of the Joshua tree (yucca brevifolia), or from the bark of the red bud or sumac. Some of the blacks and purple-browns were gained by using the stems of the maidenhair fern. Where this material was not available, or the natural black of other plant was wanting, that color was secured by burying materials in mud tinctured with sulphur, or by the simple expedient of boiling them in the liquid obtained from such mud. Or sometimes the splints were painted with a charcoal paste and buried with a covering of ashes in the damp ground.[45]

It is regrettable that more on this and other subjects pertaining to native Indian methods and practices was not written by those early Spanish explorers who could have given us first-hand information concerning many vexing problems. For, with the passing of intervening years and the overlapping of mission influence, many old customs and practices had been discontinued or modified before modern experts took up their study.

Returning to the subject of weaving, Fr. Tapis reported: "Those who are set to work at the looms, also have their tasks to perform. The weavers from the month of March to October daily weave ten yards of woolen cloth which is made into shirts, breeches and skirts. He who weaves more than ten yards is paid at the rate of two reales[46] for each additional ten yards. Seldom do they fail

[43] *Fages' Description of California*, 66.
[44] *Ibidem*, 51;
[45] See Kroeber, *Basketry Designs of the Mission Indians*; James, *Indian Basketry*, Chapters VI and VII.
[46] Real—a small silver coin of Spanish countries, valued in México at about 12½ cents.

to have one hundred yards to their credit every five days. They are paid with glass beads, which they prize, or with wheat. Those who weave blankets, nine spans[47] in length, have to finish three every day. The carders comb three pounds of wool to be woven into cloth for skirts, shirts, and breeches, but four pounds when it is intended for blankets. The spinners spin one pound of yarn a day for skirts, etc., and the others in proportion. These are all the tasks performed at Santa Bárbara.[48] All concerned accomplish it with pleasure, and even insist on being put to such work. From November to February the task is shortened. The weavers then make eight yards of cloth; the carders comb two pounds and four ounces; the spinners produce twelve ounces of yarn, and so on in proportion. Most of those employed finish their task before noon."[49]

In 1817-1818, a fulling mill, whose lack was noted by Vancouver, was built at San Juan Bautista. Three years later another was erected at Santa Inés. This latter mill was constructed of burnt brick and was 6 varas long and 5 varas wide, or 16' 6" x 14'. Whether the operation of these fulling mills was successful or not is uncertain. The writer has been able to find no further mention of the subject in the mission records.

[47] A span equals nine inches in English measurements.
[48] The amount of work required of other workers has been given elsewhere.
[49] Engelhardt, *Miss. & Miss.*, 2. 561.

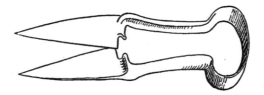

CHAPTER 16

The First Vine Shoots Sent up From Baja California

The Indians are Taught to Make Wine and Olive Oil

IN HIS ACCOUNT of the labors of Fr. Serra in the Sierra Gorda region, Fr. Palóu makes no mention of either vineyards or olive groves. We may, therefore, safely assume that the story of wine-making in Alta California, like that of weaving, began in the Jesuit missions of the peninsula. There, at Mission San Francisco Javier, Fr. Ugarte had planted the first vineyard to be set out in that region. "The excellent wine that was produced," writes Clavigero, the Jesuit historian, "served for all the Masses which were said in that peninsula, and what was left over was sent to New Spain as a gift to the benefactors."[1]

In his recital of the unusual efforts expended by Fr. Jorge Retz to secure fields for the planting of grains, vines, and fruits at his mission of Santa Gertrudis, Clavigero gives us a glimpse of the hardships endured by the Jesuit Fathers working in Baja California. Water from a small spring was conducted in a narrow ditch cut in solid rock to a field almost a mile away. "Near this," that writer continues, "another small field was made with earth carried from another place and spread over the stones, as was customary in that peninsula, using all the economy possible in order not to lose any of the little water. Besides some fruit trees they had planted a vineyard also, which gave good wine in due time. . . "

"The method of keeping the wine was also singular. Since hogsheads were un-known in [Baja] California and Fr. Retz could not have those large earthen jars which were used at the other missions, he decided to make use of some of those very large rocks which are so abundant in that country. He had them hollowed out like sepulchres and covered with boards painted with pitch. The wine was poured in and kept well in such vessels."[2]

[1] *The History of [Lower] California*, by Don Francisco Javier Clavigero, (translated and edited by Sara E. Lake and A. A. Gray), 187.
[2] *Ibidem.*, 331-332.

After Fr. Serra left Baja California for "the new missions of Monterey," Fr. Palóu became president of the peninsula establishments. In 1772, he reported to the Fr. Guardian of the San Fernando College on the state of those missions. Among other things he mentions vineyards at seven of the establishments, and wine stored at three of them in jugs of fifty and sixty quart capacity. These jugs, according to Hittell, were stoneware and had been obtained from the Manila galleons, trading vessels which had brought silks and other articles from China to be exchanged for needed products.[3]

It has been shown in another chapter that grape cuttings from Old California were planted at San Juan Capistrano, and presumably at San Diego, in the spring of 1779. These vines should have begun to bear fruit by 1781 or 1782, at most.[4] Fr. Palóu writing his *Life of Junipero Serra*, in 1785,[5] says of viniculture at San Juan Capistrano: "Having noticed from the very first that all this land was covered with wild grapevines so that they looked like vineyards, the Fathers started to plant some grafted vines which they had brought from Old California and from which they have already obtained wine in quantities not only sufficient for the service of the Mass but also for table use."[6]

Wine making, then, probably began at that mission in 1783 or 1784. Fr. Serra's letter of December, 1781, to Fr. Lasuén at San Diego, in which he deplores the lack of altar wine clearly indicates that none had been made before that time.

It is not known whether at first the Franciscan Padres followed the method practiced by the Jesuits in Baja California of pressing the juice from the grapes with the hands,[7] or if, after the European custom, they had it trodden out under the feet of the Indians. Fathers Palóu, Crespí, Murguía, Lasuén, Peña, and Miguel de la Campa Cos were all stationed for a time in the peninsula missions where grapes were grown and wine made, and they may have continued the former method for a time.

Bancroft, who probably drew upon Carlos N. Híjar's recollections of *California in '34*,[8] describes the process employed at that time as follows: "The wine of pastoral days was made after this manner: Suitable ground was selected, and a

[3] Hittell, *History of California*, 1. 283.

[4] Acc. to Bancroft, *Hist. of Cal.*, 7. 48, "During the first year there is a little increase of wood. In the second year the rooted vines may bear a few grapes. The third year 3 to 4 lbs. of grapes should be obtained from each vine. After this the stalks are self supporting. The increase in yield continues till full maturity in the sixth and seventh year." See also Nordhoff, *opus cit.*, 215-222.

[5] From his dedicatory letter, Palóu began this book February 28, 1785. And since, as he states, "it was written among the heathen surroundings of the Port of San Francisco," it must have been finished before he left that region in the late summer preparatory to his departure for Mexico.

[6] See chapter on vineyards.

[7] Hittell, *opus cit.*, 1. 283.

[8] Hijar's Ms. is in the Bancroft collection.

desvan or platform [?] placed thereon. This was covered with clean hides, and the grapes piled upon it. Some well-washed Indians, having on only a zapeta [loin-cloth], the hair carefully tied up and hand covered with cloth wherewith to wipe away the perspiration, each having a stick to steady himself withal,[9] were put to treading out the grape juice, which was caught in coras, or in leathern bags. These were emptied into a large wooden tub, where the liquid was kept two or three months, under cover of the grape skins to ferment. Such as did not flow off was put into wooden presses, and the juice into copper jars, and covered with a kind of hat. Through two or three inserted tubes heat was conveyed to the mass to aid evaporation and condensation. These jars served as a still for brandy. For white wine the first juice only was taken and stored."[10]

In 1858, Colonel Agoston Haraszthy, who was probably the most important figure in after-mission-day grape culture and wine making, wrote an article for the State Agriculture Society in which he said: "The priests and native Californians planted vines in small patches for their own use only, without regard to locality [?] or a view of improving the vine."

"Their mode of making the wine—also still in use with some—was to pick the grapes, crush them with the feet, which was the business of a big Indian, put the whole mass in raw ox-hides, made sack-fashioned for want of barrels—if barrels could be procured they used them also; and after fermentation, to draw the wine in them, or very often in hides sewed together, water-tight. If they made white wine, they squeezed the juice out of the crushed grapes and put up said juice, without stems and husks, for fermentation. From the balance they made their *aguardiente*, by putting stems and husks together in the still. Brandy was not made until lately."[11]

Colonel Haraszthy cites General Mariano Vallejo as authority for his statements.

With the account of the Padres' wine making, as with the stories of their endeavors in other industries, one is often given an erroneous impression of their lack of equipment, the crudity of their methods, and their own impracticability. The crudity of their methods was that of pioneers wherever they were found at that time. And, considering the day, there was, according to *memorias* and inventories, no great lack of equipment.

From the very first the Padres had barrels which could have been, and prob-

---

[9] It would have required more than a stick to steady one trampling out juice from slippery grapes laid upon a more slippery skin.

[10] Bancroft, *California Pastoral*, 371-372.

[11] *Transactions of the California State Agricultural Society During the Year 1858*. Printed by John O'Meara, State Printer for California, Sacramento, 1859. Page 312. Courtesy of the Wine Institute, San Francisco, California.

ably were, utilized as wine presses, a hole being bored near the botton of the barrel to allow the juice to escape into a tub, vat, or jug set below it. While it is not stated how the supplies brought up in the vessels of 1769 were packaged,[12] it is recorded that, in 1773, four barrels of Castilian wine, four barrels of brandy and three of lard were sent to the missions as an alms by Viceroy Bucareli.[13] Running through the *memorias* for years are orders for a barrel of white wine and one of aguardiente, and, in 1823, the Padres of Santa Clara ordered through W. E. P. Hartnell from his firm in Peru, eight barrels—no contents.[14] Santa Bárbara's inventory of 1834 lists ninety barrels in the wine cellar. Some contained wine, some aguardiente, while four held vinegar. One barrel was in the tannery, one in the soap factory,[15] and one filled with water was always to be found in the kitchen. The above are but isolated records. Many more might be cited.

Lacking barrels, which they assuredly did not, wooden vats could have been made to serve as presses. There were tools and lumber, even though it might have been handhewn, for their construction. And, by the time the missions were engaged in wine making, quite a number of the Indians had been trained in carpentry. There is, in fact, nothing in the mission records that would give color to Bancroft's or Híjar's description of the Padres' substitute wine-press.

While speaking of the equipment for wine making it might be well to note that besides the barrels, there were in Santa Bárbara's bodega, one large china jar of oil for cooking, four stills, twenty-one casks, or hogsheads, three large earthen jars, two small ones, and six funnels of various sizes. At San José, the appraisers listed eight large casks, four small ones, three barrels of a hundred pounds capacity, nineteen large ones, two copper funnels—one large and one small—four buckets, three augers for barrels, thirteen large earthen jars, and two stills ("uno de rosco, otro de sombrero").[16]

Wine-presses, in which the juice was trodden from the grapes, still remain at a few of the missions. Two are at San Antonio, one at San Miguel, one at La Purísima's vineyard rancho, San Francisquito in the Jalama Valley, and one at San Fernando. At San Gabriel there is an adobe building believed to have once contained that mission's three wine-presses. At San Juan Capistrano are four masonry, vat-like structures that this writer believes once served in that capacity. They are arranged two above and two in front of and below the upper ones. The two top vats have openings, or outlets, at the bottom that would have

---

[12] Except the wine, brandy, and vinegar, which came in jars. See Banc. *Hist. of Cal.*, 1. 128-129, note 6.
[13] *Palou's New Cal.*, 3. 123.
[14] Sales Book of W. E. P. Hartnell, Monterey.
[15] SBMA.
[16] Originals in SBMA.

allowed the juice trodden from the grapes to flow into the lower ones, or into vessels standing in them. Screens would have covered the openings, for they are rather large. This arrangement is very similar to one described in the book, *Agricultura General*. "In Rome," the writer of the treatise on grape culture states, "it is customary to have in the vineyard tanks, or vats, made of ladrillo or of stone well-lined, with floor either of mortar or well-bricked, and at one side near the base another small tank into which, through a small hole, the must [juice] flows, and that [the must] they carry to the casa in casks or barrels, or copper-lined vessels, and pour it into earthen jars to ferment without skins."

"In Talavara and in other parts," that writer continues, "the grapes are put in large tubs, or troughs, and the juice trodden out."

Regarding the treading of the juice from the grapes, which was a practice centuries old, Herrera writes: "The one who treads out the juice must be a man, not a woman, but a young man of good strength, who crushes the grapes well, is clean, having well-washed legs, and wearing a clean garment; he has a pole or rope placed across the top [of the press] to which he holds so that he does not fall. Those who pull the stems from the grapes must also be clean persons, as cleanliness is one of the essentials of good wine-making."[17]

From various accounts it seems certain that it was a strong Indian who trampled out the juice from the grapes, also that he was "well-washed." This practice was continued down even to 1860, and perhaps much later at Santa Clara, where, in what seems to have been the last room of the front wing, the Jesuit Brother, Asti, "reigned and supervised the wine-making in Autumn when with pants rolled up to the knees in time-old fashion, the pressers with bare feet trampled the purple grape."[18] This room, according to John A. Waddell, one-time student at Santa Clara College, extended across the width of the double row of rooms and contained both the cellar and the wine press.

One wine cellar and the ruins of another are all that exist today at the old missions, though what may lie under the rooms of the west wing of San Juan Capistrano's quadrangle is yet to be determined by excavation. Then, too, Stephen Ríos, mentioned in Chapter XIII, remembers a sort of "basement" which stood at the extreme left end of the front wing of San Miguel's quadrangle. Early photographs show buildings beyond those now existing at that mission—buildings whose foundations have never been uncovered.

At San Antonio the remains of the Padres' bodega is found under the two

[17] Herrera, *Agricultura General*, 70, 71.
[18] Waddell, John A., "Some Memories of Earlier College Days in Santa Clara." MS.

brick wine presses. Its walls are of stone and its arched ceiling of large ladrillos. It was probably floored with ladrillos, but excavation alone will determine its original state, as the room is at present partially filled with debris from the fallen walls above. Small outlets near the bottom of the presses allowed the juice from the crushed grapes to flow into tubs or other vessels which, when full, were stored in the cellar below. There the juice was fermented, some with and some without the skins of the grapes covering it.

San Fernando's wine cellar, the only one intact, is located under the northern part of that long room which extends across the entire east end of the Fathers' dwelling. It is reached from the rear of the building by descending steps which lead down past the tall wine vat to the arched doorway of the bodega. The cellar is 18′ 6″ x 41′ 6″ in size and 8′ in height from the floor to the huge handhewn beams which span its ceiling. Cool, dry, and dark, it should have made an ideal place for keeping wine.

Referring once more to Herrera's treatise, we read: "The fermenting is done in two ways. The one, where the must is put to ferment without the skins, and the other where it is fermented with the skins. With the first method the wine is clear like water, keeps better, and by nature does not have so many defects. . . Where it is fermented with the skins the wine is more golden, has more strength, but does not keep so well." (Del cocer hay dos maneras. La una, que echen el mosto sin casca à cocer, y desto se hace el vino claro, como agua, y de mas dura, y no suele tener tantos vicios. . . Lo que se cuece con casca sale mas rubio, de color de oro, y de mas fuerza, y no de tanta dura, . . ")[19]

That the mission grape was so fermented is attested to in the oft-quoted letter written June 17, 1833, by Fr. Presidente Narciso Durán to Governor Figueroa in answer to the latter's inquiry about the Padres' method of making claret, brandy, etc. "I have to remark in reply," writes Fr. Durán, "that I can say little or nothing certain about the muscatel, because there is none of it at Mission San José;[20] nor do I know it. The wine of San Luis Rey in my opinion is not the best, nor the best suited to place before a friend. I think that there are only two kinds: the red wine and the white wine. The latter, which is used for altar purposes, is rather unpleasant, because it has no sweetness whatever, but is very dry."

"The best wine which I have found at the various missions are those of San Gabriel. There are two kinds of red wine. One is dry, but very good for the table; the other is sweet, resembling the juice pressed from blackberries and so rather unpleasant. There are also two kinds of white wine. One of them is from

[19] Herrera, *Agricultura General*, 71.
[20] Fr. Durán had served at Mission San José from 1806 to 1833.

Top: PLAN FOR ALTAR at Santa Clara; niche for baptismal font in the Indian chapel at Pala. Bottom: Sanctuary ceiling at Santa Clara; the earliest known photograph of Mission Santa Clara.

▲ Fr. Peyri looks on *as the Indian artist paints the side altar of Pala's chapel.* (Miniature)

▼ The original decorations *on the walls of the sanctuary of the chapel at Pala.*

pure grapes without fermenting, I mean from pure grape juice without fermenting it with the skins of the pressed grapes. This produces the white wine. The
other of the same juice is fermented with a quantity of grape brandy. These
two make a most delicious drink for the dessert. The wine from the pure grape
juice is for the altar; the other for any use whatever."[21]

During the period of fermentation, according to Herrera, the wine must be
carefully guarded, for it is at this time that it is most susceptible to odors and fra-
grancies. Accordingly the cellar, be it made out of wood or cut from living rock,
under ground or above, must be deep, cold, dry, and dark. It must stand at a
distance from stables, sewers, wells, places of habitation, granaries and trees,
especially fig trees, which breed mosquitoes.[22]

How well the mission cellars as a whole followed these general requirements
there is little way of knowing at this date. Should the front wing of the quadrangle at San Antonio be scientifically excavated and restored much may be
learned from that mission's bodega.

To produce good wine the jugs, or jars, barrels, or casks in which it is kept,
must be scrupulously clean and well sealed. Herrera asserts that wooden casks
produce more fragrant wine than do earthen jars. On the other hand the jars
are not liable to mildew nor do they require the care that casks do. The latter
must be looked over each year, cleaned, their hoops tightened, and all cracks
filled or sealed with pitch. It is interesting to read that the hoops used on wine
casks in the Spanish wineries at that time (1777) were of strong ropes, or cords,
of hemp.

We have already seen that our mission Padres had both barrels and jars in
their cellars. The vessels used in fermenting the wine were large, wide-mouthed,
and big-bellied, while those in which the wine was kept were narrow-mouthed
and long-necked. Pottery was taught at a number of the missions and it is quite
possible that some of the wine jars used were made in the mission pottery shops.

That good wine was made at many of the missions, if not eventually at all,
is testified to in official letters, documents, and in accounts written by early
visitors. It is claimed that the vines at Santa Cruz, San Carlos, and San Francisco
did not do so well as those in other mission vineyards. William Heath Davis
asserts that the wine made at Mission San Francisco (Dolores) was from grapes
grown at Santa Clara.[23] It was at the latter mission that Vancouver reported
that in the garden "were planted peaches, apricots, apples, pears, figs and vines,

---

[21] Engelhardt, *Miss. & Miss.*, 3. 571-572 ("Archb. Arch." no. 2140).
[22] Herrera, *Agricultura General*, 72.
[23] Davis, Wm. Heath, *Seventy-five Years in California*, 6.

all of which excepting the latter promised to succeed very well. The failure of the vines here as well as at St. Francisco, is ascribed to a want of knowledge in their culture; the soil and climate being well adapted to most sorts of fruit."[24] Nevertheless, wine was being made at Santa Clara when Wilkes visited there in 1841. De Mofras wrote: "This mission is surrounded by extensive orchards and kitchen gardens, and its wine is superb."[25]

Fr. Presidente Lasuén, reporting, in 1801, on the state of the eighteen missions then founded, stated: "The Missions of San Diego, San Juan Capistrano, San Gabriel, San Buenaventura, Santa Bárbara, and San Luis Obispo raise grapes and press some wine. In most missions despite our endeavors, we have no success, since we missionaries, being all Europeans, do not know the climatic or other situations. In some missions grape culture and wine pressing succeed, in others the result is distressing; whether by reason of the soil or the climate, they are failures. . . "[26]

The wine made at this or that mission was praised by various visitors of the mission period. Langsdorff visited Mission San José and found "excellent wine, sweet, and resembling Malaga." That at Mission San Francisco which, he says, "was the production of the country, was but of ordinary quality."[27] Davis wrote that the California red wine was as good as any he had ever tasted.[28] Harrison Rogers found the wine at San Gabriel good, as did Fr. Durán, but it was wine from Mission San Luis Rey that Duhaut-Cilly took back to France with him. Speaking of that mission's gardens, the Frenchman wrote: "These gardens produce the best olives and the best wine in all California. . I carried away some of this wine, and I have some of it still." In an appended note he added: "After seven years, it has the taste of Paxaret, and the color of porto depouille."[29] And when Viceroy Count de Venadito wanted to send a gift of wine to His Majesty, Don Fernando VII, he chose that from the wine cellar of Mission San Diego—a dozen bottles of it. Moreover, in transmitting the message to the Padres, Governor Solá added: "and if you know that it could arrive sound, then a barrel of the same wine for the said viceroy. I shall esteem it highly."[30]

There has been considerable discussion about the mission grapes. Bancroft contends that there were two varieties. "During the first years of Spanish occupation," he says, "were introduced from México the two leading varieties of

[24] Vancouver, *Voyage*, 2. 18-22.
[25] De Mofras, *Travels*, 1. 220.
[26] Engelhardt, *Mission San Diego*, 153-154.
[27] Langsdorff, *Voyages and Travels*, 2. 193, 161.
[28] Davis, *opus cit.*, 6.
[29] "Duhaut-Cilly's Account," 228.
[30] Engelhardt, *Mission San Diego*, 192-193 (*Cal. Arch.*, Prov. Rec. xi, pp. 467, 536, blotter).

deteriorated yet hardy fruit of the South Spanish stock now known as the mission grape, first the reddish black grape of Los Angeles, rich in juice, then the
fruitier bluish black Sonoma, which yields a lighter wine."[31]

A letter written, in 1810, by Fr. Payeras at La Purísima, to Fr. Presidente
Tapis supports Bancroft's statement regarding the two varieties. After speaking
of other matters the Padre remarks that they had torn up the vineyard at Lalsa-
cupi (the first site of the mission at Lompoc) and had transplanted it to a location near the place which he called San Francisco, where it bore well according to
samples brought yesterday by the gardener—"two kinds of very small grapes."
In the meantime, they had made a life-contract with the Ortegas to divide the
vineyard[32] in return for the labor of caring for and cultivating it. "To them goes
the account, to us the wine and brandy (of which we require little), from one
and the other we have old and new in abundance, made here after the Mayor-
can method in new wine presses. Hence, if God grants us life, some day Your
Reverence will drink it without pellicle, without sediments, and without bad
taste, pure, and clear."[33]

The last sentence quoted indicates some of the difficulties experienced in wine
making at that mission. The Padre's reference to new wine-presses is of interest
because, at the time of his writing, that one still standing at San Francisquito
had, in all probability, but recently been erected. San Antonio's second press
was not built until 1829. The Padres rarely recorded the building of such structures. After all, the presses were merely part of the equipment.

To return to the question of the mission grapes. Wilkes, who, in 1841, inspected the vineyard at Santa Clara, remarks: "The deputy [Ignacio Alviso][34]
now conducted us through the garden, which is surrounded by a high adobe
wall, and has a gate that is always kept locked. It was from one and a half to two
acres in extent, and mostly planted with grapes, which are cultivated after the
Spanish fashion, without trellises. Some of the fruit was yet hanging, and was
generally of the sweet Malaga kind. Our guide informed me that the mission
took the first picking for the manufacture of wine and to preserve, then the
inhabitants, the women of the 'gente de razon' and afterwards the children.
Strict watch was, however, kept that they did not pull the other fruit. Only a
certain number were allowed to work in the garden, and the whole place is under
the constant superintendence of a gardener. It would be impossible to protect

[31] Banc., *Hist. of Cal.*, 7. 44, 46, note 8.
[32] The Ortega vineyard? The mission Indians would, of course, care for and cultivate it.
[33] Engelhardt, *Mission La Purisima*, 26-27. Original in SBMA.
[34] Ignacio Alviso came as a four year old child with Anza's colonists for the San Francisco region. He was administrator of Santa Clara in 1840-1843.

the fruit otherwise. They have fruit of all kinds, both of the tropical and temperate climate, which they represented as succeeding admirably well. A few barrels of wine are made but nothing can be more rude than their whole process of manufacturing."[35] Unfortunately, Wilkes does not describe the process.

Bryant, visiting John Marsh at his rancho situated near the foot of Mount Diablo, wrote: "I noticed near the house a vegetable garden, with the usual variety of vegetables. In another enclosure was the commencement of an extensive vineyard, the fruit of which (now ripe) exceeds in delicacy of flavor of any grapes which I have ever tasted. This grape is not indigenous, but was introduced by the Padres, when they first established themselves in the country. The soil and climate of California have probably improved it. Many of the clusters are eight and ten inches in length, and weigh several pounds. The fruit is of medium size, and in color a dark purple. The rind is very thin, and when broken the pulp dissolves in the mouth immediately."[36]

Listed in the book, *Agricultura General*, are the following names of the several varieties of grapes grown in Spain: Moscatel, Jaen, Heben, Alarixe (Alarije), Castellana blanca, Malvasia, Lyrenes, Prietas, Palomina, Argones, Tortozon, and Herrial (Erial?—uncultivated). Of these the Prietas and Palomina were black grapes. Whether the mission grape derived from either variety will probably never be known.

"La oliva es arbol de tanto provecho, y estíma, que no podré encarecerlo, asi para luz, como para guisados, y cosas de botica."[37]

As with the grapes and wine making, the Padres probably had their first experience in olive culture in the Baja California missions. Whether they brought olive seeds or cuttings with them when they came to their new missionary field is impossible to determine. Seeds would have been more practical, for they would have taken up less space and would not have needed to be planted at once. Considering the experiences of the various divisions of the expedition of 1769, it seems hardly credible that cuttings would have survived had they been brought along.

A belief that is quite widespread is that most of the mission fruit orchards were planted from seed. Guadalupe Vallejo, as quoted in a previous chapter, spoke of "many varieties of seedling fruits," and, in writing about Mission Santa Clara, Palóu remarked that "A goodly supply of fruit has been obtained

---

[35] Wilkes, Charles, *Narrative of the U. S. Exploring Expedition* (Philadelphia 1845, 5 vols), 5. 206-207.
[36] Bryant, *What I Saw*, 283. See also pp. 296, 316.
[37] "The olive is a tree of great benefit, and esteem, which is not possible to overrate, as much for illumination, as for culinary and medicinal purposes." *Agricultura General*, 490.

from as many of the seeds as were brought from Spain and were planted, as all the seeds brought out at first have thrived, even the grape."[38]

In *Agricultura General* are directions for planting the olive by seed, branch, sucker, root, or any of the many parts of the tree that bears bark. The use of barbados (young shoots) that come up around the base of the tree, or of strong cuttings four or five hands long and as thick as the handle of a hoe, is advised. Shoots, or suckers, as they are usually called, and the large cuttings are set out where they are intended to grow. Whereas, plants started from seeds, or fruit-stones, are slow in growing, must be transplanted, and, being seedlings, in order to be good must be grafted, or budded. All this calls for much labor and also delays the years of fruitage.[39]

Still, in view of those first uncertain months and years, it seems that if olives were started it was seeds and not cuttings that were planted. However, there is nothing in the mission records to indicate that the Padres were for several years concerned with planting other crops than wheat, beans, and corn. Those were the essentials. Olives, grapes, and other fruits could wait until more was known about climate, soil, and irrigation, and until permanent sites for the missions were found. Neither Palóu nor Fages in their early reports on the state of the missions mention fruit trees or vines. Nor does observant Fr. Font.

Shortly after 1868, when he first came to California, Elwood Cooper of Santa Bárbara began planting groves of olive trees. He did for the olive industry what Colonel Haraszthy did for the grape. In an article written, in 1892, for *The Californian*[40] he stated: "Olive tree planting is inexpensive because trees can be raised from slips and cuttings, which grow readily if properly manipulated. If grown from cuttings the plants will produce fruit the fourth year. Trees can also be grown from seeds, a plan in general encouraged, on the ground that better trees are produced. By this method, however, it takes probably twice as long to get the first fruits, with the additional expense of either budding or grafting. I have a young orchard four years old, from cuttings, planted in permanent sites, uniformly good trees and well fruited. Such results can only be expected where the best of care and cultivation is given. . . The cuttings I planted were from the Missions of Santa Bárbara, San Fernando and San Diego, and from the Tajiguas ranch. . "

In 1803, two years after Fr. Presidente Lasuén had reported on the little success that some of the mission Padres met with in their wine making, he wrote

[38] *Palou's Life of Serra* (James ed.), 213-214.
[39] *Agricultura General*, 159-161.
[40] Cooper, Elwood, "The Olive in California," in *The Californian*, January, 1892.

that "in some missions they have begun to harvest olives; and at San Diego they have already made some very good olive oil."[41]

"In 1810," Bancroft states, "olives had begun to be planted at many missions; and in 1818 olive culture was already an assured success, especially in the missions of the San Diego district which furnished other missions all the oil they needed."[42]

In view of the above reports and, taking Elwood Cooper's figures for a yardstick, remembering also that the mission groves could not possibly receive the care and cultivation that one specializing in olive culture would give those trees, it does not appear that the olive could have been planted at any of the missions much before 1785-1790. It is likewise extremely doubtful that either olive mills or screw-presses were set up, or constructed, before the coming of the artisans of 1790-1795, for those devices very definitely belong to that period or later.

Of course olives may have been ground with mortar and pestle. Fr. O'Sullivan was told by "Doña Dolores," whose mother had lived at the Capistrano Mission in the time of the Padres, that along the corridor of the east wing of the quadrangle, that is, the "Serra Church" wing, "the old Indian women used to sit in a row, and pound up the olives to make olive oil for use in the sanctuary lamp. The olives were dried first like raisins, then pounded up and put in fine cloth, and hung up to drip the oil slowly."[43] In all likelihood, this or some similar primitive method of extracting the oil was employed before the mills and presses were set up.

Mills used in crushing the olives prior to their being placed in the screw-press were standing and still in use as late as 1885, and perhaps a little later, at San Juan Capistrano and San Fernando. The one at the latter mission had been slightly modernized, though not to a harmful extent (that is from a historical point of view). At about the same time there stood, in the old olive grove at Mission San Diego, the ruined walls of an adobe building giving some meed of protection to the last of the mission oil presses.[44] These relics enable one quite accurately to picture the Padres' process of producing olive oil.

The mill has already been described in the chapter on tanning. The press, which worked on the same principle as the letter-press, consisted of a framework of two huge uprights into which a crossbar was set. A floor board, an upper board onto which the large screw was affixed, comprised the mechanism. The

[41] Engelhardt, *Mission San Diego*, 154. Original in SBMA.
[42] Banc., *Hist. of Cal.*, 2. 418, note 10.
[43] Saunders and O'Sullivan, *Capistrano Nights*, 73-74.
[44] This old oil press is now in the Junípero Serra Museum, at "Old Town," San Diego.

screw projected up through the crossbar, while a spout-like trough extended from the floor board. A tub, half-barrel, or cask was placed under the trough.

According to Herrera, green olives make the best olive oil and should be gathered by hand. And, if the oil comes out without using the millstone it is better because it does not have the flavor or the bite of the pit. Some, he says, produce oil by filling bags with olives, and, placing them in very warm water, tread upon them. If the mill is used he advises keeping it in an enclosure where it and the millstone are kept warm, for the oil does not all come out when the olives are cold. The oil should be put in clean vessels and stored in a warm place.[45]

Possibly some of the oil was produced by treading the olives in hot water. Of that we cannot be sure, but the existence of the mills and the press proves that some of it came from olives that had first been crushed by the millstone and then put into the press.

Olives for pickling were gathered by hand, as were they all as long as the trees were small. But, as the trees grew larger it seems that the fruit was either whipped off with switches or was shaken down by striking the limbs with long slender poles, just as walnuts are dislodged today. Gathered up by the little Indian children, the olives were carried, probably in burden baskets, by the women to the mill. There they were poured into the cement-lined well of the mill, where they were crushed by the revolving stone propelled by a blindfolded burro. That patient little animal was urged on by an Indian armed with a rawhide whiplash. When sufficiently crushed the pulp was scooped up from the well by other neophyte workers, stuffed into sacks, or bags, of strong hempen net and placed in the press. That machine was operated by two or more sturdy Indians, by means of a bar inserted through a hole in the socket-fitting of the screw. Under pressure the oil and juice (alpechín) ran out the spout, extending from the floor board, into the tub set below it. The oil was skimmed from the juice, poured into jars or glass bottles and stored away. The best oil was that which came out first, but, by continued working over of the pulp, more could be obtained. And there were many uses for olive oil at the old missions. It was burned in the sanctuary lamps; was used as a medicine, for cooking purposes, and even for the lubrication of machinery.

Cleanliness throughout the whole process was as necessary in the production of oil as it was in wine making. The oil, too, must be kept well covered lest insects and mice fall into it. In the event of such calamity, even as Herrera writes, olive oil must not be thrown away for there is always some use for it.

[45] *Agricultura General*, 166.

That writer also advises the use of great diligence in collecting the juice as it has many virtues. It is beneficial to trees, especially the olive, when mixed with an equal amount of water and poured into the pits around them. It rids the soil of fleas, mice, moles, and destroys bedbugs.[46]

The process of pickling olives was very simple. They were sometimes steeped in "lye" water—obtained by leaching ashes from the fireboxes under the tallow vats—washed, and bottled in salt water with perhaps a little fennel or other spice added. Or they were kept in a tub, or other receptacle of fresh water for fifteen days, the water being changed every second day, then stored away in salt water. This writer has, within recent years, seen olives "cured," or pickled, by the latter method.

Searching for information regarding the mission olives and olive oil, one gleans some interesting items from accounts written by visitors who came to California in after-secularization days. Waseurtz, writing and sketching in 1842, noted that "the old Mission of San Luis Obispo was, even more than the others, in ruins. The gardens were badly kept, though there was a splendid olive grove and the crop for the season was abundant. Only for gathering them, barrels full might have been gotten and salted, for the whole ground was covered with them."[47]

Henry Chapman Ford, the artist, who, in the 1880's sketched the buildings of Mission San Fernando, wrote in his *Notes*: "There are two orchards of olives, probably containing the largest [olive] trees in the State, the trunks of some being two feet in diameter. They are of a different variety from the common Mission olive, the fruit being nearly double the size and highly valued for pickling. . . "[48] It is said that these olives had been the pride of Fr. Ibarra's heart.

Speaking of the "different varieties" of mission olives, Elwood Cooper advanced the theory which perhaps explains the apparent diversity. "Some claim," he wrote, "that there are several Mission varieties, while others that all came from the same original stock first brought here by the Mission Fathers, and that while there are different types it is the result of climatic conditions or location. I am inclined to this latter opinion because there is an apparent difference in the size and shape of the fruits in different locations, while all of them reproduced in the same orchard show no difference."[49]

It has been claimed by experts that the mission olive as well as the grape, has not been identified with any of the varieties now cultivated in Europe.

[46] *Ibidem,* 167.
[47] Waseurtz, *Sojourn in California,* 47.
[48] Ford, H. C., *Notes,* Southwest Museum Collection.
[49] Cooper, E., *opus cit.*

COPIES OF TWO OF THE INDIAN PAINTINGS *of the Via Crucis (Way of the Cross) now hanging on the walls of a room that was formerly a part of the Fathers' dwelling at Mission San Gabriel.*

▲ Copy of painting of Mission San Gabriel done in 1832 by Ferdinand Deppe.

▼ Copy of painting of Mission San Francisco de Asís in after-mission days.

CHAPTER 17

The Use of Pigments Not Unknown to Our Indians

Indian Artists Learn to Decorate the Church Walls

Pₐᵢₙₜᵢₙg is an art that was not unknown to our California Indians before the coming of the White Man. While many of them have been initialed, chipped away, shot at, and otherwise defaced by ignorant vandals, there still remain pictographs to verify this assertion. Here and there along the coast, and probably in other as yet undiscovered places, are to be found on walls and in caves, painted figures and symbols which may record the travels, trials, triumphs, or defeats of peoples who lived and loved, hunted, fought and died perhaps many centuries before the time of the Indians seen by Cabrillo, Vizcaíno, or the later explorers of the Portolá expedition.

The "Painted Cave" in the hills back of Santa Bárbara; that one five miles above Mission San Antonio and at the head of Pine Canyon, and the "Painted Rock," or Piedra Pintada, in the Carrizo Plain, about fifty miles from Taft, in San Luis Obispo County, furnish outstanding examples of California's first mural paintings.[1]

No one knows what the figures and designs outlined on the walls may signify. There are delineations of men and animals, geometrical designs and various symbols of unknown portent, sketched in black, white, yellow, and brilliant red pigments. These were the colors known to the Ancient Ones and are found in their wall paintings and in their graves.[2]

There is nothing mysterious about the pigments they used. It required no "witches brew" to produce them. They were gathered from the hillsides and along the trails that led from one hunting ground to another. They are earths and minerals and their use dates from the time when one of the Ancients picked

---

[1] Kroeber, *Handbook*, 936.

[2] *Ibidem*, 936-939; Angel, Myron, "La Piedra Pintada," in *West Coast Magazine*, July, 1910; Smith, F. R., *Mission San Antonio*, 88-99; Hawley, W. A., *Early Days of Santa Barbara*, 20; Rogers, *Prehistoric Man*, 407.

up a colored stone and noted that it left a red mark on his hand. Color has always attracted the Indian.

The black pigment used by the California coast natives has usually been classified as charcoal, either bone or wood. David Banks Rogers thinks that the chief constituent of this paint was soot mixed with heavy fat. It is, he says, always found in a container.[3] In describing the pigments found in the "Painted Cave" in the Santa Inés Mountains west of Santa Bárbara, Walter Hawley states: "The black paint has been found on analysis to be hydrous oxide of manganese; . . " The white has been analyzed as white earth, chalk, or diatomaceous earth; the yellow as ochre, and the red either ochre or cinnabar. Numerous deposits of colored earths and minerals are found along or near the coast from San Diego to Santa Clara County and beyond. From these the California natives obtained the pigments with which they painted themselves and their belongings.

Fr. Crespí, accompanying Portolá's party in search of Monterey Bay, noted the fact that deposits of white and red earths had been passed somewhere in the hills near the present site of San Juan Capistrano.[4] Several persons in the party describe the canoes built by the natives of the Santa Bárbara Channel and remark that they were painted in bright colors. Fr. Font, traveling along that way a few years later, noted that the canoes were all painted with red hematite and that the poles and planks set up in the Indian cemeteries were decorated with designs in black, red, and white colors.[5] None of these diarists discloses the source of the adhesive which the natives mixed with their paints to make them adhere to objects and to render them waterproof.

The red paint on the canoes may have been either hematite or cinnabar. Both are found in the near-by mountains. Many balled lumps of cinnabar have been found in graves in old Indian village sites along the Santa Bárbara coast. In 1938, at the Museum of Natural History of Santa Bárbara, this writer was shown a drawer containing many lumps of this most brilliant of all red pigments which had been taken from Indian burial places. The source of the mineral, a mercuric sulphide, was undoubtedly the quick-silver mines near the Gibraltar Dam.

According to Mr. Rogers, abalone shells, filled to the brim with red ochre, were also frequently found in the graves.[6] This earth pigment, in varying shades, may be seen along the San Marcos Pass highway. During the rainy season the colors are particularly striking.

[3] *Ibidem*, 407.
[4] Bolton, *Palou's New Cal.*, 2. 123. Within recent years a vein of very fine yellow ochre was found in those hills and a sample brought by two Mexican boys to Fr. Hutchinson, the present pastor of the mission community.
[5] Bolton, *Anza's Calif. Exped.*, 4. 252-3.
[6] Rogers, *Prehistoric Man*, 364.

Cuts made in the cliffs when the new San Marcos road was built expose layers of a bluish-gray clay. Possibly this is the blue clay of which Don Pedro Fages wrote when, in 1775, he reported to Viceroy Bucareli on California, the state of the missions, and the Indians. Concerning the natives of the Santa Bárbara Channel, the lieutenant observes: ". . some make strings of beads, others grind red, white, and blue paint clays, and a certain kind of plumbiferous stones, which serve for the men to paint themselves with when they are celebrating and dancing or when they go to war, and which are used by the women for their usual adornment."[7] This same bluish-gray clay occurs in one of the canyons back of San Juan Capistrano. It is blue by contrast only.

Near La Purísima and Santa Inés are vast deposits of white and red diatomaceous earth in addition to the cinnabar mines previously referred to. And, according to one writer, there is an outcrop of copper ore along the range of mountains lying to the east of Santa Inés. However, there is no mention in the diaries of the first explorers of the natives' use of either green or blue paints. Nor has either color been found in the pictographs discovered along the coast or within the vicinity of villages of Indians later attached to the missions. The natural inference is that those colors were introduced by the missionaries.

That the Padres ordered and received from México pigments of many colors is proved by the *memorias*. For example, in 1797, the Santa Bárbara Fathers secured 3 pounds of cardenillo (verdigris, which at that time was used both as a paint and a medicine),[8] 3 pounds of almagre (red ochre), 2 pounds of vermellon (vermillion), 2 pounds of orange color. In 1800, their lists included 2 pounds of purple ochre, 2 of yellow ochre, and 2 of orange, 8 ounces of vermillion, and 3 bottles of linseed oil. In each of the years 1807, 1808, and 1809 they sent for 2 arrobas, or 50 pounds, of indigo.

When, within recent years, the Fathers' dwelling at La Purísima Concepción was restored, laboratory tests were made of colors found on fragments of whitewashed adobes. The tests showed that all the blue and green paints discovered were copper compounds.[9] The red pigment, it was determined, had been extracted from a deposit of red diatomite found along the Santa Inés River. Yellow ochre, in tones ranging from straw to orange, was found, and a gray which had been produced by mixing bone or wood charcoal with lime.[10]

---

[7] *Fages' Description of California*, 34-35.

[8] Fr. Font, who was suffering from sores in his mouth, "was somewhat relieved afterward by touching the sores with a little powder of verdigris" (polvo de cardenillo). Bolton, *Anza's Cal. Exped.*, 4. 218.

[9] The Fathers' dwelling was built in 1815 and the church in 1817-1818, by which time strictly primitive conditions no longer obtained. The Padres had, for some years past, been importing paints from México.

[10] Hageman, Frederick A., *An Architectural Study of the Mission La Purisima*.

When that mission's old church was excavated bits of colored designs were found still adhering to the ruined walls. These designs were pieced together for reference in the later decoration of the restored building. The original work was found to have been "done in vermillion and light Indian-red pigments on pale ochre background."[11]

While the restoration work was going on this writer discovered near the mission a vein of yellow ochre so pure and soft that it needed but to be mixed with water and an adhesive added to render it ready for use.

Before Mission San Gabriel's campo santo was restored and re-dedicated in January, 1939, an effort was made to establish the former location of two brick tombs that once stood in the plot. Excavators searching for these graves came upon a cache of rocks rich in a bright red pigment. There can be little doubt that this mineral had been gathered for use in mission days. On the grounds of the old quadrangle this writer also found stones, similar to those laid in the lower walls of the church, and containing pockets of yellow ochre.

Yellow ochre was also found near Mission San Carlos, while from outcroppings of what later became known as the New Almaden Mines, the Indians of the San Francisco Bay region had for years, perhaps for centuries, been accustomed to pick up "heavy reddish rocks" and use the cinnabar they contained to paint their faces and bodies in preparation for gala occasions or for war.

Seeing the natives with their persons painted in several colors it is not strange that the Padres at once began to consider ways and means of turning this custom to practical advantage. There can be no doubt that the church which would eventually arise at each new mission site was always in the minds of the Padres. What then would be more natural than that they should at once envision churches decorated and painted with dadoes, friezes, and ornamented ceilings? It is not a matter for surprise, therefore, to note that the Padres of San Gabriel, in 1771, the year of that mission's foundation, had ordered sent up from México "Una docena Pinzeles" (One dozen artists' brushes) and "Un libro intitulado Pintar sin Maestro, o cosa semejante" (One book entitled "Painting Without an Instructor," or something similar).[12]

What use the San Gabriel Padres may have made of this book, or whether their early churches were decorated with painted designs, is not known. The first recorded notice of a church being so decorated is found in the Baptismal Register of Mission Santa Clara. This was the church for which Fr. Serra laid

[11] Bartlett, Lanier, ed., *Mission Motifs*. Southern California Index of American Design. WPA.
[12] Copied by Arthur Woodward from an original manuscript of the MSS. Division, marked Leg. 283-61 Archivo Nacional, Mexico City.

the cornerstone on November 19, 1781, and which he, with the assistance of Fr. Francisco Palóu and Fr. Thomás de la Peña, dedicated May 15 and 16, 1784. The translated record reads in part: "The church is whitewashed inside and out-side. The walls inside are painted above and below. The entire chancel and a great part of the ceiling are also painted. The floor is a pavement of adobe flags."[13]

This was the church that was built by the Indians under the direction of Fr. Murguía, one of those Padres who had served in both the Sierra Gorda and Baja California missions. It is said that not only was he architect of the building but that he had labored with the Indians in erecting it. According to the notice in the Burial Register, it was while he was decorating the church for its dedica-tion[14] that he was seized with an illness that caused his death a few days later. That he was assisted by the Indians in the work of adorning, decorating, or painting the church, is not to be doubted. It was the custom then, as it is now, to credit the architect or the one in charge with the work performed.

Vancouver, it will be remembered, saw this church (of the second site) and remarked that it "was infinitely more decorated than might have been reason-ably expected."

Eventually the walls and ceilings, or ceiling beams, of most of the churches seem to have been decorated with painted designs. The sanctuary zone in some of them was particularly well ornamented. This was especially true of the third and fourth churches erected on the various mission sites.

After 1800, when foreign trading vessels had begun to visit the Pacific coast, the names of a number of men of different nationalities began to appear in the mission records. Were it possible to search all the Padres' old account books the presence of a surprising number of those "foreigners" would, it seems, be re-vealed. Some had deserted their ships, hiding out until their vessels had de-parted, because of the harsh treatment dealt them, while some unceremoniously took leave because this new country looked more desirable to them than did their own. Some were ship owners.

Thus, in 1828, we find at San Buenaventura George Cosme, nationality not given, serving as gate keeper for the mission Padres, and George Coleman, an Englishman, in a position of some considerable trust.[15] Robinson speaks of a

[13] James A. Colligan, S. J., *The Three Churches.*
[14] "..., y fabrico la Yglesia grande de adobes, y estando adornando la por la dedicacion, que havia [habia] de ser el dia 15 de este Mes, .. " From the *Libro de Difuntos* in the University of Santa Clara Archives. Through the courtesy of Rev. Henry L. Walsh, S. J.
[15] Engelhardt, *Mission San Buenaventura,* 63.

Scotchman, by name of Mulliken,[16] who, during his stay at Mission Santa Cruz, had taught Padre Luis Gil y Taboada some very questionable English.[17] Pedro Bruno, an Anglo-American blacksmith, was hired as mayordomo at San Juan Bautista.[18] There were others who served under the Padres. They came to California with new ideas and the knowledge of new ways of doing things, and the missionaries were not loath to accept such aids.

One of these strangers was a native of Boston named Thomas Doak. He came to Monterey as a sailor in 1816, and it is said became the first Anglo-American settler of California. Soon after his arrival he, with the help of the Indians, painted the main altar (reredos?) of the church of San Juan Bautista.[19]

Aside from that of Padre Murguía at Santa Clara, the recorded names of artists, amateur or otherwise, who painted or directed the painting of altars, walls and ceilings of the mission churches and other buildings, are but three in number. These are Thomas Doak at San Juan Bautista, Don Esteban Munras of Monterey, who, "assisted by the Indians," painted the walls of San Miguel's church and sacristy, and Señor Augustín Dávila, who, with the aid of the Indians, decorated those of the church of Santa Clara, at the mission's third site.

At the latter mission not only was the interior of the church painted, but also those figures and designs seen on the church fachada in the earliest known photograph of the mission. The pigments used were mostly cinnabar and yellow ochre. The cinnabar, Doña Piñedo tells us, was brought by the Indians from the New Almaden mines, which are located near Santa Clara.

A traveler of 1860 wrote the following description of the building: "The old church is built of adobe bricks dried in the sun, the roof is of red tiles. There is a wooden tower annexed to the main edifice, surmounted by a vane, and having a clock on the side facing the green, and a gallery around the top of the tower. The round [?] wall of the front of the church retains traces of having been painted in gaudy colors. High up over the doorway is a rude representation of Santa Clara, while on each side are roughly painted and half-erased figures of San Francisco [St. Francis] and San Antonio [St. Anthony].[20] The colors of the decorations are chiefly red and yellow; but the woodwork of the adjacent tower was once painted green. There is a small fence in front of the building and an arched wooden gateway. These were once elaborately ornate with red and yellow representations of flowers. The rains of many summers have left but faint

[16] Probably John Mulligan, an Irish weaver who came in 1815.
[17] Robinson, *Life in Cal.*, 116.
[18] Engelhardt, *Mission San Juan Bautista*, 34.
[19] *Ibidem*, 30.
[20] Not St. Anthony of Padua. That saint is always represented wearing the simple Franciscan habit.

traces of the gaudiness and glare. Fifty years ago the gaud of all this coloring, . . must have had a wondrous effect on the minds of the gazing Indians, . . Interiorly as well as on the exterior of the building, the painter has had recourse to decorative art, and his colors have been chiefly crimson and yellow. The coloring has faded now, the touch of time has taken the bloom from off the painted flowers and interfered marvelously with the intrinsic beauty of the arabesque. . . Roughly painted pictures of the incidents of the Crucifixion, and some very capitally executed oil paintings also adorn the walls. The place is diffused with a 'dim religious light,'—and has an air of holy calmness, and is in every way calculated to make a deep and ineffaceable impression upon the memory of the visitor. It made such on mine."[21]

Because so much that is confusing and erroneous has been written about this church of the third site, it seems expedient to note here that it was built in 1822-1825. Fr. Murguía's church of 1781-1784 had been badly damaged by an earthquake in 1818.[22] A temporary church was erected and roofed that same year.[23] In 1819, the Padres report that the church was finished (". . ,.y se ha concluido la Yglesia"). Where this temporary church stood is not known, but it may have been one of those buildings that stood outside the quadrangle of the third site and later served another purpose.

The quadrangle, of which a part remained until 1926, was, according to the *informes*, begun in 1822 when the Padres report that there had been erected two rows of buildings. Each was 85 varas, or 234 feet in length. The walls were of adobe and the roofs of tile. During the next year two more rows were built thereby closing the square of the new mission, and, moreover, a guardhouse, with workshop, jail, and six houses for the soldier-guards were erected. All these buildings were of adobe and had tiled roofs. There is in the Santa Bárbara Mission Archives no report for 1824, but, in 1825, the missionaries note that the church is finished and the whole mission completed.[24] No more building was reported at Mission Santa Clara after 1825, the Padres down to the close of 1832 merely noting under Fábricas (building reports): "Se han retechado las echas" (the old buildings have been reroofed), or "No hay cosa particular" (there is nothing particular, or special, to report). Santa Clara's entire establishment, at

[21] Anderson, Prof., "A Reminiscence of California, being a Visit to a Jesuit College," in *The Sunday Atlas*, Philadelphia, Oct., 21, 1860.
[22] Inventory March 21, 1851. "Esta primera Iglesia fué casi arruinada por un fuerte temblor en el año de 1818."
[23] *Informe* 1818. "Se han retechado las echas, y se ha techado tambien la nueva Yglesia." SBMA.
[24] *Informe* 1822. "Se han echo dos liensos de 85 varas de largo cada uno, todo con paredes de adobes y techo con teja.
Informe 1823. "Se han echo dos lienzos mas, y queda cerrado el quadro de la nueva Mⁿ y á mas el cuerpo de guardia con almazen y calabozo, y 6 casas para la tropa, todo de adove y teja."
Informe 1825. "Se han concluido la Sta Yglesia, y queda acabada todo la Mision." SBMA.

its third site,[25] then, was built in just four years—a feat accomplished at none of our other missions. The Indian population reached its peak here in 1827 when the neophytes numbered 1,462.

In 1840 or 1841, the tower, which was originally built of adobes, was so badly damaged by excessive rains that the top stage was taken down and rebuilt of wood. Four years later the entire belfry was encased in planking and painted. An iron cross 2½ varas (about 7 feet) high crowned the belfry.[26] Later, when the old mission had been placed in the hands of missionaries of the Jesuit Order, Fr. Joseph Carredda installed a clock[27] in the tower face. The subsequent history of the old mission buildings is fairly well recorded in photographs and in Jesuit annals.

The fire of 1926, which destroyed the church and adjoining buildings, consumed the decorated sanctuary ceiling, the reredos, and the quaint hand-carved pulpit, all believed by many persons to have been taken from Fr. Murguía's church and installed in the new one of 1822-1825. Harry Downie, however, thinks it quite unlikely that the ceiling was removed from the earlier church because of the fact that the planks comprising it had, in all likelihood, been nailed to the ceiling beams with the roughly squared iron nails in use at that time. And to have removed the planks, so secured, with the then available tools, would have been practically impossible without shattering them beyond repair.

Stored away in the archives of Mission Santa Bárbara, together with the rare old documents, is a very interesting drawing. This is a plan for a reredos, or retable. Drawn with quill and ink on the paper of the day, dated October 25, 1802, and signed by Marcos López, it has the notation "Pertenece a la Misión de Sta Clara" (Pertaining, or belonging, to the Mission of Santa Clara) inscribed upon it. Aside from the fact that this drawing, together with that of the Monterey presidial chapel, corroborates the belief that plans were drawn in those days, and that the missions and their furnishings were not always constructed by "rule of thumb," the reredos is so strikingly similar to the one destroyed in the fire of 1926 that it gives substance to the belief that the latter was taken from Fr. Murguía's church. The differences between the plan and the finished retable may well be explained by the probability that the one who executed the order did not too closely follow the López pattern. The reredos was probably brought up from México in 1803 and was installed in the Murguía church with appropriate ceremony.

---

[25] This was the establishment sketched by Waseurtz in 1843 and by H. M. T. Powell in 1850. A daguerreotype was made of it by J. M. Ford "somewhere prior to 1858," according to Charles B. Turrill, an authority on early photographs.

[26] Inventory of 1851. Copy in the writer's collection through the courtesy of Rev. Arthur D. Spearman, S. J.

[27] From its description it probably was the clock received by the Padres in 1777.

Top: Drum used in mission days by Indians of San Antonio, kept by them and recently returned. Bottom: Remains of musical instruments, the barrel organ, and lectern at San Juan Bautista and Santa Inés.

▲ MISSION MUSIC *once used by the Indian choristers of San Juan Bautista.*

▼ MUSIC USED, *perhaps by Fr. Estevan Tapis, in teaching the Indians of Mission Santa Inés.*

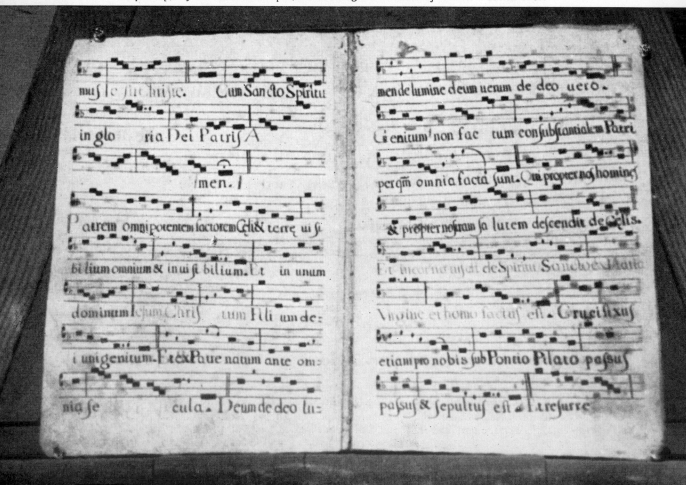

The original mural decorations at Mission San Francisco were obliterated with whitewash many years ago. Those seen in the sanctuary zone after about 1898 were executed by Miss Nora Fennell of San Francisco. It is said that the original decorations are still to be found on the wall back of the reredos. The pigment used was cinnabar. The ceiling decorations are original. The colors employed in painting the chevron design on the planks and beams are white, blue, yellow, and red, and are laid in that order. The white is probably whitewash, the red and yellow are ochres, and the blue is indigo. Indigo was used both as a dye and a paint. The red on the ceiling could not have been cinnabar, since those colors, mixed with whitewash, were laid on one after the other and cinnabar mixed with fresh whitewash turns black.

In a photograph, known to have been made not later than 1875, the sanctuary arch in this church is shown ornamented with a simulated cut-stone design. From the gradations in the shades, it appears that the "stone" may have been painted in red and pointed off with black and white pigments. Considerable black was used in mission days.

A water color drawing made of the Santa Cruz church ruins,[28] after the earthquake of 1857, pictures its ceiling decorated with the same design as that found at San Francisco. Nothing appears to be known about the wall decorations of Missions San José, San Rafael, San Francisco Solano, San Juan Bautista, and San Gabriel.

At San Miguel the murals, executed by Don Esteban Munras, of Monterey, and the Indians, still exist much as they did in late mission days. They were "touched up" in a few places when restoration work was done in 1931-1932, but otherwise have been undisturbed. They are well worth a visit to the mission for they present a study in both design and pigments.

Due to the generous gift of William Randolph Hearst and other added contributions, a number of our old missions are being re-furbished, protected from further ruin, or restored to some degree of their former architectural state. Lovely San Antonio is, after all, not to be allowed to fall into complete oblivion. Under the supervision of Harry Downie its church has been restored while the other buildings of the quadrangle are being rebuilt to be used as a Brothers' School.

At San Luis Obispo the old mission church has recently undergone many changes. Under the direction of Mr. Downie it has been enlarged and re-decorated. New doors, fashioned after those of Indian workmanship, have replaced the old ones. The old paintings have been cleaned, re-framed and given new

[28] Illustrating an article, "A Sea-Port on the Pacific," in *Scribner's Monthly Magazine*, August, 1878.

settings. Altogether, the charm and atmosphere of the mission church, as the Padres and Indians knew it, has to some considerable extent been restored.

At Santa Inés the original wall paintings remain in the chancel and in the sacristy. Those of the former have been somewhat interfered with by "restorers," but the sacristy seems to have been spared. There, in the dado, may be seen one of the best and most striking examples of mission-day mural painting. In the sanctuary zone, high up on the left hand wall, is a somewhat faded or damaged frieze painted a clear, pale blue that only azurite can produce. The altar was formerly painted this same "heavenly blue," but some time after Fr. Buckler left the mission the color was changed to an unlovely green, unlike anything found in the original pigments.

The designs employed at both Santa Inés and San Miguel are conventionalized and clearly indicate the use of stencils, but this fact does not preclude the probability of participation in the work by Indian artists, though some critics who have examined the murals are inclined to think otherwise. The idea that these natives should be able to turn out such work in stone, wood, pottery, and basketry as to excite praise from Fr. Crespí, Costansó, Portolá, Fages, Font, and others of the early expeditionary parties, and then not be capable of learning to handle brushes, paint-pots, and stencils[29] in helping to create the decorations found on some mission walls today, is utterly preposterous.

About sixty years ago much might have been seen of original mural decoration, particularly on the walls of the southern missions. But the desire for change, modernization, as well as the lack of appreciation of such priceless relics has brought about their destruction, chiefly by means of the whitewash brush. However, photographs, taken in the 1875-1890 period, have preserved many of the designs at least.

Decorations exhibiting much of Indian artistry were executed at San Buenaventura, San Fernando, San Juan Capistrano, San Luis Rey, and its dependency, Pala. Reporting to the College of San Fernando and to the Mexican government, in 1819, Fr. Commissary Prefect, Mariano Payéras, wrote: ". . the mission San Buenaventura has placed its church and sacristy, including the chapel dedicated to Saint Michael,[30] in such condition that, since it was all done by the neophytes under the direction of the missionaries and at little cost, it is worthy of praise to God."[31] In 1820, the Padres of this mission note in their annual report that

---

[29] "Traditionally," writes Lanier Bartlett, "this wallpaper like appearance [at San Miguel] was effected with rawhide stencils cut by the decorators' Indian helpers." *Mission Motifs*, p. 6. Southern California Index of American Design. WPA.

[30] This chapel is shown in Robinson's sketch of San Buenaventura.

[31] Engelhardt, *Mission San Buenaventura*, 42-43.

in the year "special attention was given to beautifying the church." No mention is made of the artist or artists employed, but again, there is little logic in thinking that Indian workers who could fashion that mission's pulpit and confessionals,[32] conceded by all who have examined them to be of Indian workmanship, would not also, with the aid of stencils, be able to decorate the walls of their church. One remnant of the original painting is still to be found on a wall of the old baptistry.

Indian motifs—animals, an emblazoned sun, triangles, and other geometrical designs; a hunting scene where an Indian, disguised in a deerskin, is shown shooting a deer with bow and arrow; flowers and other objects have, within recent years, been discovered under layers of whitewash at San Fernando.

At San Juan Capistrano, in the ceiling of the dome over the altar zone of the old stone church, are yet to be seen some of the original decorations. Some are carved and others are both carved and painted. The colors used are red, blue, pale green, and gray. According to legend, a large red star was painted on the ceiling of the dome that formerly existed over the center of the transept. Until about 1900, there was a niche in the wall of a room in the northeast corner of this mission's quadrangle. It was decorated with a checker-board design done in red and yellow ochres. George Wharton James photographed this detail.[33]

Butterflies, flowers, and angels in blue and gold were painted by the Indians on a side altar at San Luis Rey. In describing this mission Helen Hunt Jackson wrote: "Even finer than the ruins of San Juan Capistrano are those of the church at San Luis Rey. It has a perfectly proportioned dome over the chancel, and beautifully groined arches on either hand and over the altar. Four broad pilasters on each side of the church are frescoed in a curious mixing of blues, light and dark, with reds and black, which have faded and blended into a delicious tone."[34]

There were a number of motifs in San Luis Rey's church that were repeated with variations at Pala. Indeed it is hard to escape the conviction that the artist who decorated the walls of the asistencia's chapel was an Indian from the parent mission. Arches and pillars, in remembrance, it may be, of the great court at the mission; diamond-shaped and checker-board designs, potted cactus (?) slabs, a quill and ink bottle over the baptismal font niche, a mother quail feeding with her young—such were the designs that were painted on the walls of the Pala chapel. Here and there were also figures that are reminiscent of the petroglyphs

[32] The Confessionals still exist, but the pulpit was destroyed about fifty years ago. Pieces of it have, however, been preserved in the Ventura Mission and County Museums.
[33] James, G. W., *In and Out of the Old Missions*, Plate L.
[34] Jackson, H. H., *Glimpses of California and the Missions*, 93.

found in the "Painted Cave" in the Santa Inés mountains and on the famous "Piedra Pintada" (Painted Rock) in the Carrizo Plains in San Luis Obispo County.

The opportunity to study the original paintings on the walls of this little Indian chapel has passed, for they were thoughtlessly whitewashed over soon after the "exiled" Indians from Warner's Hot Springs and other small villages were established by government orders on the Pala Reservation.[35] Again an almost complete set of photographs of the interior had been taken in the years just preceding and after the restoration of the chapel by the Landmarks Club. Later the walls were repainted, but the Indian touch is no longer as evident as it was. Nor were all the original designs reproduced. The colors used in the original murals were, according to Ford, the artist, red, green, and black.[36] And those were the colors found by this investigator some years ago while making a careful study of the walls wherever the whitewash had peeled off and the old paints were showing through. The green was that soft, almost-sage yet bluish color so much used in mission days. There were several shades of red and two blacks, one hard and brilliant. These pigments were, according to legends which still persist among Mexican and Indian peoples, mixed with water with a little cactus juice added for adhesive purposes, and applied directly to the walls. One old Mexican explained that the juice used was "not from the opuntia such as is growing in the garden of Mission San Juan Capistrano, but from the *tuna Castilla*."

The history of the little chapel at Pala is very interesting. Reporting about Fr. Peyri (sometimes spelled Peiri), in 1817, Fr. Comisario Sarría writes: ". . A year and some months ago, with the permit of the government and with mine, he built a chapel about seven leagues east of the Mission, under the title of San Antonio de Pala, Pala being, in the language of the Indians, the name of the site. At this Mission [Pala] he is ordinarily occupied, but at times returning to the chief Mission [San Luis Rey]. . "[37]

Mission Indians have lived at Pala from the time of the building of the chapel. The settlement was never abandoned by them. Items in Fr. Mut's[38] account book verify this statement, for expenses incurred in visiting that community are set down from the year 1866 to 1886. In 1885, this entry was made: "Reparos de la Capilla de Pala, véase el diario (Repairs of the chapel of Pala, see diary),

[35] James, G. W., *Picturesque Pala*, 43.
[36] From Ford's small notebook in the Grant Jackson Collection in the Southwest Museum at Los Angeles.
[37] Engelhardt, *Mission San Luis Rey*, 203-204.
[38] Rev. José Mut, a Catalonian, serving at San Juan Capistrano from 1866 to 1886.

$214.67."[39] From time to time Padre Mut jots down donations or subscriptions from the Indians. During the disorders that followed secularization, Indians from Pala went over to the parent mission and, securing the statue of the patron saint, took it over to their chapel for safe keeping. There it has remained to this day. It was in the upper triangular section of the altar panel painted on the wall back of this statue that the design of the feeding quail was found.

In fancy this writer sees Fr. Peyri indulgently, yet critically, watching as a young Indian artist decorates the walls of the chapel, using here and there the White Man's stenciled designs yet managing, through the introduction of motifs of his own race, to give the whole a thoroughly Indian character.

Another phase of Indian effort with brush and paint is represented in a series of paintings of the Via Crucis (the Way, or Stations, of the Cross), now hanging in one of the old mission rooms at San Gabriel. Painted at San Fernando, according to all available information,[40] these pictures, admittedly of Indian workmanship, have been the subject of the most absurd and impossible stories. A few years back a newspaper writer startled his readers with a sensational account of the paintings, placing their potential value, as he said, at $1,500,000. The pigments used were, he claimed, made from the crushed petals of flowers. He proceeded at length to describe the process whereby those petals were transformed into pigments, assuring his readers that there was nothing imaginary about the process; that it was still used by the Pueblo Indians of Arizona and New Mexico.

To demonstrate the erroneousness of the claim that the pictures were executed with flower pigments, it will be necessary to give a short sketch of their history. In 1887, they were found stored away in the lower room of the belfry of the "Plaza Church" in Los Angeles. In 1893, they were exhibited at the World's Columbian Exposition held in Chicago. Back in Los Angeles, in 1902, they became a part of a Chamber of Commerce exhibition. Stored afterwards in the basement of St. Vibiana's Cathedral in that city, they were finally given by the Bishop to the Claretian Fathers at Mission San Gabriel. There they were first hung in the church. Then, fearing that they might be considered "cheap," the pastor had them removed and hung in an outside corridor. Here for some twenty years they were mercilessly subjected to the vagaries of wind, sun, and gritty dust. And, even though they were protected by the corridor roof, they were, nevertheless, exposed to the dampness of rain and fog.

---

[39] *Libro del Padre Mut*, p. 91. Copy by Maj. Bruce Condé in E. W. collection.

[40] From *Herald-Express* Files, under date Nov. 15, 1887; "A California Loan Exhibition," by Auguste Wey in *The Californian*, Sept., 1892; Holway, Mary Gordon, *Art of the Old World in New Spain*, 104.

After the publication of the sensational story of their value together with the details of the flower-pigment making, the paintings were taken down from the corridor wall, dusted off, and hung in a room which was once a part of the mission Fathers' dwelling. Despite the years of rough treatment accorded them, the pigments today are probably almost as bright as they ever were. This writer does not hesitate to declare that no flower pigments, had it been possible to produce them, could possibly have withstood the long years of exposure to which the paintings were subjected. Desiring expert opinion on the subject, a letter was dispatched to Winsor and Newton, Limited, manufacturing artists' colourmen of London, England, a long-established and highly reputable firm. Their answer reads:

> . . . there is no reason to believe that it has ever been possible to prepare permanent pigments from flowers.
> Dyes can be extracted from leaves, berries or wood of certain plants, but, with the exception of alizarin from madder root, these dyes are always more or less fugitive, and, in those cases where the dye can be combined with an organic base so as to form a lake pigment, the resulting lake displays the same impermanence as the parent dyestuff.
> Examples are Persian Berry, Quercitron and Red Wood lakes. The natural colouring matter present in the petals of flowers is even more fugitive than those mentioned and therefore still less likely to be of any value for the preparation of permanent pigmentary colours.

Regarding the truth of the statement that the Pueblo Indians of Arizona and New Mexico produced paints from flowers, a letter sent to the Laboratory of Anthropology at Santa Fe, New Mexico, elicited this reply:

> "The 'flower paint' legend is quite widespread in New Mexico, and unfortunately has appeared in print. All of the references, including the label in the State Museum, refer to one author, Gilberto Espinosa in *New Mexico Magazine*, March, 1935. He gives no verification for his statement. I have talked with one artist and writer, . . , who has done considerable research on santos, bultos, and other ecclesiastical works of the Spanish-Colonial Period in New Mexico. She quoted this author about ten years ago and now is going to re-write her article and change the statements previously made. . . After many years of going over this type of material she sees no justification for the 'flower legend.' "

The paintings of the Via Crucis are unique and should be carefully preserved. It is to be hoped that no effort will ever be made to "restore" them, for they represent a phase of Indian endeavor that is fast disappearing. It is because of this fact that they are priceless. The pigments used in painting them were the same as those employed in decorating the walls of mission churches and other buildings—earths, minerals, and one vegetable, indigo. According to Fr. Sugranes, formerly of Mission San Gabriel, the Stations were painted by a San Fernando Indian named Juan Antonio.[41]

[41] Sugranes (Rev. Eugene), *The History of Mission San Gabriel*, 77.

CHAPTER **18**

The Native Indian's Primitive Musical Instruments

Training the Indian Youths to Become Choristers

WHEN, IN 1602, Vizcaíno sailed into the Santa Bárbara Channel, he was astonished to see two Indian fishermen in a canoe "rowing so swiftly that they seemed to fly. They came along without saying a word to us," the narrator writes, "and went twice around us with so great speed that it seemed impossible; this finished, they came aft, bowing their heads in the way of courtesy. The general [Vizcaíno] ordered that they be given a cloth, with bread. They received it, and gave in return the fish they had, without any pay, and this done they said by signs that they wished to go. After they had gone five Indians came in another canoe, so well constructed and built that since Noah's Ark a finer and lighter vessel with timbers had not been seen. Four men rowed, with an old man in the center, (singing) as in a *mitote*[1] of the Indians of New Spain, and the others responding to him."[2]

Fr. Antonio de la Ascensión, one of the three priests of the Discalced Order of Carmelites who accompanied Vizcaíno, was impressed with the friendliness and docility of the natives. As was the custom of the day, he wrote a report of the expedition and concluded it with an outline of "The Method to be observed in Subduing and Settling the Realm of the Californias." That he was deeply impressed by the singing of the Indians while they were rowing their canoes is evidenced by the suggestions found in Chapter XVI of his manuscript.

"And it would be well," he writes, "to bring from New Spain minstrels, with their instruments and trumpets, that the divine services may be celebrated with solemnity and pomp. Likewise it would be well and proper to choose from among the Indians some of the brightest, selecting among the young men and boys such

---

[1] Mitote—an Indian dance.
[2] Bolton, *Spanish Exploration in the Southwest.* "Diary of Vizcaino", 87-88. Charles Scribner's Sons, New York, 1916.

as appear the most docile, talented and capable; that they should be taught and instructed in the Christian doctrine and to read the Spanish primers, in order that along with the reading they may learn the Spanish language, and that they may learn to write and sing, and to play all the musical instruments; because a good foundation makes the edifice firm, and according as care is given in this matter to the beginnings, so will the middle parts and the ends be good."

"It is a very easy matter, by this method, to teach the children our language, and they, as they grow up, will teach it to their companions and to their children and families, and in a few years all will know the Spanish language, which will be a very great boon; . . "[3]

That the zealous Carmelite Father should have outlined the policy later followed by the Franciscans in training native boys and youths of California seems more than a coincidence. It seems rather to indicate a practice established by the missionaries who followed close upon the heels of the military in the Spanish conquest of México and other lands of the western hemisphere. For music, vocal and instrumental, was necessary to the proper celebration of divine services and the Padres would soon have realized that only in the natives lay their hopes for either. Therefore, the early training of the boys was essential. And specialized training required segregation, a practice followed by the Franciscan Fathers of the California missions from the very earliest years.

It was recorded in the early diaries that the members of Portolá's party going up the coast, in 1769, had been both amused and annoyed by native serenaders of the Santa Bárbara Channel who came dancing and blowing shrill whistles for their entertainment. Nevertheless, both Fr. Crespí and Costansó agreed that in their dancing and singing the natives kept such good time with the movement and noise of "hollow reeds," which they held in their hands, that they produced real harmony. The pipes, or whistles, however, "were very disagreeable and only served to annoy us." Fr. Crespí reported that the noise of the pipes grated on their ears.

Later, in 1812, when the missionaries answered that series of questions regarding the Indians' origin, their advancement under the mission system, their fondness for music, etc.,[4] they noted that in their uncivilized state the natives of various localities had such musical instruments as timbrels (small hand drums), whistles made from the bone of the foreleg of the deer, flutes made from the elder tree, and rattles. They had, moreover, a well-developed sense of rhythm and a fondness for both music and song.

[3] *Ibidem, Report of Father Ascensión,* 128.
[4] The Padres' original replies to those questions are preserved in the Santa Bárbara Mission Archives.

▲ THE CEREMONY OF "WASHING THE FEET" *was performed at all the old missions.* (Miniature)

▼ THE CEREMONY OF "CHASTISING JUDAS ISCARIOT" *was celebrated on Saturday of Easter Week.* (Miniature)

▲ THE FEAST OF CORPUS CHRISTI *is celebrated annually by the Indians of Pala.*

▼ "MAKING THE WAY OF THE CROSS." *The mission Indians enjoyed such ceremonial devotions.* (*Miniature*)

There is no doubt that as soon as the most necessary things connected with the beginning of a mission had been attended to, the boys and young men were selected for training in the various tasks involved in the management of the mission activities. It is presumed that they were chosen according to their ability and physical fitness. Some were to become makers of adobes and tiles, some to do blacksmith and carpenter work, others to look after the live stock, or to work in the fields. From among the boys about nine years of age were chosen those who were to be trained to serve as pages, acolytes, bell-ringers, choristers, and players of such instruments as violins, bass viols, guitars, flutes, drums, and triangles.

Fr. Owen de Silva, who has made an extensive and sympathetic study of our mission music, the Padre instructors, and the Indian choristers and instrumentalists, thinks that at first the singing was done by the whole congregation.[5]

Meanwhile, the Padres were selecting the boys most likely to succeed as singers and musicians. They were chosen, without doubt, because of the quality of their voices, their intelligence, and their aptitude. They were to be taught to read and write and were the envy of the other boys, for all were fond of music and delighted in taking part in any celebration. Moreover, the colorful uniforms worn at some of the missions served as an added attraction. That many of those black-eyed, "shock-headed" boys would strive for a place in the choir or orchestra is obvious.

Much that is of interest is to be found in the Padres' answers to the question about the Indians' fondness for music. The Padres of Mission San Antonio, Juan Sancho and Pedro Cabot, write: "They like music very much. They play the violin, and bass-viol, the flute, the trumpet, the drum, and any other instrument given them. They also have a flute of their own, which they have kept from Gentile days. This flute, open at top and bottom, is played like the dulcet flute. It is from three to five spans in length. When five spans in length, the flute sounds eight notes perfectly. The Indians play a number of pieces on it, almost all merry and in the same time. The five-span flute has eleven holes. The other flutes sometimes have more than eleven holes, sometimes less. Another instrument of the natives is a wooden bow with a catgut string. It produces but one note. They have no other instrument of their own, but their songs are numerous. They sing at their dances and on other occasions. As we [Padres] are not professional musicians we cannot send you copies of the songs. All we are able to say is that they sing in variable pitch and tone, and that their melodies ascend and descend by seconds, thirds, fourths, fifths, and octaves. The only time that

[5] Fr. Owen da Silva, O. F. M., *Mission Music of California*, Warren F. Lewis, Publisher, Los Angeles, 1941 (hereinafter referred to as *Mission Music*), 6.

they sing anything like part music is when many sing together; then some sing an octave higher than the others. Very many of their songs are joyous; others, however, are sad. In all their singing there is never any consecutive thought; they simply name birds, places, etc. They have used these instruments and songs from time immemorial. They sing Spanish airs to perfection and easily learn whatever is taught them, be the music plain or figured. They form a choir, and can do a part Mass, but cannot sing by sight."[6]

Of the Indians of San Juan Bautista, Fr. Felipe Arroyo de la Cuesta writes: "They are fond of music and song. They learn anything with ease, and can even play their pagan tunes on our instruments. These pagan tunes are many and various. They have songs for their games but the men do not sing them the same as the women. They have songs for burials, for recovery from sickness, for the time of war, for the chase, for the dances of the men, for the dances of the women, for entertaining the children, and for the telling of stories and fables. In their songs there is no sequence of thought; many of the singers do not even understand the individual words, because these words were taken from other tribes and languages. Some of their songs are sad, others very cheerful, depending on the occasion or the motive for singing and dancing. Their instruments are a stick split down the middle and a stick mounted by a sort of hollow ball containing tiny stones or gravel, the shaking of which produces a noise. Their sense of time is admirable; they keep together even in their unusual motions and shoutings. They also blow small whistles made from the bones of the goose and the deer. Most of the natives, if not all of them, smear their faces with paint in the most ridiculous way. They wear feathers in their hair, on their forehead, and even on their shoulders, in imitation of wings. This renders them hideous. They also imitate the bear, the coyote, and other animals."[7]

Frs. Estevan Tapis and Francisco Xavier Uría, reporting on the Indians of Mission Santa Inés, note: ". . . They no longer hear such chants nor instruments [i. e., their native ones], but in their place are heard devout songs and harmonized instruments. The violin, the baja violon [bass viol], (instruments made by the neophytes themselves, as also the tambora), the sweet German flute, the trompa, the bandola, are those they know and use in the functions of the church. They are fond of music, and they learn easily by memory the sonatas which they hear, or which are taught them."[8]

Concerning his Indians' fondness for music, Fr. Antonio Martínez of Mission

---

[6] Fr. Owen, *opus cit,*. 5.
[7] Fr. Owen, *Ibidem*, 5.
[8] Engelhardt, *Mission Santa Ines*, 21.

San Luis Obispo writes: "I have not been able to ascertain whether the Indians have any fondness or not for music. What I know is that they have among themselves a variety of songs, and I have seen with some of them some wind instruments made of sticks from elder trees. They possess none of our instruments; but when they have become Christians, I have seen them learn to play the violin, the bass-viol, the flute, the guitar and the bandola. They, in fact, are inclined to learn whatever is taught them." And, Fr. Antonio Rodríguez, his companion friar, signs, "So it is."[9]

Fr. José Señán, of San Buenaventura, notes: "They are now quite eager to sing and play on the instruments, string as well as wind, and they easily learn by ear and sight. In paganism they used only a flute-like thing made of elderwood, as also a bone whistle, with which the players produce a shriek and violent trill, at the same time making strange and ridiculous contortions of the body. . . "[10]

Fr. Josef Barona and Fr. Gerónimo Boscana, at San Juan Capistrano, write concerning their neophytes: ". . It must be observed that they easily learn to play any instrument, no matter what it may be."[11]

The Padres of San Diego observe: "These neophytes have not and never had other musical instruments than the timbrel which has a disagreeable sound. However, the Fathers have procured some musical instruments, and the neophytes play them with some ability; they would be proficient if they had someone to perfect them, for they are very fond of our musical instruments."[12]

Not all the Padres were musicians, consequently not all the Indian choirs and orchestras were as good as they might have been. Such may or may not have been the case at San Francisco where Kotzebue, in 1816, attended the festival of St. Francis. "The orchestra," he writes, "consisted of a violoncello, a violin, and two flutes; these instruments were played by little half-naked Indians, and were very often out of tune."[13]

There was, however, no missionary who was unacquainted with music, as he might easily have been of agricultural or architectural arts, for he had been accustomed to singing in the choir from the earliest days of his training. Three or four times a day he was required to take part in this exercise. Moreover, as Fr. Owen writes: "Whether they were destined for the foreign missions or for work at home, they had to learn how to sing, and how to play a musical instrument."[14]

[9] Engelhardt, *Mission San Luis Obispo*, 53.
[10] Engelhardt, *Mission San Buenaventura*, 39.
[11] Engelhardt, *Mission San Juan Capistrano* 60.
[12] Engelhardt, *Mission San Diego*, 183.
[13] Mahr, *Visit of the "Rurik"*, 59.
[14] Fr. Owen, *Mission Music*, 19.

The California Padres, therefore, whether masters or not, were able to lead their little Indian boys in both vocal and instrumental music.

When Duhaut-Cilly, his trading done, went to take leave of the Padres of Santa Bárbara it happened to be Palm Sunday. Accordingly, as he writes: "I attended the ceremony for the day, which took place with extraordinary pomp. Branches of palm leaves, elegantly decorated with flowers and braids of the leaf itself, were distributed among all the *gente de razon;* the Indians had simple olive branches. The severity of Lent did not permit the padre to let us hear his music in the church. His Indians executed merely some chants with much taste and sweet melody: they made us hear Spanish and Latin words to the prettiest Italian airs."

"After Mass we returned to the padre's reception-room, and the musicians gave a serenade to the commandant general [Governor Echeandía]. There were a large number of musicians, and all in uniform: although they executed tolerably some French and Italian morceaux, I noticed that they had succeeded better in the chants. At last I returned to the ship and we set sail immediately."[15]

Going on down the coast Duhaut-Cilly visited San Luis Rey. There, "On the evening of the 11th [June, 1827]," he relates, "volleys of small shot, and fires lighted on the place, announced the festival of the following day [that of St. Anthony]. It began with a high Mass, sung by the Indian musicians. As many as those at Santa Bárbara they were far from equalling them; it must also be said that most of the instruments which they used, made in the mission, were of very inferior quality. Immediately after the mass came the bullfights, lasting a part of the day."[16]

Telling of a visit to Mission San José on a feast day, Alfred Robinson writes: "Mass was commenced, and Padre Viader [from Santa Clara] at the usual period of the ceremony ascended the pulpit, and delivered an explanatory sermon relative to the celebration of the day. The music was well executed, for it had been practiced daily for more than two months under the particular supervision of Father Narciso Durán. The number of musicians was about thirty; the instruments performed upon were violins, flutes, trumpets, and drums; and so acute was the ear of the priest that he would detect a wrong note on the part of either instantly, and chide the erring performer. I have often seen the old gentleman, bareheaded, in the large square of the mission beating time against one of the pillars of the corridor, whilst his music was in rehearsal."[17]

---

[15] "Duhaut-Cilly's Account," 164.
[16] *Ibidem,* 229.
[17] Robinson, *Life in Cal.,* 124.

Robinson wandered into the church at Santa Bárbara one day and found that "the musicians attached to the choir were practicing, and played some fine airs; rather unsuitable, however, to the place. It was not unusual, both here and at the churches of other missions, to hear during the mass the most lively dancing tunes."[18]

The reason for the adoption of French and Italian airs, a custom noted by Duhaut-Cilly, Robinson, and others, may lie in the explanation given de Mofras after he had listened to music performed at Santa Cruz by the visiting Indian musicians of Santa Clara. Writing about the latter mission, the Frenchman remarks: "Santa Clara has always been one of the leading missions. The ideal situation and the mildness of the climate attracted the natives, and the Spanish Fathers gave so much thought to their education and instruction in the mechanical arts that they became skilled carpenters, blacksmiths, and even masons."

"Music was also taught with marked success, and their neophyte orchestra was known throughout the land. One of the Fathers purchased from a French whaler thirty complete uniforms and organized a band of musicians. Our party was privileged to attend some of their performances when at Santa Cruz on September 14, 1841, the fete day consecrated to the exaltation of the Holy Cross, and it was not without keen surprise that we heard musicians brought over from Santa Clara, singing the *Marseillaise*, as the congregation rose, and escort the procession singing *Vive Henri IV*. After mass, upon asking one of the Fathers how these Indians happened to know these airs, I was informed that one of his predecessors had brought a small organ from France and that the Indians, after hearing the airs, had instinctively arranged the songs for use by the various instruments."[19]

Hand, or barrel-organs, were to be found at other missions besides Santa Clara. One was presented by Captain George Vancouver to Fr. Fermín de Lasuén, whom the Englishman greatly admired.[20] This was probably the one that was listed in the San Carlos inventory as "1 órgano de Sigianuela [Ciguenuela?] con tres cilindros decompuesto" (One hand organ—literally 1 organ of small crank—in disrepair, with three cylinders),[21] for at the time of Vancouver's visit, Fr. Lasuén was Padre Presidente and was residing at San Carlos. In 1829, another such organ was received at Mission San Juan Bautista, while in that same year one was confiscated by customs officials at San Diego.[22] Judge Benjamin

---

[18] *Ibidem,* 57.
[19] Mofras, *Travels,* 1. 221.
[20] Banc., *Hist. of Cal.,* 1. 522.
[21] Mission San Carlos inventory, 1835. SBMA.
[22] Banc., *Hist. of Cal.,* 3. 139.

Hayes tells of one being brought to San Diego from San Francisco. It had been used at the latter mission, in days gone by.[23] Edwin Bryant found one in San Luis Obispo's organ-loft,[24] and perhaps there were others at other missions.

Señorita Encarnación Piñedo describes the uniform mentioned by de Mofras: "Rev. Father José Viader taught the Indians to perform on musical instruments and to sing. The younger ones sang and the older ones played in the band, which consisted of a clarinet, flute, cello, bass and small drums, cymbals and triangle. The leader of the band was Joaquín, a neophyte. With a rod he led the musicians, striking with it whomsoever among them made a mistake. In the course of time the band dressed in blue uniforms with a red stripe along the length of each trouser leg, and a red cap with a tassel."[25]

A search through the inventories of 1834-1851 reveals the fact that some of the missions were quite well equipped with musical instruments. For example, at San José, in 1842, there still remained four bass-viols, one contra-bass, twenty violins, one drum, two triangles, one cilindro (hand-organ) with its case and three cylinders, one book of choral music written on parchment with leather cover, some masses and various other unclassified pieces of music, and twenty-six uniforms for the musicians. The latter were very much damaged and soiled.[26]

At Santa Clara, in 1851, the Jesuit Fathers, into whose keeping that mission had just been placed, found in the music room one bass-viol, three medium sized ones in good condition, thirteen violins, three medium sized ones all "en buen estado," three large ones somewhat damaged, flutes, one drum, one bass drum, one choral written on parchment with leather cover ornamented with bronze, two triangles, various sheets of music, one stand and two bronze cymbals.[27]

At Santa Bárbara, the inventory taken in 1834 shows that the mission possessed at that time four flutes, three clarinets, two trumpets, two bass viols, one Chinese (viol?), three drums—one large—, twenty violins, three triangles, four music stands, and the uniforms of the musicians.[28]

There can be no doubt that musical instruments were made at some of the missions; on the other hand, *memorias* and account books record the purchase of violins, flutes, drums, trumpets, oboes, mandolas, and strings and parts for various instruments.[29]

[23] Hayes, *Pioneer Notes*, 229.
[24] Bryant, *What I Saw*, 357.
[25] Piñedo, "Early Days."
[26] Inventory of Mission San José, 1842. SBMA.
[27] Inventory of Mission Santa Clara, 1851.
[28] Inventory of Mission Santa Bárbara, 1834. SBMA.
[29] *Memorias* of Mission Santa Bárbara, SBMA; *Memorias* of Mission San Buenaventura, Lib. Miss. Sn. Buen; *Hartnell Account Book*, Lib. B. A. Soberanes, Salinas, California.

Of the music stands mentioned above, and others once standing in mission choir lofts, only two exist. One is at Santa Inés and the other at San Juan Bautista. At the latter mission may also be found one of the old barrel-organs mentioned in the inventories. Here and there one occasionally hears of a violin said to have been used in mission days, but it is usually so crudely wrought that it is doubtful that any Padre musician would have countenanced its use in the mission orchestra.

Phases of this subject that have always intrigued this writer are, first, the place of practice for those playing musical instruments, and second, the method of instruction employed. Robinson has said that the musicians at San José practiced in the inner court, but at San Antonio it seems that a walled space at the side of the church was chosen for that purpose. It is described in the inventory as "1 plaza pequeña con su puerta y llave" (a little court, or plaza, with door and lock). This probably refers to that yard which lay at the rear of the church on the right side. It adjoined a row of rooms built against the orchard wall. Part of this row was erected in 1819 to provide a dormitory for the young men.

This walled-in court would have made an admirable place for practicing, particularly if the Padre instructor had, as is done in Spain today,[30] written the music on one of the whitewashed adobe walls. At our old missions the notes would have been done in red, black, and yellow! And the pigments used would have been the same as those employed in decorating the church walls. That the broad white walls of the mission buildings were used for some such purpose is indicated in the San Gabriel Padres' reply to the question regarding the Indians' inclination to read and write. "One or the other has an inclination to read and write," they observed, "and the young are apt in drawing characters on the wall with carbon when they want to mimic [imitate?] us. . . " [31] It is only a hint, but there it is.

Fr. Owen, who has examined numerous books and sheets of music written by mission Padres for their dusky pupils, explains the significance of the colored notes found on some of the old manuscripts. "Perhaps," he writes, "the most engaging feature of the Old Mission music is the colored notation. Due to the crowding of two, three or four parts onto a single staff of five or six lines, it was often difficult to follow an individual voice, especially when the voices crossed. Some inventive padre, and local tradition says Fray Estevan Tapis of Mission San Juan Bautista, overcame this problem by the use of colors. There are no set rules for the use of the colors. Padre Tapis himself uses but red and black. Padre

---

[30] *National Geographic Magazine*, March, 1929, p. 325; December 1932, p. 762.
[31] Engelhardt, *Mission San Gabriel*, 99.

Durán denoted four part music as follows: white notes outlined in red for the first voice (tiple); white notes outlined in black for the second voice (contralto); solid red notes for the third voice (tenor); and solid black notes for the fourth (bass). Some of the four part scripts effectively employ yellow for the first voice, red for the second, white outlined in black for the third, and solid black for the fourth. At Mission Santa Bárbara a three part Mass employs yellow, red and black. If the music were two part, red and black were generally used. Thus it was easy for a chorister to follow his respective part as it wound its way among the others. And where did the padres get their colors? They have faded little through the years; they are still bright and beautiful."[32]

Recorded on the pages of secular and mission history are the names of a few of the Indians who mastered the system of colored notation as well as the unique method of teaching music devised by Padre Narciso Durán while serving at San José.[33] Among those of outstanding ability are Antero, Toribio, and Juan de Dios of Santa Bárbara whom, as Fr. Durán noted: "it cost me twelve years of labor to teach."[34] Antero was not only a gifted tenor but an accomplished player of the bass-viol as well. Bancroft says that his "excellent tenor voice filled the church and was admired by foreigners as well as Californians."[35] (There is, or was a few years ago, just such a singer at Pala whose voice, of peculiar Indian quality, was such as to attract visitors from miles around.) Then there was old Rogerio Rocha, whom old-time residents of San Fernando still remember and speak of with pride. Rogerio was said to have been born in 1801. He was both a chorister and a flutist of considerable talent. Moreover, he was so well-versed in the various church services that when his wife died, in about 1886, Rogerio was master of ceremonies. "The service," Mr. H. N. Rust observes,—"the impressive funeral service of the Catholic Church—was conducted by Rogerio himself with all the dignity and beauty that belong to it. Mr. Romulo Pico, who was present, says that it was the most impressive funeral he ever attended."[36]

Concerning the Indian singers' and instrumentalists' ability to master and render acceptably the numerous hymns, chants, and Masses sung in the mission churches, Fr. Owen writes: "Judging from the few complete choir books and scattered fragments of the old music that still remain, as well as from the historical accounts, we gather that the repertoire of a Mission choir was quite exten-

[32] Fr. Owen, *Mission Music*, 13.
[33] Fr. Duran served at Mission San José from 1806 to 1833.
[34] Engelhardt, *Mission Santa Barbara*, 242.
[35] Banc., *California Pastoral*, 234.
[36] Rust, Horatio N., "Rogerio's Theological School," in *Out West*, Sept., 1904. Rogerio had been trained as a blacksmith. He spoke Spanish as well as his native tongue, and could conduct church services in Latin.

▲ "TAILING A STEER." *Duhaut-Cilly gives an excellent description of this sport (?).*

▼ INDIAN WOMEN of *Tucson, Arizona, still play the game witnessed by Duhaut-Cilly in 1827.*

Top: THE INDIAN VILLAGE of Agua Caliente (Warner's Hot Springs) in 1902. Center: A temescal on the Soboba Indian Reservation. Bottom: Indian home at Agua Caliente.

sive. Although the music was simple, including the figured masses and motets, it was no mean accomplishment for the neophyte choristers to be able to sing plainchant *Asperges* and *Vidi Aquam*, the Proper of the Mass for Sundays and Principal Feasts of the year, one or two plainchant masses, a few two or four part homophonic masses, numerous hymns for Benediction with the Blessed Sacrament, and hymns to the Blessed Virgin and the Saints. Even when we take into account that the Proper of the Mass was simplified, as it was by Padre Durán, who left out most of the Graduals and Offertories, and set all Introits to the melody of the *Gaudeamus*, and all *Allelujas* and Communions to standard melodies of the VI Tone, it still speaks well for the Indian choristers that they were able to sing so much of the sacred Liturgy."

"Moreover, they at times sang Vespers or Compline, knew the various Litanies, and had special hymns and lamentations to accompany the mysteries of the Rosary and the Stations of the Cross. On solemn occasions they sang the *Te Deum*, and at funerals they were capable of rendering either the incomparable plainchant melodies or the four part *Requiem* and *Libera*."

"Holy Week, commemorating the Passion and Death of the Savior, was especially well observed. The padre and a four part chorus even sang the Passion on Palm Sunday and Good Friday. They also sang the three Nocturnes of *Tenebrae* on the various nights of Holy Week and the *Mandatum* on Holy Thursday, when, with the choir singing 'Mandatum novum do vobis,' the padre, like the Master before him, humbly washed the feet of his poor disciples."

"The Patronal Feast of the respective Mission, the Month of May, the great Feast of Corpus Christi with its procession, as well as occasional Novenas were other occasions that made a special demand on the choristers and players. And *Los Pastores* in December! Musicians and singers practiced long and well for that eagerly awaited play, which so charmingly and tunefully tells the story of the First Christmas."[37]

Written by a Padre musician and instructor himself, no higher tribute could be paid the Indian choristers and instrumentalists, and indeed, none is needed.

Some fifty years ago there appeared in *The Land of Sunshine*, a Southern California magazine, several articles illustrated with the words and music of a number of Indian songs—songs that they had inherited from their fathers and their fathers' fathers before them.

In 1891, David P. Barrows[38] witnessed the celebration of the feast[39] of St.

---

[37] Fr. Owen, *Mission Music*, 10.
[38] Later to become Major General Barrows through participation in World War I.
[39] Feast—in the sense of religious festivals of rejoicing; solemn, or more commonly, joyous anniversaries.

Louis (August 25) by the Indians of the Cahuilla Valley. He was greatly impressed with their songs, and, after repeated visits succeeded in setting them down on paper. They were later harmonized by John Comfort Fillmore, Professor of Music at Pomona College.

In describing his visits with those people, Mr. Barrows notes:[40] "Songs play a large part in the life of the Coahuia [Cahuilla] Indians. There are war songs, gambling songs, songs for ceremonial dances, songs for the women, songs for the dying and the dead. And frequently it is a common thing to hear the high piping voice of some little child singing away as she plays, all unmindful of her surroundings. . ."

"There is not space here to describe the game of *peon*. It is played by eight men, four on a side, with a bright fire between them. Such is its varying fortune that it may last for hours. I remember once watching through a game, when, as the finally defeated participants wrapped their blankets around them and turned their backs to the fire, the eastern sky was reddening behind Torres mountain and it was four o'clock in the morning. The game throughout is filled with intense excitement, and the pent-up feeling of the players breaks out in strange barking sounds, made by forcing the air from the lungs in quick, successive cries. At a little distance it sounds like the baying of hard-run hounds. At certain parts of the game the players sing their *peon* songs, which are sustained throughout by the crowd of old men and women in the outer circle about the fire."

". . One of the fiercest games of *peon* I ever saw played was at a summer feast at Coahuia in 1892. It was a time of great rivalry between hosts and visitors. The spirit of the mountain Indians had broken out repeatedly in boasts about 'the Coahuia valley'. The *peon* game was played by four Coahuias against four Diegueño Indians from Mesa Grande. The following on this occasion was the *peon* song of the Coahuias. It was sung with bravado and defiance. It won them the game."

PEON SONG

HE-YO | CO-YA-WI-A | TO-YA-MA-LA-MA-LA | NE-HE-WE-YA | WE

---

[40] In his article "Some Coahuia Songs and Dances " in *The Land of Sunshine*, December, 1895.

". . . I will close with the death song of my friend, José Maria. One of the last times I visited him, as we sat together in the sunny little patio before his jacal [hut], I asked him for a song. He reached out his hand and groped feebly for mine, for José Maria is blind and near to his end, and thus he sang me his death song, Ne-sun-ha-he-wi-wi. 'My heart is leaping within me. My body is burning. I am low with sickness. Perhaps, now I am dying."

"The music it will be observed is very near to the primitive song. Just a single cord sung feelingly over and over. . .'"

DEATH SONG   (3 TIMES)

NE- SUN-HA-HE- WI-WI, NE- MA-NA-HE- WI-WI, NE- MUK-NE-HE- MU-TO.

At about the same time that David P. Barrows was making friends of the Cahuilla Indians, two women, Anna B. Picher and Jeanne C. Carr[41] of Pasadena, were becoming interested in a little group of Indians living at San Gabriel. The last of that mission's neophyte family, these Indians dwelt in battened frame houses that were hidden behind the pomegranate hedge that bordered the one-time mission garden and orchard. There were gathered together Luisa Serrano, the last Capitana; Victoria, the official perfiladora (maker of drawn work) of San Gabriel; Theodora, the last of that mission's famous basket weavers, and a few others of their tribe.

Luisa had often sung to Miss Picher songs remembered from the days of the Padres and songs that had been handed down to her by her own people. One day by prearrangement with Luisa, Miss Picher came, accompanied by Professor Arévalo, a Mexican musician, for the purpose of capturing the words and melodies of the songs most often on the lips of the old Indian woman.

"When we were quite ready," writes Miss Picher, "Luisa sang; over and over, bar by bar, when asked to, she repeated the songs we had come to secure. As she sang, I understood syncopation at last, and believed in the value of my long struggle with thorough-bass and harmony. I found all these in her melody.

---

[41] Anna B. Picher wrote, under the pen name of Auguste Wey, several articles for the *Land of Sunshine* and *The Californian* magazines. Jeanne C. Carr is best known for her article "Among the Basket Makers," published in *The Californian*, Oct., 1892.

When she had finished singing the chant of El Capitan, she rose and danced it for us. . ."[42]

This and three other songs were recorded by Professor Arévalo, but, apparently, only the song of the Captain survives.

Such were the songs that the natives sang when the Padres first saw them. They were kept alive during mission days, and they are sung today when Indians gather for ceremonies of their own. Truly, a people that can retain its native songs and games through almost two centuries of change and adversity has a sturdiness of character that is very admirable.

[42] Auguste Wey, "The Captain's Song," *The Land of Sunshine*, December, 1896.

CHAPTER 19

Pageantry: Religious Ceremonies and Festivals

Indians Attracted by the Pomp of Such Occasions

RUNNING THROUGH the story of the workaday life of the mission Indians are pages illumined with the color, pomp, and solemnity of religious pageantry. From the ceremonies of the blessing of the flags, and of the ships about to sail for San Diego and Monterey, through those of the founding of the first mission, the taking possession of the land at Monterey, the laying of cornerstones, the blessing of churches, and the celebrating of the various feast days of the church calendar, the pageantry was most impressive.

That the natives of California were affected by the ceremonies which they witnessed, albeit, at first, from behind bushes and trees, is not to be doubted. Color, ceremonial costume, and ceremony have, from time immemorial, deeply impressed the Indians. In their native state, paints, brightly colored feathers, ceremonial songs and dances had supplied their inborn love for such things.

That the Indians would be attracted by glittering ornaments, colored beads, trinkets, and bits of cloth was a fact known to all the early explorers. That the beautiful many-colored vestments, shining silver vessels, lighted candles, music and solemn ceremonies would irresistibly draw them to the church was equally well known. Lured by color, music, and ceremony they could but answer the summons of the far-reaching call of the mission bells. Gálvez was aware of this truth when, as Palóu tells us, ". . he wished to adorn the new missions as if they were cathedrals, for, as he said to the reverend father president, they must be beautified as much as possible, and the vestments must be the very finest, so that the heathen might see how God our Lord was worshipped, and with what care and purity the Holy Sacrifice of the Mass was said, and how the house of God our Lord was adorned, so that by this means they might be induced to embrace our Holy Faith."[1]

---

[1] Bolton, *Palou's New Cal.*, 1. 56-57.

That Fr. Serra was in accord with this belief is shown in Palóu's account of his work among the Indians of the Sierra Gorda. That the labors accomplished in that field guided Serra and his fellow toilers in their work in the "new vineyard" cannot be doubted. Through the celebration of the various feast days of the church, through religious observances, and devotions, the natives of the former region "became as thoroughly Christian as if they had always been such."[2] And, by continuing the same methods and observances, it was expected that similar results would crown the efforts put forth in New California. To that end the missionaries neglected no opportunity for impressing the natives with the beauty and solemnity of various celebrations.

Therefore, when, in May, 1771, ten additional missionaries from the College of San Fernando arrived at Monterey to take charge of the five new missions that were to be founded, Fr. Serra took advantage of the circumstance to celebrate with as much pomp as possible the feast of Corpus Christi, which that year fell on May 31st. One who has witnessed this celebration at Mission Santa Bárbara, or San Luis Rey—or even at Pala, the little Indian mission, will be able to visualize, in part at least, the magnificence displayed in that procession of 1771.

It was headed by the military resplendent in their dress-parade uniforms, the red coats of the Catalan volunteers contrasting with the tan of the "leather-jackets," or soldados de cuera, as they were called. Seated on their gaily caparisoned horses, the soldiers fired occasional volleys from their muskets, as was the custom of the day, the sound of the firing supplying, no doubt, the lack of musical instruments. Following the soldiers came three servers, the one in the center carrying the processional cross while the other two bore tall candlesticks with lighted candles in them. After the acolytes, or servers, came the incense bearer, walking backwards and swinging the glittering silver censer before the celebrant, Padre Serra, who, bearing the Sacred Host, and accompanied by two priests serving as deacons, walked beneath a silken canopy upheld by four stalwart men. The Padre Presidente and the other priests were vested, some in copes and some in dalmatics of several colors and glittering with silver and gold braid and fringes. The acolytes and those who carried the canopy were probably Christian Indians from Lower California and soldiers from the presidio. The handful of neophytes[3] of Mission San Carlos followed in procession around the square from one ermita (wayside altar) to the next. With the blue waters of the bay before them and the low hills covered with dwarfed and crooked oaks

---

[2] *Palou's Life of Serra* (James ed.), 31.
[3] By the end of 1771, twenty-three Indians had been baptized.

for a background, what a picture that would have made for the artist! It was a sight never again to be seen in California.

But to properly tell the story of the pageantry of the church in mission days it is necessary to begin with the first Sunday of Advent, which, in the Catholic Church, is the beginning of the ecclesiastical year. Starting with the Sunday nearest to the feast of St. Andrew, which falls on November 30th, Advent is a season of preparation for the festival of the Savior's Nativity, just as Lent is one for the "great feast"[4] of Easter. Special hymns and Masses are chosen for each.

During those few weeks before Christmas the Indian choir and orchestra were kept busy practicing not only the hymns and chants for the special church services, but also for the *Pastorela*, or Nativity play, enacted at most if not all the missions on Christmas Eve. But before the celebration of "Los Pastores" came that of "Las Posadas" (the inns), a play commemorating the journey of Mary and Joseph from Nazareth to Bethlehem and their nine-day search for shelter. This play, which dates far back in Mexican[5] and Spanish history, is re-enacted yearly in the former country and recently has been revived by the little Mexican colony of "El Paseo" (Olvera Street) in Los Angeles.

A visitor in México a few years back wrote: "A colorful phase [of the Christmas season] is the after-dark procession in which everyone, including the children, take part. Little figures representing Mary riding the burro, followed by Joseph and the angel, are on display in pine twig-decorated litters. Participants carry candles and sing the litany. The processional halts before the house destined to admit the weary travelers. In song the merry-makers awaken the sleepy master of the house. The 'casero' answers singing and tells them to stop disturbing him in his rest. He threatens them with beating if they do not go away, but when properly convinced of the importance of the wayfarers, doors are wide open, letting them in amid great rejoicing."

"Among the less religious, 'the posadas' are limited to dancing and breaking the 'piñata.' An earthern jar filled with prizes is hung conspicuously high. One of the company is blindfolded, whirled about and sent off in the wrong direction, armed with a stick with which he endeavors to break the 'piñata.' Members of the group keep it out of reach for some time but after several have made attempts at bringing the contents down someone succeeds and there is a merry scramble in which everyone tries to capture some of the treasures for himself."[6]

On the last night of "Las Posadas," that is, on Christmas Eve, the play "Los

---

[4] Feast—See Chapter XVIII, note 39.
[5] Cubas, Antonio Garcia, *El Libro de Mis Recuerdos*, 291-300.
[6] Travel Section, *The Los Angeles Times*, Nov. 10, 1940.

Pastores" was given. It is said that the Indians eagerly looked forward to taking part in this performance in which the scene of the Nativity was represented.

The celebration began with the illumination of the mission buildings, the lighting of bonfires, and the firing of rockets. The bells rang merrily calling the neophytes, the soldiers of the guard, the mayordomos and their families to the church, and, on this night of nights, "la nocha buena," there were few laggards. From the choir loft came the clear, melodious voices of the Indians, their singing mingling with the sweet, haunting music of flutes, violins, bass-viols, and trumpets rendering the old hymns and chants taught them by the Padres. Then the Padre celebrant sang the Midnight Mass and the service closed with the injunction—"Ite, Missa est" (Go, it is the dismissal).

Immediately there came strains of lively music from the loft, announcing the beginning of the long-awaited drama, the *Pastorela*, or Nativity play, perhaps that one composed by Fr. Florencio Ibañez of Mission La Soledad. Then through the great, wide-flung doors of the church came the procession of actors, the Indians and others within the church crowding along the side walls and facing the center aisle the better to view the enactment. (There were no pews or benches in mission churches, the worshipers standing or kneeling upon the tiled floors).

Accounts[7] differ somewhat as to some of the characters represented in the play, but always there were the Archangel Gabriel, Satan, or El Diablo, the shepherd of Bethlehem, a hermit, a clownlike fellow, and a number of girls representing angels. The Archangel was clothed in a blue garment bespangled with gilt stars, a larger star being fastened with wire above his forehead. El Diablo wore a flaming red costume and carried a rod tipped with red paint to simulate heat. The hermit with long white beard was clad in nondescript apparel and carried a "tattered missal and sin chastening lash." The shepherd, clothed in sheepskins with wool side out, carried a crook. The girls were dressed in white and had veil-like head coverings, each being adorned with a star. Bartolo, the clown, had no real part in the play, his sole purpose being to amuse the onlookers, especially the children.

"The story of their performance," explains Robinson, "is partially drawn from the Bible, and commences with the angel's appearance to the shepherds, his account of the birth of our Saviour, and exhortation to them to repair to the scene of the manger. Lucifer appears among them and endeavors to prevent the prosecution of their journey. His influence and temptations are about to succeed

[7] Colton, Rev. Walter, "Three Years in California"; MacFarland Grace, *Monterey, Cradle of California Romance;* Chase and Saunders, *The California Padres and Their Missions,* 271-276; Robinson, *Life in Cal.,* 78-80, 202.

DRAWN WORK BY INDIAN PERFILADORAS *of Los Angeles County and lace made by Indian women of Mesa Grande, San Diego County.*

BASKETS MADE BY INDIAN WOMEN of Pala. *The old basket makers are fast disappearing and Indian basketry will soon be one of the lost arts.*

[the hermit and shepherd were beguiled by the Tempter and were lingering at a game of dice] when Gabriel again appears and frustrates their effect. A dialogue is then carried on of considerable length relative to the attributes of the Deity, which ends in the submission of Satan. The whole is interspersed with songs and incidents that seem better adapted to the stage than the church."[8]

In the final act of the play Gabriel leads the shepherd, the others following, to a covered platform erected just outside the altar rail, and, drawing aside the covering, discloses a manger, or crib, in which an image of the Child has been placed. On one side of the crib is a small statue of the Virgin Mary and, on the other, one of St. Joseph.

The Padre then invites the spectators to come forward and view the Niño Santo in the manger. The bells in the belfry ring out merrily and the drama is ended.

There was probably no California mission where on Christmas Eve the scene of the Nativity was not re-created, for these Padres were all Franciscans and it was St. Francis himself, who, with the permission of Pope Honorius III, introduced into the Franciscan churches the custom of representing the manger of Bethlehem.

At Mission Santa Clara, according to legend, there were two rooms which adjoined the church on the cemetery side. The first was the baptistry and is shown in a daguerreotype of the early 1850's. The second was known as the "Bethlehem" from the fact that the manger, or crib, was represented in it each year at Christmas. One may picture the "Pastorela" being enacted just without this room, a velvet curtain concealing the Nativity scene until the conclusion of the play. Then, the screen being dramatically drawn aside, the manger, the figures of the Child, Mary and Joseph, with perhaps an animal or two, are displayed within the room. Christmas hymns, are sung by the Indian choir accompanied by violins, bass-viols, flutes, trumpets, bandolas, and the joyful sound of the mission bells fills the church. This was an event that the Indians long and eagerly awaited. And how coveted and striven for were the actors' parts in that appealing drama!

According to Mexican custom, as related by Cubas, in the above described scene a statue of St. Joseph knelt at one side of the crib and one of the Virgin Mary at the other. In front and in symmetrical positions were an ox and a mule, next came the three royal Magi, the first being a Spanish king, the second an Indian, and the third a negro.[9] In México today, the three Magi are not added to

[8] *Ibidem* 79.
[9] Cubas, *opus cit.*, 299.

the group until the feast of the Epiphany which occurs on January 6th.[10] It is on that day, too, that the little Mexican children put their shoes out on the window sills for the three Kings to put presents in as they pass by, for it was on that day that they came bringing "gold and frankincense and myrrh" to the Christ Child. There is no Santa Claus in México.

One wonders if the little Indian children were given sweets and trinkets on that day. Doubtless they were after the lessons of the day were recited. They had no shoes to set out.

Various festivals are observed by the Catholic Church in the interval between Christmas and Easter, or Holy Week, but little or nothing has been written about their celebration in mission days. Within recent years there has been revived among the Mexican people of Olvera Street and the old "Plaza Church," the ceremony of "La Benedición de los Animales" (the blessing of the animals).[11] There, on the appointed day, domestic animals and pets—horses, cows, cats, dogs, birds, squirrels, chickens, ducks, and even goldfish are brought in procession from the picturesque little Mexican street to the courtyard of the old pueblo church where each in turn is blessed by the smiling officiating Padre for its health and fertility.

Surely this custom was followed in mission days, especially in those first years when it was so vitally necessary that the flocks and herds increase as rapidly as possible. Moreover, it is not reasonable to suppose that the Padres would bless the newly planted fields, the crops, the water as it was turned into new ditches, and not bless the live stock.

On March 19th, came the feast of St. Joseph, foster-father of Jesus and patron saint of the expedition of 1769. Gálvez had chosen St. Joseph, his own patron saint, and had, as Palóu relates, "sent out a circular letter charging the missionaries that every month on the 19th day, they were to celebrate High Mass in all the Missions in honor of this most Holy Patriarch, concluding it with the litany of the saints, in order to obtain the most complete success for the expedition."[12] And this, Palóu says, Fr. Serra did to the end of his days.[13]

At the mission founded in 1797 and named in honor of St. Joseph, his feast was celebrated with great solemnity and festivity. Robinson attended one such observance in company with Fr. José Viader and some of the mission Indians from Santa Clara. His eye-witness account of the fete contains many interesting

[10] This custom is also followed at St. Joseph's Church in Los Angeles, where the scene of the Nativity is elaborately depicted each Christmas season.
[11] A ceremony still observed in Grandmother Spain.
[12] Palou's *Life of Serra* (James ed.), 58; Bolton, *Palou's New Cal.*, 2. 16.
[13] Palou's *Life of Serra* (James ed.), 266.

details, part of which—that describing the training and performance of the Indian musicians—has already been recounted in a previous chapter.

"After mass was concluded," he writes, "we passed out of the church to the priest's apartment through a shower of rockets, which were fired off incessantly in every direction. Dinner was served early to give us time to witness the performances of the Indians; and as there were many strangers at the Mission, a very lengthy table had been prepared, so as to accommodate all. An abundance of good things appeared and disappeared, till at length the cloth was removed; cigars were smoked, and the good old friars retired to enjoy their siesta, whilst we repaired to the front corridor to behold the fun."

"At a signal from their 'Capitan,' or chief, several Indians presented themselves at the corner of one of the streets of the 'Rancheria'[14] and gradually approached us. They were dressed with feathers, and painted with red and black paint: looking like so many demons. There were several women amongst them. Soon they formed a circle and commenced what they called *dancing*, which was one of the most ludicrous specimens of grotesque performance I had ever seen. It did not appear to me that they had any change of figure whatever; but fixed to one spot, they beat time with their feet to the singing of half a dozen persons who were seated upon the ground. When these had performed their part, they retired to an encampment beyond the building and another party appeared, painted and adorned rather differently from the former, whose mode of dancing, also, was quite dissimilar. They retired after a while, and arrangements were made for a bear fight. Whilst these amusements were going on, the Padres had risen, and we were called to chocolate; but the enthusiasm of the Indians hardly gave us time to finish, when we heard them crying *'aqui traen el oso!'* (Here they bring the bear!) He was soon ready, though almost dead from confinement, and the bull made but a few plunges, ere he laid him stiff upon the ground. This part of the amusement concluded, Deppe[15] and I walked to the encampment, where the Indians were dancing in groups, as we had seen them at the mission. Around the large space which they occupied were little booths, displaying a variety of ornaments, seeds, and fruit. All was hilarity and good feeling; for the prudence of Father Narciso had forbidden the sale of liquor. At sundown the bells were rung—rockets were let off—guns were fired; and long after supper, . . we could hear from our beds the continued shouts of the multitude."[16]

[14] The "ranchería" was the neophyte Indian village which stood in front of the mission establishment and was laid out in streets.

[15] Ferdinand Deppe, German supercargo of the vessels of Henry Virmond, German merchant of Acapúlco and the city of Mexico, who "did a large business with California."

[16] Robinson, *Life*, 124-126.

Duhaut-Cilly witnessed a similar celebration, though held in honor of St. Anthony, at San Luis Rey, but of the main sports event, the bull fight, he declares: "This exercise offered nothing very remarkable: it took place in the inner court. Each rider proceeded to tease the bull, which rushed with lowered head, now upon one, now upon another; but such is the agility of men and horses that they are almost never overtaken, though the bull's horn appears to touch them every instant... The bull was not killed as in Spain. After it had been provoked, tired, teased for a half-hour, a small gate giving onto the plain was opened; no sooner had the animal seen this way of escape, than it made for it with all speed; the horsemen flew like arrows in its pursuit; the swiftest, upon reaching it, seized it by the tail; and, at the same instant, giving spurs to his horse, he over-threw the bull, sending it rolling in the dust; only after this humiliating outrage was it permitted to gain the pasture in freedom. This exercise, demanding as much agility as firmness from the rider, is what is called in the country *colear el toro* [to overturn the bull]."[17]

While this performance was going on the spectators were standing on the flat roof of the arcade behind the picturesque ladrillo-latticed railing that extended along the outer edge of the corridor roof on all four sides of the great courtyard. Truly here was another picture for the artist! The Indians and visitors, all dressed in their gayest best, crowding the roofs behind the balustrade; the black-haired, black-eyed girls from the monjerio, each dressed in "a red flannel petticoat and a white shirt"; the gaily bedecked and caparisoned men and horses below engaged in what might well become a combat to the death for man or beast. That excitement did run high is noted by the French visitor. "The next day," he writes, "after the ceremonies and the procession of the consecration, the games began again in the same manner as the day before; but this time the bull fights were disturbed by an accident. One of the Indian girls, sporting upon the mission terrace, fell over the railing upon the pavement of the court, from a height of twenty feet, and broke her head."[18]

Duhaut-Cilly describes some of the games played by the Indians after the bull fights had ended. "While the *gente de razon* amused themselves thus variously [in racing, etc.], the Indians, on their part, betook themselves to their favorite games: the one which seems to please them the most consists in rolling an osier [willow] ring, three inches in diameter, and casting upon the ring, while rolling, two sticks, four feet long, in order to stop it in its course. If one of the two sticks, or both together, go through the ring, or if the ring rests upon

---

[17] "Duhaut-Cilly's Account," 229-230.
[18] *Ibidem.*

the two sticks, or upon only one of them, a certain number of points is counted, according to the amount of hazard. When a pair have played their game, two opponents begin again, and so alternately, until the match is finished. According to M. la Pérouse, this game is called, in the Indian language, *tekersie*."

"Other Indians, like the Bas Bretons, gathered into two large bands; each, provided with a stick in the shape of a bat, tried to push to goal a wooden ball, while those of the opposing band strove to drag it in a contrary direction.[19] This game appeared to attract both sexes alike. It happened, indeed, that the married women having challenged the single women, the latter lost the game. They came, crying to complain to the padre, that the women, making an ill use of their strength, had taken unfair means to stop their arms as they were going to strike the ball. Fray Antonio [Peyri], with a gravity worthy of the judgment of Solomon, made them give an exact account of the affair. . . When the Indian girl had ended pleading her cause, he raised his head and declared the game void;.."[20]

The Frenchman also witnessed the Indian dances. His impression of those performances differs considerably from Robinson's, probably because he was more interested in the Indians than was the Bostonian. "When night came," he writes, "I went with Fray Antonio to see the Indian dances, which appeared to me as interesting as they were strange. They were lighted by torches whose effect was to seem, by contrast, to spread a sad veil over the starry vault of the sky. A dozen men, having no other clothing than a cincture, the head adorned with tall feather plumes, danced with admirable rhythm. This pantomime always represented some scene, and was performed chiefly by striking the feet in time, and making with eyes and arms, gestures of love, anger, fright, etc. The dancers held the head erect, the body arched, and the knees a little bent. Sweat, rolling down the entire body, reflected, as in a burnished mirror, the fire of the torches; and when it annoyed them, they scraped it off with a flat piece of wood which they held in their hand."

"The orchestra, arranged like a semi-circular amphitheatre, was composed of women, children and old men, behind whom one or two rows of amateurs could at least taste of this spectacle. The harmony of the songs governing the time was at once plaintive and wild: it seemed rather to act upon the nerves than upon the mind, like the varied notes from an Aeolian harp during a hurricane.[21] From time

[19] This game is still played by the Indians of Mission San Xavier in Arizona.

[20] "Duhaut-Cilly's Account," 230-231.

[21] Some few years ago this writer and her husband attended a ceremonial "sing" conducted by the Navajo Indians of Monument Valley, Utah. Camped on a slight "bench" at the foot of a cliff, and above the Indian encampment, she listened night after night as those people practiced for the coming event. The sound of their songs as it reached her ears was like the eerie, high-pitched singing of telephone wires strung in open, lonely places—once heard, never forgotten.

to time the actors rested, and at the moment the song stopped, everyone breathed at the same time into the air with a loud noise, either as a mark of applause or, as I was assured, to drive away the Evil Spirit; for, though all are Christians, they still keep many of their old beliefs, which the Padres, from policy, pretend not to know."[22]

In 1816, when Kotzebue visited San Francisco, he and his party were invited to the mission for the celebration of the feast of St. Francis. Regarding the games played by the Indians of that mission, the Russian captain writes: "This being a holiday, the Indians did no work, but, divided into groups, amused them-selves with various pastimes, one of which requires particular dexterity. Two sit on the ground opposite each other, holding in their hands a number of thin sticks, and these being thrown up at the same time with great rapidity, they im-mediately guess whether the number is odd or even; at the side of each of the players, a person sits, who scores the gain and loss. As they always play for something, and yet possess nothing but their clothing, which they are not allowed to stake, they employ much pains and skill on little white shells, which serve instead of money."[23]

The penitential season of Lent, observed as a remembrance of our Lord's forty days of fasting in the desert, begins with Ash Wednesday whose date is not a fixed one, being dependent on that of Easter, which varies from year to year. Easter falls on the first Sunday after the first full moon after March 21st. Ash Wednesday is the first of the week-days (the Sundays are not counted) of the six and one-half weeks preceding Easter. Palm Sunday, the Sunday before Easter, was observed with much ceremony in mission days, as Duhaut-Cilly's account given in the preceding chapter indicates.

"The ceremonies of Holy Week were especially impressive," Encarnación Piñedo writes. "On Holy Thursday a solemn high mass was chanted, the In-dians joining in the responses, and at the end of the mass, the clergy and acolytes, robed in their richest vestments and carrying crosses and lighted candles on poles, and the people in gala attire, formed a procession which reverently issuing from the church, escorted the Holy Sacrament around the plaza and back to the sanc-tuary, where it was deposited with every manifestation of deepest devotion. During the ceremonies solemn hymns and psalms were chanted and prayers were offered to the divine Redeemer, while incense was constantly burned, sometimes ascending in clouds. . . "

"In the afternoon of Holy Thursday, the ceremony of the washing of feet

---

[22] "Duhaut-Cilly's Account," 231.
[23] Mahr, *Visit of the "Rurik"*, 61.

took place. The oldest Indians in the rancheria were crowned with flowers and brought to the church, where they were seated on benches prepared for the occasion. The priest in his alb, and carrying a white towel and a pitcher of water scented with bay leaves, then washed their feet and wiped them, after which he ascended the pulpit and preached the sermon on true Christian humility and brotherhood, typified by the ceremony just performed, . . ."[24]

Fr. Owen tells us that the neophyte choir sang "*Mandatum novum do vobis*" while the Padre washed the feet of the Indians.

In his Sierra Gorda mission, according to Palóu, Fr. Serra not only washed the feet of the twelve oldest Indians but ate with them. He then "proceeded to the sermon of 'washing of the feet,' and at night made the procession with the image of Christ crucified in the presence of all the people."

"On Good Friday," Palóu continues, "he used to preach in the morning on the Passion, and in the afternoon the Descent from the Cross was represented with the greatest vividness by means of a lifelike figure which he had ordered made for the purpose and which had hinges. He handled the subject in his sermon with the greatest devotion and tenderness. The body of Our Lord was placed in a casket and then used in the procession of the Holy Burial. It was afterward placed upon an altar which he had prepared for this purpose and at night another procession was made in honor of Our Lady of Solitude, and then the day finished with a special sermon on the subject."[25]

On Good Friday, 1935, this writer witnessed from the choir loft of the church of San Carlos del Carmelo, the celebration of the "Descent from the Cross" as it had been observed by Fr. Serra and his fellow priests in their Sierra Gorda missions—a ceremony that is rarely performed in California. It was a never-to-be-forgotten experience.

The great doors of the church were closed. Sunlight came filtering through the colored glass of the small windows, set high in the church walls, catching up here and there some figure or detail in the old paintings hanging there. A curtain of purple velvet concealed the altar. Ranged in front of this screen was the Calvary Group, a large Crucifix, a statue of Our Lady of Sorrows, and one of St. John, the Evangelist. Six lighted candles, three at each side of the group, shone like stars through the gloom of the sanctuary. These candles, together with those carried by the acolytes in the procession that slowly made the Way of the Cross along the side aisles of the church, and the mellow sunlight from the windows furnished the only illumination of the darkened interior. The ceremony was of

---

[24] Piñedo, "Early Days."
[25] *Palou's Life of Serra* (James ed.), 29.

three hours duration and throughout that period there came through the door that opened upon the bell chamber the soft but insistent and far-carrying cooing of many white pigeons who made their nests in the bell tower.

The priests celebrating the Mass were black-robed, the acolytes, the choristers, and the worshippers were all from the little community of today, but, if one has really learned to concentrate it is not difficult to brush such tangibles from the scene and people it with the mission padres and the dusky neophytes of long ago.

Picturing the Indians kneeling on the tiled floor, or standing, as the celebration demanded, this watcher wondered if they were as startled as she was, when, at the proper moment in the ceremony, the nails were drawn from the hands and feet of the lifelike, life-size figure of the Christ on the cross, and the arms allowed slowly to fall to its sides. Then, gently, carefully the figure was taken down, the knees bending as if it were a human form. Following the custom established by Fr. Serra, this act was performed as the procession making the Way of the Cross reached the thirteenth Station. At the fourteenth Station, commemorating the burial of Christ, the figure was carried out the front door of the church, around the plaza and back into the Mortuary chapel, the choir singing the "Reproaches" even as the Indian neophytes did in mission days.

That was pageantry at its best and who can measure the impression it had made on the minds of the Indians?

In those days the ceremony of the Via Crucis (Way of the Cross), or "Christ's journey to Mount Calvary," was, according to Encarnación Piñedo, performed at Santa Clara in the afternoon of Good Friday. "Three men," she writes, "enveloped in vestments of white linen carried a very heavy crucifix from one station to another."

At that mission the Stations, crosses only, were erected along the famous "Alameda" half way to the pueblo of San José. At San Carlos Mission they were set beside the road that led to Monterey. Captain Frederick William Beechey left what is probably the best description of the latter. "The ride from the presidio to San Carlos on a fine day," he notes, "is most agreeable. The scenery is just sufficiently picturesque to interest, while the hills are not so abrupt as to inconvenience a bold rider. The road leads principally through fine pasture lands, occasionally wooded with tall pine, oak, and birch trees; but without any underwood to give it a wildness, or to rob it of its park-like aspect. Before the valley of San Carmelo opens out, the traveller is apprized of his approach to the mission by three large crosses erected upon Mount Calvary; and further on by smaller

▲ ART WORK IN TILE. *The picturesque chimney still stands at Mission San Juan Capistrano.*

▼ THE HAND-CARVED PULPIT *formerly at San Buenaventura: the original iron cross at San Carlos.*

The tower of San Carlos del Carmelo—*the crowning glory of the California missions.*

ones placed at the side of the road, to each of which some history is attached. . ."[26] It is claimed on good authority that portions of the latter crosses may still be found along the way.

At San Buenaventura, it seems, the Stations at one time marked the path that led from the mission church to the little chapel of St. Michael built near the beach by Fr. José Señán.[27] In his Sierra Gorda mission Fr. Serra "made in procession the Way of the Cross from the Church to the Chapel of Calvary which he had ordered erected on a hill outside of town and within sight of the Church."[28] In view of this circumstance one wonders if therein does not lie the significance of the large cross set up some time in mission days on the top of the hill back of the mission dedicated to St. Bonaventure.[29] Was that hill the Padres' Mount Calvary?

There is much in the mission records that substantiates the assertion that many customs established in the Sierra Gorda missions were continued in those of California.

On Wednesday, Thursday, and Friday nights of Holy Week a special ceremony took place. This was the *Tenebrae* (darkness) service, so named from the act of extinguishing one by one fourteen of the fifteen lighted candles in the Tenebrae candlestick. This rite occurred after the singing of the "Lamentations" by the Indian choristers. The tune to which those mournful lines were sung is considered "the saddest melody within the whole range of music."[30] After the fourteen candles had been extinguished, and during the chanting of the "*Benedictus*," the six candles on the altar were also put out. The shutters were closed and curtains drawn across the windows. The fifteenth candle was next removed and placed behind the altar. The church became quite dark. And then, following the recitation of the psalm "*Miserere*," there came a terrifying noise caused by the striking together of wooden clappers[31] accompanied by a creaking, clacking, grinding, and clanking sound produced by the whirling around and around, or the shaking of the wooden matracas[32] (ratchets or rattles), symbolizing the confusion of nature at the time of Christ's death.

---

[26] Beechey, *Narrative*, 2. 86-87.

[27] This chapel was destroyed by floods in 1832. It is shown in a sketch reproduced in Robinson's *Life in California*.

[28] Palou's *Life of Serra* (James ed.), 29.

[29] The original cross, according to the late E. M. Sheridan, was destroyed in a storm. Another raised in its place was blown down in 1875. A scroll board which had been affixed to the cross above the cross-arms bore the initials "I. N. R. I." (IESUS NAZARENUS, REX IUDAEORUM—Jesus of Nazareth, King of the Jews). Early photographs and sketches show such scroll-boards on a number of the original mission crosses.

[30] Sullivan, *Externals of the Catholic Church*, 143.

[31] Just as was reported in the San Francisco *Chronicle*, April 20, 1935, of the Good Friday rites celebrated in St. Peter's Church, in Rome, when "priests banged with their prayer books on their kneeling benches to signify the confusion of Nature at the passing of the Savior."

[32] There are matracas at San Juan Capistrano, San Carlos, San Luis Obispo, and Santa Bárbara.

The *Tenebrae* service is celebrated today at both Santa Bárbara and San Luis Rey. At each of those missions two highly trained choirs unite in singing the chants mentioned above. The ceremony is most solemn and impressive and the music is magnificent.

On Holy Saturday came the ceremonies of the blessing of the salt, the new fire, the baptismal water to be used in the ensuing year, as well as the paschal candle, the litany and the Mass being chanted by the Indian singers. With the blessing of the paschal candle came the singing of the "*Exsultet*," considered one of the most beautiful chants in all the Catholic Church's liturgy.

On this day, too, was performed the ceremony of chastising Judas Iscariot, the betrayer of Christ. An effigy was constructed, dressed in man's clothing and strung up on a yardarm set in the mission plaza. It was then shot at, stoned, spat upon, reviled and beaten with sticks. Miss Frances Hannon, long-time resident of San Gabriel, well remembers when this ceremony was observed at the mission there.

Then, "Anticipating" the joy of Easter, with the singing of the "*Gloria*" of the Mass on Holy Saturday,[33] the church bells, which had been silent since Holy Thursday, were rung joyously. Statues and paintings were divested of their purple wrappings and the curtain concealing the altar, once more resplendent with flowers, gleaming silver candlesticks, and unveiled statues, was drawn aside.

On Easter morning the Indians assembled in the church and, dressed in their cleanest, gayest garments, joyously took part in the feast of the Resurrection of our Lord.

Children of nature, they responded to the colorful and solemn ceremonies of Holy Week accompanied, as they were, by music and song ranging from the saddest to the most joyous known to man, as only unsophisticated peoples can respond, and the impressions received through participation in those ceremonies must have been most enduring.

On May 3rd, the Finding of the True Cross was commemorated with appropriate ceremonies. The month of May brought also the feast of San Isidro, el Labrador (St. Isidore, the Ploughman), patron saint of those who cultivate the soil.[34] In San Isidro, New Mexico, Spanish-Americans to this day meet on May 15th to pay homage to this saint. The one day festival begins with early Mass

[33] "The Mass of Holy Saturday was originally the midnight Mass of Easter Sunday, the conclusion of the long ceremonies of the vigil. . . . Century after century the time of the ceremonies and consequently of the Mass, was put earlier, until it came to pass that the nocturnal Mass of Easter Sunday became the morning Mass of Holy Saturday." Sullivan, *Externals*, 147.

[34] See Jameson, Mrs., *Sacred and Legendary Art* (London, 1888), Vol. II. 778.

and continues with the carrying of a statue of San Isidro through the fields. Four men carry the litter upon which the statue stands, the assembled people following in procession singing and chanting the prescribed hymns and prayers. Never, they say, does San Isidro fail to bring them bountiful crops.

Even so we may picture the gray-robed Padre, ritual in hand, preceded by the Indian acolytes bearing censer, sprinkler, and holy water vessel, leading the procession into the newly planted field or vineyard to ask the Lord's blessing on the crops. A statue, framed painting, or banner having a picture of San Isidro painted on it, was carried in the procession. That newly planted fields, vineyards, and orchards were blessed, there can be no doubt, for, under date of March 15th, 1819, Fr. Señán, at San Buenaventura informed Captain José de la Guerra, of the Santa Bárbara presidio, that he had blessed the new vineyard of Ranchito de San José.

Moreover, we may be very sure that when the mission dams and aqueducts were finished there was a ceremony of thanksgiving for the completion of the task and a blessing of the water as it was turned into the new ditches that led to mission, fields, mills, and tanneries. Happily, there are still practiced here and there, mostly in the San Diego district, old ceremonies that have been brought down to us from mission days. At San Antonio de Pala, in May, 1913, water was brought from the headwaters of the San Luis Rey River to the farms of the little Indian community. It was a government project, but the work was, for the greater part, done by the Pala Indians. The aqueduct was laid along the line of the old one constructed in Padre Peyri's time, and, after the work was finished a fiesta was planned.

"The morning of the fiesta dawned bright and clear. Every member of the tribe was there in his or her best. The ceremonies opened by a solemn high mass conducted by Father Doyle, and assisted by the Franciscan Fathers from San Luis Rey. Then a grand parade was held, everyone marching happily to the head of the ditch. There Father Peter Wallischeck, Superior of the San Luis Rey home, blessed the water which poured itself for the first time over the Indians' lands since the old ditch crumbled away, and as he did so he stood on the very spot where Padre Peyri stood when, with his Indians, they said a prayer of thanksgiving over the successful completion of their labors, a century previously."

"The rest of the day was then spent in the pleasures of the table mainly provided by an old-fashioned barbecue, a baseball game and the inevitable game of *peon.*"[35]

---

[35] James, George W., *Picturesque Pala*, 55-59.

A photograph of the above ceremony shows at least eighteen horsemen riding as escort, eight on each side of the procession, representing the military of mission days. As one writer has remarked, "nothing could be done without the military taking part in it."

As has been noted in the chapter on the mission water systems, most of the grainfields depended upon the winter rains for the necessary moisture. When these rains were late in coming or not sufficiently abundant the Padres, as Fages remarked, "stormed Heaven with ceaseless petitions for rains, whenever their fields needed them, until they succeeded." Corroboration of Fages' statement is found in a letter, written by Fr. Serra at San Carlos, April 22nd, 1778, and sent to Fr. Lasuén at San Diego, wherein the Padre Presidente declares: "The news that the wheat and other grain is falling behind for want of rain, grieved me very much. Tomorrow, with the help of God, will begin my especial supplications."[36]

Robinson describes one such ceremony that took place at Santa Bárbara. "The season for rain had set in," he writes, "but as yet none had fallen. The hills and fields were parched by the heat of the sun, and all vegetation seemed partially destroyed. Everyone cried for rain! One wished it for his corn, another for his beans, another for his wheat, and all for their pasturage, the scarcity of which was likely to cause trouble among their cattle. At this important crisis, the holy father of the mission was besought, that the 'Virgin [Virgen] de nuestra Señora del Rosario' might be carried in procession through the town, whilst prayers and supplications should be offered for her intercession with the Almighty in behalf of their distress. This was complied with as was customary on such occasions, and conducted in the following manner. First, came the priest in his church robes, who, with a fine clear voice, led the Rosary. On each side of him were two pages [acolytes, or servers], and the music followed; then, four females, who supported on their shoulders a kind of litter, on which rested a square box containing the figure of the Holy Virgin. Lastly came a long train of men, women and children, who united in the recital of the sacred mysteries. The figure was ornamented for the occasion with great finery, and every one who pleased, had contributed some rich ornament of jewelry or dress, for its display. In this manner, they proceeded from the church, through the town, to the beach; chanting verses between the mysteries, accompanied by violins and flutes. From the beach, they returned to the church in the same order when the prayers were concluded."

"After this performance, all looked for rain with as much faith as our

---

[36] Engelhardt, *Mission San Diego*, 98; SBMA.

countrymen look for the steamer from Liverpool on the thirteenth or fourteenth day after her time of departure! Should their expectations, however, not be realized, the procession would be repeated until they were."[37]

At San Juan Capistrano, which, until the advent of the automobile, was often spoken of as a "sleepy little hamlet rich in memories of mission days," there occurred, according to the story, in the 1890's, a series of years of scanty rains. During one of the dry winters when the hills around the village were as brown as in the summer time and the cattle were dying in the canyons, the ranchers persuaded Doña Polonia[38] to take the children out into the hills to pray for rain. She consented and had a litter, a sort of palanquin, made upon which was placed a paper bedecked niche containing a crucifix and a picture of St. Vincent. This litter, supported on the shoulders of four persons, was carried in procession for three days. Up the hills and over the mesas to the north, east, and west of the mission went Doña Polonia and the children singing litanies and hymns and praying the rosary. On the third and last day, though there was not a cloud in sight, a violent storm arose and the rain-drenched party was finally rescued and brought back from near the seashore in three large wagons—their mission accomplished![39]

Similarly, in 1823 or 1824, at Santa Clara, according to Secundino Robles,[40] Fr. Magín Catalá led a procession asking Heaven for relief from the long drought that had extended throughout the winter and spring of that year.

In the after-mission days many of the old customs, celebrations, and feasts established by the Franciscan Padres were kept alive by secular priests who came to take their places. Notable among the latter were Rev. Doroteo Ambris at San Antonio; Rev. José Mut at San Juan Capistrano; and Rev. Antonio Ubach at San Juan Bautista from 1860 to 1865 and thereafter at San Diego where he spent the remaining years of his life, his death occurring April 27, 1907. These three priests are remembered particularly for their interest in the remaining handful of Indians at or near the old missions, and for the desperate efforts that they made to keep white vultures from robbing their charges of the little parcels of land which had been granted them.

Fr. Mut's account book which he kept with scrupulous care from August 17, 1866, the day on which he took charge of the parish of San Juan Capistrano, to June, 1886, when he was transferred to Mission San Miguel, is replete with

---

[37] Robinson, *Life in Cal.*, 157-158.
[38] During the time when there was no resident priest at San Juan Capistrano, Doña Polonia, midwife of the pueblo, was captain of the children.
[39] Saunders and O'Sullivan, *Capistrano Nights*, 17-22.
[40] Engelhardt, *Holy Man of Santa Clara*, 147-148.

items that tell of his traveling to the Indian settlements of Santa Margarita, Las Flores, Pala, Pauma, Rincón, Temécula, San Jacinto, "the rancho of the Cahuillas," and to San Luis Rey. It is said that he usually walked to those places and that he went barefooted. Here and there in the book[41] one finds mention of contributions for Holy Week ("para Semana Santa"), for Corpus Christi ("collecta para Corpus Christi"), and for the feast of St. John of Capistran, the mission's patron saint. This last feast occurs on October 23rd.

It is in those same little communities that one may witness today some of the celebrations observed by the Franciscans in mission days. At Pala, for example, the feast of Corpus Christi[42] is celebrated with such sincerity by the Indians there that people of other races and creeds come from miles around to join the procession or to watch as it starts from the little adobe chapel and wends its way around the plaza lying in front of the mission,[43] stopping at flower bedecked ermitas (wayside altars) set at certain intervals along the way. When this writer first witnessed this celebration in that little town, three Indian horsemen, representing the military of days gone by, headed the procession and fired their pistols at appropriate moments. Today the town marshal, Remíjio Lugo, afoot and alone, fires his pistol while his son, in answer, rings the old mission bells. The little flower girls, so long trained by Mrs. Salvadora Valenzuela, one of the last of the Pala basket makers, scatter rose petals in the path of the Father celebrant who walks under the silken canopy carrying the Sacred Host. Indians from other settlements walk in procession with those of Pala, each contingent carrying a banner, the singing of the Indian choir providing the link connecting the ceremony of today with that of bygone yesterdays. And, as in mission days, a barbecue and games follow the religious ceremonies.

In the Sierra Gorda, as Palóu tells us, Fr. Serra "instructed them to prepare and decorate arches in the road where the procession of Corpus Christi would pass. Four chapels were placed along the way with their respective altars where our Crucified Lord might rest, and after the singing in each one of them of the corresponding anthem, verse and prayer, an Indian stood up (generally a little boy) and recited a praise to the Divine Sacrament, of which two were in Spanish and two in the Pame dialect, which were very touching and which increased the devotion of all. When they had returned to the church a Mass was sung and a sermon preached on this most Holy Mystery."[44]

---

[41] Rescued from a burning trash heap by Jesús Aguilar.

[42] Corpus Christi occurs on the Thursday after Trinity Sunday. Trinity Sunday follows Pentecost, which occurs 50 days after Easter.

[43] In about 1902, Pala became a true mission when the Bishop appointed a priest to take charge of that parish.

[44] *Palou's Life of Serra* (James ed.), 30.

One of the most gracious of mission-day customs has been recorded in a photograph made in about 1920. Seeing a copy of this picture in the writer's scrapbook, Fr. O'Sullivan of San Juan Capistrano exclaimed: "I must tell you about that. It was Acú's custom to come each year to bring to me the first fruits of his vines. This year (the time of the photograph) he came bearing large bunches of very luscious grapes, saying 'first fruits go to the Father.' Thinking that this was one of those old customs that should be preserved in picture form, I said, 'wait a minute.' And, hastily getting my camera I got someone to take the picture as you see it." And so was made what is probably the only authentic picture in existence of a mission Indian bringing "Las Primicias" (the first fruits) to the Father.

On October 13, 1934, there took place at Santa Isabel, in San Diego County, what was called the "observance of the annual harvest festival." According to a newspaper clipping, five hundred Indians and one thousand whites had gathered for the two-day festival. All the afternoon of the first day barbecued beef and Indian-cooked foods were served to residents and visitors alike. In the evening a procession, led by three men each carrying a large cross made of sheaves of grain, was formed at the fiesta grounds from whence it proceeded to the chapel where a Mass of thanksgiving was sung. After Mass came the bonfires and games so loved by the Indians. On the second day the religious ceremonies were repeated and then came another barbecue. Then followed the games of *peon*, *pelota*, *gome*, and *monte*—played by the older men, for the younger ones have taken to baseball.

Interesting details missing in the newspaper account are supplied by Guadalupe Vallejo in her description of this ceremony as it was observed at Mission San José. "A special ceremony," she states, "was connected with the close of the wheat harvest. The last four sheaves taken from this large field were tied to poles in the form of the cross and were then brought by the reapers in the 'harvest procession' to the church, while the bells were rung, and the father dressed in his robes, carrying the cross and accompanied by boys with tapers and censers, chanting the *Te Deum* as they marched, went forth to meet the sheaves."[45]

Fr. Lapointe, worthy successor of Frs. Mut and Ubach, for some twenty years attended Santa Isabel from El Cajón. He it was who revived or kept alive there many of the old customs and ceremonies celebrated by the ancestors of the present-day Indians.

[45] Vallejo, Guadalupe, "Ranch and Mission Days."

La Fiesta de todos los Difuntos (All Souls' Day) was observed on November 2nd. On that day, after Mass was said in the church, the congregation followed the Padre, accompanied by his servers, into the cemetery (campo santo) where prayers were said, hymns sung, incense burned and holy water sprinkled over each candle-lit grave.

This ceremony is still observed in the little Indian settlements of San Diego's "back country." Visiting Santa Isabel in January, 1938, the writer found graves in the picket-enclosed campo santo still adorned with faded, fluttering paper streamers and flowers, together with the remains of consumed candles—remnants of the religious rites of All Souls' Day. If one really seeks to acquire a background for the study of the old missions, he should spend some considerable time around these Indian outposts.

There were other fetes and fiestas, besides those already mentioned, that were celebrated by the gray-robed Padres. The feast day of the patron saint of each mission was never forgotten. On such occasions neophyte Indians and Padres from a neighboring mission and the Spanish colonists were sometimes invited to join in the festivities, as early writers attest.

There was the ceremony of the blessing of the newly acquired bells, their hanging and ringing. Much was made of these occurrences and the Indians enjoyed it all. The ceremony itself appealed to them and, moreover, it gave them—at least those who were at the mission and not away on the ranchos—a holiday from work. [46]

The laying of the cornerstone of a new church was a great occasion. The account of the celebration held in 1781, at the second site of Mission Santa Clara is of particular historic interest in that both Fr. Serra and Fr. Crespí took part in the ceremonies. The record of this event is found in the old Baptismal Register now in the archives of the University of Santa Clara. Translated it reads as follows:

On the 19th of November, in the year of our Lord 1781, in this Mission of our Seraphic Mother, Santa Clara of Thamien, after having on the afternoon of the preceding day, erected in this place the Standard of the Holy Cross, we had the blessing and laying of the cornerstone of the temple or church, which was commenced on the said day as a house of our Great God and Lord, with the title of the glorious Santa Clara of Assisi, Virgin, Abbess and first Mother of her most celebrated Order. All this happened yesterday and today with much solemnity and in exact accord with the Roman Ritual. The celebrant at both these functions, that is to say, at the blessing and erection of the Cross, and the blessing and laying of the cornerstone, was Fr. Junipero Serra, President of

[46] January 25th, 1817, Fr. Vicente Sarría, comisario prefecto of the missions, issued a circular to the Padres in which he declared that he had noted that the neophytes were made to work on St. Francis Day. He would have that day celebrated solemnly, though with the understanding that, . . it was not a day of obligation, hence not a sin to work on that day. Engelhardt, *Miss. & Miss.*, 3. 44.

these missions, assisted and accompanied by Fr. John Crespi, Minister of the Mission of San Carlos of Monterey, and by two from this Mission, Fr. Joseph Anthony de Murguia and Fr. Thomas de la Peña, and Don Jos. Ramon Laso de la Vega, official ensign of the Presidio of our Father St. Francis, as laic patron. He was accompanied by soldiers who were here. All conduced to the greater importance and solemnity of the celebration. In the cavity of the cornerstone were enclosed a cross, images and several coins, a signification of the Church treasury. And in order that everything may be recorded, we the following affix our signatures.

> (signed) Fr. Junipero Serra, President
> Fr. Jos. Anthony Murguia.
> Joseph Ramon Laso de Vega.
> Fr. John Crespi.
> Fr. Thomas de la Peña.[47]

Recalling to mind details of other ceremonies previously described, it is not difficult to invest this one with its proper measure of solemnity and pomp. The religious rites to which the presence of the Father President gave added significance, the ensign acting as patron, the soldiers firing their muskets, the bountiful repast which followed the ceremonies, the games indulged in later—all made the occasion one long to be remembered by neophytes and other participants alike.

When a mission church was finished it was blessed and dedicated. After the dedication of Santa Bárbara's church of 1815-1820, the Padres wrote a very detailed account of the celebration in order that future generations might know exactly what took place. This account is found in that Mission's Baptismal Register under the heading "Nota Singular y Instructiva." Translated, it reads:

Inasmuch as the infant whose Baptism has just been entered (in the Register on September 13, 1820, number 4,181) is the first to be baptized in the new church of the Mission of Santa Barbara in Upper California, we missionaries in charge have deemed it proper to give here a true account of what took place at the dedication of the new church and of the celebrations, so that in the future there may be evidence for it and it may be transmitted to posterity.

Three religious, missionaries of as many other Missions of New California, came to honor the occasion and to assist us, namely Rev. José Señan, Vicário Foráneo to the Rt. Rev. Bishop of Sonora, Vice-Prefect, and missionary of San Buenaventura; Rev. Fr. Luis Martínez, of Mission San Luis Obispo; and Rev. Fr. Gerónimo Boscana, of Mission San Juan Capistrano. Neither the missionary of Santa Inés nor the one of San Fernando, though both of neighboring Missions, could come because they were managing their respective Missions alone; nevertheless they allowed their neophytes to come with their musicians and dancers, whom our alcaldes had invited for that purpose by sending commissioners from among themselves, as they are accustomed to do and as the Fathers permitted.

The dedication took place on September 10, of this same year (1820). With his suite and company corresponding to his authority, the Padrino, Colonel of the Military and Governor of this Province, came down from Monterey, he having been invited for that purpose. Although he had been invited for September 7, the Vigil of the feast of the Nativity of the Most Holy Virgin, whose feast day had been assigned for the celebration, he did not arrive till September 9. The ceremony then began on the appointed day, the feast of the Name of Mary. On that afternoon, *the afore-named* Rev. Fr. Presidente accompanied all the priests, the Honorable Padrino Solá, the

⁴⁷ James A. Colligan, S. J., *The Three Churches*, 9.

captain and commander of the presidio, Don José de la Guerra y Noriega, with all his troops and officers, Don Narciso Fabregat, lieutenant of the auxiliary troops of Mazatlán, who had arrived in the preceding year with his alférez, sergeants, and corporals; and a great number of people of all stations and conditions. The *Te Deum* was chanted, whereupon solemn Compline followed, the celebrant being the Fr. Presidente, and amid the great illumination of all the altars, especially that of the Titular Saint. Then in succession, were illuminated the (azoteas) housetops, the corridors, and the tower, the last named having many flags of all colors. Immediately the musicians of the three Missions passed through the corridors, where they played with a will for about two continuous hours. Meanwhile, rockets, serpents, firecrackers, were fired (tirandose en estas cohetas, buscapies, carretillas), followed at once by the castillo de fuego artificial[48] (castle of artificial fire). Then came bull-baiting, the baitors having the same artificial fire, which caused the greatest fun and diversion. All this was repeated on the two following nights.

On Sunday, the tenth of the month, which was the feast of the Name of Mary, after the merry ringing of the many bells, solemn High Mass was sung, the Rev. Fr. Gerónimo Boscana being the celebrant, with Fr. Francisco Suñer missionary of this mission, serving as deacon, and Fr. Luis Martínez as sub-deacon. During the holy Mass the Fr. Presidente preached. On the next day, the eleventh, the coffins of the deceased religious who had died at this mission, Fr. Antonio Paterna, its missionary, and Fr. José Dulanto, of Mission San Juan Bautista, who had come down ill, and lived here to recover, but whom God called to himself, were taken from their tombs. May they rest in peace! The remains were then placed in the center of the new church, whereupon a solemn vigil was chanted for their repose, the Fr. Presidente officiating and the other missionaries assisting. With this the church celebration terminated.

Immediately after going out, the soldiers, cavalry as well as infantry, continued the festivities they had commenced on the preceding day, while the Indians had their dances and all diverted themselves as best they could.

Food, drink, and shelter were given to all who asked for or needed them; and they were given on a grand scale. To accommodate all, supplying them with whatever they needed, the Mission had at its disposal two houses of the whites, besides the barracks which did not prove sufficient. A man was appointed to serve the wine and brandy, until all had enough. Since the number of people was so large[49] it cost something; but the expenses were well applied, because without all was clatter, merriment and diversion; and thanks be to God, neither mishap nor quarrel, nor complaint occurred. It was a lively, continuous and pure blessing to the Lord and from the Lord. In order that there be evidence of this, we two missionaries signed on September 13, 1820.

Fr. Francisco Suñer[50]

For some reason, however, Fr. Antonio Ripoll's signature was not affixed to the document.

There is little to add to the Fathers' account of this the greatest celebration ever held at the old mission, except mention of the weeks upon weeks of preparation that went into making it the great success that it was. Besides the setting to rights of the whole establishment in anticipation of the coming event, there was the placing of hundreds of candles used in the illumination of the altars, the housetops and corridors; the practicing of singers and musicians; the making of long tables that extended from end to end of the corridors of the inner courtyard; the preparation of the bounteous supply of food—the barbecued meats,

---

[48] For a description of the castillo fuego, see Dane Chandos, *Village in the Sun*, 120.
[49] Santa Bárbara's Indians alone numbered 1,132 at this time.
[50] Engelhardt, *Mission Santa Barbara*, 108-111.

roast fowl, smoked tongues, hams, sausages, chili-con-carne, frijoles, tortillas, fruits preserved and fresh, nuts and raisins, food in abundance for one and all—and wine and brandy! It all meant work, long, long hours of work, and able planning on the part of Padres and neophytes, but when it was over the Padres sat down and professed themselves satisfied. It had been an occasion to be long remembered by all who had taken part in it, and, while the dedication of a church was a rare happening, the *días de fiesta* (feast days) that came throughout the year were sufficiently frequent to break the monotony of the workaday mission life, and give the Indians numerous pleasant holidays to look forward to.

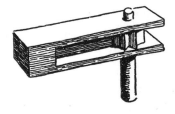

CHAPTER 20

The Tragic Fate of the Mission Indians

What Real Secularization Might Have Wrought

THE NEOPHYTE population of some of the missions began to decline at a very early date. At San Carlos, for instance, the peak in population was reached in 1795—just twenty-five years after the mission was founded—when the Indians enrolled numbered 876. Santa Cruz counted 644 neophytes, its greatest number, in 1798; Santa Bárbara 1,792, in 1803; La Purísima 1,520, in 1804; San Antonio 1,296, San Luis Obispo 961, and La Soledad 688, in 1805; San Fernando Rey 1,081, in 1811; San Juan Capistrano 1,361, in 1812; San Miguel 1,076, in 1814; Santa Inés 768 and San Buenaventura 1,328, in 1816; San Gabriel 1,701, in 1817; San Francisco de Asís 1,801, in 1821; San Juan Bautista 1,248, in 1823; San Diego 1,829, in 1824; San Luis Rey 2,869, in 1826; Santa Clara 1,462, in 1827; San José 1,886 and San Rafael 1,140, in 1831; San Francisco Solano 996, in 1832.[1]

The Mexican government finally became alarmed at the increasing number of deaths among the soldiers and Indians and, in 1804, Viceroy Iturrigaray directed Dr. José Benites, military surgeon at Monterey, to investigate and ascertain the causes. Dr. Benites visited and examined the soldiers and Indians in his district. He reported that the chief causes of deaths among both were dysentery, fevers, pleurisy, pneumonia, venereal diseases, scrofula, moist climate and continuous fogs. "The causes of the first-named diseases," he reported, "are: impure water which they [Mexican soldiers] use in the preparation of their food; want of cleanliness in their habitations and lack of inclination to cleanliness; want of care and prudence in eating when ill; the lack of vegetables and aversion for them; the continued exposure to dampness, fogs and rains in their season, when they are in the habit of letting the clothing dry on their bodies which results in eruptions. The causes of the venereal and kindred diseases

---

[1] See table of missions with dates of foundations.

among the Indians are impure intercourse, filthy habits, sleeping huddled to-gether, the sick with the others, the interchange of clothing, passing the nights in gambling and dancing on which occasions they shout and exert themselves exceedingly; finally the unreasonable use of the temescal or sweat-house from which perspiring freely they jump into cold water. Despite the zeal of the Fathers, who for the sake of charity took me to the rancheria in order to apply some remedies, the rudeness of the Indians reached such a degree that they de-clared the missionaries wanted to kill them. The sick would refuse medical aid. They would wash their sores and wounds, and would scarify them with a flint, even the eye-lids. I omit other barbarous customs."[2]

The explanation of the Indians' "rudeness" reported by Dr. Benites and their refusal to accept medical aid probably lies in the fact stated by Frs. Abella and Lucio in their answer to the question about the medical treatment given the neophytes. "The greatest favor that can be offered the sick and his relatives," they wrote, "is not to force him to take anything, because they say force makes the sick die."[3]

In writing about the San Juan Capistrano Indians' treatment of various dis-orders and diseases, Fr. Boscana substantiates the San Francisco Padres' state-ment. "In internal diseases such as fevers, pains in the side, burning fevers," he observes, "I do not know if they may have used special remedies other than bathing; what they did was to lie down naked on top of a pile of sand or ashes, the little fire in front of them being in whatever condition it might be, and a basket or pot of water at the head of the person; they were also accustomed to set for this person a little basket of acorn mush, but the sick person, if he wanted to eat, ate, and if not, he left it, and without anyone importuning him to take food, and it is to be noted that he always had someone or other at his side day and night, and thus he remained until either nature conquered or the disease conquered."[4]

The temescal, of whose "unreasonable use" Dr. Benites complained, was re-sorted to by all the male Californian natives not only as a remedy for their bodily ills but as a relaxant after fatiguing labors, games, or dances. Many writ-ers describe this "sweat-house" or "hot air bath" and tell of its effects on the Indians.[5] Robinson witnessed a ball game played by the Santa Bárbara mission Indians and those of the presidio. "Great excitement prevailed," he states, "and

---

[2] Engelhardt, *Miss. & Miss.*, 2. 608-609.
[3] Engelhardt, *Mission San Francisco*, 150.
[4] Harrington, John P., *A New Version of Boscana's Historical Account of the San Juan Capistrano Indians of South-ern California*. Smithsonian Miscellaneous Collections. Vol. 92, Number 4, Page 49.
[5] Fages, Font, Martínez, Duhaut-Cilly, Beechey, Robinson, De Mofras, Forbes, Bryant, Dr. Cephas Bard.

immense exertion was manifested on both sides, . . Many of the Indians retired afterwards to the enjoyment of their Temescal or hot air baths, which is their usual resort after fatigue, and is the sovereign remedy for nearly all their diseases. A round hovel or oven is built, generally, over an excavation in the ground. An opening is left in the roof for the escape of the smoke, and one at the side for entrance. As many persons as it can conveniently hold, enter, and make a fire close to the door on the inside. They continue to add fuel to the flame till they can no longer bear the intense heat, which throws them into a profuse perspira-tion. Thoroughly exhausted, they crawl forth from the hut, and plunge them-selves headlong into the nearest stream. I have frequently seen old men lying about on the floor of the oven apparently bereft of all strength, whilst some of the younger persons enjoyed it, and sang and laughed under its influence. The women also frequently made use of these baths, repeating them until their diseases are cured."[6]

Robinson probably errs in stating that the women made use of the baths, since a number of those persons who lived long with the Indians, and studied their habits closely, say that such was not the case. Don José Longinos Martínez, member of a botanical survey commission directed by Carlos III to explore the Spanish empire in America, visited California in 1792. In his *Journal*,[7] is found the following interesting note regarding temescals: "Each of the villages has one or more sweat houses (*temescales*) according to the greater or smaller number of people, and every day men and women[?] go into them twice, sweating streams of water. Then they go into pools or rivers of cold water, which they always have at hand. This, which truly does not seem repugnant to our habit of life, they do daily, even in the worst of the cold, which on some days is consider-able. Nevertheless, I attribute to this bad practice of theirs, which they follow from birth, the lack of that robustness that I note in those nations which do not do such violence to nature. These, however, are so addicted to it that even the missionary fathers allow them to have their sweat houses in the missions and their pond of cold water at hand, for the daily lavatory which they all perform because of their cleanliness and their fondness for soaping themselves at all hours."

And, indeed, it is true that the missionaries did allow them to build their temescals at the missions. As the San Carlos Fathers write: "The men have the daily custom of entering an underground oven, known as the 'temescal.' A fire

---

[6] Robinson, *Life in Cal.*, 105-106.
[7] *California in 1792. The Expedition of Jose Longinos Martinez* (Translated by Leslie Byrd Simpson. Huntington Lib. Publication, 1938), 42.

is built within and when the oven has become heated sufficiently, the men enter undressed. They perspire so freely that, upon coming out they appear to have been bathing. It is understood that this is very beneficial for them. For a time the attempt was made to stop them, and as a result skin diseases and boils and other ailments appeared among them. When they betook themselves to the 'temescal' again, scarcely a man was found afflicted with the itch, a disease common to the women and children who do not make use of such baths."[8]

According to the reports of the San Antonio Padres, the Indians of that mission had a temescal built at the extreme left end of the front wing of the quadrangle and close beside the creek.

As Dr. Cephas Bard writes, there can be no doubt of the beneficial value of the temescal before the coming of the white man and his diseases.[9] For, until the Spanish and Mexican people invaded California, the native Indian knew nothing of measles, mumps, smallpox, and social diseases. With regard to the last-named affliction it would be well to remember that, with the little knowledge of sanitation and contagion, as well as the lack of remedy then possessed, even by medical men, for the cure of those dread diseases, it would have taken but three or four infected persons to have corrupted hundreds and eventually thousands of others. It is, therefore, calumnious and reprehensible to lay the blame for this disorder on either the soldiers or settlers as a class.

That the use of the temescal, followed by a plunge into cold water, by patients suffering from measles, mumps, smallpox, and pulmonary afflictions would result in serious injury or fatality, is quite understandable today. But, the white man's diseases were strangers to the neophytes and the temescals were their cure-alls.

On very rare occasions was there more than one doctor at a time in all the length and breadth of California. And, according to Dr. Bard, "At the time of the founding of the Mission of San Diego, the science of surgery had hardly been separated from the trade of barber. In fact, so servile was the position of the military surgeon throughout the world in the early part of the eighteenth century that he was required to shave regimental officers."

". . . The long distance from home and the danger incidental to the position may have deterred better men, if they then existed, from coming. Those who did arrive were, with hardly an exception, grossly incompetent, and in no respect prepared for the exigencies and emergencies of the service. . . Of the

[8] Engelhardt, *Mission San Carlos*, 126.
[9] Bard, Dr. Cephas, *A Contribution to the History of Medicine in Southern California.*

surgeons,[10] Benites seems to have been possessed of the most attainments."

All of the surgeons were stationed at Monterey and persons residing in other parts of the state were obliged to rely upon the Indians, Padres, early settlers, or "foreign" visitors for medical aid in times of sickness or injury.

Our California Indians had knowledge of many herbs, plants, roots, etc., of medicinal value. And some of these the Padres were glad to employ on occasion. "One of the tribe," the San Carlos Padres note, "knows a root, a remedy against bloody dysentery. The root is beaten to a powder and this is given with a little water. Some have been cured and highly praise the remedy. The Indian, who knows, does not care to tell where the root is found, because in this way he gains a livelihood and so guards his secret. Recently we ordered him to bring it from the country and we saw that it is a root of a plant, large and tender, like the parsnip. . ."[11]

Dr. Bard, who was very much interested in the Indians and had come to San Buenaventura before the last of that mission's neophytes had disappeared, writes: "It has been reserved for the California Indian to furnish three of the most valuable vegetable additions which have been made to the Pharmacopoeia during the last twenty years. One, the Eriodyction Glutinosum, growing profusely in our foothills, was used by them in the affections of the respiratory tract, and its worth was so appreciated by the missionaries as to be named Yerba Santa, or Holy Plant. The second, the Rhamnus purshiana (the buckthorn) gathered now for the market in the upper portions of the State, is found scattered through the timbered mountains of Southern California. It was used as a laxative, and on account of the constipating effect of an acorn diet, was doubtless in active demand. So highly was it esteemed by the followers of the Cross that it was christened Cascara Sagrada, or Sacred Bark. The third, Grindelia robusta [common name gum weed], was used in the treatment of pulmonary troubles, and externally in poisoning from Rhus toxicodendron, or Poison Oak, and in various skin diseases."[12]

Dr. Bard lists many other herbs and plants used by our Indians in treating their various ailments but the subject matter would require more space than this chapter allows.

[10] Pedro Prat 1769-1771
Pedro Castran 1773-1774
José Dávila 1774-1783
Pedro Carbajál 1785-1787
Pablo Solér 1791-1800
José Castillo 1792-1818
Juan de Dios Morelos 1800-1802

Manuel Torres 1802-1803
José M. Benites 1803-1807
Manuel Quijano 1807-1824
I. Evan Pérez de Leon 1829
Manuel de Alva 1831-1840
Manuel Crespo 1832
Edward Bale 1840-1843

[11] Engelhardt, *Mission San Carlos*, 125.
[12] Dr. Bard, *opus cit.*

The Padres did what they could for the sick and infirm. As those at Santa Bárbara reported: "We missionary Fathers are careful, as far as possible, that the Mission lacks nothing in the way of medicines, very frequently needed for ourselves as well as for the neophytes."[13] And *memorias* testify to the fact that medicines were ordered and sent up from México. Then, too, there were medical books in the Padres' libraries. In San Antonio's inventory of April, 1842, the following works were listed among others: Broun, *Medicina Domestica;* Tissot, *Medicina Domestica;* Buchan, *Medicina Domestica;* and Stanciffer, *Florilegio Medicinal* (Medical Anthology).

Hospitals and infirmaries were probably constructed at all the missions and attempts made to segregate those neophytes afflicted with contagious diseases, especially the *mal Gálico,* from the others. In 1797, the San Diego Padres built four houses for the sick. Apparently, the houses formed a row fifty-two varas long and five varas wide and were roofed with tiles. San Juan Capistrano's hospital consisted of those rooms, or buildings, which surrounded the patio in the rear of the main quadrangle. Erected in 1814, this hospital contained "bed rooms and corresponding salas, or reception rooms, for the convenience of the sick. Attached to it was a chapel for the administration of the sacraments to the sick, as also rooms for the nurses and a room for medicines and other requisites of the hospital. Furthermore, a wall separating the patio of the hospital from the various shops of the mission had been erected."[14]

At San Gabriel a hospital was finished in 1814. It was 114 varas long and 12 varas wide, or 314′ x 33′. It consisted of four apartments for various classes of infirmities. To provide a patio for the exclusive use of the sick there was erected a room 100 varas long and 6 varas wide, as well as a chapel for the hospital. All were built of adobe and roofed with tiles. In 1810, the Padres of this mission had reported that their hospital was crowded with from 300 to 400 habitually infirm. At that time the total number of neophytes in their charge was 1,199.[15]

In enumerating the buildings which stood around the inner court at San Luis Rey, Duhaut-Cilly mentions the infirmary with its private chapel. "For everything," he says, "has been contrived for the convenience of the sick who could go to church through the cloisters without failing to be under shelter; but this is a refinement."[16]

At San Francisco a bathhouse was built in 1799, and bathtubs installed. More-

---

[13] Engelhardt, *Mission Santa Barbara,* 94.
[14] Engelhardt, *Mission San Juan Capistrano,* 57.
[15] Engelhardt, *Mission San Gabriel,* 86, 94.
[16] "Duhaut-Cilly's Account," 227-228.

over, a large caldron for heating water was set up and everything necessary for bathing the sick provided.[17] The rate of mortality among the Indians of this mission was particularly high. In 1806, more than 300 of them died during an epidemic of measles, while only 23 were born. The severity of the weather in this region was sometimes blamed and finally a number of ailing Indians were sent across the bay where the climate was milder. Their health improved and so it was decided to establish in that place "a kind of rancho with its chapel, baptistry, and cemetery, under the title of San Rafael Arcángel, in order that this most glorious prince, who in his name expresses the 'healing of God,' may care for the bodies as well as the souls."[18] This hospital asistencia, as it might be called, grew into Mission San Rafael. Fr. Luis Gil y Taboada, "who was somewhat versed in medical science," was placed in charge of the rancho. However, some time in 1819, Fr. Juan Amorós took his place.

It is believed that in time the Indian neophytes would have built up an immunity from white man's diseases. Certain it is that they were not all destroyed by those scourges. The considerable number of Indian neophytes and their offspring living in the vicinity of the various missions as late even as 1890 and on into the twentieth century attest to this fact. Their descendants, many of mixed blood, are still living in numerous parts of the state.

Nor could the confinement at the missions—a necessity, though deplorable, if the Indians were to be civilized—have been so injurious to their health as is often charged. The foregoing pages will have shown that most of the tasks allotted the neophytes carried with them considerable outdoor life, and the occasional leave of absence for a week or two provided some outlet for the elders' inherent urge to return to their former haunts and pursuits. That this confinement, or restriction to the mission bounds, with its imposed routine was extremely onerous to the older ones can not be doubted.[19] That they sometimes ran away to escape it and the diseases which they did not understand, is a matter of record. But neither confinement nor routine should have affected the younger ones and the children reared at the missions, for they had never known any other way of life.

" . . On September 13, 1813, the Cortes (Parliament) of Spain passed a decree to the effect that all the missions in America that had been founded ten years

---

[17] Engelhardt, *Mission San Francisco*, 137.
[18] Engelhardt, *Miss. & Miss.*, 3. 31.
[19] ". . , an irresistible desire of freedom sometimes breaks out in individuals. This may probably be referred to the national character. Their attachment to a wandering life, their love of alternate exercise in fishing and hunting, and entire indolence, seem in their eyes to overbalance all the advantages they enjoy at the mission, which to us appear very great: . ." Langsdorff, *Voyages and Travels*, 2. 171.

should at once be given up to the bishop 'without excuse or pretext whatever, in accordance with the laws.' It was provided that the friars might be appointed if necessary as temporary curates, and that one or two might remain in the district where they had convents and have been serving as curates; but with these few and temporary exceptions they must move on to new conversions, and must at once yield the management of temporalities, the mission lands having been reduced to private ownership, and the neophytes to be governed by their ayuntamientos [municipal government] and civil authorities.[20] This decree, perfectly in accord with Spanish law and policy, applied to the missions of California and of all America as directly as to those of Guiana, . . . but there was no attempt to enforce it in California, where it was not officially published as a law, and perhaps not even known for eight years."[21]

It is not the intention of this writer to devote many pages to the incidents which led up to the final secularization and spoliation of our California missions. Information on that subject may be found ably presented in many well-known works.[22] Suffice it to note that, in 1825, the Mexican administration appointed José María Echeandía governor of the Californias with the expectation that he would carry out the decree of 1813. Coming to California Echeandía found many essential conditions lacking for the successful accomplishment of the act. The territorial finances were not in good condition, the troops were dissatisfied, partly because of the uncertainty of their pay; there were no curates on hand to take the place of the Padres, and, moreover, the welfare of the entire territory was more or less dependent on the missions. If the plan did not function smoothly, chaos would result.

"The governor," Bancroft states, "recognized the impossibility of immediate action; but in accordance with the policy of his government, with his own republican theories, with the spirit rapidly evolved from the controversies with the friars on other points, and with the urging of some prominent Californians who already had their eyes on the mission lands, he had to keep the matter alive to test the feelings and capabilities of the neophytes."[23]

Accordingly, on July 25, 1826, Echeandía issued a decree of partial "emancipation" in favor of the Indians. "By its terms those desiring to leave the mission might do so, provided they had been Christians from childhood, or for fifteen

[20] See Engelhardt, *Miss. & Miss.*, 3. 95-97, for wording of decree.
[21] Banc., *Hist. of Cal.*, 2. 399-400.
[22] Banc., *Hist. of Cal.*, vols. 2-6; Hittell, *Hist. of Cal.*; Jones, Carey, *Land Titles in California;* Dwinelle, *Colonial History of San Francisco,* 54; Blackmar, *Spanish Institutions of the Southwest,* Chapter VII; Priestly, Herbert I., *The Mexican Nation,* 122; Engelhardt, *Miss. & Miss.,* vols. 3 and 4; Hill, Joseph J., *The History of Warner's Ranch,* Chapter V.
[23] Banc., *Hist. of Cal.*, 3. 101-102.

years, were married, or at least not minors, and had some means of gaining a livelihood. . . "[24] They must, however, have a permit from the presidial comandante granted on the approval of the mission Padres. Then, "like other Mexican citizens," they might go wherever they pleased.

In the meantime, the governor was preparing a plan which was approved by the California territorial diputación during the July 20—August 3, 1830, session, and was sent to the supreme government in September. "This plan," Bancroft notes, "provided for the gradual transformation of the missions into pueblos, beginning with those nearest the presidios and pueblos, of which one or two were to be secularized within a year, and the rest as rapidly as experience might show to be practicable. Each neophyte was to have a share of the mission lands and other property. The friars might remain as curates, or establish a new line of missions on the frontier as they should choose. . . "[25]

Echeandía received no reply from México regarding his plan and events were crowding him. Some Mexican friars from the College of Our Lady of Guadalupe at Zacatecas were coming to the relief of the mission Padres, many of whom were old and serving alone. The governor did not want these newcomers to assume temporal management of the eight northern missions to which they had been assigned. Therefore, on January 6, 1831, he put into effect his decree of secularization, in spite of the fact that the newly appointed governor, Lieutenant-Colonel Manuel Victoria, had, since the previous month, been waiting in San Diego to take the oath of office.

"It was," Bancroft observes, "an illegal and even revolutionary measure. . . The territorial government, as Echeandía well knew, had no power to secularize the missions. . . The decree of January 6, 1831, was for the most part in accordance with the plan of 1830."[26]

But the Californians would have none of Victoria, and, on April 17, 1832, José Figueroa was appointed by the supreme government to succeed him. At the same time "Minister Alamán disapproved in the vice-president's name Echeandía's decree of 1831: both because he had gone far beyond his authority in issuing such a decree, and because some of its provisions were not in accord, as pointed out, with the law of 1813, on which it purported to be founded; and he ordered Figueroa, if Echeandía's order had to any extent been obeyed, to restore the missions to the position they held before its publication. Yet he was to study the question closely, to ascertain what missions were in a condition to be secular-

---

[24] *Ibidem*, 102.
[25] Banc., *Hist. of Cal.*, 3. 106.
[26] *Ibidem*, 304-305.

ized according to the law of 1813, and to report such a plan as he might deem expedient."[27]

Figueroa accordingly investigated conditions and called upon Fr. Narciso Durán, president of the missions in charge of the Fernandinos and Prefect García Diego in charge of those held by the Zacatecanos to state what missions were ready to be secularized under the decree of 1813; what objections to secularization existed; and what would be the best means to be employed. The territorial diputación was also consulted.

Fr. Durán was opposed to secularization and suggested three alternate plans. "The first," Bancroft states, "was to establish a new line of missions and presidios east of the old line, secularize the old establishments into Indian pueblos,[28] and give the neophytes their choice between remaining in the pueblos or being attached to the new missions. This would effectually prevent them from escaping from civilization, and would also free the territory from the danger of attack and outrage at the hands of renegade neophytes, hostile gentiles, and ambitious foreigners.[29] This plan, though the best, was probably impracticable, because the national government could not be induced to bear the expense. The next plan, though not so expeditious, was sure, and would lead to the same result. It was to have a bishop appointed for California, a live man, not bent on living a life of ease, and to give him exclusive control of all the tithes under the protection but not direction of the governor. With the means placed at his disposal, the bishop could in a few years have in operation a seminary of ecclesiastical education, a college of missionaries, a cathedral, and all the necessary agencies for converting gentiles and furnishing curates. Then the missions could be secularized without risk."[30]

Figueroa had by this time become opposed to any "sudden and radical change in the mission system, as involving total destruction of all property with possible danger to the security of the territory." He so wrote the home government. Too late, however, his report reached the Mexican authorities for, on August 17,

[27] *Ibidem*, 325.

[28] That it was clearly the intent of the Spanish Cortes that the mission establishments themselves be transformed into Indian pueblos is seen in the following article 6 of the decree of 1813:

The missionaries from Religious Orders must immediately surrender the government and administrations of the estates of those Indians, leaving it to the care and choice of these Indians, by means of their Ayuntamientos and under the supervision of the civil governor, to nominate from among themselves those who would be to their satisfaction, and may have more intelligence in managing them, the lands to be divided and reduced to individual ownership in accordance with the decree of January 4th, 1813, concerning the reduction of the Valdios and other lands to private ownership.

[29] This second line of missions had been advocated as early as 1813 by Fr. José Señán. Fr. Mariano Payeras urged the establishment of a mission in the Tulare Valley in his report for 1815-1816, as a means of stopping stock stealing by gentile Indians led by runaway neophytes, incidental to the gathering into the church of all the gentiles in that region. See Beattie, Geo. Wm., *California's Unbuilt Missions*.

[30] Banc., *Hist. of Cal.* 3. 334.

1833, the national congress passed a bill for the secularization of the missions. In this bill no mention was made of the distribution of mission property, one of the most important issues at stake. Though, as Bancroft remarks, supplementary regulations were apparently contemplated.

Without waiting for further instructions from México, Figueroa and the California diputación proposed, discussed, and officially published on August 9, 1834, provisional regulations for the secularization of the missions. This act was quite as unlawful as Echeandía's decree of 1831, since the making of such regulations did not pertain to the territorial government. In September the taking of inventories began, starting, apparently, at Mission San Rafael. By the end of that year eight missions had been secularized and placed in the hands of salaried administrators.

Such arrangement was not in accord with the Spanish decree of 1813, either in letter or spirit. For by that act the mission establishments were to become Indian pueblos whose government and administration was to be left in the hands of the Indians themselves,[31] under the supervision of the civil governor. The Padres or secular priests would have charge of spiritual affairs only. This would have been true secularization; it was what took place in the missions of the Sierra Gorda when the Franciscans were withdrawn from that region and sent to the missions of Baja California.

That Governor Figueroa and the legislative assembly had no intention of turning over the valuable mission lands to the Indians, but merely some lots in a place selected by the commissioner, mayordomo, and the Padre;[32] that the Indians would have no voice in affairs, and that they would be forced to continue their work in the shops, fields, and vineyards is evident from the following excerpts from *Reglamento Provisional para secularización de las Misiones de la Alta California, 9 de Agosto, 1834:*

"Distribution of property and lands.—To each head of a family, and to all over 20 years old, will be given from the mission lands a lot not over 400 nor less than 100 varas square. In common will be given them enough land to pasture their stock. *Egidos* [vacant suburbs] shall be assigned for each pueblo, and at the proper time *propios* [lands that were rented] also."

"6. Among the same individuals there shall be distributed pro rata, according to the judgment of the gefe pol. [gefe politico—the governor], one-half of the livestock, taking as a basis the latest inventories rendered by the missionaries."

"7. There will also be distributed to them proportionately, half or less of the existing chattels, tools, and seed indispensable for the cultivation of the ground."

. . .

[31] See note 28 this chapter.
[32] In view of what happened to the Padres at most of the missions as soon as they were secularized, it does not appear that many of them were consulted about anything.

"Political government of the pueblos. . . 16. The emancipated [?] will be obliged to aid in the common work which in the judgment of the gefe pol. may be deemed necessary for the cultivation of the vineyards, gardens, and fields remaining for the present undisturbed."

"17. They will render to the padre the necessary personal service."

"Restrictions—18. They may not sell, burden, nor convey the lands given them; nor may they sell their stock. Contracts made against these orders shall be void; the govt will reclaim the property and the buyers will lose their money."

"19. Lands, the owners of which die without heirs, shall revert to the nation."

"General rules. . . 4. Before making an inventory of the field property the com. [comisionado] must explain to the Indians this regulation and the change it is to effect in their condition. Their lots are to be immediately distributed. The com., padre and mayordomo will select the place, give to each what he can cultivate within fixed limits, and allow each to mark his land in the most convenient way. . ."

"9. Rancherias at a distance having twenty-five families may form a separate pueblo if they wish to do so, otherwise they will form a *barrio* or ward of the main pueblo." [33]

As indicated above, the missions, after being secularized, became pueblos. San Juan Capistrano, where, in 1833, the Indians had been "emancipated" by Figueroa, was named San Juan de Argüello in honor of Don Santiago Argüello and his family. San Juan Bautista was called San Juan de Castro in honor of José de Castro. These new titles, however, did not last long.

Unfortunately, the pueblos formed according to Figueroa's regulations were not such as were intended by the decree of 1813. Here, instead of the mission shops, cellars, and storehouses being turned over to the Indians to be managed by them under the direction of a leader chosen "from among themselves," those buildings together with their equipment were placed in the hands of a hired administrator or mayordomo appointed by the governor. This administrator established himself in rooms of the front wing, often depriving the Padre, who remained as curate until a secular priest was found to take his place, of part of his living quarters. The Indians, instead of being free to engage in pursuits gainful to themselves; to manage the tannery, weavery, blacksmith shop, candle factory, tallow works, etc., for their own benefit, were obliged to plow, sow, and reap; to care for the live stock, tan the hides; shear the sheep and weave the wool into blankets to provide goods to pay the salaries of the administrator and his helpers, to feed and clothe his large family (and California families really were large in those days); to fill orders from the governor for grain, blankets, saddles, shoes and whatnot for the troops and their families.

From records, found chiefly in Bancroft's works, it appears that the Indians at some of the missions were given small pieces of land and mission goods of various sorts. Of San Francisco, however, that historian states: "If any property was ever divided among the Indians, there are no records to show it." [34]

[33] Banc., *Hist. of Cal.*, 3. 342-344, note 4.
[34] Banc., *Hist. of Cal.*, 3. 715.

But the little parcels of land allotted to the neophytes meant nothing to them, for those who had wanted it had always had land for a garden and a few fruit trees. Moreover, they had always been allowed to dispose of the produce as they pleased.

By the end of 1835, sixteen missions had been secularized,[35] lands and goods presumably having been divided among the neophytes. In November of this year the Mexican congreso constituyente passed a decree which practically repealed the secularization law. It read: "Until the curates mentioned in article 2 of the law of August 17, 1833, shall have taken possession, the government will suspend the execution of the other articles, and will maintain things in the state in which they were before the said law was made."[36] This decree was not known in California until after the end of the year. Not only was it not obeyed then but the reglamento issued by Figueroa continued in operation.

"Meanwhile," writes Hittell, "the work of secularization was going on. It furnished a rich harvest for those engaged in it. No charge of corruption or unlawful gain was made or could have been sustained against Figueroa himself; and there may have been a few others engaged in the work equally clear of offence; but the great mass of the commissioners and other officials, whose duty it became to administer the properties of the missions, and especially their great numbers of horses, cattle, sheep and other animals, thought of little else and accomplished little else than enriching themselves. It cannot be said that the spoliation was immediate; but it was certainly very rapid. A few years sufficed to strip the establishments of everything of value and leave the Indians, who were in contemplation of the law the beneficiaries of secularization, a shivering crowd of naked and, so to speak, homeless wanderers upon the face of the earth."[37]

Robinson, who was in California during those troublous times, remarks: "Many [Spanish and Mexican-Californians] that were poor soon became wealthy, and possessors of farms, which they stocked with cattle."[38] The cattle were usually borrowed from the mission herds to enable the ranchero to get a start and, it is said, were seldom returned.

Bancroft states: "The methods of mission spoliation at this period [1836-1842] were substantially as follows: The governor [Alvarado] and his subordinate officials by his authority, used the cattle and grain of the missions as freely as they used the revenues from other sources. If the government con-

---

[35] They were San Diego, San Luis Rey, S. Juan Capistrano, S. Gabriel, S. Fernando, Sta. Bárbara, La Purísima, S. Luis Obispo, S. Antonio, La Soledad, S. Juan Bautista, S. Carlos, Sta. Cruz, S. Francisco, S. Rafael, S. Francisco Solano.
[36] Banc., *Hist. of Cal.*, 3. 355.
[37] Hittell, *Hist. of Cal.*, 2. 206-207.
[38] Robinson, *Life in Cal.*, 175.

tracted a debt to a trader, the governor gave in payment an order on any mission for wheat, tallow, or hides, just as he would draw a check on the treasury. The mayordomo, being an employe of the government, obeyed the order as a rule whenever the articles called for existed at his mission. There were occasional refusals and pleas in behalf of the Indians, but of course these pleas were much less frequent and zealous than those of the friars in earlier times. How far, if at all, beyond the limits of strictly public expenses the departmental authorities went in their drafts upon the mission property, it is hard to say. The most extravagant and sweeping charges are made of a deliberate plunder and distribution of the spoils by Alvarado among his friends; but no proofs are presented, the charges have always been denied by Alvarado and urged mainly by his enemies, and they are probably false. One charge, however, is supported by evidence in the archives and by the governor's own admission, namely, that of having authorized loans of mission cattle to private individuals, on condition that a like number of animals should be returned later. Alvarado certainly had no right to make these loans; but he defended his action on the ground that he had no other means of rewarding men for patriotic services to the country, often involving the loss of their own property and neglect of all their private interests. The worst feature of these transactions was that in nine cases out of ten the loans were never repaid to the missions."

"As to the comisionados, mayordomos, and administrators who successively managed the missions, many were simply incompetent and stupid, exhausting their little energy and ability in the task of collecting their salary, filling the governor's orders so long as the granaries and herds held out, exercising no restraint or influence on the neophytes and allowing the affairs of their respective establishments to drift—not, as may be imagined, in the direction of general prosperity. Others were vicious as well as incompetent, always ready to sell any article of mission property, not only live-stock, but kitchen utensils, farm implements, tools from the shops, and tiles from the roofs, for money with which to satisfy their propensity for gambling. Still others were dishonest and able, devoting their energies to laying the foundations of future wealth for themselves and friends, oppressing the Indians, quarreling with such padres, officials, and assistants as they could not control or deceive, and disposing of the mission wealth [i. e., live stock, grains, tools, goods in shops and warehouses] without scruple, for their own interests. Finally, there were, I suppose, some honest, faithful, and tolerably efficient managers, who did as well as was possible under difficult circumstances."[39]

[39] Banc., *Hist. of Cal.*, 4. 49-51.

Writing in 1841, Duflot de Mofras declared: "Those now in control are rancheros, or farmers, who have grown rich by plundering the missions and who, under the Franciscan régime, served as majordomos, cowboys, and servants to the Fathers. . . "[40]

Dwinelle sums up the case in the following brief paragraph: "These laws, whose ostensible purpose was to convert the missionary establishments into Indian pueblos, their churches into parish churches, and elevate the Christianized Indians to the rank of citizens, were after all executed in such a manner that the so-called secularization of the missions resulted in their complete ruin, and in the demoralization and dispersion of the Christianized Indians."[41]

On January 22, 1842, the Mexican government appointed Manuel Micheltorena to succeed Alvarado as governor of California. Invested with some extraordinary powers he was to study and report on the mission situation. On March 29, 1843, he issued a decree restoring to the Padres the temporal management of twelve of the missions, on the condition that one-eighth of the annual produce of every description be paid into the public treasury.

In February, 1844, Fr. Durán reported to the Mexican government on the state of the missions in charge of the Fernandinos. The neophytes at San Miguel, San Luis Obispo, and San Juan Capistrano, he said, were scattered for want of ministers. There were 200 Indians at La Purísima, 264 at Santa Inés, 287 at Santa Bárbara, 300 at San Gabriel, 400 at San Luis Rey and 100 at San Diego. "From all of which," he observes, "it appears that three missions are abandoned, in totum, for want of ministers and resources; that there remain only eight religiosos fernandinos, with three clergymen to aid them; that only Santa Inés and San Buenaventura have the means of moderate subsistence; and that the other nine destroyed by secularization, and their neophytes demoralized, are in a state of moral impossibility of ever raising their heads."[42]

And this condition had been brought about in just ten short years.

Articles 2 and 5 of Micheltorena's decree of March 29, 1843, relate to the all-important land question. They read as follows:

"2. Since policy makes irrevocable what has already been done, the missions cannot reclaim any lands that have been granted; but they may gather in all live-stock and implements that have been loaned by the guardians or administrators, making friendly arrangements with the debtors or holders as to time and manner."

"5. The govt, priding itself in being religious as well as wholly Californian, and thus interested in the progress of the catholic faith and prosperity of the country, offers all its power in aid of

[40] De Mofras, *Travels*, 1. 166.
[41] Dwinelle, *Colonial History of San Francisco*, 54.
[42] Banc., *Hist. of Cal.*, 4. 421-422; Engelhardt, *Miss. & Miss.*, 4. 322-324.

the missions, as it will also protect private individuals in the possession of lands which they now hold; promising, however, to make no new grant without a report from local authorities and from the padres, unless in case of notorious non-occupation, non-cultivation, or necessity." [43]

The lands referred to in Article 2 were, of course, the mission ranchos, lands improved with adobe houses, granaries and corrals, or orchards and vineyards— all the result of neophyte labor. Following secularization, these valuable properties had been granted by the various governors to relatives, friends, or other persons to whom those officials were indebted for some service or favor. Usually the Indians were allowed to remain on the land for the simple reason that they were required to do the work of the ranch. Some of the grants were made with the stipulation that the Indians be allowed to remain undisturbed, though this agreement was not always adhered to.[44] All grants, according to both Spanish and Mexican law, should have carried this provision.

The Spanish and Mexican-Californians, according to the early writers, did no work that could not be performed on horseback. They were superb horsemen and delighted in displaying their skill in the use of the lazo at the rodeo, during the matanza, or in capturing a bear for a bull and bear fight. But, as Duhaut-Cilly remarked, they lived only by means of the Indians who worked for them.[45] Wherefore, the mission-trained Indian became an asset rather than a liability to those people.[46]

Article 5 of Micheltorena's decree promises that no more such grants as those referred to in Article 2 would be made, the qualifying "unless" providing a convenient loophole for future emergencies.

But Micheltorena was not allowed to finish his term of office. Certain young Californians, resenting the governor's bringing an army of "Cholo" criminals with him to California, and, desiring to run the affairs of the country themselves, to enjoy its revenues, etc., albeit under the supreme government, expelled Micheltorena and some of his men. Then, on February 15, 1845, Pio Pico senior vocal of the assembly, was declared legal governor *ad interim*. On May 29th, he received a communication from México which virtually recognized his position as governor.

[43] Banc., *Hist. of Cal.,* 4. 369, note 1.
[44] Hill, Joseph J., *The History of Warner's Ranch and Its Environs.*
[45] "Duhaut-Cilly's Account," 163.
[46] Charles Nordhoff, writing in 1873, tells of Señor M., of Laguna Rancho, who "had" Indians. "You must understand," Nordhoff observes, "that in California parlance a man 'has' Indians, but he 'is in' sheep, or cattle, or horses . . 'They [the Indians] are poor creatures,' said Señor M., with a shrug of his shoulders; 'poor creatures, but quiet; not good for much, but useful.'" They slept in a lightly enclosed shed which Nordhoff "had imagined to be the chicken-house. In the farther end, truly, the chickens were at roost, but the larger part was floored with poles, on which barley-straw was spread, and here the Indians slept —." Nordhoff, *opus cit.*, 149-151.

Pico soon inaugurated his policy of sale or rental of the missions. On October 28, 1845, he issued a decree which provided for the sale at public auction of the abandoned missions of San Rafael, Dolores, Soledad, San Miguel, and La Purísima, and of the mission pueblos of San Luis Obispo, Carmelo, San Juan Bautista, and San Juan Capistrano. The remaining ten missions were to be rented to the highest bidder for a term of nine years. In the following month an order was issued in México to the effect that all sales of the missions be suspended. This order, however, was ignored by the Californian officials and before the end of the year three missions were sold and four rented.[47]

By Pico's decree some small pieces of land occupied by the Indians were to be reserved. "The Indians were to be entirely free to remain in the service of the renters or to settle elsewhere; and they were to receive titles to their land on application. Each ex-mission community was to be governed under the laws by four celadores [watchmen], chosen monthly from among the Indians, and sub-ject to the juex de paz [justice of the peace]."[48] It does not appear that this part of the decree occasioned any change in the neophytes' condition.

Added to the injustice of taking from the Indians the lands which they had been told from the very first were eventually to be their own, was the cruel failure, with but few very rare exceptions, to give them written legal title to the little plots allotted to them. On January 24, 1846, Fr. Narciso Durán, who, as Padre Presidente in the south ceaselessly tried to secure justice for his charges, penned the following suggestion to Governor Pico: "I inform your Excellency that this mission of Santa Bárbara has been entirely given over to the lessees, and that the Indians are at liberty. To the Indians were assigned the little pieces of land which the Reglamento grants them. All has been done in accord with the lessees[49] and it seems that we have left all contented. In consequence they [the Indians] have presented to me a paper which I enclose to your Excellency but on which you will excuse the blots. Considering how laborious it would be for all to present the demands and to execute titles to each one in particular, I thought that, if your Excellency approved it, a general title might be issued, in order that some authority place each Indian in possession of the lands which to date have been assigned to them, expressing the conditions of the Reglamento on leasing, and that said general title be entered with the justice of peace, so that for all times the legal individual ownership of the Indians be in evidence, without prejudice to any declaration which unforeseen circumstances might at

[47] Banc., *Hist. of Cal.*, 4. 553.
[48] *Ibidem*, 552; Engelhardt, *Mission Santa Barbara*, 250-251.
[49] Nicholas A. Den and Daniel Hill of Santa Bárbara.

some period make necessary, though never such as would infringe on this personal ownership."[50]

There is nothing to show that the Santa Bárbara Indians were given such title to their little plots of land. However, there is evidence that Pico did grant several mission ranchos to mission Indians. Two neophytes of San Luis Rey, Andreas and José Manuel, were granted Guajome in 1845. This rancho, the ancestral home of the Couts family, contained 2,219.41 acres in a perfect square. Rancho Vista, in the same district was granted to Felipe, another San Luis Rey Indian.[51] In the San Fernando Mission district Rancho Encino, 4,460 acres in extent, was given to Ramón, Francisco, and Roque, neophyte Indians; El Escorpión, a rancho of 1,100 acres to three Indians, Urbano, Odón, and Manuel; a small tract of about 200 acres to a half-breed Indian, José Miguel.[52]

By virtue of having married the Indian woman, Victoria, Hugo Reid, Scotchman, in 1844, obtained title to San Gabriel's Rancho Santa Anita. In the words of Padre Tomás Esténaga, the first grant made to Victoria in 1841, was a "reward for services rendered for the benefit of this mission by his wife and her late husband, Pablo, who did greatly contribute to the existence of said mission." Victoria also held title to La Huerta del Cuati. This latter property she kept in her own name and later sold it to B. D. Wilson.[53]

As early as 1775, Manuel Butrón, a soldier, having married Margarita, "a daughter of the Mission," was placed in possession of a piece of land belonging to San Carlos. The tract was "of the length and breadth of 140 varas, in the form of a perfect square, . . " Padre Serra had assigned the land to Butrón "in virtue of the right of his wife." This was quite in keeping with the policy outlined in Point 30 of Fr. Serra's *Representación* to Viceroy Bucareli.[54] Comandante Fernando Rivera y Moncada gave "Royal and legitimate possession" to Butrón and his Indian wife and all their descendants.[55]

Of the Santa Clara Mission lands, in 1845, one-half league from Rancho Ulistac's acreage was granted to the Indians, Marcelo Pico and Cristóbal. In 1842,

[50] Engelhardt, *Mission Santa Barbara*, 246-247.

[51] Wolcott, Marjorie T., "The House Near the Frog Pond," *Touring Topics*, December, 1928.

[52] Banc., *Hist. of Cal.*, 4. 634; Keffer, Frank M., *History of San Fernando Valley*, 90, 94; Bell, Maj. Horace, *On the Old West Coast*, 181-193.

[53] Banc., *Hist. of Cal.*, 4. 635; Dakin, Susanna Bryant, *A Scotch Paisano*, 65-69; Robinson, W. W., *Land in California*, 71.

[54] "30. I also beg your Excellency to determine upon some reward for those soldiers or those who are not soldiers who marry new Christian daughters of that country. . Let him be given for the present a mule to go about on, if he has none, and after one year or somewhat more in the service of the mission in planting the land, let him be given from the herds of the king a couple of cows and a mule, or whatever may seem best to your Excellency. And in time we might assign them a piece of ground, so that they may plant for themselves, since there is nothing else to give them." Bolton, *Palou's New Cal.*, 3. 33-34.

[55] Engelhardt, *Miss. & Miss.*, 3. 640-643.

at San Francisco Solano, Rancho Suisun, four leagues in extent, was granted to Francisco Solano, Indian chief of the Suisunes, whose baptismal name was that of the patron saint of the mission. Rancho Tiniscasio, granted in 1841 to the Indians of Mission San Rafael, was lost to them through the ruling of the land commission.[56] Possibly they had no written title to show.

Undoubtedly there were a few more grants made to mission Indians, but they were very few. Here and there one hears of Indians clinging to pitiful scraps of paper which they claimed gave them title to their lands. Most of those scraps were later stolen or burned along with the Indians' homes when the owners happened to be absent. A few instances of the many such occurrences, and of the forcible eviction of the natives from lands which were theirs by right of possession and inheritance, are found recorded in historical works, in agents' reports to the government, and in those of the Sequoia League and the Warner's Ranch Indian commission.[57]

The "Californios" (as those inhabitants of Spanish and Mexican descent called themselves), having secured the choicest of the mission lands, were well content to have the Indians stay on the property, which was usually several leagues in extent, for, as has previously been noted, without the Indians' labor the land would be of little value to the new owners. This same policy was adopted by most of the "foreigners" who came to California, married into Spanish or Mexican families, and thereby became owners of large tracts of land. One such proprietor was Johnathan Trumbull Warner, otherwise known as Juan José Warner, native of Connecticut, who came to California in 1831 with David E. Jackson, formerly an associate of Jedediah Smith. In 1844, Warner applied for and secured from Governor Micheltorena a grant to the San José Valley, a tract of land later known as Warner's Ranch, in San Diego County. Part, at least, of this tract had previously been granted to two other applicants, but that was not unusual with California land grants.

In this Valley of San José there were five or six Indian settlements on ranchos belonging to Missions San Diego and San Luis Rey. This grant had first been made with the stipulation that it did not prejudice the rights of the Indians who lived there. The most important of the rancherías was that of Agua Caliente where there were buildings erected by the Indians, planted fields, an orchard, and several vineyards. In January, 1850, Judge Benjamin Hayes visited this settlement. He found the Indians "a good looking, pleasant sort of people and polite

[56] Banc., *Hist. of Cal.*, 3. 717-718, note.
[57] Rogers, *Prehistoric Man*, 24-28; Hill, J. J. *The History of Warner's Ranch;* Jackson, H. H., *A Century of Dishonor*, 458-514; *Out West*, March, 1902-Nov., 1903.

enough." "Some of the huts," he writes, "are commodious, one perhaps 25 feet long. The Captain's and some other houses, are of adobe; and the Captain's has a spacious corral formed by an adobe wall. In the huts are bushels of a nut whose kernel has the taste of peach—a sort of plum (I was told). They make meal of it and bread." The women were busy grinding these nuts, acorns, and wheat into meal which they sold at $2.00 per almud. One woman did some washing for the judge at $1.00 for eight pieces, "she finding soap." The men were employed in sowing grain in their own fields. At other times they worked for Warner.[58] They were, in fact, a self-sustaining people, though Warner seemed to exercise some hold over them, using the lash at times to get them to labor for him.

During an Indian uprising, in 1851, Warner and his family were driven from the ranch. Later the tract was broken up and sold to various persons. Dr. John S. Griffin, one of the prospective purchasers, wrote to Judge Hayes, his brother-in-law, for advice. Replying, the judge wrote, in part: "As to the Indian title— I regard this as mere possessory: still it is the right of possession, which is of some importance. I know of no state law or state authority, that could at present dislodge, for example, the Indians of the village of Agua Caliente. Their planting grounds surround the famous Hot Springs. This is of great value. When I was last there (1867), they seemed to regard the immediate vicinity of the Spring as their own. I paid them a dollar for my bath, at the rustic bathing establishment they have constructed, consisting of two goods boxes sunk in the ground, sheltered by a ramada, and communicating with the spring by means of a trough a quarter of a mile long."[59]

According to Charles F. Lummis, the Indians of Agua Caliente held rather more than possessory rights to their property. "It is also a matter of history," he writes, "that in 1851 the Agua Caliente Indians living at the springs revolted against Col. Warner; four ringleaders were executed by Gen. Heintzelman; a treaty was made with the Indians by the U. S. Commissioner Dr. Wozencraft, Lieut. Hamilton representing the army, and Col. J. J. Warner, the ranch owner giving the Indians their lands."[60]

Yet, in spite of their possessory rights, fully recognized under Spanish law, in spite of the treaty mentioned above and numerous other papers given them by United States army officers, the Supreme Court of the United States, in 1901, handed down a decision against the Indians and in favor of ex-Governor John G. Downey, the new proprietor, who insisted that the Indians be evicted from his

[58] Hill, J. J., *History of Warner's Ranch*, 124-131.
[59] *Ibidem*, 151-152.
[60] Lummis, C. F., "The Exiles of Cupa," *Out West*, May, 1902, p. 472.

lands. The case was given much publicity. Public interest was aroused. The Warner's Ranch Indian Commission was appointed to look over the situation and report to the Commissioner of Indian affairs, W. A. Jones, on the availability of lands suitable for a new home for the Indians who were to be ejected from the six rancherías[61] of the San José Valley. Months were spent by the Commission in examining lands offered for that purpose.

Lummis, chairman of the commission, visited Agua Caliente to talk the matter over with the Indians. "The Indian village," he writes, "consists of some forty houses; of adobe, except two or three; comfortable, substantial and neat. There is a little adobe chapel, and a new $1200 schoolhouse, with a resident teacher—Mrs. Josephine Babbitt, who has been with these people a dozen years. Several hundred acres are cultivated—careful little fields and orchards. There are irrigation ditches and a reservoir. Except the school, which was built by the government a couple of years ago, and a pipe-line to it from a spring, everything at Agua Caliente is the work of the Indians. Of the American ownership, claimed to have lasted more than 58 years, there is not one stick erect nor one stone on another for token. The improvements the Indians will have to abandon on their eviction, stand, at a conservative estimate, for $10,000. There are 154 men, women and children living on this spot. I saw and talked with four generations in one family—all born here."

"Our surrey was noted afar off; and we no sooner reached the center of the village than we were surrounded by the troubled natives, who were anxious to know their fate. Shortly after lunch we had a *junta* in the school-room, which was attended by every man at home—many had gone 90 miles for work at sheep-shearing—and by many of the women. . , I told these harried people the exact state of their case in court and at Washington, and advised them to ponder it over night. There was practically no possibility that the government would purchase their own land for them—since the Supreme Court had held it to belong to the ranch claimants, who refused to sell the 900 acres occupied by the Indians, or any less land than the 30,000 acres,[62] which was held at $245,000. They would better think over the outside country and decide what they would like best after their old home."

Lummis talked to them in Spanish. "They could all understand that," he said, "but under the stress of deep feeling they talked in the Cupeño. . ." The next day the Captain was ready with his answer. Translated by a young Indian woman, Mrs. Celsa Apapas, "in perfectly lucid English," it was: "We thank

[61] The six villages were Agua Caliente, Puerta de la Cruz, Puerta de San José, San José, Mataguay, and La Ciénega.
[62] The entire San José Valley grant covered a tract of 42,000 acres.

you for coming here to talk to us in a way we can understand. It is the first time anyone has done so. You ask us to think what place we like next best to this place where we always live. Do you see that graveyard out there? There are our fathers and our grandfathers. You see that Eagle-nest mountain and that Rabbit-hole mountain? When God made them, He gave us this place. We have always been here. We do not care for any other place. It may be good, but it is not ours. We have always lived here. We would rather die here. Our fathers did. We cannot leave them. Our children born here—how can we go away? If you give us the best place in the world, it is not so good for us as this. The Captain he say his people cannot go anywhere else; they cannot live anywhere else. Here they always live; their people always live here. There is no other place. This is our home. We ask you to get it for us. . . "[63]

But the Indians had to go, and, in 1903, they were removed to Pala, which the government, on recommendation of the Warner's Ranch Indian Commission, had purchased for them. (An "American," upon learning that the property had been declared "public domain," had acquired title to it.) In 1902, ten Pala Indian families were still living there. Pala had never been abandoned by them. According to Lummis, the removal of the Indians of Agua Caliente and those of the five other little settlements marked the first time that Indians had been driven from one spot to a better one. Even so, it was a long time before some of them were reconciled to the change.

"The Pala reservation," Lummis states, "contains 3,438 acres of land, mostly good, besides some 5,000 acres of public land added to it on the recommendation of the same commission which purchased the reservation. The latter land is of little worth except for grazing, bee-range, fuel and a 'fence' against crowding whites."[64]

But few of the Indians on other ranchos were so fortunate as those mentioned above. For instance, Las Flores, estancia of Mission San Luis Rey, where, in 1843, there were thirty-two Indian families who were cultivating fields and tending their live stock, fell into the hands of Pio and Andres Pico.[65] (This little settlement had been converted into an Indian pueblo by Don Santiago Argüello, then administrator of the mission, in accordance with Governor Figueroa's "partial emancipation" plan of 1833.)

A like fate befell other mission ranchos. All the way up and down the coast mission ranchos were taken from the Indians, who had improved them, and

[63] Lummis, C. F., *opus cit.*, *Out West*, May, 1902.
[64] "Turning a New Leaf," *Out West*, April, 1903; "The Last Eviction," *Ibidem*, Nov., 1903.
[65] Engelhardt, *Mission San Luis Rey*, Chapter VIII.

granted to "Californios" or to "foreigners." The story of the wiping out of the little settlement of San Miguel, or Cieneguita, of Santa Bárbara is particularly tragic.[66]

Had the missions been secularized according to the decree of 1813, and had the Indian rancherías "at a distance" from the missions—i. e., on ranchos—"having twenty-five families" been formed into separate pueblos according to Figueroa's Reglamento Provisional, Article 9, under General Rules, all those settlements after five years occupancy would have become legal Indian pueblos according to both Spanish and Mexican Law. Under such conditions, without molestation, and with proper supervision, there is no reason to believe that they would not have survived, provided homes for our *first* Californians and become centers of many native arts and useful trades. Those organized pueblos would each have been entitled to four square leagues of land, without special grant. And the United States Land Commission which sat in San Francisco, in 1852, to "Ascertain and Settle Private Land Claims in the State of California" would have upheld their claim as it did those of the settlers of San José and Los Angeles, the four presidial towns and the pueblo of Sonoma founded, in 1835, under Mexican law by General Mariano Vallejo. For, as Bancroft states: "The act of 1851 provided that the existence of a town on July 7, 1846, should be regarded as prima facie evidence of a land grant, . . ."[67]

But the missions were not secularized according to the decree of 1813; the Indian settlements on ranchos were not declared Indian pueblos according to Figueroa's regulations of 1834. Nor were land grants always made in compliance with Spanish law and the Mexican colonization law of August 18, 1824, and the regulations of November 21, 1828,[68] by which laws and regulations the Indians' rights were protected.

When California was ceded by México to the United States under the terms of the Treaty of Guadalupe Hidalgo, the Indians were recognized as Mexican citizens, and "the rights of property remained unchanged. By the law of nations those rights were sacred and inviolable, and the obligations passed to the new government to protect and maintain them."

William Carey Jones, "an adept in the Spanish language, and as a lawyer well

---

[66] Rogers, *Prehistoric Man*, 24-28.
[67] Banc., *Hist. of Cal.*, 6. 565-566; Robinson, W. W., *Land in California*, 41.
[68] "By the fundamental laws of 1824, the regulation of 1828, and the regulation of the departmental legislature, one condition was that in making private grants of land the lands granted must be vacant lands. Lands occupied by and in possession of Indians were not such vacant lands; for by the same laws and regulations it was provided that such grants be without prejudice or damage to the Indians, and that such land granted to the damage and injury of the Indians should be returned to the rightful owners." (New Code, law 9, title 12, book 4.) Jackson, H., *A Century of Dishonor*, 476.

skilled in the Spanish colonial titles," was sent to California to "direct particu-lar attention to the extensive tracts of land covered by what are known as 'missions,' . . ; their condition as to title and possession, etc. Article 8 in his instructions related to the Indians. "You will make an inquiry into the nature of the Indian rights as existing under the Spanish and Mexican governments, etc." He arrived at Monterey September 19, 1849, and examined various archives.

In his report, dated March 9, 1850, Jones remarked: "If it were within my province to suggest what would be an equitable disposition of such of the mis-sions as remain the property of the government, I should say that the churches, with all the church property and ornaments; a *portion*[69] of the principal build-ing, for the residence of the priest, with a piece of land equal to that designated in the original act of the Mexican Congress for their secularization, (to wit, two hundred varas square,) with another piece for cemetery, should be granted to the respective Catholic parishes, for the uses specified. . . The churches, cer-tainly, ought not to be appropriated to any other use; and less than I have sug-gested would, I think, be less than equity and justice, and less than the inhabi-tants have always considered and enjoyed as their right."

Regarding the Indian rights, Jones stated: "It is a principle constantly laid down in the Spanish colonial laws, that the Indians shall have a right to as much land as they need for their habitations, for tillage, and for pasturage. Where they were already partially settled in communities, sufficient of land which they occupied was secured them for those purposes. If they were wild, and scattered in the wilds and wildernesses, the policy of the law, and of the instructions im-posed on the authorities of the distant provinces, was to reduce them, establish them in villages, convert them to Christianity, and instruct them in useful em-ployments. It was for this purpose, especially, that the missions were founded and encouraged. . . The early laws were so tender of these rights of the Indians that they forbade the allotment of lands to the Spaniards, and especially to the rearing of stock, where it might interfere with the tillage of the Indians. Special directions were also given for the selection of the lands for the Indian villages, in places suitable for agriculture, and having the necessary wood and water. The lands set apart to them were likewise inalienable, except by the advice and con-sent of the officers of the government, whose duty it was to protect the natives as minors or pupils. Agreeable to the theory and spirit of these laws, the Indians in California were always supposed to have certain property or interest in the

---

[69] The italics are the writer's. Clearly Jones refers to the Padres' living quarters. The shops and storerooms in the quadrangle were intended by the decree of 1813 to be taken over and managed by the Indians.

missions. . . The law always intended the Indians of the missions—all of them who remained there—to have homes upon the mission grounds."[70]

Again, in spite of this report, in spite of the terms of the Treaty of Guadalupe Hidalgo, and the various other laws and regulations aforementioned, the United States Land Commission confirmed very, very few of the Indians' claims to lands. The courts held that the majority of the Indians, not having appeared before the land commission, had lost even their possessory rights to their lands. It is a pity that someone was not sent to warn them of the necessity for so doing. In 1851-1852, eighteen treaties were signed with the California Indians with the purpose of effecting a just settlement of their claims. These treaties, however, were never ratified by the United States Senate, but it seems that they may yet bear fruit.[71]

When hordes of land-seeking homesteaders, squatters, and adventurers came to California on the heels of the discovery of gold, they paid little attention to land titles, even those acquired by grant. The Indian's doom was sealed. Little by little he was crowded off his property at the point of the gun, by "floating" survey lines, by "running" fences, which continually moved in upon his holdings, and by pre-emption of his lands.

"From tract after tract of such lands," reported Helen Jackson and Abbot Kinney,[72] "they have been driven out, year by year, by the white settlers of the country, until they can retreat no farther; some of their villages being literally in the last tillable spot on the desert's edge or in the mountain fastnesses. . ."

"Considerable numbers of these Indians are also to be found on the outskirts of white settlements, as at Riverside, San Bernardino, or in the colonies in the San Gabriel Valley, where they live like gypsies in brush huts, here today, gone tomorrow, eking out a miserable existence by days' works, the wages of which are too often spent for whiskey in the village saloons.[73] Travellers in Southern California who have formed their impressions of the Mission Indians from these wretched wayside creatures, would be greatly surprised at the sight of some of the villages in the mountain valleys, where, freer from the contaminating influence of the white race, are industrious, peaceable communities, cultivating ground, keeping stock, carrying out their simple manufactures of pottery, mats, baskets, &., and making their living,—a very poor living, it is true; but they are inde-

[70] Jones, Wm. Carey, *Land Titles in California*, 22, 36-7; Engelhardt, *Miss. & Miss.*, 4. 729-731.
[71] Robinson, W. W., *Land in California*, 14-20.
[72] With authority granted by the Hon. H. Price, Commissioner of Indian Affairs, Mrs. Jackson visited California, in 1882, to ascertain the location and condition of the mission Indians. At her request Mr. Abbot Kinney was authorized to act with her.
[73] See B. D. Wilson's report in Jackson, *A Century of Dishonor*, 463.

pendent and self-respecting in it, and ask nothing at the hands of the United States Government now [1883], except that it will protect them in the owner-ship of their lands,—lands which, in many instances have been in continuous occupation and cultivation by their ancestors for over one hundred years."[74]

In reading the Jackson-Kinney report one cannot fail to be impressed by the tenacity with which those Indian people held on to their little settlements. They stayed on until they were forced to leave by having their lands pre-empted; their water supply diverted; their villages left outside reservation lines by care-less or dishonest surveyors and so subject to squatter claims; their fields, orchards, and stock ranges taken from them by white robbers.

The story told in that report cannot be retold. It should be read first hand in its entirety. In itself it is a complete refutation of the charges that the Padres did not fit their neophytes for citizenship or for private ownership of land.

Those settlements were all governed by captains. The men in season left in bands to do sheep-shearing, to work in vineyards, etc., on ranchos as far as ninety miles away. They were industrious and peaceable peoples, enduring outrage and molestation past white man's understanding, not because they lacked spirit, but because they had learned that in any conflict with the whites they hadn't a chance of winning. They "were not citizens," they hadn't the right either to vote or to be witnesses. Indians were murdered by white men, and, the only witnesses being Indians, the white men claimed self-defense and escaped any punishment whatsoever.

Had these villages and others, managed by the Indians themselves, though subject to the laws of the state, been properly protected from white man's en-croachment, there need have been no Indian Question in California. The Indian pueblos of Arizona and New Mexico are assets to those states.[75] Our Indian pueblos might well have been the same to us.

Writing the Foreword for Charles Avery Amsden's book, *Navaho Weaving*, Dr. Frederick W. Hodge observed: "There is perhaps no greater problem in Indian affairs than that of adjusting the Indian to the economic scheme. . . , and the Indian will never be adjusted to us until a sufficient number of pursuits can be devised in ways useful or satisfying to both races."

Fortunately for their survival, in any number whatever, the neophyte Indians of California had been adjusted to the economic scheme of life in this state by their training in the shops and fields of the old missions. As Benjamin D.

[74] Jackson, Helen, *A Century of Dishonor*, 459.
[75] Titles to those Indian pueblos were confirmed to the Indians by the United States congress, in 1858. See Bancroft *History of Arizona and New Mexico*, 647-648; 672-673; 756-757.

Wilson, the first agent for the Indians of San Diego and Los Angeles Counties, reported: "Under the rule of the missions they were taught to do all the farm work, also the trades, as masons, carpenters, plasterers, soapmakers, tanners, shoemakers, blacksmiths, bakers, millers, cartmakers, weavers and spinners, sad-dlers, shepherds, viñeros and vaqueros. In fact they filled all the branches of mechanics in use here. They taught the Americans to make adobes; they under-stood irrigation, planting season and harvest. They had a practical knowledge which outlives their teachers. Their women were quick to learn household duties and often married foreigners and Californians, and made exemplary wives and mothers."[76]

The Indian neophytes had been taught to deal with the Spanish people and such visitors and settlers as came to California by being allowed to dispose of the produce of their little gardens or bits of their handicraft to them, or by work-ing for them on those days when, having finished their tasks for the week, they were allowed to leave the mission, and, also, when they were sent in groups to help settlers with their crops or buildings. What they earned on their own time, they were allowed to keep and spend as they chose. What they earned when they employed the time that would otherwise have been spent in the mission shops or fields went into the community fund, since, while they were absent, the other neophytes had also been working for the community.

It has been claimed that few of the neophytes were taught to speak Spanish and fewer to read and write. Yet such writers as Duflot de Mofras, Fremont, and Bryant frequently mention the fact that the Indians whom they met "spoke Spanish fluently." Reporting, in 1846, on the condition of the mission and the Indians of San Luis Rey, of which he had been placed in charge, John Bidwell wrote, in part: "The Indians at the Mission of San Luis Rey were by no means wild and untutored. They had lived, many, if not most of them, at the mission from infancy, and had been taught to do all kinds of work by Padre Antonio Peyri, the founder of the Mission. Him they loved with a friendship truly won-derful. . . I found the Indians very intelligent; most could speak the Spanish tongue fluently. Some could read. One, a chief, named Samuel, was not only fluent, but eloquent, and no Mexican to my knowledge had so fine a command of the Spanish language."[77] Judge Benjamin Hayes found that the Indians of Warner's Ranch all spoke Spanish.

Special Commissioner Robert J. Stevens, in 1867, reported to the government

[76] Engelhardt, *Mission San Luis Rey*, 164. See also, Dakin, S. B., *A Scotch Paisano*, 70-73, for William Heath Davis's opinion of the housekeeping ability and graciousness of Victoria, Indian wife of Hugo Reid.
[77] Engelhardt. *Mission San Luis Rey*, 137 (Bidwell, *California*, 183-187. Banc. Coll.).

regarding the mission Indians: "...In fact, many of them even now read and write, particularly among the aged."[78] Those aged ones could have been educated only at the old missions.

Given the opportunity these people and their descendants might well have become expert potters and weavers, in time rivaling those of both Old and New Mexico. We might have had today picturesque villages where Indian arts and handicrafts flourished; where there were shops devoted to leather work—saddles and reatas such as were made at La Purísima, Santa Inés, and San Antonio; shops where iron was forged into brands, ornamental grilles, weather vanes, etc., like those formerly at San Gabriel and San Fernando; shops for candle making; shops for baskets, ornamental and useful; and shops for laces, the work of such perfiladoras as those of San Fernando, San Gabriel, Mesa Grande, Agua Caliente and Pala. Up and down the coast the native arts might have been kept alive and broadened, the workers furnished with a means of self-expression and livelihood. There would also have been workers for the fields, vineyards, and stock ranges, carpenters, wood carvers, adobe and tile makers, for, as Fr. Durán wrote Inspector Hartnell under date of October 25, 1839, "..., as far as knowing how to make a living, be he day laborer, a farm hand, doing chores, a fisher, etc. ... If one knows how to work the iron or wood, the others know other things; ..."[79]

Numerous testimonials to the mission Indian's industry, artistry, and capability must be omitted for lack of space, but they are readily found in the reports of early visitors, first Indian agents such as B. D. Wilson, John Bidwell, H. N. Rust, and in those of the United States army officers who were temporarily placed in charge of some of the missions for their protection.

No, the Franciscan Padres did not fail the mission Indians.

[78] Engelhardt, *Mission San Luis Rey*, 168.
[79] Engelhardt, *Mission Santa Barbara*, 205.

CALIFORNIA MISSIONS
WITH DATES OF FOUNDING

San Diego de Alcalá, July 16, 1769
San Carlos Borromeo del Carmelo, June 3, 1770
San Antonio de Padua, July 14, 1771
San Gabriel, Arcángel, September 8, 1771
San Luis Obispo de Tolosa, September 1, 1772
San Francisco de Asís (Dolores), June 29, 1776
San Juan Capistrano, November 1, 1776
Santa Clara de Asís, January 12, 1777
San Buenaventura, March 31, 1782
Santa Bárbara, December 4, 1786
La Purísima Concepción, December 8, 1787
Santa Cruz, August 28, 1791
Nuestra Señora de la Soledad, October 9, 1791
San José, June 11, 1797
San Juan Bautista, June 24, 1797
San Miguel, Arcángel, July 25, 1797
San Fernando Rey de España, September 8, 1797
San Luis Rey de Francia, June 13, 1798
Santa Inés, September 17, 1804
San Rafael, Arcángel, December 14, 1817
San Francisco Solano, July 4, 1823

Bibliography

Agricultura General. Compuesta por Alonso de Herrera, y Los Demos Autores que hasta ahora han escrito desta materia, cuyos nombres, van a la vuelta desta hoja. Con las licencias necesarias. En Madrid. Por Don Antonio Sancha Ano MDCCLXXVII.

AMSDEN, CHARLES A.: *Navaho Weaving.*

ANGEL, MYRON: *Piedra Pintada.*

ARENTZ, REV. THEODORE, O.F.M.: "Chronicle of the Franciscans, or Friars Minor, at Santa Barbara, California." Unfinished MS. Santa Barbara Mission Archives.

AUSTIN, MARY: *The Flock.*
    The Land of Little Rain.
    One Smoke Stories.
    The Basket Woman.

BANCROFT, HUBERT H.: *History of California,* vols. 1-7.
    History of Mexico.
    Arizona and New Mexico.
    Native Races.
    California Pastoral.

BANDELIER, ADOLPH, and HEWETT, EDGAR L.: *Indians of the Rio Grande Valley.* Part I. *The Rio Grande Pueblos Today,* by EDGAR L. HEWETT. Part II. *Documentary History of the Rio Grande Pueblos,* by ADOLPH F. BANDELIER.

BARD, DR. CEPHAS L.: "A Contribution to the History of Medicine in Southern California." MS.

BARING-GOULD, REV. S.: *The Lives of the Saints,* 16 vols.

BARROWS, DAVID PRESCOTT: *The Ethno-Botany of the Coahuilla Indians of Southern California.*
    "Some Coahuia Songs and Dances," *Land of Sunshine,* Dec., 1895; "Homes on Mountain and Desert," *Ibidem,* Aug., 1896.

BAXTER, SYLVESTER: *Spanish Colonial Architecture in Mexico,* 10 vols.

BEATTIE, GEORGE W.: *California's Unbuilt Missions.*

BEATTIE, GEORGE W., and HELEN PRUITT: *Heritage of the Valley, San Bernardino's First Century.*

BEECHEY, FREDERICK W.: *Narrative of a Voyage to the Pacific and Bering's Strait.* 1831. 2 vols.

BELL, MAJOR HORACE: *On the Old West Coast.*
    Reminiscences of a Ranger.

BERGER, JOHN A.: *The Franciscan Missions of California.*

BIDWELL, JOHN: "The First Emigrant Trail to California," *Century Magazine,* Nov., 1890; "Life in California Before the Gold Discovery," *Ibidem,* Dec., 1890.
    "Early California Reminiscences," *Out West,* Jan.-Aug., 1904.
    A Journey to California. John Henry Nash reprint of the 1842 edition in the Bancroft Library, Berkeley, California.

BLACK, MARY E.: *Key to Weaving.*

BLACKMAR, FRANK W.: *Spanish Institutions of the Southwest.* 1891.

BOLTON, DR. HERBERT E.: *Anza's California Expeditions.* 5 vols.
    Fray Juan Crespi.
    Outpost of Empire.
    Palou's New California. 4 vols.
    Spanish Exploration in the Southwest.

BROWN, D. MACKENZIE: *China Trade in California.*

BROWNE, J. ROSS: *Dangerous Journey.* 1864.
    The Indians of California.

BRYANT, EDWIN: *What I Saw in California.* Being the Journal of a Tour . . . and through California in the years 1846 1847.

CAMPBELL, ELIZABETH W. C.: *An Archeological Survey of the Twenty-nine Palms Region.* Southwest Museum Papers.

CARR, HARRY: *Old Mother Mexico.*
    The West Is Still Wild.

Catalogo De Construcciones Religiosas Del Estado de Hidalgo. 2 vols. Formado Por La Comision De Inventorios De La Primera Zona. 1929-1932. Talleres Graficos de la Nacion. Mexico MCMXL, MCMXLII.

Catalogo De Construcciones Religiosas Del Estado De Yucatan. 2 vols. Formado Por La Comision De Inventorios De La Cuarta Zona. Talleres Graficos de la Nacion. MCMXLV.

CHANDOS DANE: *Village in the Sun.*
    House in the Sun.

CHAPMAN, CHARLES E.: *The Founding of Spanish California.*

CHASE and SAUNDERS: *The California Padres and Their Missions.*

CLAVIGERO, DON FRANCISCO JAVIER, S. J.: *The History of (Lower) California.* Lake and Gray translation.

CLELAND, ROBERT G.: *Cattle on a Thousand Hills.*
CLEMENT, CLARA ERSKINE: *Saints in Art.*
    Handbook of Legendary and Mythological Art.
CLEMENTS, EDITH: *Flowers of Coast and Sierra.*
COLLIGAN, REV. JAMES A., S. J.: *The Three Churches of Santa Clara Mission.*
COLTON, WALTER: *Three Years in California.* 1850.
COUTS, LT. CAVE J.: *Journal and Maps of. From San Diego to the Colorado in 1849.*
CUBAS, ANTONIO GARCIA: *El Libro De Mis Recuerdos.*

DAKIN, SUSANNA B.: *A Scotch Paisano.*
DALE, HARRISON C.: *The Ashley-Smith Explorations and the Discovery of a Central Route to the Pacific. 1822-1829.*
DANA, RICHARD H., Jr.: *Two Years Before the Mast.* New York, 1840.
DA SILVA, REV. OWEN, O.F.M.: *Mission Music of California.*
DAVIDSON, WINNIFRED: *Where California Began.*
DAVIS, WM. HEATH: *Seventy-five Years in California.*
DEDRICK, PROF. B. W.: *Practical Milling.*
DE MOFRAS, DUFLOT: *Travels on the Pacific Coast.* 2 vols.
DIAZ DEL CASTILLO, CAPT. BERNAL: *The True History of the Conquest of Mexico.* Translation by Maurice Keatings, Esq. 1800.
DOUGLAS, SIR JAMES: "From Columbia to California in 1840." *Quarterly of the California Historical Society,* June, 1929. Original Journal is in the Bancroft Library.
DOYLE, JOHN T.: "The Missions of Alta California," *The Century Magazine,* Jan., 1891.
"DUHAUT-CILLY's Account of California," *Quarterly of the California Historical Society* June, Sept., and Dec., 1929.
DWINELLE: *Colonial History of San Francisco.*

ELDREDGE, ZOETH S.: *Beginnings of San Francisco.*
ENGELHARDT, REV. ZEPHYRIN, O.F.M.: *Missions and Missionaries.* 4 vols.

The Franciscans in California.	*Mission San Buenaventura.*
The Holy Man of Santa Clara.	*Mission Santa Barbara.*
Mission San Diego.	*Mission La Purisima.*
Mission San Carlos.	*Mission La Soledad.*
Mission San Antonio.	*Mission San Juan Bautista.*
Mission San Gabriel.	*Mission San Miguel.*
Mission San Luis Obispo.	*Mission San Fernando Rey.*
Mission San Francisco.	*Mission San Luis Rey.*
Mission San Juan Capistrano.	*Mission Santa Ines.*

Fages' Description of California. Translation by Herbert I. Priestly.
FAULKNER: *Plowman's Folly.*
FORBES, ALEXANDER: *A History of Upper and Lower California.* 1839.
FORD, HENRY CHAPMAN: "Notes," Southwest Museum.
FREMONT, JOHN CHARLES: *Memoirs of My Life.* 1887.

GREEN, F. E.: "The San Diego Old Mission Dam and Irrigation Works," MS. The Junipero Serra Museum, San Diego, California.
GUTHE, CARL E.: *Pueblo Pottery Making. A Study at the Village of San Ildefonso.*

HAGEMAN, FREDERICK C.: *An Architectural Study of the Mission La Purisima Concepcion California.*
HALL, FREDERICK: *History of San Jose and Surroundings.*
HARRIMAN, ALICE: "Bells of Camino Real," MS.
HARRINGTON, JOHN P.: *A New Version of Boscana's Historical Account of the San Juan Capistrano Indians of Southern California.* Smithsonian Miscellaneous Collections. Vol. 92, Number 4.
HARRINGTON, M. R.: "The Folsom Man in California," *The Masterkey,* July, 1938. Southwest Museum Publications; "Pre-Folsom Man in California," *Ibidem,* Sept., 1938; "The Age of the Borax Lake Finds," *Ibidem,* Nov., 1939.
HAWLEY, WALTER: *The Early Days of Santa Barbara California.*
HAYES, JUDGE BENJ.: *Pioneer Notes.* See Wolcott.
HEIZER, ROBERT F., and TREGANZA, ADAM E.: "Mines and Quarries of the Indians of California," *California Journal of Mines and Geology,* July, 1944.
HENSLOW, T. GEOFFREY W.: *Ye Sundial Booke.*
HILL, JOSEPH J.: *The History of Warner's Ranch and Its Environs.*
HITTELL, THEODORE: *History of California.* 4 vols.
HOLDER, CHARLES FREDERICK: *The Channel Islands of California.*
HUTTON, WILLIAM RICH: *Glances at California.*
    California 1847, 1852. Drawings by Wm. Rich Hutton.

Informes Anuales, Santa Barbara Mission Archives (SBMA).
Inventarios, SBMA, and Archives of Monterey-Fresno Diocese.

Jackson, Helen Hunt: *A Century of Dishonor.*
    Glimpses of California and the Missions.
    "Father Junipero and His Work," *The Century Magazine,* May-June, 1883; "The Present Condition of the
        Mission Indians in Southern California," *Ibidem,* Aug., 1883.
    Ramona.
James, George Wharton: *Old Missions and Mission Indians of California.*
    In and Out of the Old Missions.
    The Old Franciscan Missions of California.
    Indian Basketry.
    Picturesque Pala.
Jameson, Mrs. A.: *Sacred and Legendary Art.* 2 vols.
    Legends of the Madonna.

Knowland, Joseph R.: *California. A Landmark History.*
Kroeber, A. L.: *Handbook of the Indians of California.*
    Basketry Designs of the Mission Indians.

Langsdorff, Dr. G. H. von: *Voyages and Travels in Various Parts of the World, during the years 1803, 1804, 1805,
        1806, 1807.*
Libro del Padre Mut. Typed copy.
Lockwood, Frank C.: *Story of the Spanish Missions of the Middle Southwest.*
Los Diez Libros De Arquitectura de M. Polion. Traducidos Del Latin y Comentados Por Don Joseph Ortiz y Sanz, Pres-
        bitero. De Orden Superior, Madrid 1787. SBMA.
Lummis, Charles F.: "The Exiles of Cupa," *Out West,* May, 1902; "Turning a New Leaf," *Ibidem,* April, 1903; "The
        Last Eviction," *Ibidem,* Nov., 1903.

Mahr, August C.: *The Visit of the "Rurik" to San Francisco in 1816.*
Martínez, José Longinos: *Journal of. California in 1792,* Simpson translation.
Medsger, Oliver Perry: *Edible Wild Plants.*
Mofras, Duflot—See De Mofras.
Mora, Jo; *Trail Dust and Saddle Leather.*
    Californios.
Morrow, Honore: *Beyond the Blue Sierra.*
Mylar, Isaac L.: *Early Days at Mission San Juan Bautista.*

Newcomb, Rexford: *Spanish Colonial Architecture in the United States.*
    The Old Mission Churches and Historic Houses of California.
Newmark, Harris: *Sixty Years in Southern California.*
Nordhoff, Charles: *California. A Book for Travellers and Settlers.*

O'Keefe, Rev. J. J., O.F.M.: *The Buildings and Churches of the Mission of Santa Barbara.*
Orange County History Series. Vol. 1. 1931.
O'Sullivan, Rev. St. John: *Little Chapters About San Juan Capistrano.* 1912. Revised edition 1929. See also Saunders
        and O'Sullivan.

Packman, Ana Begue: *Early California Hospitality.*
    Leather Dollars.
Palou's Life of Junipero Serra. James edition.
Permanent Court of Arbitration. United States vs. Mexico. Pious Fund Case. Transcript of Record of Amat et al vs.
        Mexico. 1902.
Piñedo, Encarnación: "Early Days at Santa Clara," *The Owl,* April, 1934.
Powell, H. M. T.: *The Santa Fe Trail to California, 1849-1852.* The Journal and Drawings of H. M. T. Powell.
Powers, Stephen: *Tribes of California.* 1877.
Priestly, Herbert I.: *Fages' Description of California.*
    The Mexican Nation.
    The Coming of the White Man.
    Joseph de Galvez.
Publications of the Academy of Pacific Coast History. Vols. 1, 2, and 3, including:
    Diary of Gaspar de Portola During the California Expedition of 1769-1770.
    The Narrative of the Portola Expedition of 1769-1770 by Miguel Costanso.
    The Portola Expedition of 1769-1770. Diary of Miguel Costanso.
    The Portola Expedition of 1769-1770. Diary of Vicente Vila.
    The Expedition to San Francisco Bay in 1770. Diary of Pedro Fages.
    Expedition on the Sacramento and San Joaquin Rivers in 1817. Diary of Fray Narciso Duran.
    The Anza Expedition of 1775-1776. Diary of Pedro Font.
    The Colorado River Campaign 1781-1782. Diary of Pedro Fages.

REID, DR. HIRAM A.: *History of Pasadena.*
REID, HUGO: "Los Angeles County Indians." Letters to the *Los Angeles Star.*
RICHMAN, IRVING B.: *California Under Spain and Mexico, 1535-1847.*
ROBINSON, ALFRED: *Life in California.* 1846.
ROBINSON, W. W.: *Ranchos Become Cities.*
    Land in California.
ROGERS, DAVID BANKS: *Prehistoric Man of the Santa Barbara Coast.*

SAUNDERS, CHARLES F.: *Western Flower Guide.*
SAUNDERS AND O'SULLIVAN: *Capistrano Nights.*
SERRA, JUNIPERO, *Diary of.* Lummis translation. *Out West,* March-July, 1902.
SHALER, WILLIAM: *Journal of a Voyage Between China and the North-Western Coast of America, made in 1804.*
SHINN, CHARLES HOWARD: "Pioneer Spanish Families of California," *The Century Magazine,* Jan., 1891; "Mission Bells,"
    Overland Monthly, Jan., 1892.
SHULTZ, JACKSON S.: *Leather Manufacture.* 1876.
SMITH, FRANCES RAND: *The Architectural History of Mission San Carlos Borromeo California.*
    The Mission of San Antonio de Padua.
SMYTHE, WM. E.: *History of San Diego.*
SOULE: *Annals of San Francisco.*
STEELE, JAMES: *Old Californian Days.*
SUGRANES, REV. EUGENE, C. M. F.: *The History of Mission San Gabriel.*
SULLIVAN, JOHN E.: *The Externals of the Catholic Church.*
SULLIVAN, MAURICE S.: *The Travels of Jedediah Smith.*
Surveys of the Missions made in 1854. The so-called Alemany Plats.

TORCHIANA, H. A. VAN COENEN: *Mission of Santa Cruz.*

VALLEJO, GUADALUPE: "Ranch and Mission Days in Alta California," *The Century Magazine,* Dec., 1890.
VANCOUVER, CAPT. GEORGE: *Voyage of Discovery to the North Pacific Ocean and Round the World.* . . 1790-5. London,
    1798. 3 vols.
VISCHER, EDWARD: *Missions of Upper California.* 1872.

WADDELL, JOHN A.: "Some Memories of Earlier College Days in Santa Clara." MS.
WALSH, REV. HENRY L., S. J.: *Hallowed Were the Gold Dust Trails.*
WALSH, MARIE T.: *The Mission Bells of California.*
    The Mission of the Passes.
WASEURTZ, G. M.: *A Sojourn in California.* The Travels and Sketches of G. M. Waseurtz af Sandels, a Swedish gentle-
    man who visited California in 1842-1843.
WATSON, DOUGLAS S.: *Junipero Serra's Expedition into California in 1769.*
WEBB, EDITH: "Pigments Used by the Mission Indians of California," *The Americas,* October, 1945; "Agriculture in the
    Days of the Early California Padres," *Ibidem,* January, 1948.
WHETTEN, NATHAN L.: *Rural Mexico.*
WILKES, CHARLES: *Narrative of the U. S. Exploring Expedition during the years 1838-1842.* Vol. V.
WILLEY, H. S.: *An Historical Paper Relating to Santa Cruz California.*
WOLCOTT, MARJORIE T.: *Pioneer Notes from the Diaries of Judge Benjamin Hayes.*
    "The House Near the Frog Pond," *Touring Topics,* Dec., 1928.
WOOD, WM. MAXWELL, M. D.: *Wandering Sketches of People and Things in South America, Polynesia, California, etc.*
    1849.

INDEX

Note: Included with the words commonly abbreviated are the following: Alta—A.; Baja—B.; expedition—exped.; illustration—illus.; Indian—Ind.; *Interrogatorio—Interrog.*; mentioned—ment.; Mission—Miss.; Native—nat.; San—S.; Santa—Sta.; Spanish—Sp.; water power—w. p.